The
Competitive
Enterprise

10 principles
of business
excellence
for increased
market share

Geoffrey Bell

The McGraw-Hill Companies, Inc.

Sydney New York San Francisco Auckland
Bangkok Bogotá Caracas Hong Kong
Kuala Lumpur Lisbon London Madrid
Mexico City Milan New Delhi San Juan
Seoul Singapore Taipei Toronto

McGraw·Hill Australia

A Division of The McGraw·Hill Companies

National Library of Australia Cataloguing-in-Publication data:

Bell, Geoffrey, 1948–
The competitive enterprise: 10 principles of business excellence
for increased market share.
Includes index.

ISBN 0 074 71104 0.

1. Success in business. 2. Market share. I. Title.
650.1

Published in Australia by
McGraw-Hill Australia Pty Ltd
4 Barcoo Street, Roseville NSW 2069, Australia
Acquisitions Editor: Javier Dopico
Production Editor: Alice Drew
Editor: Carolyn Pike
Illustrator: Alan Laver, Shelly Communications
Designer (cover and interior): Jan Schmoeger/Designpoint
Typeset in 10/12 pt Stone Serif by Designpoint
Printed on 80 gsm woodfree by Pantech Pty Ltd, Hong Kong

'Geoff Bell has used his experience as an Australian Business Excellence Award evaluator and member of the Awards framework team to give the reader an in-depth but easy to read explanation of the 10 Principles that underpin successful enterprises. Geoff has not only provided the reader with the theoretical basis for each of the Principles but has used his experience to give examples that enable the reader to understand how those Principles might be applied in their own enterprise.'

David Clayton, Scientific Affairs Director, Abbott Australasia Pty Ltd; Chairman, Australian Business Excellence Awards Framework Development Team 1997–2000

'The book is focused around 100 questions whose purpose is to help organisations concentrate their improvement efforts. It uses helpful examples that are relevant and is written in an accessible style. The section on variation is helpful and free of much statistical jargon. This is in contrast to many works dealing with this issue. This book will be helpful to anyone interested in achieving excellence in any enterprise, public or private. It is firmly grounded in Principles that are acknowledged worldwide to be the basis of success.'

Richard Cox, CEO, Australian Quality Council

'The Competitive Enterprise provides a comprehensive prescription for achieving business excellence well beyond that which can be achieved through the application of other less integrated approaches. The application of the 10 Principles is particularly suitable for the somewhat unique Australian workplace culture and provides a means of overcoming a number of the traditional barriers to change, such as poor communication, lack of trust in management, fear and poor workplace environment.'

Allan Gillespie, CEO EnviroStar Energy; Chairman, Electricity Supply Association of Australia Ltd; Chairman, HydroPower Group Pty Ltd; Director, Australian Technology Park Ltd

'Geoff Bell has built on his long experience as an evaluator for the Australian Business Excellence Awards to develop an eminently readable explanation and self-help guide. It will allow any organisation to:

- understand the Principles behind the international business excellence frameworks;
- self-assess its own adoption of the Principles and prioritise efforts towards improvement.

This book will be a valuable addition to the tool set of every manager seeking to sustainably improve the performance of his or her organisation.'

Dr Bob Hunt, Director, Centre for Management Innovation and Technology, Macquarie Graduate School of Management, Macquarie University

'In an era of corporate failure, *The Competitive Enterprise* makes available to every employer, every employee and every shareholder a proven business health assessment tool. It provides a framework of universal Principles and details good and bad practice in organisations. This is a manual for everybody interested in their organisation's success—from Chairman of the Board to first-line supervisor.'

Jeffrey Jarratt, Deputy Commissioner, NSW Police Service 1996–2001; AQC NSW Committee

'At last a book that says it like it is—or at least how it can be—for business, or any other enterprise truly interested in sustainable success. From national Business Excellence Awards programs, particularly in Australia and the United States, Geoff has captured a wealth of compelling argument for inspired, ethical leadership operating in systems that are better by design.'

Chris Russell, CEO Innov8 Advisory, ABEF Framework team, AQC lead evaluator

'This book clearly identifies the Principles that underlie business excellence. Geoff Bell has integrated these Principles into a well-packaged, logical structure supported by sound research. Any organisation seeking to improve its operations and increase the satisfaction of all its stakeholders will find much of value here.'

Dr Ian Saunders, ABEF lead evaluator, ABEF Framework Committee; Group Leader, Applied Bioinformatics, CSIRO Mathematical and Information Sciences

Contents

Preface

I N TIMES OF INCREASINGLY TOUGH COMPETITION, what is it that makes some companies more successful than others? Just what does make a difference?

Very successful companies from all around the world have found that there are 10 Principles that make the real difference—the 10 Business Excellence Principles. These companies find that the more they can work in line with these Principles, the more successful they are. Companies that shift to the new way of business are doing significantly better than are those that do not. Better in terms of share performance, profit, return on investment and all other company results.

These Principles represent the new way for leading and managing a company. Many companies, usually the bigger ones, recognise that the 10 Business Excellence Principles work and are doing their best to implement them and are achieving huge competitive advantage. They realise that the 10 Business Excellence Principles are not just 'nice to do' but represent a set of 'business laws'. Other companies, usually the smaller ones, are behaving as though the Principles do not affect them and are falling behind, contracting, failing or being swallowed up.

When these Principles are properly understood and implemented, they can be your recipe for success. They are essential to what makes a company prosper, stay in business or go out of it.

The 10 Business Excellence Principles offer a new and practical way to sustainable profit and success for all businesses—small, medium and large enterprises—in all industries.

Most people in business—especially entrepreneurs and small-to-medium enterprises (SMEs)—just do it. They run their business the way that feels right. However, SMEs may not have the resources to keep up with what bigger players have discovered. Usually, SMEs are so swamped with daily work that there is no time for anything else. This means that the successful bigger players get further ahead because the SME has not yet found out that 'gravity exists'.

How do you find out what you need to do to implement the 10 Business Excellence Principles? What do you need to do first? Who has the time? It looks complex and difficult. Where do you begin? How can you quickly work out what you should do first to significantly improve your business?

This book is designed to help. It is structured around a questionnaire that lets you assess for yourself how well your company addresses each of the 10 Business Excellence Principles, explains why you should address each issue and shows you how to go about it.

This book describes a new way of doing things. The 10 Business Excellence Principles are not just nice to know. They determine success. We know that the more companies apply these Principles, the more successful they are. Should you be interested?

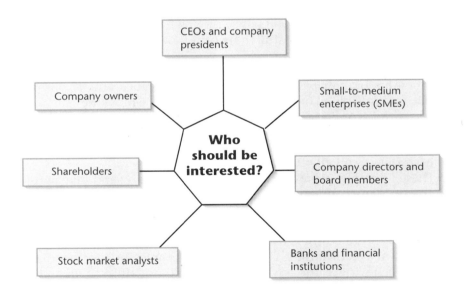

- *Small-to-medium enterprises.* You are often competing against larger players who have already adopted these 10 Business Excellence Principles into their work practices. If you are not using these Principles, will you find it harder and harder to compete? Do you know what you should be doing to improve your company significantly?

- *Company owners.* You want your company to be successful. Have you fully aligned your company and everything it does with the 10 Business Excellence Principles? If you have not, are you needlessly sacrificing performance? Why not regularly check your business health?
- *CEOs and company presidents.* Your responsibility is to make certain your company is successful. If you are not using these Principles, are you really doing the best you can for your company, its stockholders and other stakeholders?
- *Company directors and board members.* Your responsibility is to make certain the company you represent on behalf of the stockholders is successful. Are you following the 10 Business Excellence Principles? If you are not using these Principles in all your decisions, are you really doing the best you can for your stockholders? Do you appoint the CEO or president? Given the experience that companies will fail to achieve their potential if the CEO/president does not wholeheartedly role-model these Principles (see Principle 1 'Role models'), should you appoint only CEOs that will do so and dismiss those that do not?
- *Shareholders.* You make investment decisions based on the likelihood of return on your investment. How well do the companies in your portfolio stack up against these 10 Business Excellence Principles? Have you made them a critical part of your long-term portfolio decisions? Should you vote with your feet and abandon companies that do not follow these Principles? Or, those where the board appoints a new CEO/president who does not believe in the Principles? Should you demand that companies publish independent assessments against these Principles in their annual report?
- *Stock market analysts, pension fund managers.* You make investment recommendations based on the likelihood of return on your clients' investment. How well do the companies you recommend stack up against these 10 Business Excellence Principles? Have you made them a critical part of your long-term portfolio recommendations?
- *Banks and financial institutions.* You make investment decisions based on what you know about the company. Usually their ability to repay is critically determined by their sustainability and likelihood of success. How do they stack up against these 10 Business Excellence Principles? Should you use an interest margin based on the company's score? Should you devote time and resources to help your customers to adopt and manage in line with these Principles?
- *Accountants, auditors and consultants.* You advise your clients on what is important for their business to prosper. If you advise your clients to focus on accounting issues alone and ignore the 10

Business Excellence Principles, aren't you condemning those clients to continued difficulty? If companies that apply the Principles do much better, shouldn't you be encouraging your clients to give attention to the Principles? Do you run your own business according to the 10 Business Excellence Principles?

Many companies say, 'this stuff does not apply to me', 'I'm different', 'I'm too small', 'This only applies to big companies', 'I am a government department', 'I'm a not-for-profit company', 'I'm special', 'I don't believe in this bit'. But every aspect of the 10 Business Excellence Principles applies to every company—from smallest to biggest, from government organisation to not-for-profit to huge multinational, from manufacturer to service provider.

The Principles are universal. Just as for the law of gravity, they apply to your business—private or public, big or small. Companies that choose not to apply them will ultimately fail regardless of how special they feel.

The 10 Business Excellence Principles apply to all companies whether you like it or not, whether you understand them or not, whether you like them or not. This means that 'not understanding' or saying 'I am special' is something you may come to regret in the future.

Acknowledgments

I LIKE TO THINK that this book is actually the work of the Australian Business Excellence Framework (ABEF) committee that met during 1998 to develop the new ABEF and 1999 to work through the Principles. Many of the ideas presented here have come directly from the discussion of the committee. Special thanks to Dieter Markworth, Kathy Main and Alan Skinner for their insight and to chairman David Clayton who let us explore when we needed to.

I have had many excellent teachers during my journey to the point where it is possible to write this down. I have been a member of eight evaluation teams, three of which I led. Most evaluators learn a huge amount from the discussion about points of disagreement. My thanks go to all the members of those evaluation teams. I would like to especially thank Chris Russell and Brian Thomas for their excellent leadership. Marshal Herron provided extremely insightful training.

I would like to thank:

- all of the companies that I evaluated over the years as an evaluator, the Australian Quality Council (AQC) for infrastructure and permission to quote from the ABEF and training material. The material in the sections on 'good practices' and 'poor practices' began as AQC documents before I heavily modified and added to it. Specifically for the 10 Principles' material used on pages 72–3, 76, 99–101, 104, 109, 113, 119–22, 130–1, 134, 157, 162–3, 169–71, 174–5, 176–7, 189–90, 193–4, 199, 202–3, 206, 207, 211–12, 214–15, 289–90, 293, 353–4
- NIST for material from the Malcolm Baldrige National Quality Award on pages 83–4, 87–8, 115–17, 124, 155, 160–1, 229–30, 284–5, 288, 318–19, 323–4

- Cultural Imprints for Figures 1.4, 1.5, 1.6, 1.7, 2.7, 7.3
- Chris Russell for his original concepts that comprise the two text boxes on being valued in sections 7.6 and 7.8; sections 8.1, 8.2 and 8.7; and material on pages 71–2. Also for his contribution to the Honeywell Innovation Structures and Strategy as their first Innovation Manager
- The Natural Step for material in section 9.4
- Gil Friend for material in section 9.10.

My thinking has been very strongly influenced by the writings of Tice, Covey, Goldratt, Deming, Byham, Kohn and Scholtes.

I would also like to thank my business partner, Graham Le Roux, for his support, and Alex Hausner, for prodding me to write this down and his research, which clarified many issues. I especially thank my wife, Helen Bell, for her support and tolerating the mental absences and the hours of writing and research.

Introduction

The 10 Business Excellence Principles

1. The senior executives' constant role-modelling of the 10 Business Excellence Principles and creation of a supportive environment are necessary to achieve the company's potential.
2. Clear direction allows company alignment and a focus on achievement of goals.
3. Providing what your customers value—now and in the future—must be an essential influence in your company's direction, strategy and action.
4. In order to improve the outcome, improve the system and its associated processes.
5. Effective use of facts, data and knowledge leads to improved decisions.
6. All systems and processes exhibit variability, which affects predictability and performance.
7. The potential of a company is realised through its people's enthusiasm, resourcefulness and participation.
8. Continual improvement and innovation depends on continual learning.
9. The company's action to ensure a clean, safe, fair and prosperous society enhances the perception of its value to the community.
10. Sustainability is determined by a company's ability to create and deliver value for *all* stakeholders.

The 10 Business Excellence Principles

The 10 Business Excellence Principles describe what companies and researchers have come to recognise as the closest thing the business world has to a set of 'business laws'—the business equivalent of the law of gravity. You cannot 'choose' to agree with them or not. Saying you do not agree with them is like saying you do not believe in gravity. You can try to behave as though you do not believe. But that does not mean that gravity will stop acting on you and everything else.

The only way to achieve sustainable business excellence is to recognise that these Principles exist and to work with them. Why fight against gravity or behave as though the earth is flat? The Principles are working whether you like it or not.

Yes, but...

That may all be very well but you know of very successful companies that do not appear to follow these Principles. We all do. That does not mean that you have to follow these Principles to be successful. However, if you do not follow these Principles, your success will be significantly reduced.

Every Principle contributes to success—some contribute more than others, some are crucial. The extent that you are working with these Principles and not working against them determines how successful you are now and in the future.

As you will see, these Principles are commonsense. However, they are definitely not common business practice. Even the most successful companies struggle to implement them fully. Sometimes old practices are just too well established or people do not fully appreciate the extent that they are fighting against gravity. Companies that do not follow the Principles, even if they look successful, could do much better.

You can think of the 10 Business Excellence Principles as similar to the sails (or vanes or arms) of a windmill. If a company has fully implemented a Principle, it is as if that sail is fully deployed and contributes 100% to the effective running of the windmill. If all Principles are fully implemented, all sails are fully deployed and the windmill (or company) is working perfectly. If a Principle is not well implemented, it means the sail does not function well—it does not contribute all that it could to the working of the windmill (or company). Most companies are working with their sails less than 30% deployed. Very few have their sails deployed more than 60%.

The more successful large companies have been working down the path of the 10 Business Excellence Principles since the mid to late 1980s. This has given insights and learning from which you can benefit. We now know what does work and what does not work. And what good practice looks like and what it does not. It is time for the smaller companies to get the opportunity to use the same tools.

How do we know the Principles work?

These are big claims. What do we base these claims on? What is the evidence? Where is the proof? There are three sources of proof:

1. adoption of the Principles by all National Business Excellence bodies
2. analysis of the share market
3. research.

National Business Excellence Frameworks

Around the world, there are about 70 national Business Excellence Frameworks chosen by national governments to provide the best advice to businesses locally about what experts consider excellent business practice.

These frameworks are based on just three foundation frameworks, which are outlined briefly below:

1. The Malcolm Baldrige National Quality Award (MBNQA)
2. The European Foundation for Quality Management (EFQM)
3. The Australian Business Excellence Framework (ABEF).

Each of these three foundation frameworks was first developed in the late 1980s when experts around the world defined the underlying 'rules' that make businesses excellent. This was the culmination of extensive research and experience. *All* three of the frameworks are based on the 10 Business Excellence Principles. The foundation frameworks continue to be updated and modified as further research makes the Principles clearer.

National governments then selected one of the three foundation frameworks as the best advice that they could give their local business community; and rewrote that framework into the local language to give it local flavour and reflect local needs. The national frameworks serve several purposes. They:

- provide the best advice available on what is excellent business practice
- give a practical guide to companies on how to develop action plans to address and implement the 10 Business Excellence Principles
- form a basis from which people in the company can ask questions and gain a deeper understanding about how their company performs in implementing the 10 Business Excellence Principles
- provide a window through which to view a company with respect to the 10 Business Excellence Principles so that strengths and improvement opportunities can be identified

- provide a systems approach to explore *how* the company should work to achieve its goals. It leaves the specifics of *what* is done to address each Principle up to the company.

Often, national governments try to encourage use of the framework by means of a National Business Excellence Award. Each National Business Excellence Award framework describes what examiners (evaluators) for the National Award expect to see during an Award assessment.

Malcolm Baldrige National Quality Award

The Malcolm Baldrige National Quality Award (MBNQA), or Baldrige Award, is the US national framework, named after a former US Secretary of Commerce. Most national frameworks are based on this model and it is the model in most common usage. The MBNQA is designed 'to help improve the competitiveness and performance of US businesses and other organizations by promoting performance excellence, recognizing achievements of US organizations and publicising their successful strategies'.

Baldrige Awards are given in national competitions in manufacturing, service, small business, education and health care. Since 1988, 41 companies have received the Baldrige Award.

European Foundation for Quality Management

The European Foundation for Quality Management (EFQM) Excellence Model is the framework developed in Europe. It is widely used. Most national frameworks that aren't based on the Baldrige Award are based on the EFQM Excellence Model.

The EFQM was created in 1988 by 14 leading European businesses. It has a mission to be the driving force for sustainable excellence in Europe and a vision of a world in which European companies excel.

By January 2001, membership had grown to over 600 members, ranging from major multinationals and important national companies to research institutes in prominent European universities.

The EFQM believes that regardless of a sector's size, structure or maturity, to be successful, companies need to establish an appropriate management system. The EFQM Excellence Model is a practical tool to help companies do this by measuring where they are on the path to excellence; helping them understand the gaps; and develop solutions. The EFQM is committed to researching and updating the model with the inputs of tested good practices from thousands of companies both within and outside of Europe. In this way, EFQM ensures the model remains dynamic and in line with current management thinking.

The Australian Business Excellence Framework

The Australian Business Excellence Framework (ABEF) is prepared and distributed by the Australian Quality Council (AQC). The AQC is a non-profit, non-government body 'committed to promoting a national culture of cooperation for a clean, safe, fair and prosperous society. Its mission is to accelerate company improvement through the adoption of the management Principles and practices that are reflected in the Australian Business Excellence Framework'. The ABEF was developed in 1988 and is based on neither the Baldrige Award nor the European Model. However, like the Baldrige Award and the European Model, it is based on the 10 Business Excellence Principles.

The ABEF applies to all industries and sectors. It provides a framework for companies to establish effective approaches to leadership and management to enable them to survive into the future. Below are results from the 1997 winners of the Australian Business Excellence Award.

- 20% productivity increase in one year
- 247% sales increase over two years
- 600% increase in profit per employee in four years
- 100% profit increase over two years
- 150% increase in tenders won
- 500% increase in share price over six years
- 25% reduction in sick days in one year
- 100% increase in employee numbers in two years
- 66% reduction in lost time injuries in one year
- 80% reduction in product defect rates over two years
- Production faults reduced to 0.4% of previous levels over three years

Share market

The Baldrige Award published studies (see box below) that demonstrate that companies that make a significant effort to work according to these Principles do significantly better than companies that don't. This study is repeated each year with continually good results.

Baldrige index outperforms S&P 500 index by 4.2 : 1

The National Institute of Standards and Technology (NIST), which administers the MBNQA, found in its seventh annual study that the group made up of the whole company winners and the parent companies of 18 subsidiary winners outperformed the S&P 500 index by about 4.2 : 1, achieving a 685% return on investment, compared to a 163% return for the S&P 500 index.

The Baldrige index is a fictitious stock fund made up of publicly traded US companies that have received the Baldrige Award. NIST 'invested' a hypothetical $1000 in each of the subsidiary and whole company winners—ADAC Laboratories (1996 winner), Eastman Chemical Co (1993 winner), Federal Express Corp (1990 winner) and Solectron Corp (a winner in 1991 and 1997). The investments were tracked from the first business day of the month following the announcement of Award recipients through 1 December 2000. Another $1000 hypothetically was invested in the S&P 500 index for the same time period.

Baldrige index stock study: Results of 1990–99 Baldrige Award recipients

The 24 publicly traded Award recipients, as a group, outperformed the S&P 500 index by 4.2:1. A summary of the results follows.

Table I.1 1990–99 Publicly traded Award recipients

	Investment ($)	Value ($) (1/12/99)	Per cent change
1990–99 Award recipients	7282	57 185	685%
S&P 500 index	7282	19 160	163%

Research

Recent doctoral research in Australia by Dr Alexander Hausner at the University of Wollongong showed a link between the Business Excellence Frameworks and corporate success. Dr Hausner found clear evidence of a strong relationship between measurements of business excellence and bottom-line results. This research is called on throughout the book.

Figure I.1 tells an extraordinary story. First the good news. Companies with scores indicating good application of the 10 Business Excellence Principles have the highest profits, productivity and other favourable results. If you are applying the 10 Business Excellence Principles (scoring above 300 ABEF points), every 50-point improvement in ABEF score is rewarded with an approximately 3% increase in your average annual key performance indicator (KPI) improvement. Companies with high ABEF scores are significantly more successful in improving their business results from year to year.

On the other hand, if you do not follow the 10 Business Excellence Principles, you are going backwards. Companies that do not follow the Principles usually score fewer than 300 points when assessed against one of the frameworks. These companies' KPIs are not increasing. In fact, they are going backwards. If this is your company, it is not sustainable.

Unfortunately, most companies score fewer than 300 points when assessed against the 10 Business Excellence Principles. In other words, most companies are going backwards.

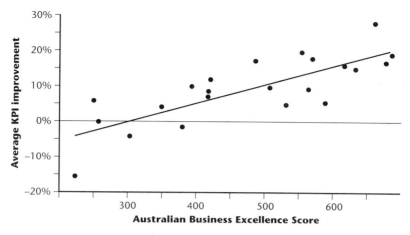

Fig. I.1 Results improve with ABEF score increase

Dr Hausner's study found that a very strong and positive correlation exists between ABEF scores and improvements in bottom-line performance indicators, including financial ones. As described above, the ABEF is one of a number of frameworks used to represent the 10 Business Excellence Principles. A high score on the ABEF or another framework would indicate a thorough application of the 10 Business Excellence Principles. Scores on the 10 Business Excellence Principles should be used as a KPI.

The study shows that high-scoring companies are more likely to:

* achieve positive improvements in their KPIs
* be better-performing.

A company has, therefore, substantial incentive to aim for evaluation scores against the 10 Business Excellence Principles that are as high as possible.

The strength of the results is very encouraging to those companies already focusing or applying the 10 Business Excellence Principles and to those trying to improve their company.

A company's success is clearly correlated with the extent of its application of the 10 Business Excellence Principles. Each company, big or small, manufacturing or service, should use this information to identify and prioritise its own improvement initiatives. This finding should be of considerable importance to small-to-medium enterprises, owners, investment analysts, shareholders and all other stakeholders.

Many companies continue to perceive the 10 Business Excellence Principles as a theory or even a fad with little applicability or benefit for their business environment. The findings described above prove that this is not a fad. It is good business sense.

Most companies (especially the smaller ones) do not know about the Principles or why they should be interested. This book fills that gap. It gives a clear explanation of why the Principles are important, how to know if you are applying them, how to know if you are not and what to do to improve.

All Principles are connected

The words used to define the 10 Business Excellence Principles can be deceptive in that they can lead people to think they are already doing them. Everyone says, 'of course we *lead*, of course we *continually learn*, of course we *value employees*'. It may be precisely because these words are in such common usage that the 10 Business Excellence Principles are so poorly understood. It is not that the Principles use jargon. The wording is precise and the Principles form an interconnecting system, each one affecting the meaning of every other. This interconnectedness can cause people to misunderstand. You find that if you leave out the bits you disagree with, you tear holes in the parts you think you do well in.

Should you use the national frameworks?

Yes. Many companies self-assess against one of the national frameworks. Use your local one. If you enter for a National Award, the evaluation teams do an excellent job and you will get an extremely useful feedback report—very inexpensive consulting for the cost of the application fee. The National Award process allows you to establish a benchmark with other companies and gives you public recognition of your progress that you can use as leverage in your marketing and with financial institutions.

However, the National Awards are not for everyone. Nor would you want the expense and work to prepare for a full inspection of your company every year.

This book gives you an alternative. Do your self-assessment with this easy-to-use book and undertake your improvements before you proceed to the national frameworks. This book explains in clear terms the 10 Business Excellence Principles that form the foundation for the national frameworks and makes the technology more widely available—especially to small-to-medium enterprises. It will help you understand what your strengths are and where you need to improve.

How to use this book

This book presents material you need to make your business more effective. It will give you an action plan to improve your business and make it more successful. To help you find the information you specifically need to help your business, the book is structured around the Business Health Assessment (BHA) questionnaire.

The most effective way of using this book is to begin by doing the BHA questionnaire and, as you go, to read the appropriate parts of the book for clarification and explanation when you think you need it. The questionnaire should take you about 1 hour. That is right. You will have a clear idea of what to do to make your business more effective after about 1 hour's work—a small investment in time.

The BHA questionnaire has 100 questions—10 questions for each of the 10 Business Excellence Principles. Each question has you examine one aspect of the Business Excellence Principles for your business.

The chapters and sections of the book correspond to the BHA questionnaire. There are 10 chapters—one for each of the Principles. Each chapter is divided into 10 sections—one section for each question in the BHA questionnaire. Each chapter explains why this particular Business Excellence Principle is important, what it means, what main concepts it contains and its implications. At the end of each section are two lists that are extremely useful to companies trying to implement these Principles. The first list describes what it looks like when you are doing it well. The second list describes what it looks like when you are on the wrong track.

Some questions and Principles are more important than others. Appendix 2 has a table of the 10 most important questions and the 25 most important questions.

Step 1 Begin with the Business Health Assessment questionnaire

- Do the BHA questionnaire. It should take you about 1 hour. If you need to, or want to, or if you are not sure why the question is being asked, or what it means, refer to the section of the book before you answer it.
- When you have finished, add up your scores. The questions and Principles where you score lowest deserve your attention. For the more important questions, see Appendix 2.
- Read in more detail the parts of the book for the questions and Principles that you scored lowest (and for the more important questions). You should be especially interested in what the Principle means, its implications on other Principles and the good and poor practices.
- An electronic version of the BHA questionnaire can be found at www.netgm.com, which automatically produces a report showing your main strengths and opportunities.
- Develop an action plan of what you intend to do to correct your main shortcomings (those with the lowest score—especially for the more important questions).
- Work to implement your plan. Spend a few minutes each day working on the important issue of improving your company. You may not

have the time and have urgent things to do but this is important. Set aside 30 minutes each day to work on improving your company. This is a small investment but an extremely important one. You will find that this investment will gradually reduce the number of extremely urgent issues you have to deal with. Your company will improve and be more sustainable.

- Don't take on too much. You can realistically tackle only a few issues at a time. Concentrate on the important ones that will make the most difference.

Step 2 Get another opinion

- Appendix 1 contains a second questionnaire for your employees to assess how well the company is achieving the 10 Business Excellence Principles from their point of view. (The employee questionnaire is aligned with the Principles, not with the sections.) Using the two questionnaires (BHA questionnaire for managers and the employee questionnaire) gives a more balanced picture. The two groups often see the company quite differently.
- At the end of each chapter, a number of questions are provided that you could ask your stakeholders in order to further test your implementation of the 10 Business Excellence Principles.
- These additional questionnaires will tell you more about your strengths and areas for improvement. Revisit your plan with this new information.
- Because the 10 Business Excellence Principles are interconnected, you might decide to read the whole book from cover to cover, to see where everything fits.
- Use the www.netgm.com website to communicate with the author and a team of experts.

Step 3 Go around again

- In about six months or a year, check the success of your action plan. Redo the BHA questionnaire. Develop and implement a new action plan. The cycle of improvement does not stop.

Good luck!

Business Health Assessment questionnaire

THIS QUESTIONNAIRE is to assess your company's 'business health' by having you self-assess how well your company applies the 10 Business Excellence Principles. Companies that apply these Business Excellence Principles usually perform significantly better than those that do not.

You need to decide for which level of your company that you are answering these questions. We suggest that you first answer for your most immediate work group. (If you are part of a large organisation, you may later choose to answer as part of the larger group of which your work group forms a part.) A full description of each question is in the text. You can answer the question without reading any of it if you wish.

You should develop an action plan to address your lowest scored questions and Principles. Read those parts of the book in detail. Implement that action plan. Set at least 30 minutes a day aside to work on your plan to improve your company. After six months or a year, redo the questionnaire and make a new plan based on those results.

The scores for all questionnaires are as follows:

0: never-ever
1: never
2: starting—just
3: starting
4: sometimes—rarely
5: sometimes

6: oftenish
7: often
8: always—almost
9: always
10: fantastic at doing it

Principle 1 Senior executives as role models

The senior executives' constant role-modelling of these 10 Business Excellence Principles and creation of a supportive environment are necessary to achieve the organisation's potential.

Score out of 10

1.1	We have a climate of trust.
1.2	We regularly measure employees' perception of senior executive's belief in the 10 Business Excellence Principles (e.g. measurement of 'trustworthiness' of the senior executive, 'fear' and overall 'morale').
1.3	Employee opinion survey results show that the employees think that the senior executives are a consistent role model for the 10 Business Excellence Principles (e.g. trustworthy, believable, with high integrity, committed to the Principles).
1.4	CEO is actively involved in leading improvement efforts (i.e. executives participate and are involved as team members in improvement teams).
→	*Go to Question 2.1 now.* That is, don't answer the following six questions until you have answered all the others. Come back to 1.5 later. It makes it easier.
1.5	Our CEO/president and all our senior executives role-model the 10 Business Excellence Principles (i.e. they believe in them, make all decisions in that context).
1.6	We have strategic plans to increase our scores on all 10 Business Excellence Principles.
1.7	We measure and report our progress with all 10 Business Excellence Principles.
1.8	The reward structure for our CEO/president and senior executives rewards behaviour that is in accordance with these 10 Business Excellence Principles (e.g. the reverse would be 'does the reward system for your CEO and executive reward behaviours that are *not* in line with the 10 Principles?').
1.9	Our senior executives have created (and maintain) a supportive environment within which alignment with the 10 Business Excellence Principles can flourish.
1.10	Our senior executives are knowledgable about the 10 Business Excellence Principles (e.g. how the Principles add business benefit and the specific requirements of a Business Excellence Framework).

Total for Principle 1

Add up your scores and write the total above. ▲
This is your score out of 100 for Principle 1

Principle 2 Focus on achieving goals

Clear direction allows organisational alignment and a focus on achievement of goals.

		Score out of 10
2.1	We have clearly defined goals (i.e. our definitions of success).	
2.2	Our strategic plan addresses meeting the needs and expectations of all our key stakeholders (i.e. owners, organisation, customers, employees, community, alliance partners).	
2.3	We use these 10 Business Excellence Principles to strategically improve the organisation.	
2.4	We have plans to reach all our targets.	
2.5	Our plans to reach new targets describe how we will change (e.g. by improving process or systems, or applying resources).	
2.6	People know what is expected of them (e.g. through being involved in the planning process, having performance agreements and job descriptions).	
2.7	Everyone is enabled (i.e. given skills, knowledge, authority, resources) to implement plans.	
2.8	We measure our progress towards our goals.	
2.9	We measure the extent that our plans are being implemented (i.e. everyone who should be carrying out our strategies and plans is doing so).	
2.10	We now do our strategic work better than we did three years ago.	
	Total for Principle 2	

Add up your scores and write the total above. ▲
This is your score out of 100 for Principle 2

Principle 3 Customer perception of value

Providing what your customers value—now and in the future—must be a key influence in your organisation's direction, strategy and action.

Score out of 10

3.1	We understand clearly what our customers value about our products and services (e.g. we ask them).	
3.2	We have a very good understanding of what our customers don't like about our products and services—the dissatisfiers (e.g. we ask our customers 'what is it about our products and services that you don't like?').	
3.3	We actively seek customer complaints and use them to make better products and services (i.e. remove dissatisfiers).	
3.4	We are working to eliminate (or minimise) all of the things that are part of our products and services but which are not of value to our customers (i.e. all those 'you must do it like this to use it' things—price, payment method and terms, ease of use, ease of access, availability, timeliness, accuracy, reliability).	
3.5	We have designed all aspects of our company to provide what our customers value.	
3.6	We manage our customer contact to ensure the contact is made easy for our customers.	
3.7	All our customer contact staff are specially recruited and enabled (i.e. provided with skills, knowledge, resources, power and authority) to make the contact easy for our customers.	
3.8	We build a relationship of trust with our customers (e.g. we keep our promises, we do not overpromise or promise to do what we cannot do).	
3.9	Our information technology systems make it easy for us to record and retrieve information about our customers (i.e. they help make the customer contact easy for the customers and easy for us to do our work).	
3.10	We measure how well we provide what our customers value.	
	Total for Principle 3	

Add up your scores and write the total above. ▲
This is your score out of 100 for Principle 3

Principle 4 To improve the outcome, improve the system

In order to improve the outcome, improve the system and its associated processes.

		Score out of 10
4.1	We understand the process capability of our main processes.	
4.2	We set targets for improvement of our processes based on the needs of the customers of those processes.	
4.3	We make and implement plans to reach our targets when those targets are outside our current capability.	
4.4	When we want a different result, we change the system.	
4.5	Our performance management system is based on an understanding of process capability.	
4.6	Our managers work on improving processes as a major part of their job function.	
4.7	We work to reduce rework and waste.	
4.8	We document our important processes.	
4.9	We measure the output and outcomes of our processes.	
4.10	The improvements we have made to our systems have resulted in improved outcomes (i.e. they move us closer to our goal and are not 'improvements' that lead nowhere).	
	Total for Principle 4	

Add up your scores and write the total above. ▲
This is your score out of 100 for Principle 4

Principle 5 Improved decisions

Effective use of facts, data and knowledge leads to improved decisions.

Score out of 10

5.1	We always base our daily operational decisions on facts, data and knowledge.	
5.2	We have criteria to stop us gathering data we will not use.	
5.3	We treat our strategies as 'experiments' and measure their success.	
5.4	We rigorously use data to check our assumptions about our business.	
5.5	We always check what we 'know' by gathering facts and data.	
5.6	We have KPIs for and measure our success in reaching our mission, vision and all our important objectives and goals.	
5.7	We use data to make comparisons between different parts of the organisation and with external organisations.	
5.8	We have processes that let us know everything that is going on in our business environment.	
5.9	We treat knowledge as a major organisational resource and manage and use the leverage of our organisational knowledge.	
5.10	We formally review our process for making decisions.	

Total for Principle 5

Add up your scores and write the total above. ▲
This is your score out of 100 for Principle 5

Principle 6 Variability

All systems and processes exhibit variability, which impacts on predictability and performance.

		Score out of 10
6.1	The CEO and senior executive clearly understand that all systems and processes exhibit variability, which impacts on predictability and performance.	
6.2	Managers and staff have been given the skills to allow them to understand variation.	
6.3	Data is always presented in such a way as to allow interpretation of the variation.	
6.4	We use control charts extensively for data presentation.	
6.5	We work to make processes more stable by reducing special cause variation.	
6.6	We work to make processes more capable by reducing common cause variation.	
6.7	We know that reducing variation reduces costs.	
6.8	We are working to reduce variation in all our products and services.	
6.9	We calculate our process capability for our main products and services.	
6.10	We work to reduce variation in the early steps of all processes.	
	Total for Principle 6	

Add up your scores and write the total above. ▲
This is your score out of 100 for Principle 6

Principle 7 Enthusiastic people

The potential of an organisation is realised through its people's enthusiasm, resourcefulness and participation.

		Score out of 10
7.1	We have created, maintain and support an environment where people volunteer their enthusiasm, creativity and resourcefulness aligned with the company's goals and objectives.	
7.2	We have formed an alliance partnership with our employees—each party working for the benefit of the other.	
7.3	We give our employees space to have their say, we show we care and we keep our promises.	
7.4	All our employees know what their job is, what is expected of them and how they contribute to the company's success.	
7.5	We make certain our employees are properly enabled to carry out their work (i.e. provided with sufficient skills, knowledge, resources and authority).	
7.6	We work to ensure our work environment provides value to our employees.	
7.7	We pay our employees well and fairly (e.g. we don't attempt to manipulate them by incentive schemes).	
7.8	We actively search for what dissatisfies our employees and work to overcome those dissatisfiers.	
7.9	We measure how our employees feel about our company (e.g. that they get value from being part of it; that they are provided with sufficient skills, knowledge, resources and authority to carry out their work; that they are given space to have their say, we show we care and we keep our promises; that there is a climate of trust).	
7.10	We measure the effectiveness of training and education (e.g. that it changed what employees do).	
	Total for Principle 7	

Add up your scores and write the total above. ▲
This is your score out of 100 for Principle 7

Principle 8 Learning, innovation and continual improvement

Continual improvement and innovation depends on continual learning.

		Score out of 10
8.1	We have created an environment of continual learning, continual improvement and innovation (e.g. employees are prepared to try new ideas, experiment, innovate and take reasonable risks; people are encouraged to take initiatives and be proactive).	
8.2	We continually innovate (adapt; provide new products and services; do things differently; copy good ideas from everywhere we can—from competitors, other industries, customers, between processes, technology, salespeople).	
8.3	We use tools and techniques to generate new concepts.	
8.4	We systematically eliminate the barriers to innovation (e.g. structures, traditions, politics, fear in the workplace).	
8.5	When we implement new ideas, all the old structures that the new will impact on are also changed (e.g. reward and recognition systems; performance management systems; technology; standard operating procedures; standards systems; communications systems; company structure; performance indicators; resources; job descriptions; performance agreements; organisation values; audit systems).	
8.6	We systematically overcome the barriers that prevent us implementing our innovations (e.g. existing stock, past investment, no time or budget).	
8.7	We take a strategic approach to innovation, implementation and continuous improvement (e.g. innovation and implementation objectives; resources provided to assist innovation and implementation, including seed funding and champions).	
8.8	We continually learn (from others, from what we do, from our mistakes, from our varied success, from our strategies and approaches, from our customers, from our competitors, from our employees, from technology, from each new idea we implement).	
8.9	We make time to reflect on what has happened or is happening, and why it is happening.	
8.10	We take a strategic approach to learning (e.g. we have learning objectives and strategies to grow our core competencies and knowledge).	
	Total for Principle 8	

Add up your scores and write the total above. ▲
This is your score out of 100 for Principle 8

Principle 9 Corporate citizenship

The company's action to ensure a clean, safe, fair and prosperous society enhances the perception of its value to the community.

		Score out of 10
9.1	We always operate using standards of ethics that are acceptable by the community.	
9.2	What we do adds value to the community, rather than costs the community money in the long or short term.	
9.3	We do nothing that will endanger the community's prosperity, health, safety or cleanliness.	
9.4	We are working strategically to reduce the harm that we do to the environment (e.g. our dependence on mining and fossil fuels, our dependence on persistent, unnatural substances, and our dependency on nature-consuming activities). We always try to do more with less.	
9.5	We work to reduce the waste and pollution our organisation produces.	
9.6	We use a set of environmental performance indicators (e.g. we monitor the environmental impact at production sites, the average environmental standard of products and profitability of our most environmentally sound products).	
9.7	We work to reduce the unintended consequences (side-effects) to the community of our actions and policies (e.g. we keep the community safe and do no harm—intentionally or unintentionally).	
9.8	We constantly work to improve our industry (e.g. its code of conduct, how it operates, sharing of knowledge on what does and does not work well, changing regulations that affect us, and regulators' and community perceptions).	
9.9	We share our knowledge about the 10 Business Excellence Principles with others to help them prosper.	
9.10	We take a strategic approach to our corporate citizenship (e.g. we plan our approach to all aspects of Principle 9; we measure our success as a good corporate citizen).	
	Total for Principle 9	

Add up your scores and write the total above. ▲
This is your score out of 100 for Principle 9

Principle 10 Value for all stakeholders

Sustainability is determined by a company's ability to create and deliver value for all stakeholders.

		Score out of 10
10.1	We have objectives, strategies and plans to address the needs of and to create and deliver value for all the company's stakeholders (e.g. owners, customers, the company itself, employees, the community, and suppliers and alliance partners).	
10.2	We deliberately invest (funds and effort) to meet the needs of each major stakeholder group. (We treat these as investment decisions to reach our goals and objectives and to meet their needs.)	
10.3	We negotiate a balance with representatives of all our major stakeholder groups.	
10.4	Our reward and recognition systems focus on the long-term best interest of the organisation (rather than the short-term interest of the executives).	
10.5	We use innovative and inventive ways to create and deliver value for all our major stakeholder groups.	
10.6	We measure the investment we make in meeting the needs of each major stakeholder group (e.g. we measure the apportionment between the major stakeholder groups).	
10.7	We measure our success in meeting our objectives for all our stakeholder groups (i.e. success including and beyond financial performance by determining how we are achieving success for each of our stakeholders by integrating and balancing their needs).	
10.8	We use a balanced set of performance indicators.	
10.9	We use leading indicators and other measurements to predict our long-term sustainability.	
10.10	We keep our stakeholders informed of our progress.	
	Total for Principle 10	

Add up your scores and write the total above. ▲
This is your score out of 100 for Principle 10

← Go back to Question 1.5 and answer the remaining six questions in Principle 1 now that you have more idea of what the 10 Business Excellence Principles are.

Principle 1
Senior executives as role models

The senior executives' constant role-modelling of the 10 Business Excellence Principles and creation of a supportive environment are necessary to achieve the company's potential.

PRINCIPLE 1 IS A CENTRAL ISSUE of the 10 Business Excellence Principles. If the chief executive officer (CEO) and the senior executive team do not believe in the 10 Business Excellence Principles and do not make all their decisions in alignment with the Principles, the business will fail. Success will not be sustainable. It is as clear-cut as that. If the CEO believes in the Principles, they can be implemented. If not, the company is on a slippery slope to failure.

Senior executives must take a deliberate role to develop the company's culture in line with the Principles. This demonstrates to employees that the senior executives think that the Principles are important and counteracts the treacle of inertia and tradition.

Company culture describes 'the way things are done around here'. It represents how the people act on what they see to be the company's 'values and beliefs'. It includes the 'norms' of behaviour that are acceptable to the company, such as working hours, decision-making processes, dress code, modes of speech and so on. It includes how the company acts to implement each of the 10 Business Excellence Principles.

The senior executives greatly influence the company's culture. Culture develops, in part, through deliberate efforts by leaders to instil 'our way of doing things' throughout the company, but also through imperceptible evolution. So you cannot just pay lip service to this. People judge you by what you *do*, not by what you *say*.

You might argue that many companies do not operate by these Principles and are still successful. The research presented in the Introduction shows that this is a matter of lost opportunities. The results indicate that the more the company adopts the Principles, the more successful it will be—as it uses more and more of its potential. Conversely, the less the Principles are adopted, the more room there is for more success. However, there are two important qualifiers to that general statement:

1. If the senior executive does not believe in these Principles, if he or she does not role-model them, does not make all decisions in alignment with them and does not maintain an environment that supports others to do likewise, then the company's benefit from the Principles will be limited. And so will its success.
2. If the company scores fewer than 300 points on any of the frameworks (Baldrige, European or Australian), it is going backwards and its prospects for survival are limited.

Why this Principle is number one

This Principle is listed as number one before any of the Principles have been described because it is of the utmost importance. It is the number one risk for a company.

Dr Hausner's research show that Principle 1 ties with Principles 6 ('Variability') and 10 ('Value for all stakeholders') for the highest correlation with key performance indicator (KPI) improvement. All three are extremely important.

It is critical that all senior executives are role models of these Principles—of the new thinking. They must be seen to believe in them absolutely and not allow their behaviour or that of others to slip back to the old thinking.

1.1 Create a climate of trust

The climate of trust runs through all the Principles. For example, it will not be the boss who does the actual work. The boss needs enthusiastic people who volunteer their creativity in dealing with customers, in finding solutions to company problems, in building new and innovative products and services. Nothing kills off volunteering, enthusiasm and creativity more than lack of trust. There is a direct relationship between trust and creativity (Fig. 1.1). As trust goes up, so does creativity and enthusiasm. Once you get above a certain level of trust, that is. Below that level, which may be different for each individual, you get no enthusiasm. The person has switched off. You get their body but not their mind. And you cannot buy trust, creativity or enthusiasm.

People do not trust the boss

Establishing a climate of trust is a lot harder than you might like it to be—even after you have adopted the new thinking and are truly working towards the Principles.

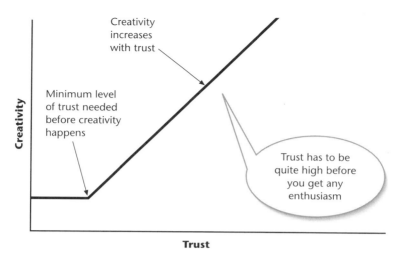

Fig. 1.1 Creativity increases with trust

For a start, your employees will distrust you. David Firth, author of *The Corporate Fool*, says that everyone is watching the boss—to see what bosses do and because what the boss does will affect them. When you watch something, you focus on it, which is like putting a spotlight on it. When you put a spotlight on someone, you get shadows that you can see at the same time as you can see the person.

Bosses have two shadows

- *Shadow 1*: The boss is saying 'challenge me', 'give me information', 'tell me what is happening'. The troops 'know' that the last person who did this was beaten to death. They know that you 'never challenge the boss, or tell what is going on'. Even if this is a myth, it is a strongly held belief.
- *Shadow 2*: Everyone knows that '*All* bosses are inherently untrustworthy and deceitful. *All* bosses are bastards'.

SHADOW 2
SHADOW 1

Spotlight

Fig. 1.2 Bosses have two shadows

3

Although the boss is saying 'we need to do new and exciting things' and would like to be treated as a trustworthy person, everyone knows not to trust the boss and that the best way forward is to believe in the shadows and not do anything. This is a huge dilemma with maybe insurmountable problems for the boss. It is at the heart of building successful companies.

There are two solutions to this dilemma. Steven Covey's concepts of trustworthiness (Fig. 1.3) and emotional bank accounts (Table 1.1) provide definite ways you can show you value, respect and appreciate a diversity of opinions.

Trustworthiness

One of the Principles that underpins Covey's work is that of trustworthiness. If you have integrity and honesty, you will keep your promises—to yourself and to others. People can trust you. Or, putting it another way, if you keep your promises, you are worthy of trust or trustworthy.

Trustworthiness represents a circle. If you keep your word, people trust you (to keep your word). If people know you are trustworthy, they are likely to believe you. That is, people will trust what you say to be the truth.

However, trust is an ephemeral thing. Despite your best intentions, it can be very easy for people to lose their trust in you. It might be the first time you break your word—the first time you do something untrustworthy. You may not even mean to. Or, it might only be one group that perceives you have broken your word. You can certainly lose your trustworthiness without deserving to. There is no guarantee of fairness.

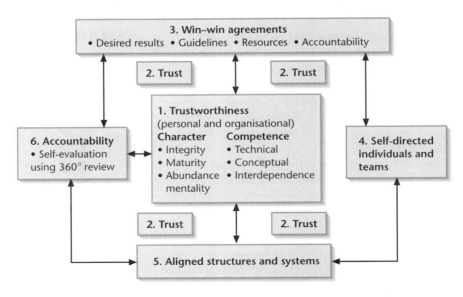

Fig. 1.3 Trustworthiness

You can quickly find examples outside the workplace. Think about your family. Your children will certainly let you know when they think you have broken your word.

Emotional bank account

To help us deal with this issue, Covey, in *The Seven Habits of Highly Effective People*, gives us the tool of making 'emotional deposits'. Covey believes that we establish 'emotional bank accounts' with each other. Just like a bank account, we can make deposits in the 'emotional bank account' or we can make withdrawals. And all of us do make withdrawals—regardless of our best efforts. The boss will make significant withdrawals just by the nature of the work place. When you align this with David Firth's work, the only conclusion is that you must constantly work on making deposits in the emotional bank account. Table 1.1 shows which actions make deposits and which actions make withdrawals.

Table 1.1 The emotional bank account

Deposits	Withdrawals
Kindness, courtesies	Unkindnesses, discourtesies
Keeping promises	Breaking promises
Clarifying expectations	Violating expectations
Loyalty to the absent	Disloyalty, duplicity
Apologies	Pride, conceit, arrogance
Seek first to understand	Seek first to be understood
Receiving feedback and giving 'I' messages	Not receiving feedback and giving 'You' messages

Source: Covey Leadership Centre, Provo, Utah.

Notice that Covey talks in terms of emotions. Most people make their decisions based on their emotions, experiences and the impact on their alliances.

As with all of Covey's suggestions, these are not quick-fix solutions. There are no shortcuts. No step can be missed in building a trustworthy character. It takes a long time to build up the deposits, yet these can be eroded in an instant with a thoughtless action or comment. You have to be seen to be trustworthy and making deposits for a long time to be truly considered trustworthy.

Communications and trust

Communication within the company is a good indicator of trust. In most companies, *all* people complain about the communications. Covey suggests that this is indicative of an environment of poor trust. If people believe that you tell the truth, there are not likely to be 'communications problems'. It is very hard to talk your way out of a problem that resulted from your behaviour and poor communication. Actions always speak much louder than words.

Integrity

Integrity means keeping your promises to yourself and to others. Integrity also contains the concept of wholeness. You keep *all* your promises, and tell *all* of the truth, *all* of the time.

Good practices

- A feeling of 'trust' throughout the company.
- A strong commitment by senior leadership to maintain staff morale.
- People can decide things and work with few rules.
- Leadership at all levels throughout the company is encouraged and developed by the CEO.
- Bosses prize surprises.
- Senior executives pay explicit attention to ethical issues pertinent to the company's situation/industry.
- A clear framework of ethics for decision making exists.
- Work is refused if accepting it will compromise the company's ethics or values, even if the work is very lucrative. A clear framework for such decisions exists and is understood by all.
- All staff can articulate the values of the company and how they are based on the 10 Business Excellence Principles, and can give examples of how the values are used to drive behaviour (especially by the senior executives).
- Plans reflect company values and basic beliefs.

Poor practices

- Bosses think they are customers.
- Senior executives 'promote' the Principles but their behaviour shows that they do not believe in them.
- Senior executives presume that saying 'good words' discharges their responsibility to participation.
- Someone else writes the CEO's speeches about this.

1.2 Measure employees' perception

Measure your employees' perception of the senior executive's belief in the 10 Business Excellence Principles regularly. For example, you should measure perceptions of 'trustworthiness' of the senior executive, 'fear' and overall 'morale'.

If you do not know what people expect of their leaders, it is difficult to provide it. 'Employees' are the 'customers' of the senior executive's 'leadership'. So, just as you find out what your customers need and then provide it, you must do the same for your employees. Poor leaders behave as though this relationship does not exist.

Old- and new-style bosses

There are two different types of bosses with fundamentally different views about people—two very different types of thinking.

1. *Old-style bosses*: These bosses think the world is predictable except for people, who cannot be trusted—'people are fundamentally bad'. They believe that someone must take charge to give order, predictability and stability, and that structures are needed to support order, viability and survival. They discourage new ideas, creativity and innovation. They believe that staff are willing servants waiting to do what they are told, while leaders control.
2. *New-style bosses*: These bosses believe that people are co-responsible for creating their own world—'people are fundamentally good'. They see companies as having a flexible role and that people have many jobs and many roles. They welcome innovation and trust people. They see influence as dependent on knowledge and skills and not position—they do not pigeonhole people—and that leaders enable and empower.

In today's world, the old-style boss is being seen as less and less relevant, while the new-style boss is being seen as increasingly relevant. Some people argue that there is usually room in most companies for both types of thinking. They argue that some people and some processes need the old style of management—where more control is needed and failure to follow rules exactly can result in poor work. Or, that 'lazy, don't care employees need a good tough boss who will stand for no nonsense and keep everything in line'.

This is not convincing. Why did you hire 'lazy, don't care employees'? You didn't! Perhaps your style of 'bossing' has turned them off. Why have you designed your processes to require such a close level of supervision? Whether or not that is the way you have always done it, given a chance, those 'lazy, don't care employees' could probably design a process that would create huge savings. For business to be successful, there is no longer any room for the old-style boss.

Hearts and minds

We hear a lot about getting people 'to bring their hearts and minds to work and not leave them at the gate'. However, as Figure 1.4 shows, much of the 'leaving hearts and minds at the gate' is the result of employees' experiences with their bosses.

Consider this. You are at a meeting with a number of other people. You have a lot to say but you are being ignored. If you are given space, enabled and empowered, you volunteer with considerable enthusiasm (Fig. 1.4, top right). If you are not, you become emotionally detached and withdraw (bottom right). If this goes on long enough, you become emotionally detached and isolated (top left). This can continue until you become so detached that you just go to work to pick up your pay. By this stage, you have definitely left your heart and mind at the gate.

Where did this begin and who has the opportunity to fix it? It began with the boss. If bosses continue to blame the employees for leaving their hearts and minds at the gates, they get nowhere. The fault is usually with the boss, not the employee. Old styles of management put people on to the left-hand side of the enthusiasm matrix and keep them there.

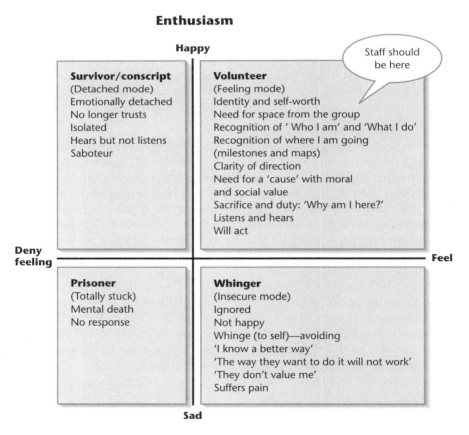

Fig. 1.4 The enthusiasm matrix

Many of the detached employees who come to work just to pick up their pay have very active lives away from the workplace. They have active lives in an environment where they are allowed to volunteer and where they feel appreciated. It is at work where they learn not to volunteer, that they withdraw and often become aggressive.

You can take over (or invade) a person's 'space' by making decisions that they should make or in which they should be involved; by taking work away from them (or not allowing them to do their work); by not considering their opinion or needs; by ignoring them; by bullying them; by put-downs; by making loud noises (or music) from which they cannot escape.

As a new-style leader, your job is to keep people in the top right quadrant. Keeping them there can be a lot easier than getting them back. Depending on how much damage was done with old-style bossing, you may have a lot of work to do to help people move from the various states of withdrawal.

How do you keep them there or get them back? As well as trust and valuing diversity, leaders have to supply several other attributes as outlined in the next section.

Good practices

- Regular measurements of: employees' perception of 'trustworthi-ness' of the senior executives; senior executives' belief in the 10 Business Excellence Principles; 'fear' and overall 'morale'. Measure the gap and act on the results.
- Close agreement between what senior executives say happens in the culture (e.g. regarding values in use, climate, ethics, creativity and innovation, company agility, valuing diversity) and what staff say happens. Measure the gap and act on the results.
- Staff evaluate the performance of their senior executives and 'management' (i.e. 360 degree feedback system). This feedback is acted upon.

Poor practices

- A culture of blame when things go wrong. This significantly discourages risk taking and innovation.
- 'Leadership' is confined to particular levels of the hierarchy.
- An attitude that all 'good ideas' come from the boss. People have to work out how to have the boss think he/she thought of the idea.
- Apparent uniformity of thought across the company, usually manifested as an unwillingness to challenge management.
- Fear of saying what is on one's mind or criticising the opinions and demands of management.
- A fear of failure.

- Blame when innovations do not work.
- Bosses hate surprises.
- Risk aversion—like a tortoise withdrawing into its shell, it is better to take no risks, that way you cannot get into trouble. Many government companies are very risk averse, seeking to eliminate risk no matter what the cost.
- Staff do not take initiative to find out how to solve problems—difficulties are simply passed up the hierarchy.
- The values statements bear no relationship to the 10 Business Excellence Principles.
- Untrustworthy executives.
- An attitude of: 'Who cares what business the customer is in. If it's legitimate in law, it's okay by me'.

1.3 Employee survey results

The results of the employee opinion survey results should show that the employees think that the senior executives are a consistent role model for the 10 Business Excellence Principles (e.g. trustworthy, believable, with high integrity, committed to the Principles).

It is important to measure employees' perceptions of their senior executives' belief in the 10 Business Excellence Principles. It is important to get high scores on that questionnaire and be seen to be doing things to improve those scores.

Set direction and have consistent values

Having consistent values means the leader does not blow in the wind like a flag—taking on the beliefs and direction of the last person he or she spoke to, or representing this cause today and representing a contrary cause tomorrow. Leaders have to be consistent, trustworthy and able to keep their word. This does not mean that you stick with the old direction no matter what when conditions change. The good leader is in the top right quadrant of Figure 1.5. Look at the dysfunctions in the other three quadrants.

Good leaders give support

Employees also respond to the leader who provides support either by 'being there' for them—explaining, showing, encouraging and acknowledging contribution (Fig. 1.6, top right)—or, from a distance, by smoothing the way, opening doors, providing resources, allowing people to look after themselves and standing up for them (Fig. 1.6, bottom right). Consider the bullying behaviour of the 'bastards' on the left—the old-style boss—that generally causes people to withdraw their enthusiasm.

Your employees will respond best if you show you care and help to provide support and build bridges to the future (top right). The saying 'I

A leader provides direction and sticks to their principles

To be consistent

• Bloody minded • Ignorant • Reliable but no vision • Asks for reports but gives no outline • 'You work it out' attitude • 'It's best to throw people in at the deep end' attitude	• Reliable and has vision • Can rely on them • Trustworthy

CEO should be here

No direction ———————————————————— **To provide direction**

• Headless chook • Weak • Wavers	• No clarity • Confusion • 'Fadist'—flavour of the month • Says one thing, does another • Followers have to 'hedge their bets'

To be inconsistent

Fig. 1.5 The consistent values matrix

A leader supports their followers

Being there

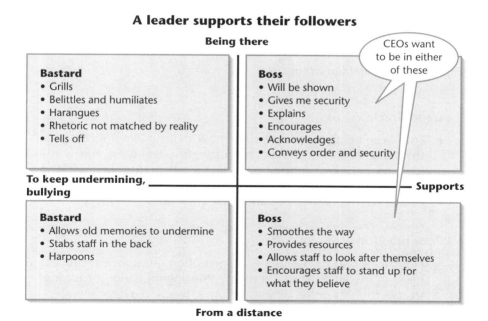

CEOs want to be in either of these

Bastard
- Grills
- Belittles and humiliates
- Harangues
- Rhetoric not matched by reality
- Tells off

Boss
- Will be shown
- Gives me security
- Explains
- Encourages
- Acknowledges
- Conveys order and security

To keep undermining, bullying ———————————————————— **Supports**

Bastard
- Allows old memories to undermine
- Stabs staff in the back
- Harpoons

Boss
- Smoothes the way
- Provides resources
- Allows staff to look after themselves
- Encourages staff to stand up for what they believe

From a distance

Fig. 1.6 The support matrix

don't care what you know until I know that you care' could be modified to 'I don't care what you want me to do until I know that you care'.

This is done by teaching, encouraging, nurturing and helping people see the future—encouraging the heart (Fig. 1.7). Notice the behaviours in the other three quadrants: dictator, petty bureaucrat, technocrat. None of these behaviours are effective in achieving an enthusiastic workforce. They turn people off.

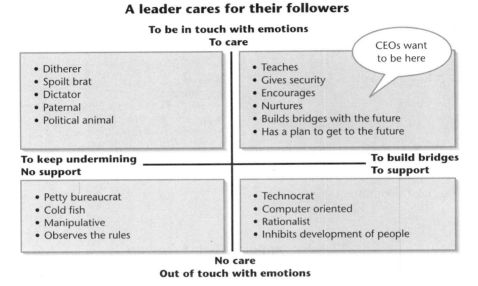

Fig. 1.7 The care and support matrix

Good practices

- Employee opinion survey results show that the employees think that their senior executives are trustworthy and believable, with high integrity, and committed to and a consistent role model for the Principles.
- People have confidence in and value their bosses' motives.

Poor practices

- Not measuring the employees' perception of senior executives' belief in the 10 Business Excellence Principles (i.e. not measuring trustworthiness of the senior executive, fear and overall morale).
- Untrustworthy behaviour.
- A climate of fear.
- Not caring about staff morale ('they will get over it' attitude).

- An attitude of confrontation, payback ('we'll teach them' attitude).
- Feuds.
- Bearing grudges for past infringements.

1.4 CEO leads improvement

The CEO should be actively involved in leading improvement efforts. The senior executives should participate and be actively involved as team members in improvement teams. In other words, it is not what you say that matters, it is what you do. Bosses who tell employees to do something but themselves do something else are not credible.

Improving the company is a fundamental role of all managers, including the CEO. The CEO has more opportunity to improve the company than any other person because of the authority he or she has. If the CEO delegates improving the company, it will not happen. Delegation of 'improvement' says loud and clear that this issue does not matter.

Experience suggests that the CEO (and all managers) should spend 40% of their time improving their part of the company. It is that important! You may say you don't have time. Make the time! This is important and you probably don't have time because your part of the company is ineffective and inefficient, and needs to be improved.

Good practices

- The CEO is actively seen to lead improvement and be involved in improvement efforts.
- Senior management 'own' processes. Line manages and executives together understand they have responsibility to ensure improvement of processes.
- Management is actively involved as team members of many process improvement teams.
- Executives see themselves as team members. They participate in a number of teams, demonstrating commitment by participation. As a team member, they usually work to build the team's capability to make their own decisions, gradually increasing the other team members' authority.
- An appropriate use of teams to solve problems and assist management.

Poor practices

- Senior executives say how much they agree with the Principles but staff say that they do not see behaviour that supports the rhetoric.
- The top of the hierarchy may 'talk the talk' but it does not 'walk the talk'.

1.5 All executives are role models

If the CEO and the senior executive team do not completely believe in the 10 Business Excellence Principles and do not make all their decisions in alignment with the Principles, the business will fail.

If you accept that these Principles describe a way of doing business that works and that leads to more and more success, then it is important to look for the major enemies of that success. Surprisingly, the first and major potential enemy is the CEO or president. If that person does not understand these Principles and does not make all their decisions to work with the Principles—rather than against them—then that person will drag the company away from its potential, regardless of how much they look like they know what they are doing.

Remember that these Principles are similar to scientific laws, like the temperature at which water boils. If your CEO behaves as though it would be more convenient for water to boil at a different temperature, then that person is failing to help the company reach its full potential. Such behaviour can result from lack of knowledge or from failing to believe that the 10 Business Excellence Principles really do mean more success.

Unfortunately, for companies and their stakeholders, the Principles represent such a huge shift in thinking for many CEOs that they cannot adopt them.

Good practices

- Executives are role models of appropriate behaviours.
- Steadfast personal commitment and involvement of the CEO and other senior executives in everything they do shows deep-felt belief in the 10 Principles of Business Excellence.
- People at the top of the company personally demonstrate their commitment to the vision, mission, objectives and values.
- Senior executives see that their main job is to reach the company's objectives and provide value to all stakeholders.

Poor practices

- Bosses delegate 'business improvement'.
- 'Business improvement' is separate from 'the business'.
- Bosses do not work to improve processes—just want people to work harder.
- The senior executives delegate this 'business excellence stuff' to change agents.
- No direct involvement by senior executives in continuous improvement.

1.6 Plan to increase business excellence scores

The 10 Business Excellence Principles are extremely important for the success of the company. You should have strategic plans to increase your scores on all 10 Business Excellence Principles.

As described in the Introduction, these 10 Business Excellence Principles are as fundamental to business as gravity. The better you are at applying them, the better your company will perform. If you choose to behave as though they do not apply to you and your company, you will perform less well and possibly fail.

If you like, you can think of them as extremely important infrastructure. That is, something in which you must invest in order to do well. The more you invest, the better your company will do. If you don't invest, you could fail.

Time conflict

Most companies are faced with a conflict. You are trying to run a company successfully and make money now and in the future. In order to make money, you have to spend time looking after your customers and the daily running of the company. If you are looking after your customers and the daily running of the company, you don't have time to work on building the infrastructure needed to improve your company.

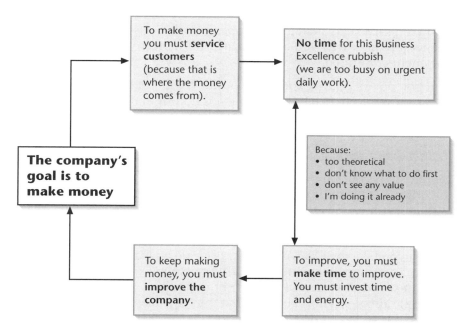

Fig. 1.8 No time to improve

On the other hand, in order to be successful and make money now and in the future, you have to build the infrastructure needed to improve your company. After all, organisations that get fewer than 300 points in the Baldrige, European or Australian Business Excellence Frameworks are going backwards and will not survive! So you will have to make time to invest in improving the company or, in the long term, you won't survive.

Figure 1.8 shows a normal time-conflict situation for all companies.

Make strategies

The best way to resolve a time-conflict situation is to elevate the importance of the issue. That is:

- make business improvement as important as daily operational issues
- determine an objective for each Business Excellence Principle
- determine what you must do most urgently (i.e. where you are weakest and would make most gains, or where you are most exposed)
- prioritise your objectives
- develop strategies and plans to achieve those objectives
- conduct cost–benefit analyses and make your investment decisions
- allocate time and resources to implement the plans
- implement and project manage these plans
- measure how well you are implementing the plans (i.e. that time and resources are being allocated efficiently and not being soaked up by other projects such as daily operations)
- measure how well you are meeting your objectives and getting the benefits promised.

If you do not do this, then your business will not be aligned with the 10 Business Excellence Principles. If you do not make time to improve your business, then your company will fail.

'I am already doing it'

People often say, 'I am already doing it'. That may be true—for some of the Principles or in some parts of your company. The experience of the evaluators for each of the major National Business Excellence Awards is that very, very few companies are doing any of this well. None are doing all of it well.

Can you take the risk? At the very least, do an assessment against the Principles using the Business Health Assessment questionnaire. Then you can see what you need to do most urgently.

People also say, 'I don't believe that the Principles are valid'. However, that is like saying, 'I don't believe in gravity'. Yet, like gravity, these Principles are known to work.

Good practices

- Business improvement is included in the strategic plan.
- The major business improvement issues are identified.
- Resources are allocated to business improvement.

Poor practices

- Accidental or contrived linkages between the 10 Business Excellence Principles and the actions of the company.
- Business Excellence practices are add-ons (i.e. they are done sometimes, done to comply with external examiners' requests) and the 'real business' is elsewhere.

1.7 Measure progress with the 10 Business Excellence Principles

You should measure and report your progress with all 10 Business Excellence Principles as this is the best way to make certain that you are doing them—'what gets measured gets done'. If you do not set up a system of measurements and insist on reports, you are demonstrating that 'this is not important', that 'no-one cares about it'. If it is not made important, people will not do it.

Measure the extent of implementation

You should measure that the people who should be doing the business improvement projects are doing them, that the resources are being allied to the projects, and that deadlines are being met. It is very easy for people to say 'I was too busy with work, I need more time'. You should not accept this excuse as it implies that:

- people could not or did not make time for the improvement project
- 'real work' is more important than improving the business.

This does not mean that you cannot be sympathetic about a lack of time because you must solve today's problems today or you might not be around to have problems tomorrow. However, if you hear this excuse often, then you have a problem, which could be due to:

- not enough resources
- the project being too difficult
- incentives that make 'real work' more attractive than improvement work
- improvement work not being seen as work
- more kudos, respect and career advancement in fighting fires and doing real work than in working to build infrastructures for tomorrow's business.

These indicate significant problems that must be solved or business improvement will always be shunted off to do later.

In most companies, projects are set up, people find good reasons not to do them and excuses for slipped deadlines are accepted. As soon as that happens, you have implied that business improvement is not important. This is not to suggest that you blame the people involved because there are very good reasons why they are not doing the projects. You need to identify and fix those problems. Blaming people is not an acceptable excuse for not fixing systems.

Measure success and failure

You should also measure to see if your improvement projects are, in fact, leading to successful outcomes. Are they effective? Is the business actually improving?

You always need to measure to see if any of your strategies are working. Business improvement strategies are strategies and so you must test to see if they are working. Success measurements would include that your rating on the Principles has improved. You could make this assessment by assessing your company using the questionnaire.

Difficulties with self-rating

Unfortunately, self-rating is difficult. When most people first come across the 10 Business Excellence Principles and do their first few self-assessments, they consistently overestimate how well they are doing. It is only with experience and understanding that people say, 'I was not as good at that as I originally thought. I am better now than I was, but those original scores of mine were from dreamland'.

In many ways it is like someone who sees a sport on television and says (without knowledge), 'That looks easy, I think I can do that easily. I give myself a 5. I am good at that'. For example, the sport may be skiing. It looks easy but when the person tries it, it is hard to do. He or she then re-rates themself to a zero, takes some lessons and puts in a lot of time to learn. This builds up the self-rating to a 7 or a 9. Then, the person tries some very difficult terrain or a race. The self-rating drops again. It will rise again when you gain skills in the area in which you found yourself weak.

Good practices

- Self-assessment against the 10 Business Excellence Principles is conducted yearly. Results are fed back to the strategic plan.
- The results of business improvement are reported with other KPIs.

Poor practices

- Financial KPIs are not included in business improvement projects. This would indicate that business improvement is an add-on and the real business of making money is done elsewhere by the real people.

1.8 Reward executives for business excellence

The reward structure for your CEO/president and senior executives must reward behaviour that is in accordance with these 10 Business Excellence Principles. The reverse would be that the reward system for your CEO and executives rewards behaviours that are not in line with the 10 Principles. This, unfortunately, is extremely common and CEOs and managers are still often rewarded:

- for overly compensating owners and shareholders in the form of excessive dividend streams that should have been reinvested in the long-term success of the company
- when customer perception of value is declining
- for selling, discontinuing or failing to maintain the company's core competencies
- when they have failed to improve the core processes and systems of the company
- when they make decisions based on gut feelings rather than data, information and knowledge
- when they fail to measure the results of their strategies
- when they fail to review their strategies and plans to see if they have been successful
- when they maintain a regime that punishes innovation and squelches the enthusiasm of employees
- when they fail to make plans or modify systems and processes to reach targets.

Appointment contradictions

For many managers, the thinking behind the 10 Business Excellence Principles is so different from the behaviour that led to their current position that they cannot acknowledge that following the Principles will result in more success for their company.

It is almost as though the reward structure that results in the selection of CEOs is based on thinking that does not lead to success for the company and its stakeholders. If that is so, then it is time that the stakeholders took much more interest in the selection and behaviour of the CEO—especially stakeholders such as shareholders and other owners' representatives.

The role of the board and the owners

The CEO must try to run the company in line with these 10 Business Excellence Principles. The board should:

- expect the CEO to do so
- reward actions that are in line with the Principles
- select CEOs for their knowledge of and adherence to these Principles
- dismiss CEOs and managers who work in ways that are against these Principles.

Boards that reward CEOs for behaviour and performance that is not in accordance with the Principles are reducing the potential performance of the company and hence reducing the value to all the stakeholders—owners, customers, employees, community and alliance partners.

Although this is not logical, you continue to see boards appoint CEOs who behave as though these Principles do not exist and who demand CEOs to do things that are clearly not in the interest of the company.

Unfortunately, you also see share prices rise when a slash-and-burn CEO is appointed; that is, a CEO who will deliver short-term profit at the expense of investing in the company and its shareholders. This is clearly illogical. The share price should fall because the long-term viability of the company is threatened.

New CEO? Beware!

Most of us have seen what happens in companies that have made significant progress towards business excellence when an old-thinking CEO replaces a new-thinking CEO. The result is usually a dismantling of the things that work and a decline towards mediocrity again. When an old-thinking CEO replaces a new-thinking CEO, the share price should drop and it eventually will. In those cases, the board that replaced the CEO has done no favours to the shareholders or to any other stakeholder.

Good practices

- CEO and senior managers are rewarded for business improvement.
- The company has strategies in place to ensure (as much as possible) that the advances in business improvement will not be lost with any change in leadership. (Experience from many companies is that new bosses often sweep business excellence progress away when they take over.)
- The 'next generation' of leaders is identified and developed for seamless transitions.

20

> **Poor practices**
>
> - Rewards for rapid returns, asset stripping or removing core competencies that harm future income.
> - Rewards for behaviour that damages the long-term viability of the company.

1.9 Create a supportive environment

Your senior executives must create and maintain a supportive environment within which alignment with the 10 Business Excellence Principles can flourish.

Experience from around the world is that well-intentioned people at lower levels do not have a chance of success if the CEO is not an enthusiastic zealot. The lower level people burn out when their efforts are a constant battle against impossible odds. The CEO can undermine (or is it over-mine?) everything they do.

The CEO and senior managers must:

- support and be seen to support the 10 Business Excellence Principles
- role-model the Principles
- make it easy for people in the company to operate in accordance with the Principles and not be constantly pulled away by inappropriate demands
- provide sufficient resources so that the company can improve itself in line with the Principles
- invest time, money and effort in meeting the needs of all stakeholders of the company (i.e. owners, customers, the company itself, employees, community and alliance partners)
- give the same kind of emphasis to business improvement objectives and strategies as operational objectives and strategies
- be seen to give importance to improving the company to be more closely aligned with the Principles
- build the Business Excellence Principles as the way the company does everything (i.e. they are not add-ons that are done occasionally or when conditions are right).

The CEO and senior managers must maintain a focus on alignment with the 10 Business Excellence Principles despite setbacks and temptations to take different paths.

> **Good practices**
>
> - Senior executives encourage behaviour in line with the 10 Business Excellence Principles.

- Senior executives create an atmosphere that accepts and welcomes innovative change that benefits the customer.
- Senior executives create a climate whereby an entrepreneurial approach is encouraged, new opportunities and prospects are sought, and there is no fear of failure.
- Managers know there is a better way and know that it starts with them.

Poor practices

- Concentration on the business as it always has been.
- No recognition of the importance or value of the 10 Business Excellence Principles.
- Company structure for the benefit of the management.
- No attempt to improve the business or do things differently.

1.10 Executives understand Business Excellence

Your senior executives should be knowledgeable about the 10 Business Excellence Principles. They should understand what the Principles mean, how they interact, how they add business benefit and the specific requirements of a Business Excellence Framework.

If your senior executives are not sufficiently knowledgeable about the 10 Business Excellence Principles, they will be constantly leading in directions that are not in the organisation's best interest. They should become extremely familiar with these Principles so that they will make fewer, avoidable errors.

Roles that demonstrate knowledge

Because of their huge influence on all aspects of the management system, the actions of the senior executives always affect how the company addresses each of the Principles.

- In Principle 1 ('Role models'), senior executives should help set the company's basic beliefs and hence its behaviour in such aspects as trust, honesty and integrity.
- In Principle 2 ('Focus on achieving results'), senior executives should help set direction and create strategies to focus the company on its purpose (mission), direction (vision), objectives (essential goals) and values (beliefs) as these provide a focus for all strategies, activities and decisions of the company.
- In Principle 3 ('Customers'), senior executives should create an environment wherein the company *wants* to align itself with providing what the customers value as the number one strategy of the company.

- In Principle 4 ('To improve the outcome, improve the system'), senior executives are the only ones who have the authority to actually fix processes and company systems so that the output and outcome of those processes and systems can produce what is required. Senior executives should understand that the only way to get a different outcome is to change the system and that they control that system. Senior executives are also the people who can move away from an environment of blame.
- In Principle 5 ('Improved decisions'), senior executives should establish a work environment that always seeks data on which to make decisions, and that routinely tests its ideas and strategies to see if they are successful. Senior executives should understand data and how it can be useful and should do their own analyses.
- In Principle 6 ('Variability'), senior executives should understand variation and its impact on their processes. They should establish routine systems to control variation, not chase random fluctuations and red herrings, and know when to hunt down a special cause of variation and how to drive out common causes of variation.
- In Principle 7 ('Enthusiastic people'), senior executives should create an environment in which enthusiastic people volunteer their hearts, minds and creativity to the benefit of the company, its customers and other stakeholders. Senior executives should enable their employees by providing knowledge, skills, resources, opportunities, authority and power so employees can do their work.
- In Principle 8 ('Innovation'), senior executives should create an environment that is constantly learning and improving—building on its knowledge and capabilities. Senior executives should establish processes that generate innovative ideas and turn them into real solutions and products.
- In Principle 9 ('Value to the community'), senior executives should work to fulfil the company's commitments (written and unwritten) to the community of doing no intended or unintended harm to the community or the environment.
- In Principle 10 ('Value for all stakeholders'), senior executives should seek to provide value to all the company's stakeholder groups—owners, customers, employees, the company itself, community and alliance partners—and work to provide the most effective balance between those competing interests for the long-term viability of the company.

Good practices

- Senior executives are literate and knowledgeable in the 10 Business Excellence Principles and the specific requirement of a Business Excellence Framework and how they are add business benefit.

- Willingness by the CEO and members of the management team to continually learn more about the 10 Business Excellence Principles and new practices.
- Executives participate in leadership development programs.
- Leaders, at all levels within the company, increase their skills through continuous learning, formal training and development.

Poor practices

- Induction training not given to executives on customer focus and company's context and ethics.

SUMMARY

What you should expect to see from your senior executives:

- strategies for action that will benefit all stakeholders
- personal behaviour that deliberately aligns to the Principles
- deliberate perseverance to 'live' the Principles
- deliberate integration of the Principles into their 'values and beliefs'
- deliberate influence on the company culture and climate to bring them in line with the Principles.

Employees expect their leaders to:

- set direction
- be consistent
- show they care and give support
- give them space
- challenge processes
- enable others to think and act
- model the way
- paint pictures of the future
- encourage the heart.

WHAT WOULD YOUR STAKEHOLDERS SAY?

HOW WOULD YOUR EMPLOYEES RATE YOUR COMPANY ON THESE?

- I can do my work without fear.
- I trust the company.
- I feel secure.
- I trust my bosses.
- This company has internal communications problems.

- The company demonstrates values that I like.
- The senior executives are open and honest.
- I am appreciated.
- I am supported.
- Everyone is treated equally.
- This company believes in the 10 Business Excellence Principles.
- The senior executives behave as though they believe in the 10 Business Excellence Principles.
- The senior executives have created and maintained an open company where I can do my best work.

HOW WOULD YOUR OWNERS RATE YOUR COMPANY ON THESE?

- This company believes in the 10 Business Excellence Principles.
- The senior executives consistently behave as though they believe in the 10 Business Excellence Principles.
- The CEO and all the executives role-model the 10 Business Excellence Principles.
- I believe in the 10 Business Excellence Principles.
- I consistently behave as though I believe in the 10 Business Excellence Principles.
- I select senior executives based on their ability to implement all aspects of the 10 Business Excellence Principles.
- I reward the CEO and senior executives for consistent application of the 10 Business Excellence Principles.
- I demand that the CEO and senior executives consistently apply the 10 Business Excellence Principles.
- I judge the performance of the CEO and senior executives by their consistent application of the 10 Business Excellence Principles.
- I monitor the company's performance against the 10 Business Excellence Principles.
- The senior executives are open and honest.

Principle 2
Focus on achievement of goals

Clear direction allows organisational alignment and a focus on achievement of goals.

I F YOU DO NOT KNOW where you want to go—that is, if you do not have a goal—getting there will be only a matter of luck and you probably will not recognise it if you do get there. If you do not focus on what you want, you will probably not achieve it. The process of focusing brings all your capability to bear on achieving the goal.

Many people try to focus on everything and consequently focus on nothing. Or, if different parts of the company are going in their own direction or running their own agenda for their own ends, this is, at best, suboptimum and is usually destructive.

Dr Hausner's research found that Principle 2 is the best predictor of a company's overall *managerial capability*. Companies that systematically focus on achieving their goals do significantly better than those that do not.

Unfortunately, even though it is important for sound management of an enterprise, focusing on goal achievement is not done well, even by the best companies, and is the third largest area for potential improvement.

In order to focus on your goals, everyone in the company must know what the direction is. You must know what your goals and objectives are, you must have strategies to achieve them and you must implement those strategies. Each department, division, section and person must know the part they are required to play to achieve the company's goals. Alignment and constancy of purpose is crucial. Everyone must be working towards the same goals using mutually agreed strategies in line with company values.

Fig. 2.1 To improve your performance, you must focus on your goals

You must measure your progress towards the goals so that you can determine if the plans are being implemented and if the strategies are effective in achieving the goals.

You must also plan to apply resources towards achieving your goal. This includes people as well as materials, capital and assets. All are usually scarce. The non-people resources and processes must be capable of providing the outcome you want. If they are not, you must plan to improve them so that they are capable. That aspect is covered in Principle 4 ('To improve the outcome, improve the system'). And your people must be 'enabled', that is, provided with the skills, knowledge, power, authority, resources and ability to implement the plans.

The goals and objectives must add value to all the stakeholders (i.e. owners, customers, employees, community and alliance partners) and be in an appropriate balance.

Finally, your strategies and actions must be in line with 10 Business Excellence Principles.

Fig. 2.2 The five ingredients to reaching goals

27

2.1 Have clearly defined goals

Principle 1 ('Role models') describes the essential role-modelling by senior executives for success in business excellence. Principle 2 looks at the next aspect of leadership—providing direction.

Setting direction—painting pictures of the future

It is difficult to overemphasise the importance of this role. People expect their leaders to be forward looking, to set direction, to paint pictures of the future. However, this is not as easy as it sounds.

Firstly, bosses suffer from the credibility problems described in Principle 1—bosses are not trusted. The extent people will believe in and take on your vision will depend on your credibility—your honesty and integrity, the extent you are trusted. Even if you can achieve credibility, there are other pitfalls waiting.

Setting direction requires much more than just writing down the company's purpose (mission), direction (vision), milestones (key goals) and values (beliefs) or giving a few speeches about it. Lou Tice, founder of The Pacific Institute, tells us that people will not do something if they do not believe in it. Cognitive psychologists tell us that we unconsciously move towards what we envisage. If we can see our-selves doing it, we will do it. If we cannot see it, we do not do it. And if we cannot see ourselves doing it, we will not do it, or we will not do it willingly. People may go so far as to sabotage ideas they do not believe in. Usually, the sabotage is unconscious but it may be very deliberate.

This is about comfort zones. You remain where you are comfortable. You do things you have done before. You mix with the same friends, go to the same places for holidays—places where you are comfortable.

It is also about our picture of 'truth'. Each of us acts, thinks and works in accordance with the truth as we believe it to be. Only when I change my 'truth' (the way I think) can I change the way I act. If you do not think something is possible, you will not try to do it. If you do not think it is possible, you will not set it as a goal. If it is not your goal, but your boss's goal and you cannot see it, you cannot begin to move towards it.

The leader's ability to have his or her followers see themselves doing the vision is crucial. That is what setting direction means in the new thinking. In the old thinking, the 'leader' described the future or issued instructions and expected everyone to follow. This does not work. It never did.

Also, people may talk of 'owning' the vision but even that is not enough. They have to be able to see themselves doing the vision. Only then will it happen.

Do you bungy jump?

'Do you bungy jump? It is very safe and great fun. I can see you doing it. You will enjoy it.' Do these words make you see yourself bungy jumping? Just because someone has tried to talk you into doing it does not make you want to race out and do it. It has to become your vision of who you are and what you do. If you are pushed towards what is, in effect, someone else's vision (e.g. you doing the bungy jumping), you will automatically push back. You will find a thousand excuses for not bungy jumping. You will sabotage the vision.

Could you be bribed to bungy jump with an incentive scheme? 'You carry out my vision and you will get this reward.' Would you bungy jump if you were paid enough? Would you be an enthusiastic bungy jumper if you were paid enough? Probably not—you might make a few jumps, but not with enthusiasm or resourcefulness, not with willing commitment. What does this mean for most incentive schemes? Will they buy people's belief in the vision? Probably not.

How far out should you set the goal?

Set your goal so it is just out of reach but still close enough so that it is believable—far enough out so that you cannot do it yet, so that there is a challenge—a stretch.

Should you know how to achieve a goal when you set it? No and yes. With some visions it may not be possible to see how to get there. In fact, only after we have set the goal do we allow ourselves to gather any information to enable us to meet that goal. Before that, there has been no need to gather the information. It might have been all around you but you did not need it so you ignored it. For example, when you are buying new tyres for your car (a goal), you suddenly have to find tyre dealers, prices, the best deal. All of that was there before you looked. It is always there. A goal is a declaration of significance—now certain information can get through. The goal comes first—then you see. If you can see how to get there, the vision may be too close.

However, do not set the goal too far out. When you are setting the vision, make it just out of reach or no-one will be able to see it—a stretch.

If you set stretch goals, people will need a map with the stages marked out. It does not matter if they do not know how to get to the next stage as long as they can see the stage.

Imagine this

Your five-year-old daughter is about to go to preschool. What if you told your daughter nothing about preschool and then on the first day grabbed her and threw her in the car, took her to preschool and dropped her off. As you drive off, you shout out of the window, 'Have a nice day'. Do we have one very frightened little child?

You do exactly this to your employees when you throw them into your vision without any preparation or support.

What should you do for your five-year-old child? For weeks in advance you should talk to her about what preschool will be like. You should help her picture it.

Your job as leader is to paint the pictures of the future. It is to prepare the way for the *next* stage.

What is the goal of your company?

In the private sector, the goal of the company is to make money now and in the future. This is because in order to stay in business, most companies have to make money now and in the future. Many companies appear to be confused about this. They behave as though the goal were cost reduction, or improvement, or technology, or customer satisfaction, or looking after employees. Important as those all are, they are only strategies to get to the goal or values you hold while working towards the goal.

In order to stay in business, most companies have to make money now and in the future. This does not mean that you should make money at any cost or at the exclusion of ethics or of public good.

In *The Goal*, Goldratt describes the 'necessary conditions' for success in reaching this goal:

- Provide a secure and satisfying environment for employees now as well as in the future.
- Provide satisfaction to the market now and in the future. (This condition comes from the idea that the market punishes companies that do not satisfy the market perception of value.)
- Provide value to the community now and in the future (Principle 9).

These conditions are described as 'necessary' because you are not allowed to violate them—ever! There are no conflicts between the necessary conditions or with the goal. They complement each other. However, there are old modes of operating that conflict with one or more of them. Those modes of operating are not sustainable.

The new thinking is that you need the approval, willing compliance and enthusiasm of your customers (Principle 3), employees (Principle 7) and community (Principle 9) in order to fulfil your goal and make money. And these conditions bring together all of the major stakeholder groups— shareholders, company, employees, customers and community.

Notice that the first 'necessary condition' carries considerable responsibility not to lay employees off. That is, you should not consider laying people off as a way to get through a period of poor cash flow. That solution leads to a vicious cycle of such periods, which do not ever seem to improve profits.

Whether your goal is to make money now and in the future or one of the three 'necessary conditions', the other three become the necessary conditions. However, you must be clear about which is which, and recognise that necessary means 'necessary' and goal means 'goal'.

Good practices

- A clear understanding of what success means for the company.
- Clearly stated mission, vision, values and objectives, which really do describe what the company is trying to achieve to be successful and are not just lip service or a 'planning exercise'.
- Alignment processes exist so that people do not head off in different directions.
- The company and everyone in it has a clear sense of purpose— why it exists, what it is trying to achieve, what its 'cause' is, what success is, what value it adds.
- A close relationship between the Board and the executive through regular meetings so that greater congruency of vision and values is achieved.
- Company is aligned overall with much congruency and consistency so that there are no political wars, with people having different agendas and going in different directions.
- A shared vision throughout the company for cultural change and improved business performance.
- Senior executives can articulate a clear strategy for growth of the company—how much, when and why the business will grow—a clear path for that growth and the risks associated with that growth.
- Plans keep faith with company values and basic beliefs.

Poor practices

- Goal-setting does not convey the sense of urgency and vision necessary for substantial change.
- No acknowledgment that the goal is to make money.
- Plans do not derive from the company's vision and values and are not supported by analysis. Although initiatives demonstrate vitality, they are not linked to the vision and values.
- Backbiting, white-anting and put downs of others and their efforts—that is, divisiveness rather than cooperation.

2.2 Strategic plan addresses stakeholder needs

Your strategic plan must address meeting the needs and expectations of all your key stakeholders and your goals and objectives must add value to all your stakeholders in an appropriate balance (Principle 10, 'Value for all stakeholders').

Stakeholders and planning

In the new thinking, good planning requires that you obtain input from your major stakeholder groups:

- shareholders or owners
- customers
- company
- employees
- community
- alliance partners.

For all of them you are asking, 'What do you want us to do?' and 'What is your picture of the future and our part in it?'. There may be conflict between these demands. Principle 10 ('Value for all stakeholders') expects the company to provide a balance between the value demanded from the company by the various stakeholder groups. The balancing process begins here at the input stage.

This input should be obtained constantly, especially immediately before major strategic planning activities. Specifically, from each stakeholder group, executives need to know the following:

- *owners and shareholders*: the required profit; rate of return; return on investment; dividend and reinvestment into the company
- *customers*: expectations about new products and services; rates of innovation; extensions to the product (especially for things you usually do not consider part of the product or service, such as financing and delivery options); how you intend to address the things customers dislike about your products and services
- *employees*: the processes that require fixing and how to fix them (you will see in Principle 4, 'To improve the outcome, improve the system', that usually the employees know what needs to be fixed to improve the system and processes to get better results but they lack the power, authority and resources to fix them); safety systems to be fixed; impressions of customer expectations and requirements; perceptions of how you are sticking to company values and ethics; perceptions of whether they are enthusiastic about the company
- *community*: perceptions that the company is a good corporate citizen; impending regulations (these usually indicate the community cannot

trust the industry or company to self-regulate); unintended consequences; things the community dislikes about the company
- *alliance partners*: definitions of which processes and systems you will
jointly manage; how you can help each other improve the services
and products you provide each other; how products and services that
you and they are about to release will affect each other; how processes
and systems that you and they are changing or about to change will
affect each other.

Systematic strategy

Dr Hausner's research found that behaving strategically is an important
differentiator between excellent companies and those that are not so
successful. Companies that make an effort to be strategic do significantly
better than do those that remain in a reactive mode.

Most companies remain at the level of just reacting to the daily
demands of their customers or threats from their competitors. This is
certainly easy to understand. Finding time to do more than meeting
daily demands is the fundamental challenge to all people in companies.

We now know that not finding time for developing strategy is a major
reason that businesses fail. Companies must be 'systematic' in their
development of strategy.

What is strategy?

A strategy is how you intend to approach an issue. Something you
plan to do to reach a goal or objective. It could be how you intend to
reach your goal, meet the 'necessary conditions' or address all 10
Business Excellence Principles. Strategies are bundles of actions. For
example, in your attempt to make money, you may decide to position
your company to address a particular market, or invest in technology
to reduce your cycle time and reduce errors, or follow your competitors
rather than lead them into new products and markets. All these are
strategies.

You will need strategies for all the things that are important to
your company. At a minimum, you will need strategies to address
your main risks and the factors that are essential to your success—
both in the short and long term.

What does 'systematic' mean?

You should know what your company is trying to achieve—its purpose
and goals for success. You should know what your company stands
for—its values, beliefs, ethics and how these will influence your

decisions. You should have systems, structures and methods to put your strategies into action—to implement them—and to ensure that everyone who should be doing them is doing them. Measure this if you can. You should measure how well other people think you are sticking to your values. You should measure your progress in reaching your goals and targets and alter your approach (strategy) according to those results.

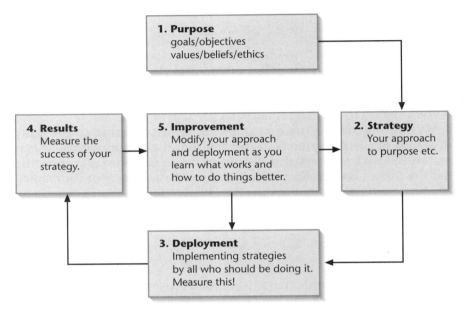

Fig. 2.3 Strategy and the improvement cycle

Strategies are experiments

It is very useful to remember that all strategies are 'experiments' (i.e. an approach to reach a desired outcome). No matter how tried and true it is, who has done it before or where it came from, every time you apply a strategy it is an experiment to see if you can reach your objective. When you think of strategies as experiments, you approach them differently. You do not cling to them and you want to know if they are working—are they achieving the results you want?; what is stopping them from working?

Just because something is popular does not mean it works. Many strategies do not work yet people continue to adopt them. For example, eating more carbohydrates to get thin is the strategy most people use following advice from nutritionists. However, they continue to get fat. Overwhelming failure has not stopped the experiment.

If what you are doing is not leading you towards your goal, it is leading you away from it. Or, it is consuming your scarce resources and stopping you from working towards your goal.

Developing strategies

Strategies can be developed in two ways—frameworks and scenarios—and you need both.

A framework helps you to organise your thoughts into cohesive strategies. There are many very good frameworks and it is not important which one you use:

- the 10 Business Excellence Principles
- Goldratt's goal and necessary conditions framework
- a customer-focus framework
- Porter's (*Competitive Strategy*) industry analysis framework of differentiation, cost, leadership or focus
- one of the national business excellence frameworks
- Goldratt's Theory of Constraints framework (i.e. improve throughput while simultaneously reducing inventory and operating expenses)
- a risk-assessment framework (see p. 39).

To be comprehensive, it is a good idea to use several frameworks in combination. However, you do not have to be exhaustive and hunt for every conceivable framework. Most companies do not have the time.

The trouble with 'framework strategy development' is that it assumes that you know in advance what you are doing. Many management writers argue that this type of strategic planning is a waste of time. This is because when many companies look back on what they did to get from some past position to their successful present position, it looks as though 'strategy' happened. The trouble is that the world does not work in reverse. When you look forward from any point in time and consider the decisions made in the context of what was happening at the time, it looks more like bumbling around than strategy.

By developing a strategy you are trying to avoid four things, each of which spells doom for companies:

1. reactive response only—the telephone rings and we do it because our customers want it
2. shopping list planning—doing a whole lot of things without any apparent reason
3. adopting strategies that are not in keeping with the goal and necessary conditions
4. not learning from what you have done or always trying to do it better.

Strategic planning activities should be scheduled at least once and preferably twice a year. In rapidly moving or start-up markets, strategic planning could occur as often as weekly. Scenarios are dealt with on page 56.

When do you have enough strategic options?

When the market is moving quickly and it is not usually clear what will work, excellent companies throw a lot of strategies and good ideas at their goal to keep moving towards it. When should you stop? Probably never.

For every change, what worked before the change probably may not work after and huge numbers of opportunities suddenly open on the other side. Options close off behind you and open in front. So, of the thousands of possible options, what should you take on? Probably, whatever you can afford to do.

Your company is faced with the same problems of choice (and it may be facing the same life and death decisions). Many classes of strategy have proponents who say they have the true and only way. You cannot afford to choose one and not the rest. The one you choose might not work for you. Similarly, you cannot afford to do them all.

> ### Fast moving
>
> Lewis Carroll's *Through the Looking-Glass and What Alice Found There* has a wonderful story about Alice and the Queen running as fast as they can go—just to be able to stay in the same place. The business world today is like that. You have to keep moving as fast as you can just to be able to keep up. Staying still, or thinking that your success from yesterday will see you through today, is dangerous fantasy. Be agile and flexible. Develop a lot of options. Keep moving!

Anticipate the future

Nothing stays the same. Thus, you want to 'position' your company for its place in the future. To do that, you need to be able to anticipate the future and continue to increase your ability to anticipate the future.

People who are good at this know everything that is happening in their marketplace—everything. This is a very big ask. However, the better you are at knowing everything that is going on, the more successful you will be.

You might call this 'reading the market'. Those who get good at it know it is more art than science—trying to work out what the market will look like and want in one, two, five, 10 or 20 years.

> To achieve this you need to know everything about:
> * what your competitors are doing and why
> * how and why your customers' expectations are changing

- how changes in your market produce new business opportunities
- how changes in the global marketplace will affect you
- how changes in thinking about technology, customer needs and the way business is done will affect you
- any technological developments and innovations that affect your products
- new ways of doing business with your customers
- changes that produce new market segments
- changes in regulations and tax
- changing community/societal expectations
- changing needs of government
- your company, its capabilities and competencies
- your people, their capabilities and competencies.

Commitments to the future

Building for the future includes a willingness to make long-term commitments to your key stakeholders—shareholders, customers, employees, the community, alliance partners and suppliers. Long-term commitments include:

- developing your employees and building long-term relationships with them (Principle 7, 'Enthusiastic people')
- building long-term relationships with your alliance partners and suppliers (Principle 4, 'To improve the outcome, improve the system')
- developing and maintaining your company's core competencies (Principle 3, 'Customers')
- fulfilling your public responsibilities (Principle 9, 'Value to the community')
- developing long-term relationships with key customers (Principle 3, 'Customers').

Good practices

- Corporate and strategic plans describe how the company will increase the value that it provides to all stakeholders.
- Senior executives see that their main job is to reach the company objectives and to provide value to all stakeholders.
- Consultation with customers and suppliers is part of the planning process.
- The company identifies strategically important partners and other alliances.
- Continual scanning of their marketplace to find opportunities that exploit their competitive advantage.
- Strategies to achieve desired outcomes are developed based on analysis of the business environment.

Poor practices

- Plans are not simple and useful.
- Executives and employees only point to owners and customers as stakeholders and do not mention employees or the community as stakeholders of the company.
- Not conducting comparisons or benchmarking in a search for industry leaders.
- Ignoring customers and suppliers as information sources in benchmarking.
- Not trying to achieve unique positioning for sustainable competitiveness.

2.3 Business Excellence Principles as a framework for strategy

You should use the 10 Business Excellence Principles to improve your company strategically. Strategies to implement the 10 Business Excellence Principles are equally important to operational strategies. You cannot leave out either side of this equation and be successful. This is because, if you do not have excellent operations aimed at making money, you will not be around in the future. However, if you do not implement strategies to bring your company in line with the Principles, you will not be around in the future.

One of the biggest reasons for failure to achieve business excellence is the failure to act on the 10 Business Excellence Principles. Most companies are faced with the dilemma of having to run their daily operations and deal with the unceasing and ever-changing demands of their customers and the constant demands of the company.

Even if companies recognise that they exist, these Principles appear to be off in a different planet and of no real practical urgency. Because the Principles are less urgent than dealing with the daily operational demands, companies think that implementing the requirements to develop expertise in using the Principles can always be put off until later.

However, we now know that companies that get fewer than 300 points in the Baldrige, European or Australian Business Excellence Frameworks are going backwards and will not survive! Regardless of excellent short-term results that might satisfy the share market, a company that can scrape together only 250 points is very bad news for shareholders.

That realisation makes acting on these Principles just as important as any operational strategy. You constantly see companies fail to achieve their full potential because they have not worked to align what they do to these Principles. Even worse, you see companies sliding backwards.

Use the Principles as a framework for strategic planning

- Conduct a self-assessment against these Principles using the Business Health Assessment questionnaire. Feed the findings into your strategic planning process.
- Measure your progress on the Principles overall and for each Principle for your company overall and for each major part. Provide help, not blame.
- Conduct an assessment against one of the major frameworks (i.e. Baldrige, European or Australian). Feed the findings into your strategic planning.

Trimming poor strategies

In *It's Not Luck*, Goldratt argues that strategy is the direction we take to reach our goal. If we violate any of the 'necessary conditions', we will not reach our goal. So a good strategy must not clash with any of them. Your first step must be to trim any strategy that clashes with the goal of making money or any of the 'necessary conditions'. Those are all poor strategies by definition.

Good strategies

Good strategies begin by developing a decisive competitive edge. Concentrate on eliminating negative factors for the market (Principle 3, 'Customers'). Change your policies to allow increased throughput, reduced inventory and reduced operating expenses (Principle 4 'To improve the outcome, improve the system').

Risk assessment as a strategic framework

Risk assessment can provide a very useful framework for the generation of practical solutions to company issues. Risk assessment should be an integral part of your planning process as it gives a practical scan of your marketplace.

There are several old thinking attitudes about risk management. These include:

1. You only need to worry about financial risk. Most audit programs are based on this thinking. The company can be completely failing to meet its objectives, but so long as all the t's are crossed and the i's dotted, the paper audit trail is available, everything is all right. The business news is full of examples of companies with financial reports signed off by the auditors which have then gone bankrupt or the executives charged with criminal behaviour. Or instances of when

the entire operating profit, painstakingly assembled through hard work and detailed improvement work, is wiped out in a single bad trade by the financial department.

2. Risk aversion—do not take any risks. Total risk aversion is usually very costly because of the large number of strategies necessary to contain the risk. It also inhibits innovation and change. The approach is still common in government where the political process punishes any 'error' and 'courageous' means do not do it.

The major risk categories, as marketed by the consulting firm KPMG, are:

- product quality
- customer service
- minimising unnecessary costs
- revenue/profit maximisation
- external disclosure reliability
- asset safeguarding
- safety
- regulatory compliance
- fraud prevention/detection
- continuity of operations
- internal compliance
- unintentional risk exposure.

Modern risk management requires you to identify your major risk factors and put strategies or 'controls' in place to reduce them to an acceptable level. You should continue to assess the risk remaining *after* your controls are in place—the residual risk.

Keep adding controls to reduce your risk until it is acceptable—to you. This gives a process for deciding the difficult issue of when to stop adding strategies. It provides a useful approach to reduce the number of strategies. If you think the risk is acceptable without that strategy, or that the cost of the strategy is more than the benefit obtained from having it, then do not add it. It's your call.

Uncertainty in decision making is dealt with more fully in Principle 5 ('Improved decisions').

Good practices

- Recognition of the relationship between improved company performance (i.e. KPIs) and the application of the 10 Business Excellence Principles to all areas.
- Company self-assessment (e.g. using the 10 Business Excellence Principles) as a strategic measurement tool that feeds strategy.
- Continuous improvement is planned.

- Thorough strategic risk assessment of the risks and threats to achieving success (mission, vision and objectives) is conducted and acted upon.
- Plans include overcoming risks to the company (e.g. risks to revenue, market share, assets, knowledge, safety, environment; risk of technology change).
- Plans examined for unintended side-effects and modified to avoid them.
- Greater use of risk-taking strategies.

Poor practices

- Not considering company improvement as a key business objective.
- No strategies to address the unintended side-effects of current strategy.
- Failure to consider unintended side-effects of policies and actions.

2.4 Plan your steps to reach your targets

You must make plans for what you need to do in order to reach all your targets. As well as needing a planned and structured approach to move the company from the present to the envisaged future, you need a planned and structured approach to improving processes, including setting and achieving targets, as you will see in Principle 4 ('To improve the outcome, improve the system').

Failure to make and implement plans to reach targets is a very frequent error. Companies often set targets without making plans to achieve them. As you will see in Principle 4, if you want a different outcome (e.g. a new target) you *must* change the system and its associated processes.

Processes and systems do not just change by themselves. Therefore, you must plan how you will go about changing processes and systems to reach those targets.

As you will see in Principle 4, plans to improve processes and systems must be developed in a partnership between senior managers and employees who have hands-on experience of the system. The employees have the knowledge about what needs to change (but not the power, authority and resources to change the process). Senior managers have the power, authority and resources to change the process (but not—regardless of what they may think—the knowledge of what needs to change).

Plans let you:

- set direction
- understand where you are and where you want to go to
- position the company and its people for the future

- establish and meet stakeholder needs
- assess and manage the risk of not reaching the goals and objectives
- foresee and plan to overcome barriers and obstacles
- generate and coalesce opinion
- align, so that everyone is working in the same direction.

Good practices

- Plans exist for how to reach targets.
- Targets are based on an understanding of the system, variation, capability and capacity. This assists in deciding realistic goals and priorities for breakthrough goals.
- Short- and long-term objectives are clearly stated in the strategic or corporate plan.
- The appropriateness and effectiveness of strategies and plans are reviewed regularly, including a deliberate review system to measure progress, adjust resources and remove barriers.

Poor practices

- Not setting targets.
- No plans made to reach targets—the 'it will happen by magic' approach.
- Targets set by 'gut feeling' or past performance levels. Goal setting is not based on knowledge of current process capability—this would assist in deciding realistic goals and priorities for breakthrough goals.
- Targets set without a clear plan to improve/modify/change processes to achieve them.

2.5 Plan to change

Your plans to reach new targets must describe how you will change (e.g. by improving process or systems, or applying resources). This is the main focus of Principle 4. If you want a different outcome, you must improve the system. In this case, you want to reach a new target. If your current system and processes were capable of doing it now, you would not need to set a new target. If your target is within your capability, you do not need a plan to reach it. It is ho-hum. If your target is outside your capability, you will certainly need a plan to reach it because you will have to change something (resources, processes, ways of doing things). When you set the target, you might not even know what you will need to change to reach the target. But you will need a plan.

The non-people resources and processes must be capable of providing the outcome you want. If they are not, you must plan to improve them so that they are capable. That aspect is covered in Principle 4. You must plan to apply resources towards achieving your goal—people as well as material, capital and assets. All are usually scarce.

Deploy assets to implement plans

The company must deploy resources and assets to implement its strategies and plans. Plans need to be resourced with money and people.

Usually the main resources needed to implement plans are people. Your strategies should include plans to have the right numbers of skilled, knowledgeable and empowered people available to implement the rest of your plans.

Make full use of all assets

The company must make the fullest use of *all* assets available to it (i.e. build, develop and apply its resources and assets to achieve its goals and objectives). This is all assets, not just the physical assets. Unfortunately, accountants usually regard assets as only those things that can be included in a balance sheet with a dollar value. We know that there are many assets that we do not yet have a way of counting, especially those assets to do with the knowledge held by people—intellectual capital, expertise.

Intangible assets

Intangible assets are often exactly those things that make the core competency of the company. For example, intellectual property, databases, knowledge, image capital, relationships with suppliers and customers, expertise.

Microsoft, Amazon and Yahoo! are examples of companies that do not hold many physical assets. However, their enormous values are shown in their intangible assets—their intellectual property.

This means that for your competitive advantage, you must look after these resources. Probably the biggest barrier to being able to do that effectively is that you cannot measure them. In fact, your main measurement system (based on very old thinking) measures their value as zero—which explains a lot of company behaviour. 'Our people are our most important resource. But they are not on the balance sheet. So they can't be important.' What you measure is what you get.

Good practices

- Plans are established to change/modify/improve the system and its processes to meet targets outside of the current capability.
- The capabilities of the company are understood and deliberate strategies are implemented to increase them.

- The core competencies of the company (i.e. those things that it does very well compared with other companies) are understood, protected and developed through deliberate strategies.
- Plans are distributed widely and responsibilities are assigned. Plans are monitored and projects managed. The necessary resources are allocated.
- A broad and inclusive view of what assets and resources are.
- Processes to determine the value provided by assets and the effect of changes in the use of assets (i.e. an economic value-added model including a 'what if' capability, statistical simulations and sensitivity analysis). Plans to maximise the value from these assets and eliminate losses from assets.
- Value is assigned to non-balance sheet assets, such as intellectual capital, knowledge and core competencies.
- Processes to manage all the company's assets to ensure that they create value for the company (including non-balance sheet assets such as intellectual capital, knowledge, core competencies).
- Documented increases in 'self-created assets', such as intellectual property, intellectual capital, image capital and knowledge, as well as in standard balance sheet assets.

Poor practices

- Rubbery, open-ended plans without targets or plans to achieve them.
- No strategies to achieve new futures.
- Only recording standard balance sheet assets.
- Intellectual capital, core competencies and knowledge are not considered assets. No strategies to grow or protect them or use them for competitive advantage.
- Learnings from analysis of overall performance not deliberately developed and not directly shown in plans.

2.6 Let people know what is expected of them

People must know what is expected of them (e.g. through being involved in the planning process, having performance agreements and job descriptions). For plans to work, everyone must know what the goal and strategies are and what part they are to play in them. Mutual agreement of the plans, strategies and roles is essential. To achieve that, communications must be very good. Plans and roles imposed by bosses either fail completely or have only very modest success. This means that your planning process must include processes for mutual agreement and for upward communication (which, as we saw in Principle 1 'Role models', must be established on a basis of trust).

People know their roles

Planning is a necessary step so that each department, division and section and each person knows their part in achieving the company goals. You might do a magnificent job in vision setting, painting pictures of the future. However, this will all be for nothing if every department, division and section and each person does not know what part they are to play in achieving that goal.

Hoshin planning and Quality Function Deployment (QFD) provide very useful tools for everyone in the company to be working towards the company's goals using mutually agreed strategies and in line with company values. They also provide excellent tools for each department, division and section and each person to know exactly their part in achieving the company goals. However, they can be a bit too complex.

Roles

Strategies get broken down into 'tactics' and 'actions' for people to do. For plans to work, everyone must know what the goal and strategies are and what part they are to play in them. People should know how what they do fits into the company's purpose. It gives direction to their job.

Everybody's job should be part of a strategy, which, in turn, is aimed at a goal or objective. Actions should be described in performance agreements and job descriptions. Performance agreements must also include processes for mutual agreement.

Performance agreements

Performance agreements and job descriptions should be products of the planning process. How else would people know what their job is? In the old thinking, bosses dictated performance 'agreements' and job descriptions were used to set pay scales for the convenience of personnel departments. In the new thinking, performance agreements are mutually agreed between boss and employee and make full reference to the obligations of both parties:

- the employee agrees to do certain tasks or activities that make up their part of the company's plan
- the boss agrees to provide skills, knowledge, authority, power, support, resources, capital, assist with suppliers (often other employees) and modify processes to make them more capable.

The job description should give description of the more general daily activities of how the employee contributes to the company goals. The performance agreement is for the special activities; the job description

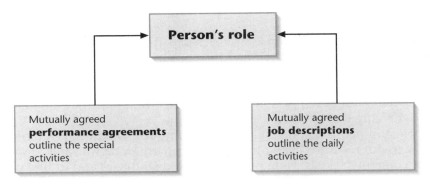

Fig. 2.4 How people know their role

handles the general activities. Both are integrally linked to each other and to the company's planning process—but not linked to personnel.

Good practices

- People know how their daily work contributes to the company's goals and strategic direction.
- Cross-functional planning teams assist in the development of plans at all levels.
- Staff surveys and focus groups indicate a high level of involvement in planning and satisfaction with involvement in planning and in decisions that affect the staff.
- Simple yet comprehensive methods of involving employees in planning and communicating plans.
- People at all levels are involved in a unified planning process—developing plans, including strategic plans.

Poor practices

- Plans decided without participation from the people who will implement them. (Few things turn people off more than not being allowed participation in decisions that affect them.)
- Planning activities restricted to particular 'levels' or departments of the company.
- Internal 'thought leaders' not involved in developing or implementing plans.

2.7 Everyone is enabled

Your people must be 'enabled', that is, provided with the skills, knowledge, power, authority, resources and ability to implement the plans. Companies often develop a strategy, set their targets and make plans to reach the targets but fail to allocate resources (people, time or funds) to the plans or provide their people with the skills, knowledge, power or authority to carry out the plans.

It is unreasonable to expect people to try to implement plans without being allowed the time, funds or equipment to do so. Nor can they succeed without:

- the skills needed
- knowing what is going on and where the project fits with other projects
- the power and authority to carry out the plans.

If it is important enough to do, then you must make time to do it and enable your people to do it. Many companies forget this part. No wonder their plans fail!

Involvement—a necessary strategy

Executives of companies often talk about 'involving' employees in decision making so they 'own' the decisions and will therefore not oppose them. The common terminology for this is 'getting ownership'. However, this is cynical and demeaning, and it misses the point.

Involving employees in decisions that affect them is necessary but it is not sufficient. You must go much further. You need to do it for the very reason that you need people to find any flaws in your proposal. The people who developed the proposal may overlook major flaws in their enthusiasm or through lack of knowledge. Other people, if you can persuade them to trust you, may find the flaws. Ask everyone who will be involved, especially end-user staff and customers, to find every reason why an idea will not work. Then systematically remove each of these flaws.

Involvement

Most companies only tell employees what to do—very few listen. Time constraints mean you cannot get to everyone—but you should try to. Set up a process that will systematically get as many people as possible to comment. And not just 'Looks good, boss' comments. You want 'why it won't work' comments—things you can use. You can bet that the person you leave out (employee, contractor or customer) could close the hole that will later sink you.

Exposing ideas to this criticism takes considerable courage and most bosses do not do it. As a result, most good ideas fail.

Having 'plans that work and that people can see themselves doing' is the objective, so involvement is a necessary strategy. Many companies get it mixed up, giving only lip service to the involvement and end up well short of the mark.

Successful work

Peter Scholtes presents a three-part model for 'successful work'. All three parts must be included to be successful. Successful work needs:

1. a clear intention or purpose—Principle 2 'Focus on achieving results'
2. an affirmation to teamwork through a commitment to values and integrity described—Principle 1 'Role models'
3. 'skilful means' by being 'enabled' to do the job.

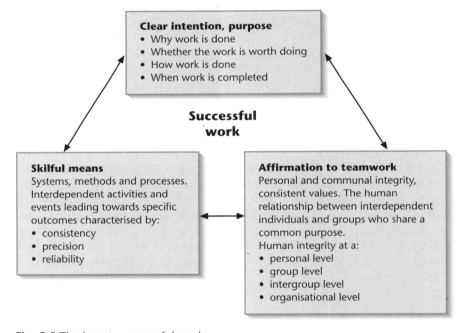

Fig. 2.5 The keys to successful work

Good practices

- The objectives of each individual and business unit are clearly linked to higher level corporate goals.
- A clear and coherent cascading system of integrated, interdependent and aligned plans. Plans and KPIs cascade to business units, teams and individuals.
- An established and maintained priority that the company is at all times moving in the chosen direction. Objectives, strategies and

activities to achieve them are prioritised. This gives focus and a unity of effort in the one direction while pursuing business unit objectives.

Poor practices

- Strategic, operational, business and departmental plans are developed and executed independently.
- Functional plans (e.g. human resources, safety, business improvement) are not linked to strategic and business plans.

2.8 Measure progress towards goals

You must measure your progress towards your goals. The results you obtain let you know if the plans are being implemented and if the strategies are effective in achieving the goals.

Measurement provides a very useful tool to focus on achieving the goal. You must measure two distinct things:

1. progress towards achieving the goal (remember a plan is an experiment to see if you can do something)
2. if the plans are being implemented by everyone (or every section or every division) who should be doing them.

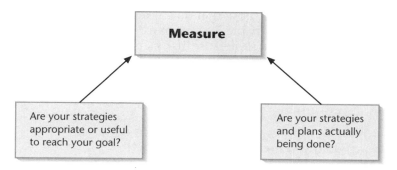

Fig. 2.6 What to measure

Measuring success

Every policy and strategy must have an objective—it must be trying to achieve something. Numerous companies fail to give meaning to what they are trying to do by failing to declare their objective. If you fail to declare your objective, and make it measurable, there is no way you will ever be able to tell if you achieved it!

At a minimum you should measure progress on all major company statements of mission, vision, values, all objectives and goals, all targets and all stakeholder demands. This is covered more fully in Principle 5 ('Improved decisions').

Many companys have an attitude of 'We thought of all these wonderful things to achieve our goals and because we are very smart, we know they will work and that we do not need to try anything else. If there was something else, we would have thought of it'. That form of ego has no place in excellent business. Excellent companies use a more scientific approach and recognise that any strategy is nothing more than an experiment about how to get to your goal.

Effectiveness and efficiency

Effectiveness asks the fundamental question, 'Are you achieving your objective?'. Efficiency asks, 'Are you working with the lowest energy or resources?'.

Effectiveness is always the more important because you must first be certain that your chosen strategies and activities are actually working towards your objective. Most companies assume they are and do not bother to check.

You must use some form of measurement to let you know if your strategies are effective or appropriate in achieving the goals. Then you can discard or modify those that do not contribute significantly to your goals and concentrate on those that do contribute significantly. This is covered more fully in Principle 5 ('Improve decisions').

As discussed above, you should use many strategies and options within those strategies. Asking which of the options or strategies is helping you achieve your goal may be the wrong question and may not be answerable. You need to know if your strategies in general are being successful and if you can discard any.

Beware: what you measure is what you get!

The biggest problem with measuring is that you drive behaviour with it. Well, isn't that what you want? It is, if the measurements are the right measurements and give you appropriate and useful behaviour (i.e. behaviour that helps achieve your goal). Unfortunately, most companies measure what is convenient, what is traditional or what they can get data on. And this may have no bearing on leading you towards your goal. Cost accounting is a very good example. It is easy to set up measuring systems for money usage, and most companies do. This leads to all kinds of measurements of 'efficiencies' on which people are assessed. It is often much more difficult to measure effectiveness—progress towards your goal. So, this is seldom measured. Because people are assessed on efficiency measurements and not effectiveness measurements, most company behaviour is pulling the company in the direction of cost reduction. This may be (and often is) away from its goal. Cost reduction looks good on the balance sheet and for the quarterly results. Unfortunately, cost reduction is seldom, if ever, the goal of the company. And because it is not the goal, achieving it may produce behaviour that takes you away from the goal.

Similarly, performance management and reward and incentive schemes may be pulling you away from the company's goal.

All strategies take up some of your scarce resources. Unfortunately, the majority of strategies have little or no effect on reaching the goal. They may work for other people, they may have worked in the past, but they may not be working now—for you. Many strategies, although they may sound good, are actually destructive of your goal. (Ernst & Young's Quality Report confirmed this by finding that some management practices are detrimental to a company's advancement.)

What is the point of continuing with a strategy if it is not assisting you to reach your goal? Would it not be better to be working on things that *do* work rather than things that *should* work? Of course it is. However, business is not a laboratory. You may not be able to find out what does work and what does not.

Recommended action

- Measure to see if what you are doing overall is leading to success.
- Use everything you can think of (and afford to use) to throw at the problem.
- Be on the lookout for new options—for new ways of doing things.
- Be on the alert for changes.
- Be vigilant and discard what does not appear to work—accept that well over 80% of your options and strategy will not be helping you towards success.
- If you can afford to, set up experiments to identify which options and strategies to discard.

Good practices

- Measurements are in place to measure success in achieving the mission, vision and objectives and behaviour in accordance with the values.
- Clear and simple KPIs so that success of the plans can be monitored. KPIs are linked to the company objectives.
- Clear cause and effect relationships between company strategy, action and results shown in KPIs.

- Success of strategies in reaching objectives is measured.
- Clear linkages between KPIs, plans, direction and daily work.

Poor practices

- Not measuring to see if strategies and plans (i.e. 'experiments' to reach objectives) are successful.
- KPIs bear little or no relationship to strategic plans.
- No measurement of progress towards achieving mission, vision, values and goals.
- KPIs not linked to company objectives.

2.9 Measure extent of implementation

You must measure the extent that your plans are being implemented (i.e. everyone who should be carrying out your strategies and plans is doing so).

Measurement is an extremely useful tool to achieve implementation. In fact, if you do not measure how much they are being implemented, it is unlikely that your plans will be implemented.

You must measure if the plans are being implemented by everyone (or every section or every division) who should be doing them.

Principle 8 ('Innovation') describes in detail the steps needed to implement a project. The secrets are:

1. discuss it to death before you do it so that you find the holes and so that everyone knows what part they play
2. measure to see if it is being implemented and that it is leading to success.

Measure implementation

You need to measure if your strategies are being implemented—if people are actually doing them. The old thinking is of the boss saying 'do this' and assuming everyone has immediately dropped everything else and is doing what was demanded. Wrong! How frequently do you hear 'We have a very good policy on that but no-one does it'?

The main way of ensuring that a company's strategies and policies are being implemented is to measure that they are. If you are serious about it, measure its implementation. If you are not willing to do this, do not waste your company's time by introducing the policy or strategy. It is just lip service.

For example, to measure implementation, you are interested in measuring actions. These could be:

- shipments made, sales calls made, proposals, tenders submitted, chargeable hours worked, projects completed, business improvement projects completed, lines of error-free code written, words written—in each department or branch
- performance agreement items ticked off.

There are a thousand good reasons for people not being able to implement mutually agreed plans. Most are solvable. However, they will not be solved by magic. They need the energy of people—usually managers—to let them happen. They take time—and you may not have time. You need to measure if plans are being implemented—to find out what barriers are preventing implementation.

Measuring implementation does not have to indicate a lack of trust. (Of course, it will indicate a lack of trust if you introduce a pattern of blame for the policy or strategy not being implemented.)

A thousand good reasons for not being able to implement plans

- Staff may not have the skills, knowledge, authority, resources, capital or time.
- The plan might completely ruin a good practical working system.
- The plan may not be practical in the field.
- The plan may require the cooperation of others who are withholding that cooperation.
- Existing processes may not be capable (see Principle 4 'To improve the outcome, improve the system').

Alignment

Companies exist because individuals acting alone cannot do the work. Bringing people together also brings together complexity. How do you ensure alignment throughout the company, everyone and every department working in the same direction towards the mutually agreed goals and objectives? This is usually very tricky.

Companies are made up of people with different values, different beliefs, different ethics, different needs, different ambitions and different temperaments. The history of humanity is of people pulling in different directions. The people in your company will do so as well. You need systems to give alignment. Alignment is created by:

- significant and meaningful involvement in developing strategies and plans
- written plans
- measurement of implementation
- everyone knowing their role
- performance agreements.

Significant and meaningful involvement ensures you get input from the people who know most about what is going on and ensure enthusiasm for implementation. By the time that you get to the identification and allocation of activities, projects and interventions, there should be no surprises.

Making where you are headed the vision of all the people involved eliminates sabotage. It also prevents the old thinking of setting the objective or target without defining the method to get there—which is cruel.

Good practices

- Deployment of strategies and actions is measured—is everyone doing it that should be doing it? Implementation against the plan is measured.
- A measurement system that supports the planning process. Performance against plans is reviewed regularly.

Poor practices

- Not measuring the extent of implementation (i.e. assuming implementation just happens).
- Not standing back and reviewing approach and deployment.

2.10 Get better at planning

You should now be doing your strategic work better than you did three years ago. You should have learned from the decisions you have made and the mistakes that you made. You should be better at finding out what is happening around you, setting targets, enabling and involving people and measuring your success.

Companies appear to move through several stages in their planning:

- Stage 1 is dominated by considerable discussion about the difference between a mission and a vision.
- Stage 2 focuses on the differences between objectives and strategies.
- Stage 3 involves discussion about what are real KPIs and what are not, what are measurements and what are indicators.
- Stage 4 has argument about key result areas and key success factors.
- Stage 5 includes the future, risk assessment and stakeholders in planning.
- Stage 6 has scenario planning with targets and milestone tracking.

The debate in each stage can become very heated and acrimonious. Yet companies have to go through the different stages as part of an important learning process. Recognise the discussion for what it is and that the stages exist. If you are in stage 1, trying to think through the difference between an objective and a strategy, you are a long way from coming to grips with scenario planning.

A culture of change

As discussed above, people automatically push back when pushed into something they do not believe in. This is one of the reasons why meaningful involvement by people who will be affected by any change is important. However, there are other factors as well. Because of personality types and cultural differences, different people respond differently to a proposed change.

Many people respond very well to crisis management: 'We have this incredibly difficult thing facing us, people! If we do not solve it we will all die or lose our jobs!'. Targets are achieved by trial and error, by trying one thing after another or all at once until something finally works—what can be described as a 'ready, fire, aim' approach, an approach where chaos is good and crises are fantastic.

On the other hand, other people hate chaos and crises and tend to hide when these occur. They need guidelines—a map—to help them work through periods of change and uncertainty. They need structure, reinforcement of past successes, emphasis of who we are and why we are good at it, constant checking on progress against the plan or map and a lot of coaching. This is shown in Figure 2.7. When structure is provided for change, these people can thrive on it (top right). When it is not provided, you get various types of dysfunctional behaviour.

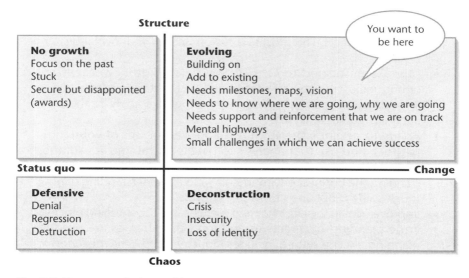

Fig. 2.7 Change works best with structure

In Japan, a target is reached through meticulous planning—incremental continuous improvement and breakthroughs.

The management literature suggests that you need a combination of these three approaches for various situations. In some instances, you need to let the panic and chaos of the crisis determine the behaviour. When you can, provide guidelines and maps. Sometimes, meticulous planning will be needed.

Scenario planning

Scenario planning is very useful for preparing for uncertain futures. No-one can see the exact future. Nevertheless, you can speculate about what various futures might look like. These futures are called 'scenarios'. In companies that use this method, the scenarios enter the daily language of the employees. For example, people work towards 'scenario five'.

Good practices

- A scenario planning process that leads to new strategy. Several probable futures are identified and likelihoods and telltale signposts are determined. These are tracked. Strategies and actions are put in place to achieve futures that are most advantageous for the company. People at all levels of the company are aware of the scenarios, talk in terms of them and track the likelihood of them being the actual future.
- A fully deployed process for scanning the business environment, including market analysis, political, environmental, social and technological aspects. This process is customised for your own industry/business type.
- More sophisticated tools than SWOT (strengths, weaknesses, opportunities, threats) brainstorming for undertaking such analyses (e.g. databases, group processes, competitive analysis, industry analysis, market analysis).
- Ability to describe the strengths and weaknesses of your competitors, and use that analysis to develop strategic advantage.
- Ability to describe the amount of effort that goes into understanding the business environment—and an understanding of how much value is obtained from this effort.
- Improvement in the efficiency and usefulness of the scanning process.
- Wide planning perspectives and long time frames are used in planning—scene setting includes industry trends, microeconomic change, demography, technology and any other environmental factors that could affect the company.

Poor practices

- A reactive or band-aid approach.
- No use made of emerging business environment factors (e.g. regional, community, demographic, reform progress,techno-logical) as part of performance assessment, learning and planning.
- A lot of environmental scanning but it cannot be seen how this is linked to strategy.
- Patchy environmental scanning, concentration on data that is easy to get or favourable to reinforcing existing beliefs about the company.
- No evidence that environmental scanning is linked to strategy.
- Reliance on brainstorming tools (i.e. SWOT) for environmental scanning (rather than thorough analysis).
- No process to monitor the effectiveness of environmental scanning.
- Narrow planning perspectives and short time frames are used in planning.

SUMMARY

Strategic planning should specifically describe the following essential factors for business success, competitiveness and profitability:

- the main requirements of your customers and markets
- your customers' perception of value—especially what drives customers' value, customer satisfaction, customer retention, customer loyalty
- what determines new markets and market share
- changes you must make to your operational performance to meet short-term and long-term growth and increased throughput
- your cost/price competitiveness
- how you will build operational capability—including speed, responsiveness and flexibility
- how you will practice—and strengthen—your competitive fitness
- how you will embed into work processes your company's knowledge and learning and any improvements gained
- how you will develop new work processes required to meet your company's goals and objectives, and disband old work practices
- how you will ensure that improvement activity is focused on reaching your company's goals and objectives
- how you will ensure the availability of skilled, knowledgeable and enabled employees
- the source and application of capital expenditures for short-term and long-term requirements

- how you will ensure reliability of supply with minimum variation
- how you will measure success and deployment of your strategies
- how you will ensure deployment (i.e. that everyone who should be doing it is doing it).

WHAT WOULD YOUR STAKEHOLDERS SAY?

HOW WOULD YOUR SHAREHOLDERS RATE YOUR COMPANY ON THESE?

- This company knows what is needed for success.
- I know what this company is trying to achieve.
- This company is focused on its goals.
- This company has clear indicators of success and I have access to them.
- This company is clearly focused on success.
- This company is well positioned for the future.
- This company is working to align itself with the 10 Business Excellence Principles.

HOW WOULD YOUR CUSTOMERS RATE YOUR COMPANY ON THESE?

- This company tries its very best to give us what we need.
- This company has built itself around providing what we need.
- This company does everything it can to anticipate what we want and to provide it to us.
- This company is focused on providing what its customers want.

HOW WOULD YOUR EMPLOYEES RATE YOUR COMPANY ON THESE?

- This company knows where it is going and has plans to get there.
- I contribute to the planning process in a meaningful way that I am very comfortable with.
- I am represented in major decisions affecting strategic planning, products and service design, process redesign and company design.
- I am given a say in this company.
- There are no surprises for me after the planning process is completed.
- All parts of the company work together to achieve the company's objectives.
- This company does not have political infighting and one-upmanship among its executives.
- I know how I contribute to the company's success.
- I know what this company is trying to achieve.
- This company is focused on achieving its goals and objectives.
- I know how we are going.

- We have clear indicators of success that I have access to.
- This company is proactive rather than 'knee jerk'.

HOW WOULD THE COMMUNITY RATE YOUR COMPANY ON THESE?

- This company includes our needs and expectations in its strategic planning.
- This company tries its very best to be a good corporate citizen.

HOW WOULD YOUR ALLIANCE PARTNERS RATE YOUR COMPANY ON THESE?

- This company includes our needs and expectations in its strategic planning.
- We work together to help each other improve our processes and systems.
- We are included in planning to introduce products and services or to change processes that would affect us.

Principle 3
Customer perception of value

Providing what your customers value—now and in the future—must be an essential influence in your company's direction, strategy and action.

YOUR MONEY comes from your customers—so provide what they think is of value to them. This sounds obvious but very few businesses do it well.

Although all stakeholder groups are important to the company, the customers provide the constant stream of money—through sales. Because it is the goal of the business to make money now and in the future, it must be focused most strongly on providing value to its customers. You can do this by providing what your customers value—what the customers really want and need and think is value for money. Everything about the business must be attuned to that end, including all the support parts of the business. That is, design your business around providing what your customers want.

Customers' perception of value must drive all aspects of the business. Most businesses only provide what they *think* their customers want, need and value. They try to sell what is convenient for them, which may not be what the customers want, need or value.

Dr Hausner's research shows that there is a strong correlation between providing what customers perceive to be of value and KPI improvement. The implication is that the more you provide what the customers value, the more you can improve the performance of your KPIs—provided, of course, you also work on the other Principles.

If you design the business primarily to provide value to owners/shareholders (the old paradigm) or to the managers (unfortunately also an old paradigm) or to the employees, the business will not make the money it could make. And, in the end, that is not in the best interest of those owners/shareholders, managers and employees.

Do not mistake this for altruism. In the end, you are not doing this for your customer's benefit. You are doing it for your own benefit. Unless you work for your customer's benefit, your *ex*-customer will find someone who will. When you provide better service, you get more money through sales by retaining your existing customers and getting more customers.

The viability of the business in the short and long term depends on you providing what your customers value—now and in the future. To do this, providing what your customers value must be a significant focus in everything about your business' design—the way it does things, its direction, strategy and action.

At first glance, Principle 3 appears concerned with the way that business identifies and sets about meeting the needs of its current and future external customers in its products and services. And most companies stop there. However, it goes much further than this and says that the company *must be designed to provide what customers value*. The company's direction, strategy and action must be designed around providing what its customers value. That is a huge shift.

Most companies are designed to meet the needs of owners/shareholders (with good dividends) or the needs of managers (with good salary packages). Some are also designed to meet the needs of employees (with good working conditions). Very few are utterly and completely designed and structured to provide what customers value. Principle 3 calls all those common practices into question.

Principle 3 also calls into question many takeovers and mergers. Many of these appear to be more aligned to providing excitement and entertainment to senior executives or to growing company 'size' by 30% to meet a stock market target than to designing the company to provide value to its customers.

Three steps

In order to design your business around providing what your customers value, you must first thoroughly understand what they value. After you have provided what you think they value, you must measure how you went.

1. Understand what your customers value.
2. Design your company to deliver what customers value.
3. Measure how well you are providing what your customers value.

3.1 Value is determined by the customer

Companies have come to realise that their customers—implicitly or explicitly—create a 'value index' by matching the value they think they will receive against the price you charge and the overall cost to them. Your customer's 'value index' includes everything about your product and service as well as things you might not consider part of your product or service but which your customers do (e.g. payment terms, delivery and costs due to inconvenience or modification).

The value your customers place on your product is based on the benefit they believe they will get from using the product.

Understanding customer needs

Most businesses have a paternal ('father knows best') approach to customer needs. 'We have been doing this for a long time. Of course we know what our customers want. We are the experts!' However, you should ask yourself, 'Do we really understand what our customers value?' and begin asking your customers what they value.

This does not suggest that you are not the expert in your product. However, the expert can and must adapt the product to meet more closely what the customer needs and perceives is of value. The first step is to admit that the customer may see your product and services differently from the way you do and may value things about it that you do not. After that shift in your thinking, the real trick is to find out what the customer really wants and perceives is of value.

Surveys

Most companies that think about this at all use a survey to find out what their customers need. This approach is *not* valid. Unfortunately, this means that most market research questionnaire tools do not do what they say they do. A questionnaire does not give you the information you need.

The reason for this is simple. Because *you* design the survey, it is designed around your belief system about your products. A survey will only give you confirmation that your customer shares these aspects of your beliefs. It gives a measurement of how well your customers like what you provide. A survey will not tell you what your customer wants. It does not tell you what to fix so you can provide better. A survey does not lead to action.

Surveys also miss the non-customers completely. Telephone surveys do not appear to work either. Many people refuse to cooperate and many lie.

Watch them using your product or similar products

A Japanese car manufacturer gained considerable knowledge about customers' needs by watching people loading shopping in a car park. They noticed that customers don't like hatch doors that whack them in the head. Customers don't like to hurt their backs when loading shopping over a lip into the trunk. Customers often have their shopping in plastic bags and don't like it sliding around in the boot.

Finding out what customers value

So how do you find out what your customers want and do not want? Ask them. Either one-on-one or use focus groups. You need to listen to what they say about your products and similar products. Watch how they use your products and similar products and learn from the difficulties they have. How you do this will depend upon the type and size of your business. For example:

- work closely with your important customers
- field trial your products and services during your research, development and design steps
- keep a very close eye on changes in technology and what your competitors offer because these have a very high impact on your customer's expectations, requirements and preferences and intention to buy or recommend
- try to understand the impact your product has on your customers' costs
- conduct focus groups with major customers and early adopter customers
- watch what customers do with products—how they use them
- train customer-contact employees in how to listen to customers
- use complaints to understand your products and services from the perspective of customers and customer-contact employees
- interview lost customers to determine the reasons they are no longer using you.

Good practices

- Use of watching, focus groups and face-to-face encounters to find out what customers need and want.
- Customer data is analysed to identify customers' needs.
- A strong understanding of their customers' current and future needs.
- Using customer input to determine what good product or service quality is and communicating that information to everyone in the company.
- Customer representatives are included in the product design team.
- Regular direct input from customers and markets in the design and delivery of products and services.
- Continual scanning of the marketplace to anticipate potential opportunities to exploit competitive advantage.
- Ability to articulate the amount of effort that goes into understanding the business environment and the value obtained from this effort.

Poor practices

- Using surveys as the sole means to find out what customers want (rather than asking them) or assuming they know what customers want.

- Discounting customer input (e.g. 'They don't know what they want. We are the experts').
- Creating products or services based on internal ideas only and then searching for a customer base.
- Use of surveys or daily contact as the only means to find out what customers need and want.
- A token attempt to 'listen' to customers—surveys are undertaken. No action is taken to address customer dislikes and needs.

3.2 Know what your customers don't like

You must have a very good understanding of what your customers don't like about your products and services—the dissatisfiers. The main questions you should ask your customers are about 'what is it about our products and services that you don't like?'. Find their dissatisfiers. These usually give the real clues to vastly superior service.

When you ask 'what is it about our products and services that our customers don't like?', you acknowledge that your customers might not like everything about your wonderful product. When you do this, you find very real gems of information. This gives considerable advantage for companies that do this.

How would your customers respond to these questions?

- What do you dislike most about dealing with this company?
- What about our products and service is not value for money?
- What don't you like about our products and services?
- What about us don't you trust?
- What about our service stops you from doing your best work?
- What about our service causes you to lose money?
- Do our response, delivery time and payment terms meet your needs? What would you prefer?
- Do you feel respected?
- Do we demonstrate values that you like?
- Are you treated fairly?

What do your customers dislike about the service you provide? Everyone likes good news and so businesses usually only ask what their customers like about the service they provide. This will give you a warm feeling but no information with which you can work. The gems are in the dislikes!

You can work out how to improve what you offer by asking what your clients dislike. This can take a fair bit of courage. However, if you can find out their dislikes, it allows you to modify your service to better meet their needs.

What about all those people who are not yet customers that could be? Why aren't they your customers? What about your ex-customers? Why aren't they your customers now?

Surveys cannot give you any of this information! Finding out about dissatisfiers needs dialogue—face-to-face contact. Watching and listening. Use surveys to *measure* satisfaction; use face-to-face contact to find out needs.

Customer contact staff and dissatisfiers

You may not even have to go to much expense to find your customer dislikes and dissatisfiers. Your sales and customer contact staff usually have a very good idea of what your customers dislike. They get told every day.

You must:

- encourage, enable and empower your salespeople to report your customers' daily problems and dissatisfiers
- provide processes so that you can listen to them reporting what goes wrong for your customers
- have processes to take this input and cause improvements in your products and services so the dissatisfiers disappear
- not shoot the messenger (i.e. blame the customer contact staff for reporting customer problems).

Good practices

- Extensive measurement of customer dissatisfaction.
- Use of watching, focus groups and other face-to-face encounters to find out what customers dislike about the company's products and services, and its competitors' and the industry's products and services.
- Customer dissatisfaction is actively sought as an integral part of process improvement.

Poor practices

- Not actively looking for what dissatisfies their customers (at all) and then not working to improve products, services and processes to eliminate these dissatisfiers.

3.3 Treat customer complaints as gifts

Customer complaints are gifts. You should actively seek complaints from customers and use them to make better products and services by removing dissatisfiers.

The customer is telling you directly what it is he or she does not like. Most organisations just make the complaint go away by fixing the problem *for that customer*. You must go further. Treat each complaint as a system failure. You are going to make sure it never happens again. Go further again. Use the complaint to modify your product and service so much that what was cause for a complaint becomes a benefit.

The new way is to think, 'Here is a gift, new knowledge. How can I make use of this to make my processes better and give my company competitive advantage? How can I change what I do so that customers never have cause to make complaints about this issue ever again?'.

An important issue in complaint management is prompt and effective resolution. This can lead to a complete recovery of customer confidence. In fact, it can lead to very loyal customers.

Cost–benefit analysis

You must examine the cost and benefit of making system alterations to fix the complaint. Some issues that your customers complain about are too expensive to fix or not possible to do. However, you must do what you can.

Fig. 3.1 Dealing with complaints

You should also prioritise what you work on so that you address the causes of most complaints with the smallest changes necessary. Effective elimination of the causes of complaints often involves aggregating complaint information from all sources so that you can evaluate it and decide what to do next for maximum improvement.

Your complaint management process should include analysis and priority setting for improvement projects based upon cost of the complaints, cost of fixing their causes and benefits that will come to you because of increased sales due to customer retention, loyalty and attracting more customers.

Many of your customers' complaints will have their origins in your own policies—how you decide to do things. You make and control those policies and you can change them. Policy changes are usually easy to do and can have a huge positive impact on your customers.

Encourage complaints

Customer complaints are so valuable that you need to encourage customers to make them. That's right! You need to create an environment where your customers feel they are an important part of your business. Only then will they take the time and effort to give you the feedback that you need to create value for them. If they feel they can trust you to act and the product is important to them, your customers will tell you their expectations about quality, delivery and price. If you are not seeking and getting clear complaints, you are missing jewels of wisdom.

You should place emphasis on obtaining 'actionable' information from your customers' comments and complaints. That is, the complaint should clearly point to the business processes you need to change. It is up to you to examine the cost–benefit of making the change.

You should ensure that your managers and employees who look after your processes receive the complaint information so that they can eliminate the causes of complaints. This must be done in a way where there is no hint of blame. People do not usually deliberately do things that cause complaints. You need joint problem solving to improve things that have gone wrong—not a climate of blame.

Good practices

- Customer comments are seen as 'opportunities for improvement'.
- A robust documented complaints process, which is managed by empowered people.
- Customer comments are shared across the company using a variety of media.
- Customers are satisfied that they are enabled to contribute to product design and their participation is valued by the company.

Poor practices

- No processes to handle complaints.
- Complaints are problematic and are treated as problem events that must be 'dealt with' rather than telltale signs of a larger systems issue.

3.4 Perception of product includes everything

You should be working to eliminate (or minimise) all of the things that are part of your products and services but which are not of value to your customers. For example, all those 'you must do it like this to use it' things (e.g. price, payment method and terms, ease of use, ease of access, availability, timeliness, accuracy, reliability).

Most businesses see their products and services just from their own eyes—what they see the product does and how much it costs to make and deliver. Customers see your product from their eyes—*what they see the product will do for them and what it is worth to them*. The gap between these views of the product is often enormous.

From the customer's perspective, your product will include aspects such as:

- payment terms and conditions
- access to be able to purchase
- advice on how to use the product
- how the product is delivered
- perceived status from using your product or service
- reliability
- the number of times they have to contact you to be able to get the product to work to their satisfaction.

Most companies see their products or services in terms of what they designed. However, from your customer's perspective, those same products and services include aspects that you probably overlooked during design. These aspects can be the source of dissatisfaction. If you work on removing them during your product/service design, this can give you a competitive advantage.

If a single deal were big enough when you are working one-on-one with a buyer, you would have worked through these issues. For thousands of small deals with anonymous customers, most companies do not bother—and lose this advantage to companies that do.

'Our new car will feature leather seats, a 10-disc CD player and central locking.'

Although it may be nice to have a car with leather seats and a compact disc player, other things may be more important to you.

You may want a car that is off the road for maintenance only once every year. When you go to the dealer, you want to be treated courteously and with respect despite your lack of knowledge. When you have the car serviced, you want to know what the bill will be in advance. You would like early warning of likely problems.

Some of the things you supply or see as part of the 'product', the consumers of the product might not like at all. Most suppliers mistakenly think everything in their product offering is what people want to buy. They fail to realise that some of the overall product is not appreciated.

Customer perception of value

In *It's Not Luck*, Goldratt presents a very compelling argument about customer perception of value.

Fig. 3.2 Customer versus company perception of value

That is, most managers' perception of the value of the products they sell is heavily influenced by the efforts required to design, produce, sell and deliver the product. Because of this, the company is likely to set its prices according to a 'cost plus margin' formula (i.e. product price is set equal to product cost plus a reasonable margin).

Value is not 'cost plus margin'

One thing that is not in your customer's 'value index' is how much it costs you to bring the product or service to the customer. Customers do not care about what it has cost you or how much trouble you have had in providing the product or service. Your costs are not part of their perception of value. When you price according to 'cost plus margin', you are thinking about this from your perspective, not your customers' perspective.

There are very few managers in the world who price on 'what the customer sees as value'. Most managers price according to the 'cost plus margin' formula. This means that opportunities for increased margins are lost because of a false assumption about what customers will pay.

Most companies are stuck in the belief that the prices that customers are willing to pay do not leave enough margin and blame the problem on the customers forcing them to cut margins or sell 'below cost'. Why assume the customer is not willing to pay more for your product and its services? Provided your package is right and your competitors cannot match the offer, you can probably ask and receive a premium, if it is in the customer's benefit. A very harmful assumption is that your product is a commodity (i.e. all products are the same and sold purely on price). Find something that the customers value that you can do that others cannot.

Do people buy only on price?

Every day you can see hundreds of examples that prove that people do not always buy the lowest price. Take cars, for example. If we all bought the lowest price car, we would all be driving the same low-price, basic model. The hundreds of different makes and models prove over and over again that we buy many things other than a basic car for the lowest price possible. We buy image and prestige as well as features and benefits, feelings, emotion and trust as well as compact disc players and colour.

Yet the myth persists that people buy mainly on price. You don't do it yourself—why do you think your customers do?

Do you create value for your customers?

Your business should try to *create* value for your customers. Few businesses actively try to create value for their customers. Most have stopped their thinking at providing what their customers think is value for money. Providing what your customers want and value may not be enough. Your product and service may become part of your customers' products and services. Each of those customers downstream from you is also trying to make money. Most businesses have been forced to understand that it is important to keep prices low as prices are passed on as costs.

So what does 'creating value' mean? A product or service that creates value adds significantly to the customer's potential to make money or to their lifestyle. Products and services that have done this have always done better than those that do not.

Good practices

- Customer satisfaction and dissatisfaction information is used to modify product design and delivery.
- Constant work to improve process capabilities to meet customer needs. 'Fix the system to please the customer.'
- Priority lists of potential customers' needs are prepared and processes developed to meet them.
- Customer input is sought when converting research and development or innovative processes to marketable products/services.

- Customers are actively encouraged and enabled to communicate their present and future needs.
- All staff care about the number and quality of units sold or services provided.

Poor practices

- Not actively looking for what dissatisfies their customers (at all) and then not working to improve products, services and processes to eliminate these dissatisfiers.
- Not acting on customer dissatisfiers.

3.5 Company designed to provide customer value

You must design all aspects of your company to provide what your customers value.

Principle 3 says that customer perception of value drives *all* aspects of the organisation—including structure, culture, design, delivery of products and services and direction. Everything about the company should be addressing its customers' perception of value—everything its people do, how they act, how the different parts of the company work together, how and which processes it improves, how its people are rewarded, which alliances it forms, its relationships with all stakeholders (shareholders, customers, employees, suppliers, community), the knowledge it accumulates, which data and information it chooses to collect and which decisions it makes and how it makes them—everything. This is taken up in each of the Principles. The emphasis here is on design of the company.

The old way of thinking is that a company is designed for the convenience and benefit of the owners, managers or employees. There are examples everywhere in almost every company. A few years ago, companies were displaying their organisation charts upside down to try to show that they were breaking with that old way of thinking. In most cases, this was just lip service. You cannot break the old habits by issuing a new organisation chart.

Owners have mistakenly believed the company should be organised for their benefit. But this confuses goal and method. The goal of the company is to make money now and in the future—for its owners. In order to do this, the company must deliver products and services that its customers see as having value to them.

Managers have always seen the company as there for their benefit—it provides them with income and identity. The behaviour and approach of managers has established the poor behaviour discussed as 'old thinking' in all these Principles.

You can go into almost any retail store and see examples of businesses designed for employees. Music played too loud, poorly displayed stock, no information on stock or options, poor lighting. Try a bank at lunchtime, with the queue out the door and all the staff at lunch.

Core competencies

Principle 3 also implies that not only must the company be aware of its market and what its customers value, it must identify its own basic skills—its core competencies—so that it can match its capabilities to the needs of its target markets.

Core competencies are what the company is very good at doing—its underlying skills, knowledge and experience, what makes it special and different from other companies. The core competency is what defines the difference, say, between a bank and a law firm. They each have developed skills, knowledge and experience in different competencies. Companies should seek to make the most of their core competencies—grow them, build them so that, in line with Principle 3, they add value to their customers.

Companies must protect their core competencies by keeping up with changes in technology and understanding about the way their industry works or may work in the future.

Better informed customers

In the modern business world, the power in the supplier–customer relationship has swung to the customers and the customer's role in that relationship has swung from passive to active. As competitive alternatives and information about them become available, customers have become increasingly demanding and influential. Any business that fails to respond appropriately is punished.

- The market increasingly punishes businesses that take a win–lose position with their customers or don't respond to their needs.
- Customers are increasingly better informed as a result of the recent explosion in readily available information.
- Customers are better able to use information for analysis and comparison.

Minimum acceptable levels

Most businesses still produce a product or service and then present it to the marketplace in the hope that it will attract customers. This is a big mistake! It is usually difficult to see any direct customer input to the product or service. Customers in the twenty-first century have much higher expectations and demand much more customer orientation.

From the customer's perspective, there are three value-related issues in any product offering:

1. *Features*: this either is or isn't present (e.g. the supermarket carries frozen pizza).
2. *Fitness-for-use*: it is fit to use (e.g. it complies with use-by dates and refrigeration).
3. *Performance*: it does the job required (e.g. the range of frozen pizzas is adequate, the frozen pizzas taste good).

You need to meet all these issues just to get to the starting line—the minimum acceptable level. To be competitive, though, most businesses must go beyond the minimum acceptable level. You can do this by identifying and acting on the gaps of specific customer segments.

Segments

It is essential that your company segments its market appropriately and determines what aspects of your offering are important to each segment. Not every one of your customers sees value in the same things. For simplicity, many businesses put customers with similar needs into segments. This simple definition may not be sufficient.

Because of your limited resources, it is essential that you focus your products and services to provide what each of your customer segments sees to be of value. An astute business will 'do its homework' and try to design its offering to fit both the immediate needs of its market segments and customers, as well as offer features that continue to attract customers in the future.

Most businesses do not do any more about their segments than grouping them. Yet it is possible to get much more out of them. In *It's Not Luck*, Goldratt presents a compelling argument that the concept of market segmentation is almost untapped by industry. This is because most managers believe that the price of a product should be equal to its cost plus a reasonable margin. This implies that most managers believe that there is, essentially, a single, fair price for a product. At the same time, different market segments have different needs. That is why they are grouped as segments. However, if different market segments have different needs, then different market segments might have different perceptions of value. This means that most managers ignore the market's differing perception of value when they set the price for their product.

This points to an overlooked opportunity. Different parts of the market might pay different prices for the same product or service. However, two segments with different perceptions of value will both demand to pay the lower price if they find out about it—there are no secrets in the long run. If different market segments have different perceptions of value, then you need to find and implement actions that cause them to think they are receiving different value for different prices.

This leads to Goldratt's definition of a segment: 'Two sections of the market are called segmented from each other *if and only if* changes in prices in one section do not cause changes in the other section'.

Let us look at the implications of this. If you impose a single price, this enables customers who have a high perception of value to pay a low price. Imposing a single price also trims away customers for whom the price is too high relative to their perception of value.

Because most businesses believe in a cost plus margin approach to pricing, this implies that they do not take advantage of the vast potential inherent in market segmentation. In other words, marketing is not oriented to take advantage of the most promising and almost virgin direction of market segmentation.

Usually businesses do their segmentation in too simplistic a manner. Consequently, most new outlets and most new improved products eat into the sales of existing outlets or products (Fig. 3.3).

You need to be able to segment the market to take advantage of the possibilities of different prices that different segments are willing to pay because of their different perceptions of value.

Read Figure 3.3 from the bottom up: '*If* the bottom is true, *then* the one above is true'.

When you operate in many market segments, you will probably have to take a different approach in each. For example, instead of being 'all things to all people', you may become a niche marketer or an expert in developing and sustaining strategic alliances. Your business will need to attune its listening and learning to the needs of each customer group and market segment, customers of competitors and other potential customers.

Choose your customers

The company must choose which customers it will accept and what to do and what not to do for each of them. You do not have to accept every arrival as a customer. You can and must choose those customers that lead you to your goal. Taking on every customer segment (and for some small businesses, every customer) should be viewed as a strategic decision because:

- the relationships that you need to build with that customer might lead you away from your goal
- you may not be capable of meeting the customer's needs, despite your wish for the revenue
- late payment by a big customer (a common tactic by big companies) may bankrupt you (i.e. you get the revenue but not the cash)
- the customer may expect you to do things that are against your value set.

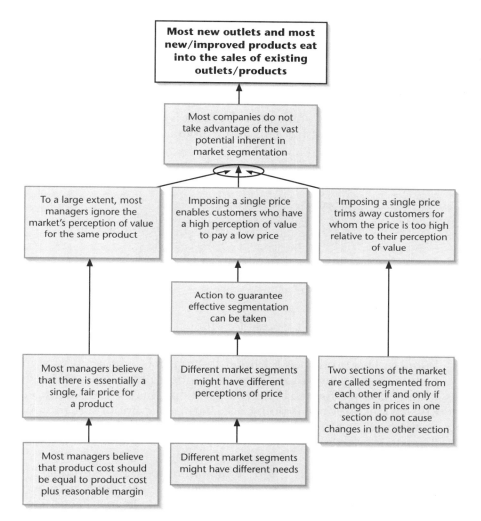

Fig. 3.3 The reality of market segmentation

You must choose what you will do and what you will not do for each customer—the services you will provide, the extent of the product offering, the nature of the relationship, the level of credit.

Which products and services

You can develop a quick matrix of which products are working well for you to help you decide whether to devote more resources to a product or to discontinue it. (This approach is much more useful than the unit cost approach, which has no validity.)

75

Compare whether your product is important or not important to your customers with how well it meets your customers' needs. This gives you four broad quadrants to assist prioritisation.

Customers, not you, define value to them. You can quantify what the customers think using gap or dissatisfier analysis. If a customer rates an issue as important and your performance as poor, then from the customer's perspective, your service/product is unfit for use. You must work to close the dissatisfier gaps in the product/service or it should be dumped.

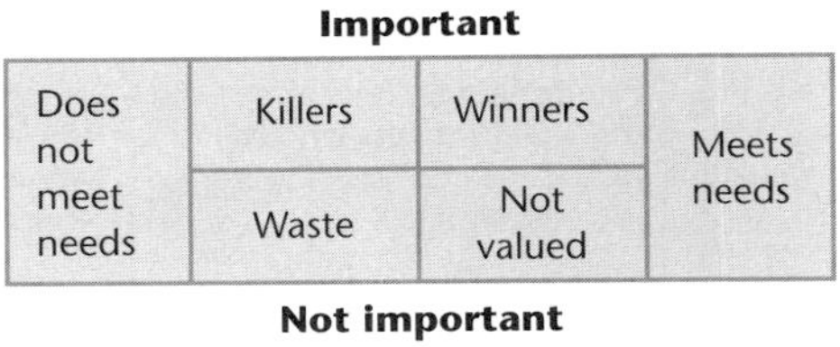

Important

Does not meet needs	Killers	Winners	Meets needs
	Waste	Not valued	

Not important

Fig. 3.4 Products and services matrix

Figure 3.4 shows the features of a product and service matrix. The features are:

- *Winners*: This product is a winner for you. It is important to your customers and your customers rate its performance as good. Maintain focus and your efforts to build your position. This is worth attention.
- *Killers*: This product is doing you harm. It is important to your customers but your customers rate its performance as unsatisfactory. Remedial action is essential. Address the dissatisfiers. This is a real opportunity for you.
- *Not valued*: Although it might be important to you, your product is not important to your customer segment. At least your customers rate its performance as good, whatever that means. Reconsider whether you are wasting resources and adding cost to your company by persisting with this product. You should raise your customer perception of importance to them or dump the product.
- *Waste*: This product is not important to customers and your performance is poor. Dump it or set it aside for the time being—you never know, customer priorities may change.

Good practices

- Caring about the value created for your customers—and *their* customers.
- Awareness that value to the customer only begins at the point of sale or service delivery.

- Alliance partnership relationships developed with major customers.
- Cross-boundary projects between the company and your customers with formal agreement of goals and responsibilities.
- Market segmentation and refinement of analysis of the needs in those markets.
- A process to choose which markets and customers the company will pursue and how to go about that.
- A process to choose which markets and customers the company will *not* pursue and how to go about that.
- Ability to articulate the strengths and weakness of your competitors and use that intelligence to develop strategic advantage.
- Customer data is analysed to identify customers and their needs.
- Customer representatives are part of the strategic planning.

Poor practices

- No direct link between the customer and vision and strategy.
- Laissez faire choice of strategy/markets—doing what has always been done or doing what is easy.
- 'Any customer is a good customer' attitude.
- 'Who cares what business the customer is in—if it's legitimate in law, it's okay by me' attitude.
- No attempt to achieve unique positioning for sustainable competitiveness.
- Patchy environmental scanning, concentration on data that is easy to get or favourable to reinforcing existing beliefs about the company.

3.6 Make customer access easy

You must manage your customer contact to ensure the contact is made easy for your customers. Every company to some extent manages its relationships with its customers. However, in the past this relationship had most to do with the convenience to the business and little to do with providing value to the customer. From the customer's perspective, the relationship you form with your customers is part of the product or service. And so is part of what the customers consider when they weigh the 'value for money' question.

In managing this relationship, you should consider customer access—how you make certain customers have easy access to do business with your business and to appropriate people for assistance when they need help and when things go wrong. Do you make it easy for them to contact you and use your business? Or, are you only available to do business at times and places that are more convenient to you than to your customers? Is your location good for your customers? Do you use technology to overcome difficulties with location and time? Can your customers contact you when they need to do so?

Clients versus customers

There is often confusion over the words 'customer' or 'client'. Many businesses have 'clients' rather than 'customers'. Others have 'buyers'. This is just different terminology or semantics. If you deliver a product or service to the person or company, they are your customers and you have to provide what they value.

You can call them whatever you like. However, a change of name might help you achieve a change of thinking. If you have been treating them as 'inconveniences' that 'stop you doing your real work', calling them something else might help. But, unless you fully take on everything that goes with Principle 3 and have everything about your company focused on providing what your 'customers' value, just changing the name you use will be just another useless fad.

End-users

Most products and services fit into a chain of products and services used by a chain of customers. All the intermediate customers and the end-user customer have different needs and perceptions of value. The concepts of customers' perception of value apply to each of them. You must meet the needs and fulfil the perceptions of value of all those downstream from you.

Consider a retailing example. In a very simple chain, a manufacturer sells to an importer, who sells to a wholesaler, who sells to a retailer, who uses a courier to deliver the product to the end-user. Each intermediate company in the distribution chain requires different things from all the companies upstream. Each intermediate company will perceive value in a different way. Each will have different dissatisfiers. The end-user pulls the chain along by demanding the manufacturer's product for its reliability, features and everything else he or she perceives is of value.

Fig. 3.5 The supply chain

Most customers do not care about the distribution chain. It is not included in their value index. However, it is in their *dissatisfaction* index if it does not work. Many companies completely forget that their customers see the distribution/delivery process as part of the product/ service. The manufacturer must ensure the entire distribution chain works well. It is a good idea to form alliances throughout this chain.

Unfortunately, when most businesses think about their 'value chain', they think about 'value' in terms of cost and from their own viewpoint (i.e. 'we machined this part or we added an instruction manual and the product is clearly more valuable than the raw material'). Such 'value added' may have had little or no relationship with what their customers 'value'.

Good practices

- The company works to make contact for its customers as easy and as pleasurable for the customer as possible.
- Documented processes exist to facilitate easy contact between customers and the appropriate people and these are used actively.
- Authority and responsibilities to support customers exist at all levels in the company.
- People at all levels of the company are put into direct contact with customers or receive ongoing feedback from the customers about the value of their work to them.
- The company maintains regular two-way communication with customers. Visits to major customers are considered essential. Face-to-face meetings are supplemented by many telephone conversations.
- Customer representatives are added to product design teams.

Poor practices

- No consistent approach to handle customers at all levels of the company.
- No-one 'owns' the customer relationship process.
- No process to capture customers' comments when they are ready to be given.

3.7 Customer contact staff are enabled

Your customer contact staff need to be enabled to handle any problem that is thrown to them by your customers. This means they must be given the skills, knowledge, authority, power and resources to solve the customer's problem. You need to take this enabling process seriously. Your customer contact staff should not always have to run back to a supervisor or manager to get permission to do something for your customers. This is very bad for both customer relations and staff morale. It infuriates your customers and tells them and your staff that the staff are not trusted.

In *Moments of Truth*, Jan Carlzon introduced the concept of the '15 golden seconds', during which front-line people in problem situations have the opportunity to respond proactively and earn the loyalty of customers. Moments of truth are opportunities to build sustainable business relationships by addressing the human need for trust and credibility—which, whether you like it or not, is part of your product and service.

Carlzon's book has many examples of employees enabled (by skills, knowledge, power and authority) to solve customers' problems. This means that they can and do solve customers' problems without having to run to a manager to get approval. This means they are trusted. Customers respond to that level of trust by giving their trust in return. This leads to loyal customers. It also leads to very happy staff, who blossom with the trust given to them.

For example, consider the differences you see in hotel staff. At one extreme, you find staff who appear to hide when they see a guest with a problem. At the other end you find staff whose body language appears to shout, 'I can tell you have a problem. Please make it my problem so I can help you'.

Selecting customer contact staff

You need very good selection criteria for your customer contact staff. These people will be the window through which your customers will see your business. They must have the right attitude, the right personality, the right values, appropriate pre-existing skills and knowledge, and be able to respond adequately to the level of trust you will place with them when they are fully enabled.

Having selected them, you will need to conduct full induction so that they:

- know the company's values and objectives and where they fit in
- have a full description of what is expected of them
- have the skills, knowledge, authority and power to respond to and solve your customers' problems
- will not injure themselves or others.

In businesses where the level of skill and knowledge needed is high, induction, including education and training, can take weeks or months before the new customer contact staff member is in unsupervised contact with customers.

The boss is not a customer

Many people think their only customer is their boss. This is definitely old thinking but is still very prevalent in government departments.

Bosses are suppliers. They provide support and resources, make certain you and your team are enabled (have the skills, knowledge, resources, power and authority to do your work), champion your cause and co-ordinate relationships with other suppliers.

Bosses are seldom customers. Unfortunately, most bosses do not understand that fact. Most bosses tend to forget who the customer is and what the purpose of the business is. This is not useful. Instead of demanding that staff work for them, bosses need to see their role as that of a supplier.

According to Principle 3, what customers value gives direction and design to the company. It is not what the boss perceives is of value. The boss cannot ever say, 'I am important. The sort of service you provide to external customers, you must provide to me'.

Are there any instances when the boss is a customer? It is difficult to think of any. When your boss asks you to do something, is it for them or for a customer? Is it to benefit the business?

Where does the manager fit in as a customer? The manager, like all employees, is a 'customer of the process'. Processes and their relationships are discussed in Principle 4 ('To improve the outcome, improve the system'). As one of many customers of the process, the manager does not have any special rights. And should not have any special power. Nor receive special treatment. Bosses who think they are special often divert processes to look after their (and not the customers') interests. This might help the boss in the short term. In the long term, it will not help the business.

Spend 40% of your time with customers

In many companies, the CEO and all senior managers spend 40% of their time with customers. This appears a very good idea. It demonstrates by role modelling (Principle 1) that customers are important. The time spent with customers should be to identify those things that the customers do not like and then to proceed through a process of mutual problem solving with the customer and the members of the problem-solving team. This should be at the senior management level because senior managers can effect most change as they have authority to control the most processes.

This 40% rule could be cascaded throughout the company. This will bring your customers into close relationships at all levels of your company—solving problems for mutual benefit, a high value-adding process.

If it is done as a slogan or imposition (with no substance, under-standing or concept of mutual benefit), then forget it. If it is done with the intent of modifying processes and systems in the company so that more of what the customer perceives to be of value is delivered to the customer, it might work. You could measure this to ensure it is implemented.

Good practices

- Customer contact staff are specially selected, trained in customer service needs, the company's products and services, and enabled and empowered to resolve problems.
- Documented processes to enable excellence in relationships with customers in the quality assurance system.
- Formal customer service standards are communicated throughout the company (e.g. using service level agreements, workshops, im-provement projects, working visits, presentations, data on expectations, satisfaction and performance, internal magazines).
- Troubleshooting by staff beyond the call of their responsibility to nurture customer relations.
- Executives and managers at all levels spend at least 40% of their time with customers. This is measured.

Poor practices

- Customer service seen as work for the most junior people in the company.
- Customers are regarded as a nuisance.

3.8 Customers need 'relationships'

You must build a relationship of trust with your customers. For example, you must keep your promises; do not over-promise or promise to do what you cannot do.

Businesses have come to realise that although features and benefits may be important, they are often more important to the company than to the customer. Often the 'relationship' between the customer and supplier is of primary importance to the customer—and this can provide significant competitive advantage.

Relationships are formed between people. As described in Principle 1 ('Role models'), trust and keeping promises are crucial in all relationships between people. Customers clearly value trust in the relationship. The surest way to harm a relationship is to break your promises and so damage 'trust'. This means you can build ongoing relationships by *keeping your promises and building trust*. You can do this in two main ways:

1. do not over-promise (i.e. do not promise what you cannot deliver)
2. when there is even a *hint* of failure to deliver, move heaven and earth to deliver—even if it is not your fault. Your customers will remember that you went completely out of your way to solve their problems.

Addressing the human need for trust and credibility is part of your product and service.

When customers think that they get value for money, there is a chance they will become repeat buyers. If your product appears like a commodity (i.e. there is nothing to distinguish it from the rest) and there is no relationship, then why wouldn't your 'buyers' shop around for the lowest price. If you do not take the trouble to establish a relationship, there is no reason for the 'customer' to stay loyal to you. You need to offer a sustainable relationship to your customers as part of your products and services.

Loyalty, positive referral and customer advocacy

A lot has been written about the value to you of getting your customers to keep coming back to buy from you—it is more expensive to get new customers.

Let us look at this from a few perspectives. Firstly, the majority of companies behave as though this were not true. Most spend money on advertising (attracting new customers with promises) but little on making certain their products and services are of value to their customers (or live up to the promises).

Secondly, much of the activity aimed at making sure customers are 'loyal' or 'advocates' appears very shallow—slogans only, rather than being backed by plans and changing processes to address Principle 3. Slogans also imply a promise. If the promise of the slogan is not delivered, this leads to lack of trust and a broken customer relationship.

You get loyal customers, positive referrals and customer advocacy when you keep your promises, including those in advertising. Make certain your products and services live up to the promises you make about them.

All stakeholders

The concept of designing the business to provide what your customers value can be extended beyond the direct customer to all stakeholders (i. e. owner, employees, suppliers, alliance partners, community). Although the customer is the primary receiver of the core products and services, each stakeholder can be considered as a 'customer' for their particular component of what they receive from the company. To some extent, the company must be organised around providing maximum value to each stakeholder group. In Principle 10 ('Value for all stakeholders'), how the company must find a balance, acceptable to the stakeholders, between those competing needs is examined.

Small businesses will be mainly concerned with customers, suppliers and employees. As the business grows, it will become increasingly involved with more stakeholders and their concerns. Large companies should have strategies and goals for each stakeholder.

Good practices

- Measurements include customer loyalty, emotional attachments to and feelings about the company, its products and its commitment to the community. Progression beyond customer satisfaction to loyalty and customer advocacy.
- Emotional response to those 'moments of truth' is included in the measurement system. 'Feelings' and 'emotion' give a more discriminating understanding than just 'satisfaction'.
- Partnerships/intimacy with customers for innovation and joint innovation.
- People 'own' customers and their needs and expectations.
- Seconding good resources to customer companies.
- Customer user groups set up by the company and managed by customers.

Poor practices

- Over-promising through advertising and slogans.
- False or misleading advertising.
- Failure to keep promises.
- Unethical behaviour.
- Lack of trustworthiness.

3.9 Customer information systems

Your information technology (IT) systems make it easy for you to record and retrieve information about your customers (i.e. they help make the customer contact easy for the customers and easy for you to do your work).

One of the main pieces of company design needed is strategic use of an IT system to record all this listening and learning about customers' needs, requirements and relationships.

The IT system should make it easy to store and retrieve information about your customers.

The word 'retrieve' in that sentence is very important. Many IT systems store data in ways that are not convenient for the users of the data. What a huge waste! It usually means that the data is not used. Consequently, the customer contact staff, who should be relying on that data, are hamstrung.

It can be very useful if you can have your IT system physically placed in your customer's and supplier's workplace—gathering data directly from the place where it is hot. Such an arrangement implies considerable trust on both sides. It can be very beneficial to both parties—each working on providing their speciality (core competency) to the business relationship and exchanging the relevant data to make each jointly successful.

Good practices

- Common systems are used to exchange important account information from a number of sources across the company through an array of methodologies. These systems are easy to use and highly accessible, making customers' input accessible to staff in all areas of the company—especially product design.
- Interconnected information systems, some enabling customer access.

Poor practices

- No customer records kept.
- Customer records difficult to access.
- Customers kept waiting while their records are accessed.

3.10 Customer measurements

For Principle 3, three different types of measurement are needed: two for perceptions and one for specifications.

Firstly, you must measure how satisfied the customers are with what they receive—their perception of value received. This tells you how successful your work is at eliminating dissatisfiers, building relationships, creating value and keeping up with technological changes in the market. Figure 3.6 on page 86 shows that you have several customer segments and that your products and services, in the general case, will not exactly meet the needs and expectations of any of them.

Secondly, you must measure the gap between what your customers value and what you provide. These gaps can be measured by survey.

Both of these measurements are about perceptions. Perceptions are important and must be gathered and quantified—an increasingly complex task. Your response to the perceptions of customers and other stakeholders will increasingly influence and alter the entire structure of your company.

Meaningful perception measurement

To be meaningful, you should measure customers' perception formally. This means you must have a process for asking, recording responses,

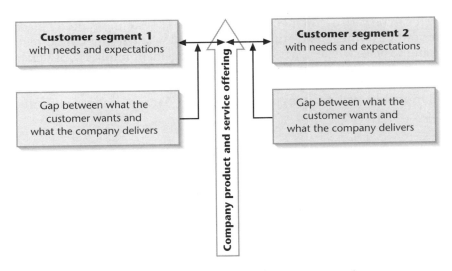

Fig. 3.6 Gaps between what you provide and what customers value

analysing responses and modifying the way your company goes about its business. You can record the anecdotes and compliments (e.g. 'Bill Smith said we did very well'). These help with the warm inner glow. However, you need graphs that shows increasing satisfaction or decreasing dissatisfaction.

It is also important to determine customer satisfaction relative to your competitors. The easiest way to do this is to ask your customers 'Are we better than our competitors?'. The information you get from such an analysis can be used to better understand the factors that influence your market and improve your performance relative to your competitors.

Specifications

The third measurement is more technical. You need to measure how closely your products meet your customers' 'specifications'. If you were a cement manufacturer, your customers would specify how much clay and lime they want in the cement you deliver to them. They might even impose penalties if you go outside those limits. You would need to manage your processes to deliver within those specifications and measure as you go. (The technical aspect of this is dealt with in Principles 4 'To improve the outcome, improve the system' and 6 'Variability'.)

This type of measurement is not a perception. Notice that you can (and should) measure it before your product or service reaches your customer.

The customers of most companies have specifications of some form or another. The most common specifications are speed of response and accuracy—often called 'cycle time' and 'defects'. (Even the cement example above is a form of defect measurement—acceptable within a range.)

Good practices

- Extensive measurement of the satisfaction gap between what the customers value and what the company provides.
- Indicators developed for the customer specifications for all the major processes, products and services. At a minimum these include timeliness, on-time delivery, numbers of times any rework was necessary, anything deliberately specified by the customer, anything customer research has identified as important to the customer and which the company controls (or should control).
- Customer satisfaction and dissatisfaction indices are determined from customers surveyed and benchmark data.
- Service level agreements or customer charters with important customers.
- Minimum standards of performance are set. Meeting these standards is always targeted especially at the level of the customer interface. This applies to all operational areas of the company.

Poor practices

- Customer perception of value received is not measured.
- The only measure of success is results of surveys that have been averaged together (e.g. '75% of our customers report they are satisfied or very satisfied').
- Indicators of quality are defined internally without reference to the needs of customer groups.

SUMMARY

Customer perception of value is a strategic concept. It is directed towards customer retention, market share gain and growth. It demands constant sensitivity to changing and emerging customer and market requirements, and the factors that drive customer perception of value and retention. It demands awareness of developments in technology and of competitors' offerings, and a rapid and flexible response to customer and market requirements.

When you are working to provide what customers value, you must take into account all aspects of the product and service that do and do not contribute value to customers and lead to customer satisfaction, preference and retention.

Customer perception of value and satisfaction may be influenced by many factors throughout the customer's overall purchase, ownership and service experiences. These factors include your company's relationship with the customer that helps build trust, confidence and loyalty. Customer perception of value also includes those characteristics that differentiate products and services from competing offerings.

Customer perception of value means much more than defect and error reduction, than merely meeting specifications or reducing complaints, even though defect and error reduction and elimination of causes of dissatisfaction make important contributions to the customers' perception of value. Your success in recovering from defects and mistakes is crucial to building customer relationships and to customer retention.

The systematic approach to Principle 3 is:

- Understand what your customers want.
- Eliminate what they dislike. Actively hunt for complaints and dissatisfiers.
- Turn their needs and wants into clearly stated 'specifications'. If possible, these should be specified in formal agreements (e.g. service delivery agreements).
- Segment your market—some customers may pay more.
- Make access to you and your products and service easy for your customer.
- Actively try to make everything about your company work to deliver value to your customers.
- Enable your customer contact employees (by providing skills, knowledge and authority) to 'make things right for the customer'.
- Measure customer perception of value, satisfaction and loyalty.
- Work to close the gaps between what your customers value and what you provide by modifying your products and services.
- Measure how well you meet your customers' specifications (including the ones you guessed at).
- Work to get closer and closer to your customers' specifications by modifying your processes.

WHAT WOULD YOUR STAKEHOLDERS SAY?

HOW WOULD YOUR EMPLOYEES RATE YOUR COMPANY ON THESE?

- I understand what my customers value.
- I understand what the company's customers value.
- We actively try to find out what our customers *dislike* about our products and services.
- We use customer input in product and service design.

- We use customer feedback/complaints to improve our service.
- Our products and services are of value to our customers.
- Customer feedback is a gift that we use to improve our products and services.
- Everything about this company is focused on providing what our customers value.

HOW WOULD YOUR CUSTOMERS RATE YOUR COMPANY ON THESE?

- This company focuses on providing what we value.
- This company provides products and services that we value.
- The employees of this company are exceptional in providing service we value.
- We trust this company and its employees.
- Employees of this company go out of their way to please.
- We feel this company uses our input to improve products and services.
- This company actively seeks what we don't like about its products and services.
- This company uses our feedback about what we don't like to improve its products and services.
- This company is always trying to find new ways to delight me.
- This company creates value for me.

HOW WOULD YOUR SHAREHOLDERS RATE YOUR COMPANY ON THESE?

- This company is organised to provide what its customers value.
- This company is steadily working to increase the value it provides to customers.
- This company invests in providing value to its customers.

HOW WOULD YOUR SUPPLIERS RATE YOUR COMPANY ON THESE?

- This company is our customer. We work to provide products and services that are of value to it.
- The products and services that we provide are of value to this company.
- We are working with this company to ensure we understand more of their business so that we can provide what they require.
- We are working with this company to ensure our products continue to increase value to this company.
- We are working with this company to ensure our products create less and less costs to this company.

Principle 4
To improve the outcome, improve the system

In order to improve the outcome, improve the system and its associated processes.

*A*LL SYSTEMS DELIVER exactly what they are designed to deliver. If you want a new outcome, you must change the process. If you do not, you will get the same result.

This Principle is one of the five most important Principles. Dr Hausner's research shows that Principle 4 is in the group of five Principles with the highest correlation on both business excellence score and improved business results and has the highest correlation with the business excellence score and the fourth highest correlation with improved business results. The others are Principle 1, 'Role models', Principle 2, 'Focus on achieving results', Principle 6, 'Variability' and Principle 10, 'Value for all stakeholders'.

We saw in Principle 2 ('Focus on achieving results') that all successful companies set goals, targets and objectives—and make plans to reach those targets. Principle 4 requires that those plans must involve change to the *processes and systems* so that the new targets can be reached.

Despite its importance, applicants for the National Business Excellence Award only do moderately well at Principle 4.

Most companies (although not the successful ones) fall into the trap of believing that all they need to do to reach their targets is to work harder. Working harder is not the answer. If you set a target that is outside the capability of the system to deliver it, you will have to change the process.

If you follow the 'work harder' thinking and do not work to change processes to reach new outcomes, all you get is burnt-out people and failure.

In *Out of the Crisis*, Deming makes the point that 94% of problems are caused by the systems and processes. That means that only 6% of problems can be attributed to individuals. Thus, we must shift the focus of blame away from inadequate people. The people are doing their best. Instead, concentrate on fixing the systems and processes.

4.1 Understand process capability

Process capability is the capability of a process to deliver, produce or perform to specifications, a result, a target or anything. Process capability is a fundamental concept. It underpins Principle 4. It is arguably the most important concept of business excellence.

All systems, including your company, produce exactly what they are designed to produce. To get a different outcome, you must modify the system. If targets are outside your capability, you must change the system in order to achieve them. Working harder is not the answer. Incentives or training are seldom the answer—although they are the most often tried methods. A manager's job is to improve the system.

Consider some examples:

- The Sydney central business district (CBD) is about 8 kilometres from Sydney airport. How long does it take to get to the airport from the CBD? When asked this, the informed traveller would say about 30 minutes. Could you do it in 5 minutes? Impossible! What if we trained you better? No. What if we gave you a bonus if you did it? Well, you would like the money, but it is still no. What if we had a helicopter waiting? Ah, that is better. You could do it then. However, you changed the process. The process will deliver exactly what it is capable of delivering. No amount of extra money, training or working harder will get more out of it.
- In Sydney, the trains are supposed to run on time. 'On time' is defined as leaving within 3 minutes of the scheduled time. Would this be acceptable in Tokyo? Definitely not! Would incentive pay get the trains to run on time? At one stage, the train drivers were being measured on achieving 5 minutes—as though it was their fault. Consequently, and because they could not control the system, the drivers began to skip stations. It solved the on-time statistics but was a tad annoying to passengers (customers) who wanted to get on or off at the skipped stations. What causes trains to leave late? The conventional wisdom was that it was 'wheelchairs'—the time taken for a wheelchair to board the train. They studied 'late leaving trains' and the astonishing result was found that the real cause of 'late departures' was 'late arrivals'. If the train arrived late,

it departed late. To solve this, they had to find out what caused late arrivals? The answer—unserviceable trains or breakdowns. Getting to that point required a shift in thinking—away from blaming wheelchairs or train drivers and towards acting on the real process issues.

Escapologist

A few months ago, there was television coverage about a skydiver escapologist. He jumped from a helicopter while wrapped up in chains and handcuffs. He jumped out at 4000 feet. From that height, he had 25 seconds before he hit the ground. It takes 7 seconds for his parachute to deploy properly. How quickly should he be able to get out of those chains? If he takes 18 seconds, he just makes it. If he takes 18.1 seconds, he is dead. Would you be happy if you could get out of the chains on average (or even most of the time) in just 18 seconds or less? Definitely not!

Let us assume that escapologists don't have a death wish and look at this process—especially his process of improvement. Would you try to get out of the chains for the first time while dropping to earth? No way! This is not an example of 'do it right first time'. You would do it in the comfort of your lounge room until you could do it every time in less than 10 seconds. Next, you would move to more difficult places (e.g. with wind, noise and cold) and practice until you could do it every time in less than 10 seconds. That 10 seconds is his process specification. He is going to keep working on his escape process until he can do it every time in 10 seconds. In this case, training (or at least practice) does work—it helps remove all the little kinks in the process. Would an incentive work? If he had not improved his capability by practice, would a million dollar incentive have made him fast enough?

- New South Wales has an excellent roadside service for vehicle breakdowns, the NRMA. The NRMA tells its customers it will respond to calls for service within 60 minutes—except on wet days. And they do. Their systems are capable of delivering service within 60 minutes 95% of the time. What would they have to do to be capable of delivering service within 45 minutes 95% of the time? Would it help to make the roadside mechanics work harder? Of course not. What about the other parts of the system? Traffic flows? The road network? Radio dispatch? The kit the mechanics carry with them? The age of the fleet their customers drive? The number of roadside mechanics scheduled at any time? All of these are parts of the system that delivers roadside service.
- How long does it take to be served in your local restaurant? Can they do it quicker? What is their service time capability? What

about the quality of the food? What is their capability for that? Would incentives work to change the quality of the food? If you offered to pay more (or less!), would the food quality improve? Or, would they have to change their process (new chef, new cooking methods, new kitchen, new menu) to achieve that? Does the process determine the outcome?

Good practices

- The capabilities of the company are understood and, where necessary, deliberate strategies are implemented to increase them.
- Process capability is calculated for all major processes, products and services.
- Training conducted in process mapping, continuous improvement and process management. Process improvement models developed.
- The company uses systems thinking to see relationships between the processes and the overall system. Systems thinking and teamwork are reinforced, including cross-boundary improvement objectives and joint planning.
- Benchmark studies in process improvement are conducted.
- Benchmark with others in your industry and more widely in business.

Poor practices

- No understanding of the concept of process capability—the 'work harder' approach.
- No understanding of process or process capability. No sense of the capability of the systems.
- Core processes not defined.
- No attempt to look outside the company: 'It's too hard to get information. It's very competitive, you know'. No attempt to look outside the industry: 'We are different. What could we possibly learn from someone else?'.

4.2 Set targets

You must set targets for improvement of your processes based on the needs of the customers of those processes. Targets are important. They are uniting in that they give direction and focus and so are very important for Principle 2 ('Focus on achieving results'). You do not have to know how to achieve them when you set them, otherwise you will always be working in the world that you know and within which you are comfortable and that is too restrictive these days. If you do not know how to reach them or if they are outside your process capability, you will need a plan of how to reach them. If you do not have such a plan, then all you are doing is wishing that you will reach your target.

Now that you understand the need to improve processes and systems in order to obtain a different outcome, how do you go about doing it? This is discussed below under systems and processes in general, the role of employees, the role of the managers, knowing what to improve, the role of suppliers and the role of standards.

Good practices

- Targets are based on an understanding of the system, variation, capability and capacity.
- Targets are set during planning.
- Targets are set for all goals, objectives and key processes.
- Targets are set that are measurable.
- Targets are set based on customer needs and specifications.
- Targets are set when processes have to change to new capabilities.
- Targets are set beyond current capabilities whenever you need to change.

Poor practices

- Targets are not set—at all.
- Objectives and required outcomes are not stated.
- Objectives and required outcomes are not measurable.
- Targets are based on past performance plus (or minus) 10%.
- Targets are based on gut feelings, a slogan, an accounting formula or as a response to head office demand.
- Targets are known to be unachievable.
- Targets are well within capability.
- Targets are unethical or clash with company values.

4.3 Plan to reach targets

The old thinking appears to be that 'if people would only work harder, we would do better'. This thinking assumes that the problem is with the people—people are to blame. Consequently, people's performance is appraised. But, systems and processes are not improved and targets are set without clear plans to achieve them. As Scholtes puts it in his lecture series, we know that:

- processes must change to meet targets outside capability
- processes do not improve themselves
- to change, you need to plan and to implement the plan
- process design determines company performance

- you cannot improve the whole by improving each part
- understanding and managing variation is a key to process improvement.

By what method?

To a large extent, Deming, in *Out of the Crisis*, summarised all of Principle 4 with his constantly asked question for which he was renowned, 'by what method?'. In this apparently simple question, he forces appreciation that if you want a different outcome you will have to change the system. He constantly observed that companies continue to set targets without making any plans to achieve them. Deming reminds us that everything is a system and we are part of it. To meet the new target, you may have to change your core competencies.

Fig. 4.1 People are part of a system

Peter Scholtes, the author of *The Team Handbook*, reminds us that a company is an aggregate of people, working within systems and processes to accompiish some purpose.

SIPOC

SIPOC is an acronym for the chain supplier–input–process–output–customers. That is, *suppliers* make *input* to your *processes*, which turn it into *output* for your *customers* (Fig. 4.2). It is a useful concept when thinking about systems and processes.

Of course, all customers and suppliers in the chain are caught in the capabilities of their own systems. Scholtes says that in this systems view, all work is an interdependent series of factors and events that produce some output (e.g. products and services) that serve some purpose (e.g. needs of customers). If there are problems with the output, it is because there are problems in the system.

Internal customers

We will now look at the way people are affected by and can assist in improving processes.

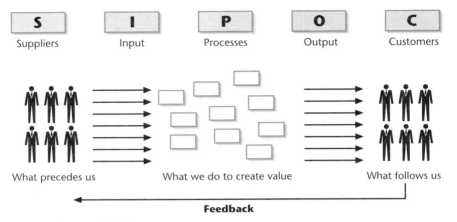

Fig. 4.2 The SIPOC chain

What is presented in Principle 3 ('Customers') about external customers applies to internal customers also—with one exception. Internal customers are really caught with one supplier. Internal customers usually cannot go somewhere else in the company to get what they really need. These people are customers of the process. For example:

- A person in an assembly line who is receiving shoddy work from up the line cannot get that work from someone else. He or she has to work with that supplier.
- A person who requires information from people in the company to do his/her work finds that it is consistently late and inaccurate. He or she has to work with those suppliers.
- A person constantly finds that his or her boss does not inform him or her enough of what is going on to be able to do the job—the boss withholds information (or authority) when delegating. The person has to work with that supplier.
- A person does not point out the flaws and problems with the boss's proposal. He or she wants to keep his/her job or does not want to be seen as 'negative'.

All these examples show a 'captured customer'. The solution is to enable those internal customers to say to their suppliers 'what you supply to me is not satisfactory'. That can be a huge thinking shift. Very few businesses have begun to make the shift.

Gemba

Gemba is a very useful concept in our understanding of internal customers. *'Gemba'* is Japanese and means 'the place where actual work is being done'; there is no equivalent in English. It is often translated as 'shop floor'.

Scholtes says that your company is made up of many systems and work flows. Not all of them are *gemba*. Only those systems that relate directly to a flow of work that adds value to the customer are *gemba*. *Gemba* work is provided directly to the customers. Not everyone works in the *gemba*. Only those who are part of the value-adding/value-creating flow as it heads towards the customer are part of the *gemba*.

This means that there are two different systems: the *gemba* and those who *support* the *gemba*. The *gemba* measures its success in how well it serves customers. The non-*gemba* measures its success in how well it serves the *gemba*.

Why is this concept important? The intent is not to establish yet another new hierarchy of importance among people—a new internal pecking order. The purpose is to help identify system functions.

Consider these:

- Very few managers are in the *gemba*, yet every decision they make is felt in the *gemba*.
- Everything is felt in the *gemba*—every policy change, plan, decision or process change. Often, those in the *gemba* will not know why or who changed something. They just see that something that did work will no longer work.
- It is extremely important that those in the *gemba* have a say in decisions that affect them.
- Do not keep those in the *gemba* waiting, do not disrupt the flow of the *gemba*. You will see later the importance of managing bottlenecks. The *gemba* usually has its hands on the bottlenecks.
- Very few of the people in your company are actually doing *gemba* work. Most people are engaged in work that supports the *gemba*. The ratio of *gemba* to non-*gemba* might be an important performance measurement for you. Many companies find they have about five people in the non-*gemba* for each person in the *gemba*. However, the ratio you have now (by Principle 4) is exactly the number you need to produce your current output. Your processes are designed to need exactly the level of support you have. If you want to change the ratio, you have to change the processes. A useful way of removing bottlenecks from the *gemba* is to have non-*gemba* people do those bits of the *gemba*'s work that is really non-*gemba* (e.g. paperwork and administration).
- Training should improve the way the *gemba* works. However, training will also disrupt the *gemba* and so must be implemented in a way that minimises that disruption.

THE COMPETITIVE ENTERPRISE

- The more you can enable the *gemba* the better—provide those in the *gemba* with skills, knowledge, power and authority to make decisions.
- Do not have *gemba* people doing things just for the sake of doing things.
- Almost all non-*gemba* people work with information.

Many companies have made significant advancements by just considering the work the *gemba* is doing and freeing up the *gemba* as much as possible from non-essential work.

Table 4.1 *Gemba* versus non-*gemba*

Gemba	Provide service to the gemba
Product or service design	Most management services
Product development activities	Customer research, marketing
Service development activities	System or process design
Potential customer contact and sales	Human resources
Delivering products or services	Plant or facilities repair and internal maintenance
Instructional and other after-delivery services for the customer	Payroll and other financial services; accounts payable and accounts receivable
Routine customer maintenance services	Purchasing
	Administrative services
	Training and education
	Budgeting
	Management information services
	Information technology services

Improve your support processes

Now a significant thing happens. Although the number of those in the non-*gemba* is usually far greater than those in the *gemba*, and everything those in the non-*gemba* do is felt in the *gemba*, most companies spend *all* their process improvement efforts on the *gemba*. However, you can usually make considerable easy gains by improving the non-*gemba*.

Because they are not directly involved in product and service delivery, support processes are not usually designed in the same detail as product and service delivery processes. You should design and operate your support processes so that they also provide value to your customers (in line with Principle 3, 'Customers').

Management and improvement of non-*gemba* support services should proceed in a similar manner to that for *gemba* processes, and include evaluation, in-process measurements and satisfaction of internal customers with the services provided.

Good practices

- Plans exist for how to reach targets. Plans are established to change/modify/improve the system and its processes to meet targets outside of the current capability.
- Improvement indices are constucted for all key, core and support processes.
- Suggestion schemes are implemented. Total visibility of all suggestions and each suggestion goes directly to the person who can implement it. (A central assessment of suggestions implies people cannot be trusted to work to the best of the company.)
- Design team is surveyed to identify level of deployment.

Poor practices

- Targets set without a clear plan to achieve them.
- For output to be improved, individuals must 'work harder, smarter' approach (i.e. blame the people).
- No training in quality tools, group process and statistical thinking.

4.4 For a different result, change the system

In its training manual, the Australian Quality Council says that when you want a different result, you must change the system. Everyone (including you) can only operate within the capabilities of the current system. If you want a different result—change the system.

All systems deliver exactly what they are designed to deliver. If you want a new outcome, you have to change the process. If you do not, the outcome will probably stay the same. Working harder does not work. The 'system' is made up of many interconnections and inter-dependencies.

Companies must use their internal systems and business processes to respond to the needs of their influential stakeholders. Complexity arises because of the interdependencies and interconnectedness of processes and activities within the company as well as external forces and processes acting on the company. From a systems perspective, nothing in the company can be thought of as isolated. Therefore, no intervention is totally discrete.

Senge's system laws

Senge, the guru of systems thinking, in *The Fifth Discipline* proposed a set of laws that he considers apply when problems are resolved at an inappropriate level of complexity:

- Today's problems come from yesterday's solutions.
- The harder you push, the harder the system pushes back.
- Behaviour grows better before it grows worse.
- The easy way out usually leads back in.
- The cure can be worse than the disease.
- Faster is slower.
- Cause and effect are not closely related in time and space.
- Small changes can produce big results—but the areas of greatest advantage are often the least obvious.
- Dividing an elephant in half does not produce two small elephants.
- There is no blame.

Reactive decisions

In the old thinking, people made their decisions in reaction to what was happening around them. Such event-driven actions are characterised by the following:

- Analysis does not consider the system, its complexity or interactions, or how people will react.
- Analyses and decisions are based on old data and information.
- Gut feelings are used instead of data.
- Analysis is superficial.
- Power and authority dominate decision making.
- Little time for diagnosis.
- Poor quantification of resource requirements.
- Little consultation with concerned parties.
- Poor identification of risks or barriers.
- Poor identification of potential consequences on other parts of the systems or to other stakeholders (suppliers, customers, community, innocent bystanders).
- Targets are assigned without knowledge of the systems' capability to produce them and subsequently plans are not made to modify/improve/change the system so the targets can be reached.

Event-based reactive decisions are unlikely to result in system level improvement. Event-driven improvements fail to consider the effect of the improvement on the system as a whole and can subsequently undermine your ability to reach your objectives.

Who is making these decisions?

The negative effects that the 'improvement' has on other parts of the system are often ignored or thought to be bad luck. For example:

Manager: We have been having major problems achieving our monthly production targets over the past six months. Last month, my boss really got stuck into me over falling behind the target. This month, I've instructed our warehousing people to ensure the full delivery targets are achieved, irrespective of the stocks in our local distribution stores.

Warehouse Supervisor: I'm going to have to work additional overtime to get all of the material delivered this month. I'll be in difficulty over that. I wish the manager had talked this decision through with me.

Local Store Supervisor: Where am I going to put all that stock? I need to hire some additional space. That's going to be expensive!

Accountant: Our costs of inventory and overtime are becoming excessive. Who is making these decisions?

Systems thinking characteristics

System level improvement requires an understanding of the system and its interdependencies. The nature of the relationships determines both the outcomes and the unintended consequences. This approach to improvement—the new thinking—is characterised by:

- historically relevant data on which the analysis is based
- in-depth analysis at a dynamic level of complexity
- several models in decision making
- appropriate time for diagnosis
- sound quantification of resource requirements
- considered targets
- appropriate consultation with concerned parties
- sound identification of potential consequences.

You can probably see very good relationships between these factors and Senge's laws. These issues are discussed throughout each of the Principles.

Good practices

- Understanding that for output to be improved the system must be improved.
- Constant work to improve process capability to meet customer needs—'fix the system to please the customer'.
- Measurement and process thinking is well developed or deployed.
- Recognising the value of innovation for the vitality it brings to the drab push for reliability.
- Senior executives have created an atmosphere that accepts and welcomes innovative change that benefits the customer and the

company and makes processes easier and simpler to use or with less variation in their output.

- People view process management and improvement as a natural part of daily work. Staff are involved in continuous improvement.
- Continuous practice of effective change management. Continual search for best or better fit.
- Process improvement incorporates creative problem-solving process.
- Internal customers send 'things' back to internal suppliers and complain.

Poor practices

- A 'work harder' approach. This shows no understanding that improved performance can only result from an improved system and process.
- Large amounts of energy expended to 'beat the system'.
- People feel like they are helpless against the 'system'. 'The system' is anonymous and undefined.
- People are engaged in mindless work—the purpose of which they do not understand and whose outcome and process they cannot control.
- No process of company self-development.

4.5 Performance management

Your performance management system must be based on an understanding of process capability, that is, on what the system is capable of doing. If it is not, then you will:

- randomly give praise and sanction in response to how the system has allowed people to do their work
- give praise and sanction to those who do not deserve it
- fail to give praise and sanction to those who do deserve it.

Performance appraisals should be confined to appraisal of the system and what about it most needs to be fixed.

Performance appraisal

The process capability concept has a major impact on the way companies understand and use performance management.

The performance appraisal is deeply rooted in the old thinking. It is a simplistic solution to a complex problem. It assumes that people are the problem—they are withholding their labour and if only they would work harder all would be all right. The performance appraisal entirely overlooks the concept of process capability—that to get a different outcome you must change the system. It also demonstrates a poor understanding of variation (Principle 6).

Most people perform in the 'average' band of performance, fully constrained by the system and processes within which they work. Those systems and processes do not produce exactly constant results—they vary, and as a result, people's performance varies. Someone who does well (in the system) one day will most probably not do so well the next day. What is the purpose of commenting on someone's 'performance' in such situations?

Remember those NRMA roadside mechanics? Should we assess each individual on the percentage of time they responded in 60 minutes? Does it help at all to measure this performance? Some cars are harder to fix. Also, the one thing customers do not want is for their car to be towed. If you put the mechanics on a tight 'time to fix' schedule and appraise them on meeting it, they will call for cars to be towed. After all, they do not want to look bad just because someone's car would not start. It is quicker to get it towed. Which is exactly the opposite of what the customers want.

The performance appraisal system forces behaviour that is not in the best interest of the customers and hence is harmful to the company.

False assumptions

Scholtes says that the performance appraisal is built on the following assumptions—all of which are false.

- Problems result from individual dereliction of duty.
- Successful work requires holding people accountable for the achievement of measurable goals.
- There is a reservoir of withheld effort that must be coaxed or coerced out of people.
- Managers can and must motivate and control the workforce.

What prevents people doing their best work?

The only reason to have discussions with people about performance is to discuss what is wrong in the system and processes within which those people work that prevents them from doing their best work. This could include:

- problems with suppliers (including you as the manager, fellow workers, other departments)
- impossible demands
- steps in the process
- understanding customer needs

- necessary skills and authority
- communication bottlenecks.

Usually, there is so much fear in a company that this discussion can never truly take place. As a result, all performance appraisal schemes result in:

- hiding mistakes
- putting a positive spin on everything possible
- dissembling—or straight out lying
- cynicism
- poor morale.

Influencers of performance

Personal appraisal schemes generally pay little heed to the complex systems that cause 80–90% of workplace problems. Table 4.2 shows the causes of poor performance. All are valid reasons for poor performance, yet few are considered in most performance appraisals.

Table 4.2 Causes of poor performance

Training and education	External influences	Morale	Resources
Interactive skills	Goals	Health	Supplies
Decision making	Reward system	Work conditions	Facilities
Problem solving	Feedback	Personal concerns	People
Business knowledge	Supervisor	Workplace conflict	Time
Product knowledge	Work load	Recognition	Data and information
Customer knowledge	Job description	Being appreciated and valued	Tools
Job satisfaction	Measurement	Security	Space to volunteer

The performance of people is always controlled and limited by the capability of the total system in which they work.

How do you break out of this destructive old thinking?

The necessary shift is away from blaming the person and towards working to find solutions to the systems problems.

Unfortunately, almost everything about the business world today is stuck in this damaging appraisal–reward, carrot and stick, incentive, stimulus–response thinking. It is worse in the upper parts of the company where the rewards are so high because of the high-value reward and incentive schemes. It is now the way we do things and is probably the biggest barrier to success.

Firstly, performance management systems must be about system performance and take process capability into account. Secondly, you must establish a process that agrees on tasks to reach the objective and then assess the process to see if they were completed or not. Thirdly, you must ensure that the only discussion about performance is about what is wrong in the system and processes within which that person works that prevents him or her from doing their best work. Identify problems with suppliers (including you as the manager, fellow workers, other departments), impossible demands, steps in the process, understanding of customer needs, necessary skills and authority, and communication bottlenecks.

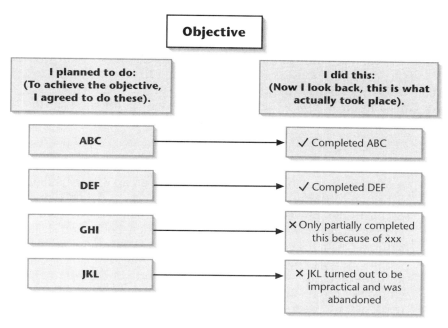

Fig. 4.3 System performance appraisal

Blame and scapegoats

Because 94% of workplace problems are caused by complex systems, human error is much rarer than people think.

When things go wrong—and they will—you should be asking tough questions about the system rather than hunting for someone to blame. Ask 'why' questions, rather than 'who' questions. Make no effort to find a person to blame. As Deming put it in *Out of the Crisis*—assume there is something wrong with the system and ask severe questions, ask tough questions, ask challenging questions. As the Japanese put it—ask 'why' five times to get to five levels of system failure.

When you hunt for scapegoats, you:

- tell the people in the company to look out, they may be next—blamed for something over which they had no control
- fail to fix the system problem, and as a consequence, the problem will reoccur—and someone else will get blamed.

Stakeholders should be very wary of all companies that have a culture of hunting scapegoats. It usually means that they do not fix their problems.

Dead wood

Old-thinking companies talk about their 'dead wood' and the need to trim it. In the new thinking, there is no dead wood. The only relevant questions are 'why did you hire dead wood?', or 'why did you hire good wood and then kill it off?'. (It is worth thinking about the value of dead wood. People build houses out of 'dead wood'. In an old growth forest, dead wood is essential for the viability of many life forms, such as possums and birds. Old wood is probably essential for the viability of businesses—it might store the knowledge.)

Good practices

- A performance management system based on an understanding of process capability and variation and which seeks to identify system problems that prevent the employees from doing their best work, provide the employees with the skills, knowledge, power and ability to further assist the company reach its goals, and recognise success.
- 'Feedback' sessions are devoted to 'what can the company and its management do to improve systems and processes so the employees can do their work?' and 'what other enablement factors (e.g. skills, knowledge, resources, authority) do the employees need to do their work?'.
- Employee performance is assessed in a context of systems thinking and knowledge of process capability.
- People are not blamed when things go wrong.

Poor practices

- 'Work harder' reward structures and incentive schemes.
- Performance appraisal schemes used instead of management of process.
- A culture of blaming people when things go wrong—scapegoats.

4.6 The manager's job

The job of the manager is to ensure that the business process is managed, controlled and improved. The process workers know what to change but do not have the power to change it. The bosses have the power to change but do not have knowledge of what to change.

At every level, managers must work with their people to improve design of those parts of the company's systems for which they are responsible. This is called 'working on the system' but it can only be enacted by people who 'work in the system'.

A team approach is needed whereby the manager brings his or her power and view of complexity. The process worker brings his or her detailed knowledge. The manager's role is to empower and enable—to be a coach, to open doors, to provide contacts when needed, to ensure the complexity of the system is considered, to value the detailed knowledge of the team, to provide the power to implement mutually agreed solutions to system problems.

The old-style company

The old view of the company focused on pleasing the managers and controlling the workforce. It is false logic and does not lead to sustainable success. It grew out of old military models. It is still a favourite of government. (Much of the material presented below is adapted from concepts presented in seminars by Peter Scholtes.)

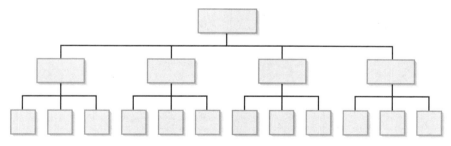

Fig. 4.4 The structure of the old-style organisation

The features of old-style management are:

- It is very useful for finding out 'who was derelict in doing their duty' (i.e. 'who is accountable').
- The company's relationship to its customers is not clear. Customers are implied.
- 'Please the boss' is the rule. The boss is the real customer. The implication is that the company exists to look after itself and primarily its bosses.

- The assumption is that the company will succeed if everyone does his or her job as directed.
- For the output to be improved, individuals must work harder or smarter.
- Quality is an event resulting from individual (or team) effort.

The new business

The new business focuses on providing value to the customer and improving the systems, processes and methods by which to create and deliver goods and services to the customer.

The features of the new business are:

- Management is implied rather than a focus of attention.
- Quality is the net result of interactions within the system.
- The steps of the system are interdependent.
- For the output to be improved, the system must be improved.
- The manager becomes responsible for how his or her part of the system serves the needs of the system's customers. In this thinking, the boss is more a supplier than a customer—a huge shift in thinking.

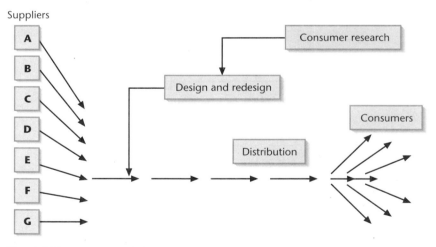

Fig. 4.5 The structure of the new organisation

The people who do the work understand the work

The issue of who knows what to change and who has the power to make changes is complicated. A company's systems are all those processes, actions, tasks, interconnections and relationships that are essential for meeting the needs of all its stakeholders. This includes its resources (machines, information, people, buildings) and its structure (policies, plans, methods, strategies, communication). Superimposed on this is a management system that manages those processes, actions and tasks. This management system must understand those processes, manage them and improve them.

The old thinking was that the managers are best able to do that. Managers controlled and directed everything. It was their right. They had been appointed as the owners' representatives and it was their job to get the lazy, shiftless and ignorant workforce to work. Managers knew best. Managers 'manage', workers 'do'. This was almost regarded as a natural law.

The new thinking recognised the folly of this approach. There is another law—the further people are from the hands-on work, the less they understand it. Put in terms of the *gemba*—the further people are from being part of the *gemba*, the less they understand *gemba* work. The people in the *gemba* understand everything about their work. If they do not, you are in big strife. How can they do their work if they do not understand it? Yet, the old thinking is that they understand nothing— and many companies still believe that. Figure 4.6 shows that the supervisor understands, say, 90% of the work, the supervisor's manager, say, 60%. The senior executives and CEO, say, 5%. And that is being generous. In these days of downsizing and young, inexperienced managers with Masters of Business Administration, the knowledge of the process can drop off even more quickly.

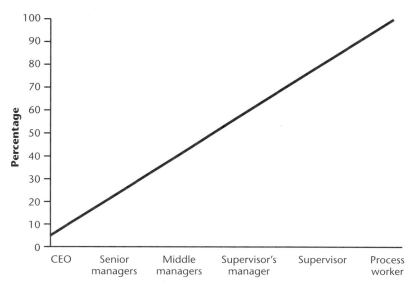

Fig. 4.6 The level of understanding the process in a company

Based on this thinking, who should design, manage and control the processes? The *gemba* of course.

What is the role of supervisors and managers?

This has been one of the biggest problems in shifting to the new thinking. The old controlling and directing behaviour of the supervisors is just not suitable any more. What should they do now? They should provide support, give strategic direction and work to improve processes. They act as suppliers to the *gemba*. They become part of the team that supports the *gemba*. They recognise that although they may sometimes be customers of the process, they are *never* 'customers' per se.

The problem with this thinking shift is, where do the supervisors and managers learn this new behaviour? Supervisors and managers are usually a little older and have 'experience'. Often, everything they know and saw during their job history supports the belief that the real way forward is by control and giving directives—that is, it supports the old thinking. Why should they change to this new nonsense? They know it will soon pass. That is why Principle 1 (the role-modelling of the senior managers) is so important. You constantly have to act to counter the move back to the old-style control thinking.

Many companies have responded by getting rid of the middle layer. After all, it is clearly the problem—not only do they want to stay with the old control thinking but they appear to be a wasted resource. The problem with that approach is that the middle layer of supervisors and managers has huge knowledge of how and why things work the way they do. They might not know the details of the process but their knowledge of the process is gold—as companies found out that threw them away.

So what do you do? You have to bring the managers and supervisors with you. They are valuable contributors—you have to let them contribute in a valuable way. Just as you have to enable your other employees, you have to enable your supervisors and managers. That includes all the senior managers too. (Remember, enable means provide skills, resources, knowledge, structure, power and authority to be able to contribute fully.)

Understanding and living according to this new thinking is yet another skill supervisors and managers have to acquire. They need the space and time to acquire that skill and forgiveness and support through the mistakes they make while doing so. There is a lot to do. They will not do it by osmosis overnight. Remember the old thinking where the instant people were appointed as supervisors or managers they immediately acquired all the knowledge necessary to make all the decisions? Didn't you ever wonder about that magic process?

What is the role of the supervisor in the new thinking? It is that of team leader—helping the team, facilitating (i.e. 'making it easy'), coaching, mentoring, using their experience and knowledge to add a level of guidance, encouraging the diversity of opinion within the team to contribute. But there is another role.

Working to improve process is the boss's job

Now we come to the paradox. The discussion above describes who knows what needs to change. But who has the power to make the changes?

Although the people who work in the system know most about it, invariably they have the least ability to make changes to it that will really matter. There are several reasons for this.

Processes in most companies are usually complex with many interfaces to suppliers and customers external to your part of the company. All of these affect the processes people work in. Workers in the process seldom have time to do any more than just exist within this complexity. They seldom have the time, knowledge, understanding or contacts to see it as a whole. It is not until you see it as a whole that you can see what affects what. The new understanding about systems is that you do need to understand the complexity before tinkering and adding simple solutions to what are usually complex problems.

Working in a process is like riding a bike. You can be so caught up in the riding that you cannot see if riding is still appropriate. For example, if the objective is long-distance transport, you might be better driving a car, catching a plane or telecommuting. You might not be riding very well. It is useful if someone independent—a coach—can help. Remember, that working (or riding) harder is not a solution.

The person best placed to take that independent view is the boss. The boss is independent of the process yet with knowledge of it and with the *power* and *authority* to help.

That 'power and authority' is the critical part and is at the heart of the paradox. Although the process workers have most knowledge of their work (especially what makes it not work), they have little or no power to change the things about it that really matter. For example, they might need a change in supplier to get better quality material, to change the approval cycle to have fewer steps, to use different software to store and retrieve more relevant customer information, a change in the process that would increase throughput by rescheduling bottlenecks. These are seldom within their control.

As you go up the company's hierarchy, there is more and more power to control the complexity of the system and its processes (Fig. 4.7). You might have to go several managers up the line to get sufficient independence, power, authority and ability to see the necessary complexity. Nevertheless, at each level it is the boss's job to fix the process. Everyone else is too busy riding bikes.

People work *in* a system. Improvement occurs when people are enabled to also work *on* the system.

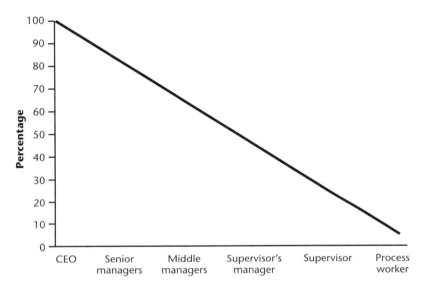

Fig. 4.7 The level of ability to improve the processes in the company

The paradox

The process workers know what to change but do not have the power to change it. The managers have the power to change but do not have knowledge of what to change. A paradox!

What does the manager do to solve this? In the old thinking, the bosses assumed that because they had the power and could see complexity, having detailed knowledge was irrelevant. They just gave orders and made their changes.

This usually led to simplistic and ineffective solutions. In the new thinking, a team approach is needed whereby the manager brings his or her power and view of complexity. The process workers bring their detailed knowledge. The manager's role is to empower and enable—to be a coach, to open doors, to provide contacts when needed, to ensure the complexity of the system is considered, to value the detailed knowledge of the team, to provide the power to implement mutually agreed solutions to system problems.

The job of the management system is to ensure that the business process is managed, controlled and improved. At every level, managers must work with their people to improve design of those parts of the company's systems for which they are responsible. This is called 'working on the system' but it can only be enacted by people who 'work in the system'.

That is a fantastic role, hugely empowering of the manager. And, if it is done right, hugely empowering of the staff as well. Unfortunately, most managers do not know it exists. Most bosses are stuck in the thinking that their job is to give people orders to work harder.

Management has three roles

1. To ensure focus on the company's goals and objectives by using key result areas (KRAs), measurements (KPIs) and plans (Principle 2, 'Focus on achieving results').
2. To be a role model of the 10 Business Excellence Principles (Principle 1, 'Role models').
3. To design, implement, monitor and improve the internal processes that produce and deliver products and services. Analysis of the processes that cause those outcomes and all their interfaces and influencers is another way to focus and give alignment.

These three roles are completely integrated.

Do not downsize before you improve the process

This is a significant warning. In these days of extreme downsizing (rightsizing), almost all businesses have lost the managers who had the knowledge or time to undertake their role of process improvement. Almost everyone is running at a thousand miles an hour just to function in the job. There is no time to examine it, let alone to improve it. The message is 'Do not downsize before you improve the process'. If you do, you will not be able to improve it. This is another reason why downsizing is often false logic.

Good practices

- All key, core and support processes have process owners who are responsible for process performance, maintenance and improvement.
- Managers become responsible for how their part of the system serves the needs of the system customers.
- CEO/owner leads improvement.
- Senior management 'own' the processes. Line managers and executives together understand they have responsibility to ensure improvement of processes.

- Senior executives see themselves as team members. They participate in a number of teams—demonstrating commitment by participation. As a team member, they work to build the team's capability to make their own decisions—gradually increasing the other team members' authority.
- An appropriate use of teams to solve problems and assist management. Management is actively involved as team members of many process improvement teams.

Poor practices

- Bosses not working to improve processes—just wanting people to work harder.
- Not enabling process workers to improve processes (by supplying skills, knowledge, resources and authority).
- Bosses think they are customers.

4.7 Rework

Rework is bad news. Rework is pure waste. Doing the same thing over and over is usually a huge cost. It is waste of time, energy and resources. It increases your costs when you are constantly fixing something that should have worked—you have to employ people to do that rework. Your customers hate it. It stops you moving on to do things that are more productive. Worst of all, it means your processes are unreliable. Rework time is definitely wasted time. If you can reduce your amount of rework, you can make a huge difference.

Most of the time people spend at work is on redoing work, fixing up things that have gone wrong—the package you delivered was incomplete, one piece of information you wanted is not there, invoices were not right, you get yet another telephone call about something you thought was fixed.

For most businesses, preventing and fixing their rework issues can be the source of huge windfall profits. Reworked is treated as the norm—'the way we always do things here'—and there is usually huge amounts of it. Removing rework reduces all the costs tied up in fixing old problems. When you are not fixing old problems, you can move on and solve the real problems of today and prevent the problems of tomorrow.

Eliminate waste and rework

Make a list of the biggest sources of your rework (what takes up most of your time), measure the time spent on it, try to find the core problem that causes your rework and change the way you do things so that there is never any rework. For example, if you are always getting calls about a certain issue that you thought you had dealt with, assume the problem is with the way *you* deliver. Change the way you do it. Aim at getting no more calls of that type.

People who charge by the hour for their services might argue that rework is a good thing because it allows them to make additional charges to their customers. This is false thinking. Do customers always pay for the rework? Does being stuck on work for past customers prevent you from taking on new ones? Is the money tied up in work in progress, unbilled work or write-offs huge? Do your customers really thank you for eventually getting right what should have been right from the first? Don't your customers see it as just another rip off?

Unfortunately, because much firefighting is to do with rework, and because old-style businesses often appoint good firefighters as managers, many managers need a constant supply of rework around them. This allows them to show how good they are.

Standardise your processes, develop and work to checklists. This lets you be consistent in your output and reduces variation in what you deliver.

Design quality and prevention

You need to build problem and waste prevention into products and services and efficiency into production and delivery processes. This is called 'design quality' and it includes creation of fault-tolerant and failure-resistant processes and products. It is important because the further 'upstream' you can correct a problem, the less expensive it will be. The costs of preventing problems at the design stage are lower than the costs of correcting problems that occur 'downstream'.

You should emphasise 'upstream' opportunities for fault correction, innovation and improvements at early stages in processes. These yield the highest cost benefits and take greatest advantage of improvements and corrections. Such upstream intervention should also include the company's suppliers.

Speed at the 'product generation' cycle time—the time from design to introduction—is a major success factor in competition. Design quality is often compromised during this stage and may cost the business considerable funds to rectify at a later stage. A rigorous design quality process (including deliberately testing to destruction and finding all possible weaknesses and problems) aimed at designing out problems can turn what might have been an expensive nightmare into a money generator. 'Who has time?' you ask. It is not a matter of time. It is more a matter of the way you approach product or service development.

Partnership development and supply chain management

You need to be very careful whom you choose as your suppliers. It should be very clear that getting good material is critical to producing good products. If you always choose the supplier offering the lowest price, it is very likely you get junk or unreliable supply or material out of specification or unresponsive service.

External suppliers include distributors, dealers, warranty repair services, transportation, contractors and franchises, as well as companies that provide materials and components. Suppliers also include service suppliers, such as health care, training and education providers. Suppliers' goods and services may be used at any stage in production, design or delivery.

If the supplier is important enough to you, you may want to build partnership alliances with them to better accomplish your goals. Strategic alliances can offer entry into new markets or provide a basis for new products or services. Alliances also allow you to blend your core competencies or leadership capabilities with complementary strengths and capabilities of partners, thereby increasing your overall joint capability. For many businesses, alliance partnerships are an increasingly important way to achieve objectives.

You need to distinguish between upstream and downstream alliances (Fig. 4.8). On the upstream side, as companies get better and better at running their processes, it soon becomes very apparent that the supplier of products and services is critical to the management and improvement of processes. If you get junk from your supplier, you will be hard pressed not to produce junk. The computer industry uses the acronym GIGO— garbage in, garbage out. You should work with your suppliers to help them improve their processes. Establish win–win partnerships with suppliers rather than the old thinking of 'screw them'.

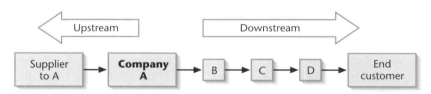

Fig. 4.8 The supply chain

The more you can increase the useability of your incoming goods and services, the less it will cost you to provide high-value goods and services to your customers. Put the onus on your suppliers to provide what you want so that you do not have to spend your valuable time and resources fixing it up to the point you can use it. You will be better off if that is done in a partnership so that both you and your suppliers understand each other's needs. This is the exact complement of Principle 3 ('Customers'). In this case, you are the customer. Make certain you are treated like one.

You should do this for all your *important* suppliers. Important here refers to how it will affect the products and services you supply to *your* customers. You should choose with care whom you have as a supplier. Quality of goods and service becomes a very strong selection criterion that far outweighs price. (You could save $9 by choosing a cheap part but end up with a $3 billion liability cost.) Because consistency of supply becomes important, companies reduce the number of suppliers so that only one supplier supplies each component. This reduces variation. Every supplier does things differently. It also means you have fewer suppliers with whom to establish partnerships. The old thinking is to have many suppliers so none of them can hold you over a barrel and so you can play one off against the other. The new thinking knows that this is false economy.

It is extremely important to improve the ability of your suppliers and partners to contribute to achieving your goals. You might do this by: improving your own procurement and supplier management processes (including seeking feedback from suppliers and internal customers); joint planning; rapid information and data exchanges; use of benchmarking and comparative information; customer–supplier teams; training; long-term agreements; or joint improvement projects. You should establish your long-term objectives, methods of regular communication, methods of evaluating progress, and methods for adapting to changing conditions.

On the downstream side, two issues lead to alliances:

1. Because almost every company is in the middle of someone's supply chain, when company A was establishing partnerships with its suppliers, company A's customer (in this case B) was establishing a supplier partnership with it.
2. Further to this, when company A passes its products and services in turn to companies B, C and D, and D sells it to an end customer, how well B, C and D can do in providing what the customer values (Principle 3) will significantly affect company A's sales. Company A is very interested in forming alliances with B, C and D so that they all do the right thing by A.

Good practices

- Working to eliminate *all* rework.
- Indicators for numbers of times any rework was necessary.
- Reducing variation is seen as a direct way to reduce costs.
- Working to obtain consistent products and services.
- Working to make processes more stable by reducing special cause variation.
- Relationships with suppliers are seen as a basis for performance improvement.

- Strategic alliance relationships are developed with major suppliers.
- A relationship with suppliers of 'innovating together'. Key suppliers are invited to participate in process improvement and product development activities. Joint continuous improvement teams established between the company and supplier. A formal improvement initiatives committee, which includes supplier's representatives, is established.
- Electronic communication channels are opened between companies and suppliers (e.g. suppliers are connected to the company's electronic networks).
- The company carefully evaluates suppliers before appointment and ensures the ongoing standards of supply are maintained at a high level. New suppliers are assessed according to their business experience, references, certification to relevant standards and commitment to the 10 Business Excellence Principles.
- Performance measurements for suppliers are established. Regular reviews and monitoring of suppliers' standards.
- Audits are conducted on suppliers. Audit outcome is communicated to suppliers.
- Supplier certification processes are in place that include encouraging, guiding and educating suppliers in quality assurance systems and procedures.
- Processes are established to help suppliers improve their processes and process output.
- Programs are in place to reduce the overall number of suppliers.
- Leading companies establish fewer but higher quality relationships based on trust, reliability and mutual integration of core competencies, with commitment to continuous improvement on both sides.
- Streamlined supply processes and adoption of 'just in time' delivery supported by computerised planning. For important suppliers, integrated manufacturing resource planning processes (e.g. Theory of Constraints, Material Requirements Planning II) to reduce lead times to a minimum.
- Suppliers (and focus groups) surveyed to identify level of deployment, satisfaction and dissatisfaction with the partnership relationship. These results have been acted on through several cycles.

Poor practices

- Rework is not recognised as waste.
- Not working with suppliers to improve those suppliers' processes.
- A confrontational, 'control' mentality when dealing with suppliers.
- No effort to understand supplier systems or to educate suppliers about your company systems.
- No efforts made to help suppliers improve their systems and outputs.

4.8 Document your processes

One way of reducing variation in processes so that their output is consistent is to document them. Then, people working in the process can follow the documented procedures. This means that everyone in the process does not have to discover and invent it for him or herself every time. This lets you be consistent in your output and reduces variation in what you deliver. Several international standards give good guidance with the process of standardising your processes.

Standards-based control schemes use documentation to clearly describe all the process and product/service control criteria required for maintaining stable and capable performance of the business process at each point. Process maps, process descriptions and checklists are all useful in documenting processes. They all have different uses. By following the documentation, people can be following a previously identified 'best' or 'standardised' practice.

Most companies that document their processes find enormous value in just carrying out the documentation. The documentation process causes discussion about the work process and uncovering of its problems, difficulties and inconsistencies.

As described previously, the people carrying out the tasks and using the schemes have expert local knowledge about how the process actually works and the nature of the problems in the process. Their involvement in both design and improvement is a basic requirement for being able to use the control scheme as intended. If the people who should use them did not design them or do not fully agree with them, or if they think they are impractical, they will not use them.

It is usually a responsibility for operational management to work with the people to design and improve local control schemes.

Problems with documented systems

There are five types of failure with the use of control schemes, which have many things in common.

1. The company insists that the control process always be followed and will not allow it to be modified or improved. This makes for very rigid processes that resist improvement even if they need it. The output of the process may be constant but it may be junk—not a desirable outcome.
2. People give only lip service to the control process because they know it leads to nonsense results. This occurs most often when the process workers are excluded from the design of the control scheme, and when process workers are not allowed to modify the formal process. In these cases, if they can or if the process is important enough, the process workers usually abandon the documented process and use

one that really works. This has the undesirable effect that there is, in fact, no standard process and that process variability is not controlled.

3. 'Our processes are extremely good. If only our people would follow them.' This occurs because of the failure to recognise that people are part of the system and contribute to system variation through their interactions within the control schemes. If the process descriptions really *are* good and *are* practical, then people would use them. If employees will not use them, there is probably something wrong with the process descriptions, not the people. The old thinking is that everything would be perfect if it were not for those 'useless employees'—the 'if only' syndrome.

4. The processes have become so documented that they are boring. People do not enjoy working with them. There is no variety. (This is discussed again in Principle 8, 'Innovation'.)

5. Your documented standards must not restrict your agility. If your documentation entrenches the way you do things to the point where you cannot respond to changes and new situations, your business can become stuck.

Checklists

Checklists are often of the most practical value for people doing routine work or precision work carried out infrequently but for which the omission of small details can be critical. Checklists are widely used by military to ensure control of processes.

Checklists are an important control. Many companies find that providing staff with checklists and process maps is an important step to providing consistent responses. Military organisations have found checklists particularly useful in tension-filled situations that have been thought through in advance but which the individual on duty at that time may not have experienced.

Control design

Traditional quality control or quality assurance designs are strongly focused on 'after the event' methods, such as inspection, testing, sampling and sorting. Because of their design, these often give information too late to be of much use in preventing costly failures. You need proactive or 'before the event' controls.

There are three types of control design:

1. feedback
2. feedforward
3. cognitive.

Feedback is a reactive, 'after the event' control. For example, 'the clothes are wet, it must have rained'. Feedback relies on some form of output—often variation outside of specification—to trigger a reaction. By then, it is all over. However, you can stop making the same mistake again and (if manufacturing) you can prevent the faulty part going to a bottleneck. Goldratt points out the cost if you put rubbish through a bottleneck (see later).

Feedback from the problem back to the cause is usually slow. Meanwhile, problems continue and get worse. The cost of running the process in between the problem occurring and you finding it can be very high—a combination of process and product costs. In addition, some faulty products get through your screening and become complaints. The cost increases.

Inspection does not guarantee no errors—it is too late. They have already happened. You have already made the rubbish, as the Australian Quality Council example demonstrates:

> 'We rely on final inspection to sort out the rejects from the prime product. There's a delay of about 2 hours between the production operation and the inspection process. We make about 4000 widgets per hour; these are valued at $100 each. Last night, we had a deep scratch on the product, rendering it useless. Cost us 8000 units before it was discovered and corrected. It was at a bottleneck resource. $800 000 down the drain!!!'

However, inspection can stop you making the situation worse.

Feedforward is a proactive, 'during the event' control that is based on an input measure. For example, 'the clothes are wet because it is raining now'. It requires a sound diagnostic knowledge of the process to quantitatively 'model' its action triggers.

Cognitive control design is a predictive, 'before the event' control that is based on some form of intelligent prediction. For example, 'clouds brewing and winds are getting stronger, it will rain soon and wet the clothes'. It is complementary to feedforward. You need sound diagnosis combined with broad knowledge and input from all your senses to provide flexible and adaptive predictions.

There are many parallels between weather and business (e.g. winter is coming, brass monkey will shrink; days get shorter, soup will be in demand). Even squirrels know that there are lead indicators. Another example of a lead indicator is the Internet. It is changing the way business is done, how information is sent and consumed. You know it will cause change but how, where, what and why?

Modern approaches to control require an in-depth understanding of the complex interactions, process flows and interdependencies within your business system and how they determine your outputs. Such sophisticated understanding is the basis for feedforward and cognitive control designs.

In terms of effectiveness, the preferred sequence for control design is:

Cognitive is better than *feedforward*, which is better than *feedback*.

This does not mean that feedback controls are not required. It does mean that predictive and preventative control design is more effective than reactive control design. Squirrels die if they do not prepare for winter.

Service controls

Service presents an even worse case. Services are not amenable to feedback control design. Customer complaints and surveys are useless for day-to-day control. Poor service simply passes through and out of the system. You end up with annoyed customers. For everyone that does complain, 10 are equally annoyed but cannot be bothered to tell you.

There are few quality assurance nets for services and usually the service part of the business has the biggest impact on customers. Poor service costs you because annoyed customers do not come back. This is bad news because it costs more to get new customers than it does to retain your existing customers—which is why companies put effort into building customer loyalty.

Quality assurance and the 10 Business Excellence Principles

Many people think they have 'done quality' when they get their five ticks from the International Standards Organisation (ISO). As you can see, the 10 Business Excellence Principles are very different from ISO checklists. There is still a strong role for a quality assurance process because quality assurance:

- lets you standardise the way you produce so that what you produce is consistent
- gives you the chock that stops your processes falling back into the chaos they once were in—back to the old way of doing things. Once you have spent the time and effort to improve your processes, you want people to use them.

In the past, ISO qualification has concentrated mainly on the standardisation aspect of Principle 6 ('Variability'). Because ISO qualification is about 'standards' and 'standardisation', it will always retain that emphasis. Currently, the ISO is trying to move to include more of the 10 Business Excellence Principles; for example, ISO 9004 is an attempt to recognise the importance of the 10 Business Excellence Principles in all companies.

Good practices

- All key, core and support processes mapped and flowcharts drawn.
- Process improvements are locked in place using quality assurance procedures until the next improvement.

122

- Procedures for design control are written and distributed.
- Quality assurance systems are developed and frequently audited and include flexibility to improve.
- Working to make processes more capable by reducing common cause variation.
- Common cause variation is identified.
- Reducing variation is incorporated into design control procedures.

Poor practices

- Procedures are difficult to update, modify or replace.
- Resistance to changing 'the way we do things around here'.

4.9 Measure process outputs

Measurement is critical to all process improvement. You must know the:

- quality and consistency of inputs
- quality and consistency of outputs
- volume of inputs and outputs
- progress towards targets
- capability of the process.

Related forms of measurement are discussed in other Principles. Principle 3 describes meeting customers' specifications. Principle 6 looks at dealing with variation in measurements obtained. Principles 2 and 10 look at measurements to ensure you reach your goals, objectives and targets and balance your stakeholder needs.

In Principle 4, we are concerned mainly with process measurements. Useful measurements include:

- throughput measurements, including rates of throughput
- ratio of throughput to maximum capacity
- process capability
- ratio of throughput to process capability
- inventory (all types, e.g. raw materials, work in process, finished goods, delivered but not paid for)
- operational expenses
- cycle time
- response time
- maximum overdue
- idle time on bottleneck
- number of orders shipped on time
- value of orders shipped on time
- throughput dollar days (to control what you were supposed to do but did not do)

- inventory dollar days (to control what was done that should not have been done)
- number of orders that have been shipped compared with number of orders that could have been shipped
- waiting time (for information or another part)
- queuing time (for a person or a machine).

You often need to set performance levels, specifications or standards to assist on-the-job decision making. Measurement of in-process specifications is important and must be done as early as possible in a process to minimise problems due to deviations from expected performance. When deviations occur, corrective action must be applied to restore the process to its specifications. Proper correction involves identifying and changing the root cause of the deviation. The correction could be technical, a process adjustment or involve human factors. Corrections should minimise the likelihood of this type of deviation occurring ever again, anywhere in the company. Measurement with specifications is described in detail in Principle 6 ('Variability').

You must evaluate, by measurement, how well the process meets the different needs of the various customers of the process (internal and external). You should use the methods described in Principle 3 ('Customers').

Good practices

- Measuring the outputs of all key, core and support processes.
- The rate of improvement is measured for all key, core and support processes.
- Special cause variation is identified.
- Working to reduce the variation in all major processes, products and services.
- Extensive use of control charts—which are understandable—to present and help understand data.
- Working in the levels of five or six sigma (see section 6.8).
- Making use of the concepts of variation and trends to assist decisions based on measuring and monitoring of processes.
- A comprehensive set of measurements is built into the production process to ensure minimum variation and consistently high quality of products and services.

Poor practices

- Not measuring process outputs.
- Statistical manipulation of data to support a position rather than analysis of the system.

- Only one or two indicators to indicate quality of product or service supplied (e.g. 'in full and on time').
- Measurement and process thinking is poorly developed.

4.10 Your 'improvements' must be real improvements

Most companies fail to improve because what they 'improve' does not help them towards their goals and objectives. You need to choose carefully what to work on. All 'improvement' work takes time, effort and resources. Spending that time, effort and resources must lead you towards your goals and objectives.

We have all seen quality circles and the experience of most people is that they do not work. Although they are popular for a while, they end up achieving very little. Many of us have seen a big song and dance about 'successful' teams that have saved their company $18 000—big deal. If you are going to spend the time, effort and resources, the team should be aiming at bringing hundreds of thousands to the bottom line, not saving a few tens of thousands.

The problem is that people do not know what to work on. The other problem is that most local improvements do not contribute to global improvement of the company—to the goal.

The chain analogy

In his insightful book *Critical Chain*, Goldratt gives a useful analogy that helps us understand that working on a lot of small improvements does not achieve much. It also shows two very different philosophies of management.

Consider the company as made up of a number of links in a chain— a purchasing link, a distribution link, a manufacturing link, a customer service link, an invoicing link and so on. Goldratt points out that when we believe that containing cost is all-important and work to reduce it, this is analogous to reducing the weight of the chain. Every link has its cost. If we want to know the total cost of the company, we can sum up the total cost of all the links. The weight of each link is analogous to its cost. In this cost–weight world, 'improve' implies that if you reduce the weight of any one link, you will reduce the weight of the whole chain. Which is a good thing, isn't it?

Suppose you are in charge of a department in a chain of companies— one of the 'links'. You are told to 'improve'! After some time you come back and tell your boss that with ingenuity and diligence you have made your link 100 grams lighter—you have saved some money. Your boss is delighted. By making your part of the chain lighter, you have reduced the weight of the whole chain. In this cost–weight world, if we induce many local improvements, we will have improved the company. This is certainly the prevailing philosophy of management in almost every company around the world. It is consistent with celebrating when a team saves $18 000.

However, the goal of most companies is to make money now and in the future. Making money implies that throughput is important. In our chain analogy, in the 'throughput world', *strength* is the important property—not weight. The *linkages* matter, not the links. The weakest link determines the chain's strength. Strengthening any link other than the weakest link will not strengthen the chain.

What are the implications in our example? Firstly, let us assume your link is not the weakest—there will be only one weakest link. You have been told to improve and you come back and report that with considerable diligence and ingenuity, you have made your link four times stronger. Is your boss impressed? Of course not! Your link was not the weakest link. Making your link stronger did nothing to make the chain stronger—to improve throughput. Thus, most local improvements do not contribute to global improvement of the company—to the goal. Inducing many local improvements is not the way.

The Pareto rule

When we work in the cost world, it does not matter which improvements we work on. Because we want the most bang for our efforts, we prioritise according to the *size* of the problem. We use the Pareto rule—80% of problems originate from 20% of causes.

Unfortunately, in the world where throughput is important, we should consider only those improvements that 'strengthen' the throughput chain, that is, give us more throughput (while simultaneously reducing inventory and operating expenses). That means that the Pareto rule is no longer sufficient.

Bottlenecks and constraints

In most businesses, the key to making more money is to increase throughput (while simultaneously reducing inventory and operational expenses). What stops throughput? Bottlenecks or constraints.

Most processes have constraints. If the constraint is a physical bottleneck, you might be able to find it by looking for a pile of work in front of it. In *The Goal*, Goldratt points out that constraints (or bottlenecks) are not good or bad. Bottlenecks can be very useful in process improvement work but they do need careful management.

An hour lost at a bottleneck is an hour lost to the whole plant. That is:

$$\text{An hour lost at a bottleneck} = \frac{\text{total annual revenue from the plant}}{\text{number of hours the plant works}}$$

You lose time at bottlenecks (among other things) by having the bottleneck work on rubbish. If you can stop the bottlenecks from processing rubbish, you can save that time for the whole system. The rule here is to put inspection in front of bottlenecks.

Goldratt makes several important points:

- The theory of constraints gives us a new set of rules for how to identify which problem to work on and how to go about it.
- Always put your quality control in front of your bottlenecks. There is no point having your bottleneck work on defects.
- The majority of constraints are not physical constraints. The vast majority of constraints that prevent us from making more money are our own policies—the way we do things—our own standard operating procedures. Surely, these should be the easiest things to change. As you have seen throughout Principle 4, the barriers you build in by hanging on to the way you do things and demanding people work harder are significant obstacles.

Service companies should not reject this by thinking this applies only to manufacturing. Many service companies set their processes up just like factories (e.g. banks, law firms, insurance companies).

The five steps of bottleneck management

1. Identify the system's constraints (bottlenecks).
2. Decide how to exploit the constraints (run at the maximum). Do not waste any time at the constraint.
3. Subordinate everything else to the above decision (make sure everything else marches in tune with the constraints). Protect the constraint from problems occurring at non-constraints.
4. Elevate the system's constraints (bottlenecks). Add more capacity to the constraint. Clone them.
5. Warning! If in the previous steps a constraint has been broken, go back to step 1. Do not allow inertia (from a previous solution) to cause a new system constraint.

Queues and waiting

Most things you work on will spend more time waiting than they will spend being worked on. Working out where things spend their time can greatly assist you to determine what part of your process you should work on to get most benefit.

Consider a file in a law firm. The percentage of the total cycle time that the file is actually being worked on is usually very small. Most of the total time the firm has the file, it is not being worked on. It is either waiting in a queue with other files for someone to work on it or it is waiting for information.

Most companies make the mistake of trying to reduce cycle time by reducing the time a file (or part, or inquiry) is being worked on. Wrong! Tackling the queue or the waiting time gives much bigger gains. For example, if one of your bottlenecks is waiting for information, begin action on it as early as possible in your process. That is, request the information as soon as you possibly can.

Files, parts or inquiries spend their time:

- being worked on (very small percentage)
- queuing for someone (or a machine) to work on them (a big percentage)
- waiting for missing information (or another part) (a big percentage).

An example of the five-step process in a service company

1. You identify your bottleneck as your leading technical expert (e.g. a lawyer or a person building your database or website).
2. You add helpers (who are cheaper and lack experts' skill) to do the legwork or rough work to which the expert will add the finishing touches. You capture the legal knowledge in forms, precedence letters and your computer system that non-legal people can use. This leverages your knowledge. You make certain you get every hour you can out of them—no meetings or training (or meetings and training during lunch or weekends or periods of slack). Beware! Too much of this breaks Principle 7 'Enthusiastic people' and will lead to burn-out. The steps below are better.
3. Everyone else moves to support that person. You put quality control in front of the person. You have someone else check what goes to the person to make certain it is accurate and valid. You do not have them work on quotes, tenders (you might not get them) or freebies.
4. You add capacity. Eventually, you add another expert.
5. You check to see if the person is still a bottleneck.

Inertia

The inertia of tradition in your own policies and standard operating procedures is often your only bottleneck preventing you from getting more throughput and making more money.

Every time you do something for the first time, you establish a tradition. Because it is tradition, it has become 'the way we have always done it', even if you or no-one else remembers why.

There is a story about guns used in military parades. The story is that the gun crew (of seven) roared up in their truck with the gun mounted in its trailer. They leapt into action, uncoupled the gun, swung it around and fired off their twenty-shot salute. One man stood at attention behind the action the entire time. A dignitary pointed out the immobile man and asked, 'What does that person do?'. A flurry of questioning revealed that no-one knew. A month later, the dignitary received an answer: 'He holds the horses'. It was 1999. Horses had not been used with artillery for almost 80 years. Inertia had kept the process unchanged.

You, too, have processes where people are doing things that are no longer required. Every time you change a process, you make redundant many actions of the old process. You must clear up such redundant actions. They can be your most significant barriers to reaching your goals and objectives.

For example, the local fast food restaurant, El Kebab, is in the food court at the shopping mall. El Kebab opens from 8.30 a.m. to 5.30 p.m.—a long 9-hour day for them. A large crowd occupies the food court from 6 p.m. to 11 p.m. for its evening meal. Other fast food stores do a huge trade. But not El Kebab, it is closed. Why? A policy.

An example of the five-step process in a manufacturing company

1. You identify your constraint as your expert (Bert) who does the final assembly. All parts go through his work station. Late orders are always piled up in front of him.
2. You do not let Bert work on other machines although he has a tendency to want to work on the upstream machines when there is a lull. You should have a pile of work in front of him that is sufficient to see him through any breakdown or delay in the upstream machines. You use small batches at the upstream machines (batch sizes of one if need be). You put your quality control in front of Bert so that he does not work on scrap.
3. You have every other person work in support of Bert. You release material to the floor based on the time you want Bert to finish the job, less all the *waiting* time and a liberal allowance for Murphy's law to disrupt and cause breakdowns. You allow others to be idle— as long as Bert has enough to do. You do not release material just to keep people busy. You let Bert's work schedule determine the lunch break of everyone. Do you have any policies that restrict the way Bert works (e.g. don't give him an air-conditioner)?

4. You have others do the less expert part of Bert's work. For example, if the surface needs to be cleaned (not an expert job), employ a non-expert to do that and to carry the completed work to dispatch. The small extra expense of employing a non-expert will be more than covered by Bert's increase in throughput.
5. After you have done those steps, is Bert still the constraint? Or has it shifted to the market? Or is it now a company policy?

Good practices

- Process improvement data is collected that demonstrates the impact of improvement efforts—sustained trends, analysis, learning and comparisons.
- Process indicators are measured and reported regularly across the company. Everyone in the company has a clear sense of 'how we are going'.
- KPIs extend into the key process and have clear review practices— strong emphasis is placed on using data and trends for decision making.
- Continuous improvement is planned.

Poor practices

- Assuming that all 'improvement' and change is for the good.
- Not measuring to see if 'improvements' helped move the company towards its objectives.
- Comparisons/benchmarking not used in the search for industry leaders. Customers and suppliers not used as information sources.

SUMMARY

A structured approach to managing and improving the operational efficiency and effectiveness of business processes would include the following:

- *Identification and ownership.* You should identify, map and manage your core support processes and operational processes. Responsibility for the management of these should be assigned.
- *Customers of the process.* You should identify your internal customers of your processes, identify their needs and expectations and ensure adequate feedback in customer/supplier relationships for the requirements of all customers of the process to be met.
- *Measurements and targets.* You should set present and future targets for process performance levels; measure process performance and

capability and use in-process and outcome indicators to measuring effectiveness and efficiency.
- *People participation.* You should encourage and enable your people (provide them with adequate skills, knowledge, resources and authority) to understand the processes with which they work, bring people at all levels together to understand the systems within which the processes sit in order to control and improve them. Managers must work to improve processes.
- *Process improvement.* You should establish techniques to understand the stability and capability of processes; systematically improve processes through innovation (Principle 8) and reduction of variation (Principle 6) (e.g. performance gap analysis, determine root causes, re-engineering, eliminate special cause variation and reduce common cause variation).
- *Process execution.* You should standardise processes in order to ensure a high level of confidence that output requirements and customers' expectations are consistently met.
- *Compliance with standards.* You should integrate compliance to relevant standards into the broader process management system.
- *Comparisons and benchmarking.* You should learn from others ways to increase speed and effectiveness of the way you improve your processes, products and services. You should use this information to improve the way you do things.

WHAT WOULD YOUR STAKEHOLDERS SAY?

HOW WOULD YOUR EMPLOYEES RATE YOUR COMPANY ON THESE?

- This company understands what its processes are capable of delivering (its process capability).
- This company uses its understanding of process capability to improve its processes.
- This company deliberately works to improve its processes.
- We are enabled (provided with skills, knowledge, authority and power) to change the processes in which we work.
- Our managers spend considerable time working to improve processes (i.e. making it easier for us to do our work).
- Systems are improved when things go wrong and people are not blamed.
- Our knowledge is actively sought when processes need to be improved.
- Decisions that effect the *gemba* are never made without involvement of the *gemba*.
- When processes need to be improved, our managers/team leaders draw on the experience of all people who have knowledge of the processes.

- Our performance management system is based on the capability of the processes to deliver.
- We have plans to reach all targets.
- Our managers are team members rather than bosses.
- My needs as an internal customer of the process are considered and met.
- I have measurements of all the main processes that affect me.

HOW WOULD YOUR CUSTOMERS RATE YOUR COMPANY ON THESE?

- This company regards my complaint as a 'gift' to improve its products and services.
- This company uses complaints to improve the way it does things.

HOW WOULD YOUR SUPPLIERS AND OTHER ALLIANCE PARTNERS RATE YOUR COMPANY ON THESE?

- This company has made considerable effort to understand what I am trying to achieve, my problems and my processes.
- This company has helped me understand my processes.
- This company has worked to minimise any difficulties of our two companies working together.

HOW WOULD YOUR SHAREHOLDERS RATE YOUR COMPANY ON THESE?

- This company sets targets for improving its outputs and outcomes.
- This company makes plans to reach its targets.
- This company implements its plans to reach its targets.
- This company works towards increasing its throughput.
- This company manages its bottlenecks and constraints to maximise its throughput.
- This company does not suboptimise by improving processes that do not matter.

Principle 5
Improved decisions

Effective use of facts, data and knowledge leads to improved decisions.

PRINCIPLE 5 IS THE POWERHOUSE that drives all the other Principles. It ensures the data on which the decisions about all the other Principles are based. It is the third part of the essential combination of:

- make plans to do things
- implement those plans
- find out if those plans worked.

This Principle is important because of its huge influence on all the other Principles. Principle 5:

- is the life blood that lets you align your company's operations with its strategic directions
- focuses on the information you need to manage the company, measure effectiveness of performance, drive improvement of performance and increase competitiveness
- requires use of non-financial and financial information and data.

Information and analysis can themselves be sources of competitive advantage and productivity increase.

Dr Hausner's research indicates that this Principle is important for both improving your company's KPIs and increasing your business improvement score. Unfortunately, most companies do not do it well. Of the 10 Principles, Principle 5 ranks an equal last with Principle 6 ('Variability') in terms of how well companies that have applied for a National Business Excellence Award have been rated by evaluating teams. This means that there is considerable room for improvement. This is because most companies do not use facts and data at all in their decision making. Instead, they prefer to base their decisions on hunches and unproven assumptions.

Measuring progress towards your goals and implementation of your strategies can be the single most important step you can make in getting better results. Until you take this step, your company assumes that it is making progress and that things are happening. After it begins to measure, the company finds that all is not as it would hope.

5.1 Manage by fact, not by gut feelings

The old thinking is that by some magic, not only do bosses know everything, but they know everything without looking at any data. If any data is consulted, it will be the budget—and usually only the expenses part of the budget.

Although we are in an 'information age', decisions are still largely being made by gut feeling, past experience, best guess or habit. In most companies, the right hand *still* does not know what the left hand is doing—or even if there *is* a left hand. We may have the technology, but do we base decisions on information?

The new thinking is that of management by fact. Acknowledgment that measurement and analysis of performance is important. Such measurements provide crucial information about results, key processes and outputs. As you saw in Principle 2 ('Focus on achieving results'), this provides an important focus on achieving results—meeting your goals and objectives. In this new thinking, many different types of data and information are needed for performance measurement, including information on customers, products and services, operations, markets, competitors, suppliers, employees, costs and processes.

Data and information are needed for planning, improving your operations, reviewing your overall performance and comparing your performance with competitors or with best practices' benchmarks.

In Principle 5, we look at how we gather, analyse and make decisions based on that data, information and knowledge. In Principle 6 ('Variability'), we will look at how to use data to improve our processes.

What you need to do

Principle 5 requires that you have a process for converting data into meaningful information. And that you use this information in a preventative, proactive way to assist with decisions to continually improve processes, outputs and results at all levels of the company. Principle 5 requires that:

- you have an effective performance measurement system
- you carefully select and use measurements and indicators to track daily operations and overall company performance

- your measurements are aligned and integrated so all measurements work together to the same ends
- your measurements allow company-wide measurements and comparisons
- your performance measurements allow you to track work group and department contributions towards key company targets
- your data and information are accurate, reliable and valid. If they are not, all attempts at interpretation will be scorned.

You should collect and use data and information to:

- inform your decisions about the needs of your important stakeholders
- meet the needs of your important stakeholders
- inform your decisions about your core activities.

You should have processes to deal with the uncertainty contained in missing information when making strategic decisions. You seldom have information about all aspects of your decision before the event. How do you cope with making informed strategic decisions when you do not have all the information?

You should keep your performance measurement system up to date to meet your current business needs. This is an extremely difficult ask. Information technology (IT) is usually a significant expense for most companies. Most companies become locked into a technology they purchased at a point in time. Unfortunately, technology moves forward very quickly. Yesterday's technology could not do what is easy today.

Although graphs and charts can assist in transmitting information, the graphs and charts are not in themselves the purpose of collecting the data—although many companies appear to think so. The most important purpose of collecting data and sharing information is to use it for decision making.

How do you analyse the decision-making process itself over time? Has your decision making been effective? Were data, information and knowledge used in an appropriate way? Were decisions made at the appropriate level?

Good practices

- Widespread competency at collecting and interpreting data to measure the results of daily work.
- Systems make it easy to display first-level analysis of data (e.g. charts and graphs).
- Written procedures exist that describe methods to analyse data at different levels of the company.
- An understanding at each level of the company how the information is analysed and used at the next level and how it is collected and analysed at the previous level. Respect each other's needs and processes.

- Prominently displayed local and business performance data. Staff can explain the data and the implications for the customer and the company.
- Extensive use of control charts—which are understandable—to present and help understand data.
- Awareness sessions are conducted to improve understanding of data, information and variation.

Poor practices

- Employees not enabled to actively participate in the workplace or to make decisions through the provision of adequate skills, knowledge, power, resources or authority.
- Bosses do not do their own analyses—they delegate analysis to 'assistants' or 'statistics units'.
- Measurement and process thinking are not understood or thought relevant.

5.2 Don't gather unnecessary junk

One of the most difficult issues is what data to collect. Gathering data costs money. Storing it so you can find it again costs more money. Setting up a system to find the exact piece of data you want when you want it costs even more money. So do not gather data you will not use.

One of the greatest difficulties is to stop gathering data that you do not want. Most companies are so swamped with useless data that they cannot find the useful data on which they might be able to make a decision. The temptation is to gather everything because we do not know what we will want, so we had better gather everything. Frequently, companies describe their policy as 'we measure everything that moves'. This is very wasteful and very impractical.

You have to decide in advance what you will need and do not collect information just because you might need it. Unfortunately, people gather information to eliminate risk because they know that as soon as they decide not to gather some data, they will need it. Many of us have been in the situation where the boss asks, 'We need this piece of data. Why don't you already have it?'.

The widespread availability of electronic recording in databases has also led to unnecessary collection. Data is so easy to collect that people shovel huge amounts of data into electronic databases. Of course, the hope is that some day it will be useful. Many companies find that the expensive database that they built with the expectation that it would be full of vintage wine turns out to be full of rusty old cans—if they can extract anything at all.

Collection criteria

Companies that follow Principle 5 well have collection criteria to help decide what to collect. The people who will be using the data should design the criteria and describe how they will use it. That is, the customer of the process should design it.

Collection criteria should be based on good frameworks. These frameworks are usually at six levels:

1. The data and information needed to *conduct daily work* (e.g. customer account data, transaction data, data collected on forms, tolerance of a part, mixture details of a batch).
2. The data needed to *manage those processes* (e.g. numbers of transactions, throughput, flows on inventory, rework, timeliness, accuracy, tolerance of batches of parts, capability estimates and calculations, targets, benchmarks and comparisons with other companies—Principle 4).
3. *Stakeholder needs data* (e.g. owner needs, customer needs [Principle 3], employee needs [Principle 7], community needs [Principle 9]).
4. *Performance data* for the company (e.g. performance against the vision, mission, goals, objectives, strategies and KPIs—Principle 2).
5. *Knowledge* (e.g. experience and learning from success and failure— Principle 8).
6. *Strategic data* and information (e.g. market behaviour analyses, competitor information, competitor behaviour analyses, technology trend analyses, political trend analyses, market and currency forecasts, scenarios—Principle 2).

Your frameworks and the data collected using them should be reviewed periodically to:

- ensure that the data is used
- ensure that it is still what the users want
- determine whether some other data should be gathered instead or as well.

Don't let IT experts decide what you should collect

Unfortunately, design of collection criteria is very often left in the hands of the IT specialists. This never works. Many companies fall into the trap of handing the design of the data-gathering system over to IT people—because 'they are the experts'. This frequently happens because many people are overawed by IT experts. However, for all their expertise, your IT people are not the customers of the data. They are suppliers of an expertise. They may be experts at the technology but they are not experts at deciding what to collect.

Your IT people are suppliers and, like all suppliers, they must supply what their customers want. The IT involvement during design should be restricted to advice on what is possible. Even then, considerable effort needs to be exerted to ensure that the IT specialists deliver intuitive (you should not need a manual), user-friendly systems that provide what you would have designed if you had those particular skills.

We have all seen computer systems that were so unfriendly that no-one could use them (with the possible exception of the designer). Most IT departments hold their companies to ransom because they have special skills. Unfortunately, they seldom deliver what their internal customers want.

Information versus data

There is an ongoing debate about the difference between information and data. It appears to be semantics. The definitions are that 'data' is raw, unprocessed material. 'Information' has been processed, analysed, interpreted or summarised. 'Analysed' means that some 'meaning' is interpreted from the data, preferably a prediction or a cause and effect relationship, that was not apparent before the analysis. Another way of thinking about this is that information is data that has been processed to the point that it can assist your decision making.

However, this distinction is too restrictive. What you often find is that the results of one person's analysis, their 'information', becomes the next person's 'data'. As you go further up the decision-making tree, what for one level is the final piece of information obtained after much analysis and interpretation is just the input (together with the results of other analyses) for those in the next level to begin their analysis.

Fig. 5.1 The relationship of data and information

Although the debate has raged for many years, the distinction between data and information has little value except to IT professionals and to show the different levels of uses the customers of the process have for data and information. So, forget it. It is more important to know how you use the data or information for making decisions.

Good practices

- Written criteria exist for the selection of data. These indicate sampling procedures, types of data, frequency of sampling and users' requirements of the data.

- Collection criteria for data are evaluated against your vision, mission, goals and strategies or strategic plan. Your planning process and KPIs drive data collection and analysis.
- Quality assurance procedures describe sampling frequency, reliability and standardisation.
- Data collected according to criteria that define what data needs to be collected in line with the needs of users of the data. Data that does not have a user is rejected and not collected.
- Staff and customer feedback channels on the usefulness of data, its collection, analysis and presentation.
- Staff surveys and focus groups indicate widespread satisfaction with consultation on what data people need, including its frequency and form.
- Staff surveys and focus groups indicate widespread understanding of what data is collected, why it is collected and how it is collected.

Poor practices

- No criteria to stop gathering data.
- Data collected about everything—no system to define what data needs to be collected.
- The data collection is not simple and not clearly linked to key processes.

5.3 Strategies and decisions are experiments

Why do you need data and information at all when you make a decision? Aren't your instincts good enough?

The business world is becoming more scientific as the better companies take a more scientific approach to their decision making. Every strategy you choose, every decision you make, is only an *experiment* that you hope will take you towards success. Can you afford to do the experiment without finding out if it works? Of course not! You must measure to see if it works—to find out if you made a successful choice.

In the scientific world, decisions and questions are based on data. Which comes first—the data or the question you need answered?

Incorrect science

Karl Popper said that in the old thinking of science, the scientist begins by gathering data—carrying out careful experiments and making useful observations. These findings were systematically recorded and published and, in the course of time, scientists in that field noticed things about the data. Features would emerge that would let scientists write down hypotheses—statements of a law in nature that fit all the facts and explain how they are causally related. The individual scientist would then try to *confirm* these hypotheses by finding evidence to support them. Such verification would prove the new law. And the existing barriers of our ignorance would gradually move back.

A scientific law cannot be broken

In *Popper*, Magee said:

> It is worth having a brief discussion about the word 'law', especially as we are calling these Principles the equivalent of scientific laws. A law of nature cannot be broken. A law of society, on the other hand, prescribes what we may or may not do. It can be broken. If we could not break it, there would be no need to have it. We do not legislate against someone being in two places at the same time. A law of nature is not prescriptive but descriptive. It tells us what happens—for instance, that water boils at 100°C. It cannot be broken because it is not a command: water is not being ordered to boil at 100°C.

This process is called induction and was the way science was conducted. It is still how most companies think about gathering and using data. The trouble is that it does not work.

The question comes first

For the new-thinking scientist, the question comes first. In fact, you cannot gather any data unless you know which question you are trying to answer. For example, look out of your window and write down what you see. How can you possibly do this with any meaning? You cannot do it unless you know what question you are answering. Should you be writing about people, buildings, trees, the colour of the sky, the clouds? What was the topic? What question were you trying to answer?

Asking the question before collecting any data is a huge shift in thinking. However, there is an even bigger one. It is about the type of question you ask. Is it a question to confirm your belief (the old thinking) or a question to challenge it (the new thinking)?

You can never confirm your beliefs

The breakthrough to the new thinking comes from the realisation that you can never *confirm* your hypothesis. You can never prove it true. It does not matter how many times you have seen evidence to support your belief. For example, Magee, in *Popper*, describes how you may have a belief that the sun revolves around the earth. Every morning you see the sun rise and move across the sky. This confirms your belief. You can, in fact, make tables to predict with great precision exactly when the sun will rise on each day for the next 10 000 years. Do any of your precise observations or predictions make the belief true? Even if you see it confirmed every day? Does the accumulation of thousands of confirmatory observations (and this may come as something of a shock) increase the probability of it being true? No way!

Collect data to prove your beliefs incorrect

If you cannot prove your that hypothesis is true, what can you do? You can try to prove it is false. Although scientific laws are not verifiable, they are falsifiable. This means that scientific laws are testable in spite of being unprovable. They can be tested by systematic attempts to refute them.

This new thinking of science has changed our understanding of our physical world and provided us with leaps in technology.

It is time the business world applied these concepts to the way that it makes decisions. It certainly indicates a different type of data collection. It means that instead of gathering data to confirm your beliefs, you should be trying to find data that will refute them—to find data that will prove your beliefs incorrect. It means floating ideas that you hope to have shot down. It means deliberately testing the edge of what you know. That is far too challenging for most people. The easier thing to do is to look for evidence that confirms your opinion only—ignoring all contra-evidence. Unfortunately, although it is easier, it does not lead forward.

You will have seen people defend their position even when there is evidence to disprove what they have proposed. That type of posturing is extremely wasteful—it holds you in the past. That might have been good enough in an old business world. It is not good enough any more. When you have been proved incorrect, build a new hypothesis.

All swans are white

Suppose you believe that 'all swans are white'. To refute this, you should be looking for swans that are not white. If you find just one black swan—which is easy to do in Australia—you have disproved the hypothesis. Alternatively, you can go down the unproductive paths of 'that's not a swan' or the common one of 'the person who saw it has no credibility'.

You should formulate your theory as unambiguously as you can to expose it clearly to refutation. Another commonly made mistake is to keep reinterpreting the evidence to make certain it fits with your beliefs. You should not evade the unpalatable by rewording, redefining or refusing to accept the reliability of inconvenient information.

However, don't abandon your beliefs too lightly—make certain they are tested rigorously. When we discover that some things we predicted did not occur, this adds to our knowledge and we should begin again by building on what we know now.

We can never accumulate enough evidence to prove that our theory is true. At no stage can we ever prove what we know to be true. The history of science is of disproving what was once known to be true.

Good practices

- Positive trends shown on the major indicators that the company uses to judge its success, in combination with a rational explanation of what the company is doing to ensure the positive trends continue.
- Performance is reviewed against plans regularly. A user-friendly set of performance indicators shows implementation and performance against plan.
- A measurement system that supports the planning process.

Poor practices

- Not measuring to see if strategies and plans (i.e. 'experiments' to reach objectives) are successful.
- Mistaking action for success.

5.4 Check your assumptions

'What are these people on about? In the business world, we do not make hypotheses!' Wrong, we do indeed. We call them assumptions and our companies are full of them. We make assumptions about everything, every person and every situation. Our assumptions give us our 'mind set'—our mental attitude about how we approach everything. They are usually based on experience and are very often wrong. We usually make no effort to challenge our assumptions and they remain the biggest barriers to effective decision making in all companies.

What is described above is a fundamental shift that happened in science during the last century. The business world has not yet moved to this thinking, which is largely why it is still swamped in unusable data. It is time the business world took a scientific approach to the expensive process of gathering and storing data—and to the very expensive process of decision making.

Whether you like it or not, your beliefs about the world affect the way you see the world and consequently your decisions. There is significant evidence that it is difficult for each of us to alter the beliefs/assumptions/hypotheses we form first. (This is why it is always important to get your story to the boss first.)

Good decision making begins with asking the right questions

When you combine these concepts you see, as Goldratt suggests in his book *The Haystack Syndrome*, that information is the answer to the question asked. This suggests that the secret to good decision making begins with asking the right questions. Asking the right questions leads to getting useful information on which you can then base your decisions.

If you ask the wrong questions, you get rubbish information. If you do not challenge your assumptions, your decisions can be very unsound.

Challenging your assumptions

In almost all situations where people who would like to agree but cannot do so and cannot compromise, the resultant conflict is probably due to different assumptions being made by the different people. In his books *The Goal* and *It's Not Luck*, Goldratt gives a very useful tool for uncovering assumptions and challenging them.

1. First, write down the problem clearly by answering these five questions (Fig. 5.2):
   (a) What *action* do they complain about?
   (b) What do you want?
   (c) In order to satisfy what need, do they insist on what they want?
   (d) Why is what you want so important to you, or what is jeopardised by what they want?
   (e) What is your common objective?
2. Check that you answered the questions in the correct order. That is, in order to have (e), they must have (c). On the other hand, in order to have (e), I must have (d). Next, in order to have (c), they must have (a). But in order to have (d), I must have (b). The conflict between (a) and (b) should be clear and no compromise possible.

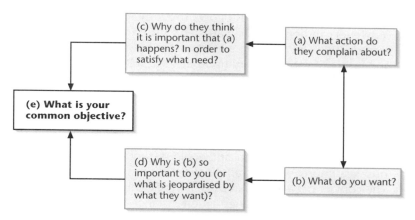

Fig. 5.2 Flowchart to challenging your assumptions

3. Read what you wrote to the people involved. If what you wrote is wrong for them, do not argue, cross it out.
4. Uncover the assumptions. Read your answers again. This time, add the word 'because' and answer the implied question, as follows: 'in order to have (e), I must have (d) because...' and so on. Complete this for all steps, including '(a) is mutually exclusive to (b) because...'. There is often more than one assumption per step. Find as many as you need.
5. Examine the assumptions. Can you break a step by finding something to destroy the assumption? Some useful hints are:
   (a) Concentrate on the step with the assumptions that irritate you most.
   (b) Find a solution at the (c) and (d) level. Do not argue at the (a) and (b) level.
   (c) For each assumption ask 'Is there another result?'. Keep challenging the implications of the assumptions. You are looking for a thinking shift.
6. If you can find a different approach for a major assumption, the problem disappears.

'I don't have time for this business improvement crap'

This situation faces almost all companies:

- Most companies are trying to be successful in the long term. This is objective (e).
- In order to be successful, everyone in the company, from the CEO to the most junior employee, and every system must provide value to the customers—described in Principle 3. This is (d).
- In order to provide value to customers, each person in the company is working flat out to look after customers or to look after those people who are serving customers—described in Principle 4. This is (b).
- All that is very clear and follows the Principles described here. However, remember Dr Hausner's findings described in the Introduction—in order for a company to be successful now and in the future, it must be very good at these 10 Business Excellence Principles. Dr Hausner's research shows that unless the company can score more than 300 points, it is going backwards and will not be successful in the future. This is (c).
- Being good at these Principles does not happen just by chance. In order to be good at these Principles, a company must take time to work on them. (The complaint would be 'I don't have time for this business improvement crap. I have a business to run'.) This is (a).
- The conflict between (a) and (b) is very clear. People must spend time to improve the business's performance on the Principles but no-one has time to do so.

144

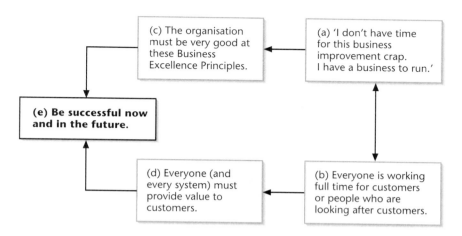

Fig. 5.3 Flowchart on conflict for success now and in the future

Good practices

- Data demonstrates the impact of improvement efforts—sustained trends, analysis, learning and comparisons.
- Attempts made to predict the future using data and information.
- Data gathered from a variety of sources (especially stakeholders) and through analysis into information that is used in decision making. Interconnect information systems—enable some for customer and supplier access.

Poor practices

- Not able to make cause and effect relationships between KPI results and company action. People cannot say 'we did this here and that is the result'.
- No links between operational and financial measurement.
- Seeing trends where there are no trends; missing trends where there are trends.

5.5 Get the facts

At a basic level, Principle 5 says to use facts to check what you 'know'. This might sound like a contradiction but it is not. A very common mistake by almost everybody is that they 'know' the reasons for things and act according to that knowledge. Well, it might come as a huge surprise that people do not do this well. A lot of the time most people are wrong about what they 'know'.

Remember the example of the Sydney train company with the late trains in Principle 4. They 'knew' it was 'wheelchairs' that caused late trains. They 'knew' that having to delay the train while someone in a wheelchair got on the train was the cause of the trains being late. It was a 'known fact' until someone gathered some real data. Wheelchairs accounted for less than 0.1% of late trains. All the planning about wheelchairs (while helpful for the people in the wheelchairs) was of no use to getting the trains to run on time.

Having the real facts, instead of imaginary ones, allows you to give attention to issues that might make a difference. Get the facts!

There are many examples of employees who are thought not to care about the company. They are said to be lazy. They are always late, always having to leave on time and distracted and inaccurate in their work—clear signs that they do not care. Right? Wrong! When the boss finally gets around to finding out the facts, we find a sick child or a sick spouse that requires constant attention and resultant poor sleeping patterns. It also tells us something about the degree of trust in the workplace—what repercussions was the employee frightened of that prevented immediate disclosure? These are very different problems from being 'lazy' and require a very different response. Get the facts!

What assumptions are you making (and acting on) about the causes of problems in your processes and with your employees? Get the facts!

Managers often 'know' that one of their staff is lazy and slow, always making mistakes. However, when you check the facts, you find out that the data supplied to them is always wrong and they are having to spend many hours trying to get accurate data, or you have not provided them with adequate training. These are very different problems from being 'lazy'. Get the facts!

Useful tools

Often facts need to be organised in some way to make them more useful—more easily interpreted. For example, it is easier to extract useful information from a graph than from pages of numbers.

Although there are a great many analysis tools, you really only need to be familiar with about 20. About half of those take 5 minutes to become expert at using. The Memory Jogger II is a useful pocket-size compilation of the most commonly used useful tools. You should be familiar with all of them.

Get computer literate—at least enough to do your own analyses. It is amazing how many executives and senior managers cannot use even the simplest computer equipment or who have all the analysis done for them because they 'don't have the time'. The person who does the analysis gets significantly more information than the person who gets the analysis delivered to him or her. Good analyses generate questions.

When you do the analysis yourself, you get to explore those questions yourself. Remember, your actions say very loudly what you consider important. Delegating analysis says using data to make decisions is not important.

Warnings about three common tools

The *Pareto rule* lets you focus your efforts on the most important issues. The Pareto rule is that 20% of sources cause 80% of the problems. This is very useful. However, its main use may be in the 'cost world'. Remember the chain analogy in Principle 4? If you prioritise according to the size of the problem, you may not improve the company. In the world where throughput is important, you should be concerned with only those improvements that strengthen the throughput chain, that is, give you more throughput (while simultaneously reducing inventory and operational expenses). That means that applying the Pareto rule on size alone may not be appropriate.

Brainstorming is a commonly used analysis tool. Brainstorming belongs to a group that includes fishbone diagrams, affinity diagrams and force field analyses. Be aware that brainstorming does not give facts (neither does the rest of the group). It is a way of collecting opinions and arranging those opinions into groups. All these 'opinions' need to be checked subsequently by *gathering facts*.

Multivoting is often used to prioritise among a number of potential ideas. It has two main problems:

- the vote is only opinion and needs to be verified by facts
- the issues getting the most votes may just be the popular, obvious issues, while often you are looking for the new, the innovative.

An analogy can be made with your favourite dish at your favourite eating place. What makes that food your favourite is probably the very, very small amounts of flavour or the skill of the chef. Multivoting can give votes for bulk but neglects the flavour. That is, an issue that gets the most votes may not be the most important.

What will you do when you get the data?

A useful rule of thumb to ask about collecting data is, 'What will you do as a result of getting the data?'. Most non-operational data is seldom used to inform a decision. For example, most customer or employee survey information is not used for anything. Often, these surveys are so badly designed that they cannot be used to inform a decision. This is usually because surveys give you information that you already know— warm fuzzy information or ratings on such. These surveys are a waste of company time and money and are probably conducted because someone said this data should be collected. If you are not going to do something with the data or will not be able to do anything with it, do not gather it.

Companies often plan to conduct yet another survey that will tell them nothing they don't already know or can guess at with a high degree of accuracy. If it will tell you what you already know, do not gather it!

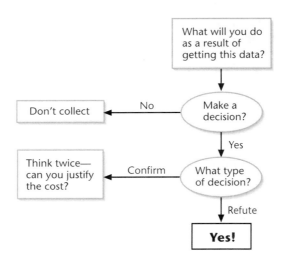

Fig. 5.4 The rationale behind gathering data

Good practices

- Data and information used to prove clear links between operational activities and company outcomes. This has many implications as it shows that the company knows it is working to improve outcomes and to do that it has established a number of strategies. It then uses this data and information (not gut feelings) to track if the strategies have been implemented and are achieving the desired outcome.
- The concepts of variation and trends are used to assist decisions based on measuring and monitoring of processes.

Poor practices

- No clear linkage between decisions and integrated information.
- Deterministic models used to make decisions.
- Superstitious management interventions.
- No understanding of variation—expecting exactness and using only deterministic models for displaying data and decision making.

5.6 Measure your success

Most companies do not measure to see if they are being successful. However, if you do only one thing that will make a huge difference it would be this: measure your progress towards your important objectives and goals. When you do this, it implies that you:

- are interested in success and therefore may achieve it
- know what success is for you
- understand that your strategies to achieve success may fail.

Effectiveness and success

The most important measurement you can make is to see if you are reaching your objectives (i.e. being effective). However, many companies make the mistake of thinking that doing things is the same as success. For example, you watch a documentary on television about cheetahs. A cheetah chases an antelope—a lot of action, animals running, swerving. Is this success? It might be if the cheetah catches the antelope. However, antelopes often get away. So, let the cheetah catch its antelope. Is this success? It will be if the cheetah is able to eat it. Often a lion or hyena will take the antelope from the cheetah. Success (for the cheetah) is an eaten antelope and a sleeping contented cheetah. (On the other hand, success for the antelope is escape. For the lion, success is a stolen and eaten antelope—or cheetah.)

The vast majority of companies do not think through what success is. They mistake the chase (action) for success.

Every company must work out what success means for it—and then measure to see if that success is being achieved. Every project, every strategy must have an objective—so that you will know what success will look like. You must measure if the action on the project or strategy is achieving (or has achieved) success (i.e. reached its objectives). These objectives must be linked to the overall success of the company.

Key performance indicators

You saw in Principle 2 ('Focus on achieving results') that measurement is a useful method to provide focus. In their analysis of what will make them successful, most companies decide on five to six major objectives. These are often called key result areas (KRAs)—areas where it is strategically important to get results. Common KRAs are improved:

- financial performance
- customer satisfaction
- operational performance
- employee morale.

In order to give focus to these, you should measure your success in achieving those objectives. These measurements are usually called key performance indicators (KPIs). As you saw in Principle 2, KPIs will be of two types—measurements of success (are you achieving the objective?) and measurements of implementation (is everyone doing it who should be?).

As well as their KRAs, companies should also write down their mission and vision statements and statements of values. KPIs should also be developed for progress towards the mission and vision and implementation of (or adherence to) the values. The set of KPIs you use should cover all your stakeholders and all your KRAs.

There are a number of very useful approaches to this. One is the balanced scorecard approach originally proposed by Kaplan and Norton. Figure 5.5 shows a modified version of the balanced scorecard that is more in line with the Principles described here, which gives the main ideas to address. You need to identify and develop under each idea the KPIs that are relevant to you. A number of lists of KPIs can be found throughout this book (see sections 4.9, 6.7 and 10.7).

Choose carefully—what you measure is what you get

What you measure will significantly affect the behaviour of your employees. People will behave so that they look good (or at least not look bad) in the measurements.

Because the KPIs ask significant questions of the company and significantly drive behaviour, choosing the KPIs are important decisions. Do not be afraid to change, modify or drop KPIs—although such changes should not be done lightly. Too frequent changes indicate instability and lack of focus. However, getting them right is very important.

Here are some examples of KPIs that usually do not work.

- A seemingly good KPI can lead to unintended poor focus. For example, a company might have a policy that 95% of service calls will be dealt with on the day for which the service was booked. This sounds like a very good indicator to focus the attention of service crews. However, it needs very hefty back-up—what of the steadily accumulating 5% for which they did not turn up on the day? You need another indicator to pick them up or they get left behind in the mad scramble to deal with the next day's calls. Assume that on average the service crews can achieve the '95% dealt with on the day' target. However, this means that every day a new batch of 5% is added to those customers who you did not get to service. If the service crews are flat out to do the 95%, then you need two other things—other service crews, independent of the first measure, whose job it is to mop up the 5%, plus an

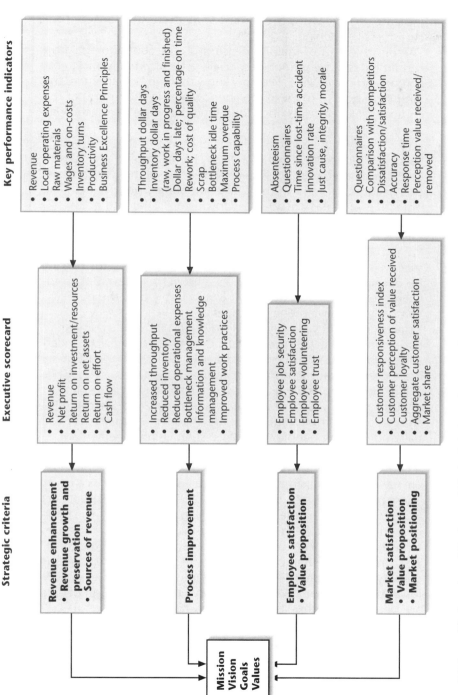

Fig. 5.5 A modified version of Kaplan and Norton's balanced scorecard

indicator to measure the extent that there are 'unserviced' customers left behind.

- The old thinking of mainly measuring cost containment gave certain types of behaviour—especially a focus on efficiency, cost cutting and downsizing. We now know these to be harmful to the long-term goal (e.g. make money now and in the future) of the company. Nevertheless, for a long time they have driven the way companies behaved.
- When activity is measured but effectiveness is not, almost inevitably success is judged in terms of activity. For example, 'We need to establish an Internet site to increases sales'. Establishing the Internet site becomes an end in itself and someone's pet project. The objective—increasing sales—is forgotten. That the activity—establish an Internet site—is just an experiment to try to increase sales is never acknowledged.
- When costs are measured but effectiveness is not, almost inevitably success is judged in terms of cost. In many companies, the penalty for overspending expense budgets is often more severe than for failing to increase revenue. This would imply that the goal of a company is to save money. Madness!
- Using percentages can give misleading results. Many companies have a policy for a 95% success rate. Companies often fail to understand what a 95% success rate means—'95% of our customers are extremely satisfied!'. It also implies a 5% failure rate. A 5% failure rate becomes a big problem when you have a large number of customers. If you have 20 million customers and 5% can tell a story about a terrible experience they had with your service, you have one million people who can testify. Using a percentage in this case is masking the problem (i.e. one million war stories).
- A common conflict occurs when team goals are set but individuals are rewarded. For example, 'We must all work together as a team. Those people in the sales team who get 100% of their sales quota get to go to Hawaii'. This means that the people who work in the background to support the sales representatives, and on whom the sales representatives depend, cannot be rewarded. Why should they help?
- The strangest is when companies plan to kill or injure so many employees each year—'Our target for lost time injuries is 20% lower than last year'. What do you do when not enough people are killed or injured? Kill or injure a few more?

Measure your implementation

Measuring the extent of implementation is extremely important. Without these measurements, people assume that implementation is uniform across the company.

Measuring the extent that initiatives or policies are deployed can be a very powerful method of achieving alignment in large companies. For example, a police service introduces a policy of always arresting offenders at domestic violence incidents. Measuring the extent that this is carried out in each division or precinct can show considerable differences in the way the policy is implemented. In line with Principle 4 ('To improve the outcome, improve the system'), this can lead to questioning why it is not happening—what systems are preventing it?

Evaluation checklist

There are many issues to consider when developing your KPIs and deciding what you need to measure. Below is a checklist that is useful in determining the kind of issues for which you need measurements.

Table 5.1 Evaluation checklist

Issue	What to measure
Effectiveness	Has the strategy achieved its objectives?
	Was it successful?
	What are the results achieved? How do you know?
	Were the results because of the change? How do you know?
Appropriateness	Does the strategy add value to the company or your customers? How do you know?
	Is it closely connected to the company's goals?
	Is it still what you want to do?
	What are the good and bad consequences (to all stakeholder groups) of not doing the process, abandoning the product or discontinuing the strategy?
Implementation	Was it done? How do you know?
	Is everyone doing it that should be doing it? How do you know? (You will usually have to measure this with data!)
	Has behaviour altered?
	Was the level of implementation the same everywhere?
Throughput	Number of orders shipped
	Value of orders shipped
	Maximum overdue
	Idle time on bottleneck
	Number of orders that have been shipped compared with number of orders that could have been shipped
	Work-in-progress inventory

153

Table 5.1 Evaluation checklist (*continued*)

Issue	What to measure
Process capability	What is the process capable of delivering?
	How is it measured? (You will usually have to measure this with data!)
	How capable is it of achieving your targets? (You will probably have to calculate this.)
	How do targets match the process capability?
	What is being done to improve the capability of the process to meet targets?
Customer perception of value	Do the customers feel they receive value? How do you know? (You will usually have to measure this with data!)
	What do your customer dislike? (Both internal and external customers.)
Quality of service	How do you measure the service delivery design (up to the instant before you deliver it to the customer)?
	How do you track and measure quality (accuracy, timeliness, reliability, validity)?
	How do you track rework?
Efficiency	In delivering its services and objectives, is the strategy, project or unit operating with the minimum resources, taking the minimum steps in its processes? How do you know?
	What is your response time? What is it compared with what your customers want or what your competitors can do?
	What attempts have been made to remove steps and what results have been achieved?

Good practices

- A clear link between the strategy of the company and what it measures.
- KPIs linked to company objectives.
- Indicators that reflect what is important to customers and other stakeholders.
- Clear linkages between direction, KPIs, plans and daily work.
- Clear and simple KPIs to monitor implementation and success of plans. Trend data is used to identify successes or opportunities for improvement of the strategies.
- Progress on all KPIs measured automatically each month, quarter or year and the results published internally.

> **Poor practices**
>
> - KPIs bear little or no rel
> - KPIs not linked to company objectives.
> - KPIs relating only to financial side.

5.7 Make comparisons

Comparative information is important because:

- comparative and benchmarking information might alert you to competitive threats and new practices
- you need to know 'where you stand' relative to competitors and to best practices
- comparative and benchmarking information often provides impetus for significant ('breakthrough') improvement or changes
- you need to understand your own processes and the processes of others before you compare performance levels
- benchmarking information may assist business analysis and decisions relating to core competencies, alliances and outsourcing.

Selecting exactly which comparisons and benchmark information you will use is very important. Selection criteria should include a search for the best performers (both within and outside your industry and markets).

The search for the best selection criteria is a crucial element. Just because the company next door will share data with you does not make it a good benchmarking partner. You might both be among the very bad. You constantly need to find the best performance or best practice in your industry and in your market.

Keep looking outside your company and your industry. Many breakthrough ideas come from adapting practices, products or service offerings from another industry. It is often easier to benchmark outside your industry than within it because companies outside your industry:

- are not competitors and may share information with you
- have not been confined by your industry's conventions.

How have other industries reduced their response time? For example, if response time means getting there quickly, all the following industries would have much to learn from each other: police, fire, ambulance, taxis, roadside service, couriers, fast-food delivery, tow trucks.

The search for the best never stops. New practices and new leaders constantly emerge and industries and technology constantly change. Today's best practice will probably look very ordinary next year.

Lead and lag indicators

Almost all traditional KPIs are lag indicators in that they tell you about what has happened. You can use these indicators to project into the future. However, that assumes that the future will be similar to the past—and that is seldom true. KPIs can be extremely useful for monitoring process performance and as measures of success in reaching desired outcomes. However, as predictors of the future they are of limited value. They are like driving a car while looking only in the rear-vision mirror. You need a different type of indicator to predict the future. Lag indicators usually measure the output of a system or process. They include all financial KPIs (including revenue, expenses, sales, quantities sold, return on net assets, return on investment, profit).

An example of a lead indicator is 'storm clouds brewing, wind getting up; it might rain'. Squirrels and geese can predict winter snow.

Useful lead indicators are measurements of your attempts to influence your future by undertaking activities that are thought to lay foundations for future success; for example, investment made in capital, training, product development, innovation, knowledge or technology. Notice that these investments are also among the first that companies cut when they need to show better results to shareholders.

Shareholders should be very wary of such tactics. Investment in capital, training, product development, innovation, knowledge and technology are investment in the future of the company. Continuity of investment is a very useful predictor of sustainability. Cuts to investment mean exactly the opposite—taking money out of the company now to maintain the illusion of success is a smokescreen that is increasingly seen through by shareholders and analysts.

Dr Hausner's research indicates that scores on the 10 Business Excellence Principles are extremely good lead indicators.

Accurate, available, valid, reliable, timely

Data or information that is not accurate, not available, not valid, not reliable or too late is useless to you when you are making your decisions. So you need processes to make certain the data and information is accurate, available, valid, reliable and timely. None of this will happen by chance.

You saw above that asking the right questions is important. However, even if you are asking the right questions, you might still be getting useless data and information. You cannot assume that because you are using a computer to gather it, the data will be accurate or available. Your experience is probably exactly the opposite. Our experience with databases is that they are usually full of 'dirty data', that is, data that is full of errors (e.g. incorrect dates, wrong units, numbers reversed, missing digits, wrong formats, missing values). Sometimes these errors appear small or insignificant. However, they all mean that the data is unreliable and hard or impossible to use.

Cleaning up a database so that it can be used is often the single most expensive and difficult part of any analysis. It is far better to put the data through a set of good 'data scrubbing' tools to trap any errors during collection. For example, do not let the person collecting the data move on if they have left out required data. Make estimates of the data you are expecting and reject data that is out of range.

Accurate, available, valid, reliable and timely data is critical for generating factual information and making decisions. The computer saying of 'garbage in garbage out' applies. Where the measurement is direct through some form of mechanical or electronic device, it is important that repeatability and reproducibility studies are carried out to ensure confidence in the method of measurement. Instruments should be regularly checked for calibration.

You also must ensure that the measurement is measuring what you think it is measuring (i.e. it is 'valid'). Otherwise your measurements are measuring something entirely different and any interpretation you make will be misleading and meaningless.

You also need to be sure that your analysis is valid. For example, people often make errors when analysing surveys. It is incorrect to assume that survey responses will balance themselves out when aggregated. For example, you cannot add the 50% 'very satisfied' to the 50% 'very dissatisfied' to get an 'average satisfied'. It would be like adding apples and bananas. You should delve into the reasons for those answers. (Was the question inappropriately worded for its audience?) Any one of those 50% who were dissatisfied may give you real material to work with.

It takes hard work to make certain the data is accurate, that you can get it out of the computer, that it is about what you think it is about (i. e. valid), that you would get the same result each time (i.e. reliable) and that you can get it when you want it.

Good practices

- Benchmarks within the industry and outside as they search for the best.
- Comparative data for best in class and best in region for all KPIs.
- Corporate data is chartered and made readily accessible to staff.

Poor practices

- No comparisons with the outside world.
- A 'we are different' or 'we cannot get external data' attitude.

5.8 Know what is going on

You have to know what is going on in your marketplace. You need to know everything about:

- what your competitors are doing and why
- how and why your customers' expectations are changing
- how changes in your market produce new business opportunities
- how changes in the global marketplace will affect you
- how changing paradigms about technology, customer needs and the way business is done affect you
- any technological developments and innovations that affect your products
- new ways of doing business with your customers
- changes that produce new market segments
- changes in regulations and tax
- changing community/societal expectations
- changing needs of government
- your company, its capabilities and competencies
- your people, their capabilities and competencies.

You need good processes that deal with this inflow of data to categorise it, analyse it, make sense of it, determine implications and make predictions from it. The relevant piece of data should be available to the person who needs it when he or she needs it. This is a big ask.

However, the alternative is that you blunder along, not knowing what is going on, making uninformed decisions, trying to pretend you are isolated. That even when you go to the trouble of collecting the data, you cannot find it later or cannot or do not analyse it or try to make sense of it.

Unbelievably, most businesses do the latter. Do you? It is hard work and takes considerable effort to do otherwise.

Swamped with junk e-mail

Junk e-mail is an example of how companies deal with data. Junk e-mail is a significant issue in many companies. In this information age, companies have to find ways to deal with internal junk e-mail, endless meetings, constant policy changes and incessant telephone calls. Today, senior managers can expect to receive more than 300 e-mails a day. How can anyone be expected to do anything with them? Most managers spend 90% of their day in meetings. How can this time be well spent? Many large companies send out at least one significant policy change a week. How would you find it in all the junk e-mail, let alone be able to work out its impact on your systems and processes?

This is all a huge 'information/knowledge' process. What is your method of dealing with it? You now have technology that swamps people with junk information. You need criteria to filter out the junk from this material, just as you need criteria to screen out the 'dirty data' when you are collecting data.

Why do you need to be informed?

Many senior managers demand to be notified of everything that happens and consequently are decked out with pagers and mobile phones. However, some useful questions are 'Why do you need to be informed? ', 'What will you do as a result?'. If you are constantly asking to be more informed, it might indicate that you do not trust your staff or the decisions they make. Is this because you have not enabled them to make decisions themselves (i.e. given them skills, knowledge and power so they can make sound decisions)? Or did you hire people you cannot trust? Or is it that you have such a chaotic management system that you are being judged by your ability to keep track of everything that is going on?

In the days of the Roman Empire, you selected your manager and watched him and his baggage (they were 'he's' in those days) disappear over the hill to look after things in some far distant place. And that was the last you saw or heard for a few years. You did not talk on the telephone several times a day. Or exchange faxes and e-mails. You could not! Communication took weeks or months—far too long to handle a crisis! There is no way that you could maintain the illusion of direct control. You could not ring him up or he could not ring you. You could not fly over to sort things out. Therefore, you had to choose well. Someone you could trust to do the right thing. You made certain that person had the right values, the right skills, sufficient knowledge and knew what you were trying to achieve and the way you do things. We seem to have gone a long way backwards since then.

Of course, you need communications. You need to know what is happening. It makes up your information and knowledge base. You must ensure that when you set up your informal communications system, that you are not destroying trust, you are not removing the authority to make decisions or setting up a time-wasting system.

Analysis of company performance

Analysing the company's performance is an excellent way of assessing its overall health. Good analysis will go a long way towards you being well informed. Analysis should guide the company towards attaining essential business results and important strategic objectives.

Although they are important, individual facts and data are not enough. Individually, they do not give you 'the whole picture' so that you can make sound strategic decisions or set priorities. Information and data from across your marketplace and from all parts of the company must be analysed to assess overall company health.

Analysis systems should include:

- examination of progress towards success in achieving your mission, vision and all your important objectives and goals
- full marketplace information
- scores on the 10 Business Excellence Principles
- financial and non-financial information and data
- resource, cost and revenue implications
- implications for implementation of decisions
- implications for people (especially those in the *gemba*)
- implications for processes (especially bottlenecks and key processes).

Good analysis requires that you develop an understanding of the cause and effect connections between your processes and your business results. These cause and effect connections are often unclear.

Examples of helpful analyses

Analyses that companies perform to gain an understanding of performance vary widely depending on company type, size and competitive position.

Companies have found the following examples useful:

- correlation between improvement in product/service quality and market indicators, such as customer satisfaction, customer perception of value, customer retention, customer referrals and market share
- cost and revenue implications of customer complaints and problem resolution effectiveness (and the reverse when you don't act on them!)
- effect on market share of customer gains and losses and changes in customer satisfaction
- improvement in KPIs such as cycle time, rework, defect levels and waste reduction, revenue, inventory, cost and quality trends relative to competitors
- correlation between revenue per employee and product/service quality, operational performance indicators, financial performance, operational expense, inventory and asset utilisation
- net earnings originating from performance improvements in throughput, inventory reduction, waste reduction, cycle time reduction, operational expense reduction
- comparisons between business units showing how quality and operational performance improvement affect financial performance

- contribution of improvement activities to cash flow, working capital use, asset utilisation and shareholder value
- profit impacts of customer retention
- market share versus profits
- trends in economic, market and shareholder indicators of value
- relationship between revenue per employee and employee/company learning
- financial benefits from improvements in employee safety, absenteeism and turnover
- benefits, costs and effectiveness of education and training
- benefits, costs and effectiveness of improved company knowledge management
- correlation between employee retention, motivation and productivity, and indicators of employees' perception of value
- cost and revenue implications of employee-related problems
- allocation of resources among alternative improvement projects based on cost/revenue implications and improvement potential
- cost/revenue implications of new market entry, including global market entry or expansion.

You must provide a sound analytical basis for decisions—and then keep reviewing it to see if what you are doing works.

Withholding data

One reason for not knowing what is going on occurs when people do not pass on the data and information they have. This can be inadvertent ('we didn't know you needed it') or it can be deliberate because of disgruntled employees or another corporate power play ('see how they get on if they don't know X').

Often you can have everyone in the hierarchy saying 'I don't know' and still expecting a decision from the top. This is unrealistic. It usually indicates a climate of fear or a lack of trust of the senior people (Principle 1, 'Role models').

Good practices

Decision making based on asking 'good' questions, for example:

- What is your purpose? Will the decision assist you to reach it?
- Will this make a difference for the company?
- Is the decision in line with your values?
- Will this make a difference for the customer?
- Will this make a difference for the *gemba*?
- What are the unintended side-effects?

- How much of the core information pertinent to decisions is unknown?
- What assumptions have you made?

Poor practices

- Information is not shared.
- The data reported is not comprehensible and its relevance is not communicated.
- Management makes all decisions.
- Decisions are mainly based on experience, tradition or gut feelings.

5.9 Treat knowledge as a resource

You should treat knowledge as a major company resource and manage and use the leverage of your company's knowledge. You need knowledge about:

- your market
- what is happening around you
- your customers and their needs
- your employees and their needs
- how you do things and why
- decisions you have made and why you made them
- what you are intending to do.

That knowledge is the lifeblood of a successful company.

Just as information is produced when you analyse data, you produce knowledge when you learn. In Principle 8 ('Innovation') the importance of learning is described. The knowledge produced by your learning is a company resource that must be available in a useable form for decision making.

Most often, the knowledge previously gained by the company is lost and is not available or is disregarded. If you ignore your prior learning, you may have to pay the school fees again.

Every company contains knowledge obtained from its business experience as well as the experiences of every person associated with it. You should:

- identify your sources of knowledge—existing and potential, external and internal
- validate what you 'know'—ensure that knowledge is soundly based and not hearsay, old paradigm or based on invalid assumptions
- generate knowledge and learnings—by analysing data, information and what you have learned in business experience, learnings by improvement teams, from the expertise of people within the

company, from reflection on consequences, from courses, conferences, market analysis, research findings and reviews

- manage knowledge—capture, store (e.g. in checklists, databases) and share knowledge
- make knowledge available and accessible across the company—be able to retrieve the knowledge you want when you want it, be able to find research and policy information
- embed knowledge—in the company's procedures and systems
- use knowledge—in decision making, strategy development and other activities to improve company performance
- encourage sharing knowledge—make available, encourage by use of technical and human processes (e.g. meetings) or reward and recognition systems, prevent hoarding
- use the leverage of your knowledge—to add to the company's value, prepare for future challenges and provide value for all stakeholders, exploit innovative thinking and experience
- retain company memory—capture the knowledge of people in systems and procedures, retain the experience of those who leave the company, retain details of why things are done and decisions made
- safeguard your knowledge—protect your intellectual property and intellectual capital
- develop and retain core competencies—the underlying skills, knowledge and experience that the company is very good at doing, those things that make it special and different from other companies; make the most of these core competencies and increase them.

Checklist knowledge

Checklists, forms and standard operating procedures are very useful ways of capturing knowledge. A checklist or standard operating procedure can be used to store experience and expertise in a way and at a time when it is not urgently required so that it can be brought to hand when it is. Even experts can forget things—especially when under pressure. A form can be used to capture the expertise of experienced personnel so that less experienced people can record customer information.

Checklists, forms and standard operating procedures are the simplest forms of expert systems. They can be designed and compiled by experts so non-experts can use them, even without the experts being present. They are an excellent way of using company learning.

Sources of knowledge

An emerging trend in companies is to call the company's librarian or IT manager the 'knowledge manager', or the education and training coordinator, the 'learning' coordinator. This appears to show a considerable lack of understanding of what is meant by 'knowledge' or 'learning'. There are at least five major sources of knowledge:

1. *Experience*: having done it or something like it before. This includes professional and all other types of education and training, on-the-job experience, life experience, family experience, reading.
2. *Network*: someone in your network knows the answer or has the experience at how to do it. As a rule of thumb, this works more than 80% of the time. Someone among the people you talk to most of the time has done 'it' before or knows how to do 'it'. Find this person. Ask for help (this often allows people to volunteer).
3. *Position*: people often know more about what is going on because of their position in the company—meetings they attend, the network they are in, 'being in the know'. It is the responsibility of all people to share their knowledge so that others can make meaningful decisions. Bosses who hoard knowledge often do so because they have to be the one with the answer. (In the section below, the habit of confidentiality and how damaging it can be to companies is discussed.)
4. *Location*: people in head office often know more of what is going on than those in some remote branch office on the other side of the country or the other side of the world.
5. *Personality type*: different personality types will place more value on different types of knowledge. Some people value practical experience as the only source of know-how, while others value theoretical analysis.

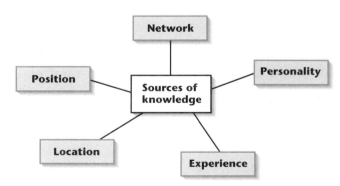

Fig. 5.6 Sources of knowledge

Untapped knowledge

It is astounding how many companies fail to fully utilise the experience and learning of their employees. You repeatedly see employees with extensive skills and experience in their communities but who have no credibility in their companies. The man who is the president of his local Apex club, the woman who has raised five children, the woman who coaches softball or teaches aerobics, the woman who runs a care centre for homeless or disabled people. These abilities are seldom recorded on any company 'skills register'.

Probably the biggest overlooked and untapped source of knowledge is 'parenting'. A large percentage of employees are parents. Parenting takes much the same skills as managing—encouraging, coaching, enabling. Why not use (and build) those skills? This would be a real win–win situation: employees would get better parenting skills and companies would get to recognise and use a wealth of potential.

Confidentiality

Some discussions and written material are often classed as confidential and given a limited distribution. And rightly so. You probably do not want your opposition to know what you are doing—timing can be very important in announcing decisions or actions. No-one likes to have a confidential discussion and then find it in the newspaper the next day.

However, treating all discussions by executives or the Board as confidential is a habit that can be very damaging to the company. There is no doubt that keeping some things confidential is sometimes necessary. Keeping all things confidential is, however, very damaging to trust. It says very loudly that 'we the executive don't trust you'. Employees respond to lack of trust by withdrawing—enthusiasm, resourcefulness.

Consider the effect of making the discussion confidential. It means that everyone not included in the confidential discussion is now working without relevant knowledge. In many companies, this means that all vital knowledge is held by a trusted few at the top. Everyone else in the company is denied knowledge often essential to do their job, to make useful decisions or to offer suggestions.

Confidentiality is also often used when the executive of a company is doing something that is unethical, unlawful or that the other stakeholders will not approve of.

Good practices

- Knowledge is used as an input to strategy and decision making.
- Lead indicators for determining the rate of knowledge acquisition and innovation rate.
- Celebration of the search for knowledge that benefits the company.
- Systems and processes for capturing and making available the knowledge of individuals for the benefit of the company. A growing repository of knowledge that is well sorted and can be accessed easily.

- Use of technology, such as an Intranet, for sharing knowledge.
- Staff can give examples of how they would go about obtaining new knowledge they need in order to create value for a stakeholder.
- Processes to counter 'group think' in decision making.

Poor practices

- Using only financial data for decision making.
- No systematic approach or strategy to link all data in use in the company.
- Data not easily available to the people who need it.
- Data stored in various locations without easy accessibility. Information scattered across the company so that no-one has a big picture.
- No method of sharing of information between people or groups. The 'right hand does not know what the left hand is doing' or that there is a left hand.
- No systems to capture knowledge (e.g. no-one can find the new policy three months after it is issued, no document control, overseas visits or conferences do not result in a presentation or trip report).
- No processes to recognise or avoid 'group think'.

5.10 Review your decision making

The important issues about decision making are:

- At what level are decisions made? How do you ensure that decisions are made by the people who have the knowledge to make decisions about process? How do you prevent bosses monopolising the decision-making process?
- How do you enable people to make decisions—by providing skills, knowledge, information, power and authority?
- How do you decide on what information you base your decisions?
- How do you ensure you are asking the right questions?
- How do you seek to understand and challenge your assumptions?
- How do you ensure you are making your decision based on full knowledge of what is really going on—that you are not missing relevant information; that your data is reliable, accurate, valid and timely; that your information has not been distorted to tell a false story?
- How do you keep challenging your thinking?
- How do you ensure that the people who need the data receive what they need and not what someone else thinks they need?

- How do you deal with uncertainty? How do you make decisions even though important data and information may be uncertain or unavailable?
- How do you review your decision-making process?

Reviewing decision making

Most companies assume they are good at making decisions. Perhaps they are but good companies are always looking to do better. One way to do this is to review how you make decisions. You should use the checklist above to review several:

- routine daily operational decisions
- process improvement decisions
- management decisions (e.g. plan implementation and system performance)
- significant and important strategic decisions.

Strategic decisions

Principle 5 adds a different aspect to many decisions. With the old ways of thinking about business, you saw companies acting in ways that showed little clear benefit for the company. For example, exactly how will the proposed merger provide what the customers value?

Owners, executives, managers and investors need clear and easy rules of thumb to follow so they can assess strategic decisions.

In Principle 2 ('Focus on achieving results') we discussed company goals and the necessary conditions to reach those goals. The goal for most companies is to make money now and in the future. In *It's Not Luck*, Goldratt identified three necessary conditions for success in reaching the goal:

1. Provide satisfaction to the market now and in the future (the market punishes companies that do not satisfy the market perception of value).
2. Provide a secure and satisfying environment for employees now as well as in the future.
3. Provide value to the community now and in the future (the community punishes companies it considers are not good corporate citizens and takes away their right to operate).

These four guidelines—one goal and its three necessary conditions—*must* be the underlying basis when deciding strategy.

- Reject any strategy that contradicts or leads you away from any of the four guidelines.
- Make certain your strategies are in total alignment with all four guidelines.

Uncertainty

In strategic decision making, most of the information needed to make the decision is unavailable, unknown or unreliable. We have all heard of 20/20 hindsight vision—when we look back, with all the information, we understand things perfectly. Unfortunately, no-one has perfect foresight vision. Although the emphasis in Principle 5 is for companies to base decisions on data and information, at the strategic level such data is usually absent. Nevertheless, the strategic decision must still be made.

How do you know that the risk is acceptable? How do you reduce the risk?

Use the concepts described throughout Principle 5 to:

- determine what information you should have to make the decision
- find what you can to close the gaps in your information
- challenge your assumptions
- use 'what if' analysis, simulations, decision trees and scenarios to determine the impact of different decisions
- assess the risk of the decision at different levels of uncertainty
- if you can, leave your options open—don't make the decision irrevocable unless you have no choice.

This 'uncertainty' caused by unavailable data and information on which to base strategic decisions should not be confused with 'variability', which is discussed in Principle 6.

Why don't people use information?

This approach to data, information, analysis and decision making appears completely logical. It makes good sense to know how the company is performing. Yet, it is rare to find anyone doing it. People in companies everywhere find all kinds of reasons why this cannot be done. Why don't people use data to manage?

One reason stems from the need to make themselves look good for the incentive scheme. When these exist, there is a real fear of performance data.

Consequently, people *dissemble*. They put the best possible light on the story that they can. They manage the *data* to make themselves look good or at least not bad. They use indicators that show only success. They discard indicators that might imply failure. They argue (against Principle 6 'Variability') that 'the (slight) upturn last month indicates a reversal in the previous downward trend'.

They lie. They modify graphs. They lose, omit or fail to display data that does not show a positive trend. They also provide data that will discredit others and so take the heat off themselves.

When all senior managers are fully engaged in this form of KPI warfare, it is very difficult to determine the real situation in the company.

These forms of survival are learned very early in a manager's career, usually as a result of seeing the ritual slaying of some poor manager who let his or her guard down. 'Managing the numbers' is usually where most managers spend most of their time. If they do not do so, they are out of a job—overall, a strange unintended consequence of performance incentive schemes.

If people were not so concerned that they would get the blame for poor performance (which is often out of their control), they would be more willing to provide data that showed real performance—and manage 'performance' rather than the 'data'.

The solution is to stop blaming people and not have the slightest hint that a person's value to the company is linked in any way to performance data.

Good practices

- Open analysis of past decisions for future improvement.
- Strong emphasis is placed on the use of KPI trends for decision making.
- Decisions link to the company mission, vision and values.
- Rationale for decision making is shared and understood. Each level throughout the company publishes information, data and analyses used in its decision making.
- A clear framework of ethics for decision making.
- Work is refused if accepting it would compromise the company's ethics or values, even if the work would be very lucrative. A clear framework for such decisions is understood by all.

Poor practices

- No measurements of the unintended consequences of current strategy.
- Manipulation of statistics to support a position rather than analysis of the system.
- Post-event rationalisation of decisions. We did this and now we look back it was because of X.
- Stakeholder groups not informed of rationale for decisions.

SUMMARY

Principle 5 is concerned with how you obtain and use data, information and knowledge to support decision making at all levels of your company.

Data is defined as raw numbers and facts (which include perceptions). Information is data that has been processed through presentation, analysis, interpretation or prediction to give it meaning. Knowledge is created when information is shared and decisions are analysed. Every company contains knowledge from its own business experiences as well as the life experiences of every person in the company. Decisions should be based on information and knowledge. Your aim is to base your decisions on a thorough understanding of the environment in which your company operates.

You must determine what data should be collected as well as how data is handled, stored, analysed and interpreted to create information. This includes all data needed anywhere in the company: measurements of process performance at the departmental or operations level; internal measurements of performance at the company level such as KPIs; and measurements of strategic success. This includes data collected on a routine basis for control and improvement as well as data collected for special purposes. To assist and inform your decision making, you need to integrate information from various sources.

At the level of collection and interpretation, you should consider:

- data selection—your criteria and processes to determine what data should be collected; your processes to prevent collecting data that is not useful to you; how you define the measurements for which you want to collect data; and how selected data relates to your company's objectives and goals
- data collection and storage—your systems and processes for capturing and storing data; how you will take 'samples' (rather than having to measure everything); how you will store the data and information (e.g. reports, databases, libraries, electronic systems)
- data integrity—how you (automatically) ensure data is accurate, valid and reliable, secure and timely
- retrieval of information—your methods to ensure that you can obtain the exact piece of data or information when you want it; your policies on who can access information
- analysis and interpretation of data—your methods of summation, aggregation and presentation to enable analysis of data; how you interpret and make predictions; how you check the accuracy of your predictions; application of valid statistical analysis
- analysis competency—how you develop abilities of staff throughout the company to analyse, interpret and link data and information
- links to company objectives—how your analysis links operational activities and company goals and objectives and so increases your probability of success.

At the level of integration and use of information for decision making you should consider:

- decision systems—your process to ensure that whenever possible, your decisions are based on data, information and knowledge

- routine decision making and prediction—your processes to use data and information for routine management, for improvement activities and to predict future performance (e.g. forecasting)
- uncertainty—how you deal with the issue that some information you need for decision making may be uncertain or unavailable; and how you deal with this uncertainty to minimise your risk
- variability—how you ensure that variability of data is understood by decision makers at all levels, how you create an understanding of variation and process capability, and use this understanding in the decision making
- use of reports—how you make decisions as a result of monthly and quarterly reports; how you decide who is responsible for responding to particular information at the various levels of the company
- communication with stakeholders—how you choose what information is communicated to stakeholders, and how this choice reflects company priorities.

WHAT WOULD YOUR STAKEHOLDERS SAY?

HOW WOULD YOUR EMPLOYEES RATE YOUR COMPANY ON THESE?

- This company bases all its operational decisions on facts—data and information rather than rumour and gut feeling.
- This company does not gather data that it does not use.
- This company demands reports that no-one uses.
- We are enabled (provided with skills, knowledge, authority and power) to make decisions about processes in which we work.
- This company constantly challenges its assumptions.
- This company evaluates its performance using indicators of success such as KPIs.
- I understand all the company's KPIs and my contribution to them.
- This company has a balanced approach to its KPIs with data about employees' needs given significant weight.
- This company has KPIs and measurements that force me to work against the company's best interests.
- I have measurements of all the main processes that affect me.
- This company uses data to make comparisons with other companies to find better ways of doing things.
- This company makes good use of the knowledge held in the company.

HOW WOULD YOUR SUPPLIERS RATE YOUR COMPANY ON THESE?

- I understand the KPIs that affect me and my part in achieving them.
- This company understands my KPIs and its part in achieving them.

- This company bases all its operational decisions on facts—data and information.
- This company uses data to make comparisons with other companies to find better ways of doing things.
- This company has helped my company understand the use of facts and data in decision making.

HOW WOULD YOUR SHAREHOLDERS RATE YOUR COMPANY ON THESE?

- This company bases all its decisions on facts—data and information.
- This company evaluates its performance using KPIs.
- This company has a balanced approach to its KPIs with all stakeholders' needs given significant weight.
- This company does not suboptimise by having KPIs that drive it into internal conflict.
- This company has a very good process for handling uncertainty when making strategic decisions.
- This company does not cut its investment in capital, training, development, innovation, knowledge and technology in order to pay dividends.
- This company publishes in its annual report its investment in capital, training, product development, innovation, knowledge and technology.

Principle 6
Variability

All systems and processes exhibit variability, which affects predictability and performance.

VARIATION MEANS LACK OF CONSISTENCY. Lack of consistency means additional cost and rework. And rework is a total waste of your resources. In most companies, rework is the largest consumer of managers' and employees' time. Reducing your variation usually means reducing your costs. People who understand the concept of variation are more likely to understand those of *process capability*, which we explored in Principle 4 ('To improve the outcome, improve the system'). Consistency means that your products will more often do what they are supposed to do and that your customers will be more satisfied.

Reducing your variation can give considerable competitive advantage. Reducing your variation gives more stable products and services (and hence more satisfied customers) and less wasted effort on fighting fires.

Variation affects us in five ways:

- Variation can lead us to react inappropriately to random events—this uses our time and energy unnecessarily and we can make the situation worse by our well-meaning interference.
- Errors (variation) accumulate from one step to the next in our processes.
- A funnel effect occurs in complex processes with errors from many different sources accumulating. This means that the final product can (and will) have errors from many different sources.
- Variation means rework and rework is a waste of time, energy and resources. Having less rework means less employee expense and

gives you time to move on to things that are more productive. You can increase your throughput.
- You can reduce your rework throughout your process by constantly working to achieve smaller and smaller variation. This also means you can provide products and services that are of more value to your customers because your products will more often do what they are supposed to and your customers will have less rework to do to be able to use them. The result is an increase in customer satisfaction.

Dr Hausner's research indicates that Principle 6 has the second strongest correlation with KPI improvement (after Principle 10 'Value for all stakeholders'). It has the fourth highest correlation with the business excellence score.

Unfortunately, Principle 6 is also equal last (together with Principle 5 'Improved decisions') in how well companies are at implementing it. Let us assume that it is a strong driver of success. If this is so, there is a lot of unused potential by not implementing it. If companies were to implement Principle 6 better, they would achieve significantly better business results—they would be more successful.

6.1 People understand variation but forget it at work

Everyone intuitively understands variation and variability. We all know that the weather is not *exactly* the same every day, or that when we commute to work it does not take *exactly* the same time every day, or that no two people are *exactly* the same, or that no two concert performances by the same group are *exactly* the same.

Maybe the 'exactly' is being exaggerated but that is the point. You intuitively know that no two things or events are *exactly* the same. They vary.

Variation is something normal that you see every day. You see it as a range of results around an average. The Australian Quality Council cites the following as examples:

- The waiting time at the counter averaged 10 minutes; the shortest time was 3 minutes and the longest time was 25 minutes.
- The average height of students in the class is 1535 mm. The tallest child is 1610 mm and the shortest child is 1390 mm.

Sometimes we may be only interested in the range. For example:

Temperatures vary over a 24-hour period and the weather report usually gives the range by quoting the highest and lowest temperatures:
- 'Today's high was 25°C and the overnight low was 12°C'.

Outside of work, most people see variation as the norm and people are tolerant of expected variations. Our friends are different ages, shapes, heights, skin colours; daily temperatures go up and down; we don't expect the forecasters to get it exactly right; the newspaper is delivered around dawn; our train is often a few minutes (or seconds) late; we finish work at different times every day.

We expect that things will vary over an implicit range and we feel comfortable about that. However, we do get concerned when we think or feel that the variation is abnormal:

> - 'Over the past few months, my train has been more than five minutes late twice. We were then told that it had been cancelled.'
> - 'Paula is doing well at school and her reports have been satisfactory. However, with her latest report, we have been asked to come to the school to have a discussion with her teacher.'
> - 'My car has been going well since I bought it. But, just in the last week, it has been difficult to start so I may be heading for some problems.'

We innately sense from the accumulation of our life experiences that events like these are in some way special. We are able intuitively to separate them from the common, normal events.

> If you think any of these, you don't understand variation:
> - 'We can learn a lot by studying the cause of each thing gone wrong.'
> - 'Whenever things get better or worse, we can learn why.'
> - 'Each problem or mistake has a human cause.'

Demanding a report on why the weather is different today

In fact, variation in the workplace is no different to that which is routinely encountered and coped with in the community. The difference occurs in the workplace when people in positions of authority in management do not understand the basics about variation and deliberately intervene in normal variation situations. This is like demanding a report on why the weather is different today.

Knowledge about variation can lead to understanding:

- the causes of variation and how to respond appropriately
- tampering—how leaders, despite good intentions, can increase variation.

Deterministic models

Unfortunately, many of the management models currently being promoted by consultants and used by companies do not take variation (or its accumulating effect) into account. These deterministic models are often built by accountants or engineers who may see the world in such a linear fashion. They fail to understand that the output of a process is *not* the sum of the average outputs from the parts of the process.

For example, if machines (or people) A, B, C and D (each dependent on the one before) can produce 10 parts per hour on average, then in a deterministic model, the output of the process should be 40 parts per hour. All the accountant needs to do is measure the 'variance' from that 40. In a deterministic world, any deviation from 40 *must* be due to slackness.

However, the output from that four-step process depends on the variation of each step, and interdependency between the steps, as well as their average output.

Deterministic models can be useful in helping to understand the links in the process. However, to be useful for prediction, they need to be made into statistical models by including estimates of variation.

Good practices

- Demonstrating an understanding that *all systems exhibit variation*, which affects productivity and the people working within those systems.
- Working to eliminate *all* rework.
- Employee performance is assessed in a context of systems thinking and knowledge of process capability.
- People are not blamed when things go wrong.

Poor practices

- No understanding of the concept of process capability—the 'work harder' approach.
- Blaming people for problems over which they have no control—or giving credit to those who are lucky.

6.2 Managers and staff understand variation

When it comes to our business life, we usually forget our intuition and suddenly expect that everything we produce, every service we give or receive, every person we deal with, will be *exactly* the same every single time. Or that when we run our process we will get *exactly* the same result every single time. We intuitively know this cannot happen but we behave as though it were so.

Unfortunately, most managers are trained to think that variation is abnormal and must be controlled. Traditional month-to-month management reporting, such as exception reports, budget variances and month-to-month comparisons, is typical of this old thinking. People are often asked to explain what has happened, particularly when the 'variance' is unfavourable!

The wobbling pen

Most management systems are built without an understanding of the concepts. Consequently, owners/managers/bosses blame people rather than fix systems.

Try this. Stand up. Take your pen and balance it on your outstretched finger. Make certain your hand or arm is not resting on a table or some other support. Balance the pen so that its point is *exactly* still. *Do not allow the pen to wobble!* Have you done that? Why is the pen wobbling? You can give many excuses about why the pen is wobbling but what were your instructions? Why can't you do this simple task?

An example of a graph of the tip of your pen plotted against time is shown in Figure 6.1. The wobbling is variation.

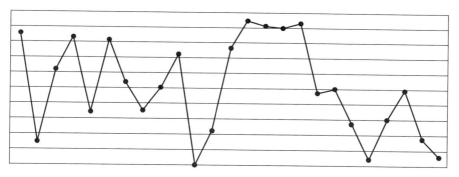

Fig. 6.1 The wobbling pen is an example of a common cause of variation

Stupid questions

The question 'Why are *you* letting the pen wobble?' is a stupid question, a boss's question. The question is stupid because, given the process we set up, the pen *must* wobble. Employees know that the boss's job is to ask stupid questions such as 'Why are *you* letting the pen wobble?'. Bosses know that it is the employee's job to answer such stupid questions. Employees also know that they can usually offer nothing better than excuses. They are caught in a system that they did not create and which they cannot control and the boss is demanding answers to such questions. The question implies that the individual can control the pen, which is clearly not the case in the example.

It is a widespread belief that asking the question, 'Why are *you* letting the pen wobble?', is useful. It has led to incentive and reward schemes that mean 'I will reward you for not wobbling the pen'—an impossible task. And to performance appraisals of 'keeping the pen still'.

Another stupid question is 'What caused *that* (particular) wobble?'. This implies that each individual wobble has a cause that can be 'tracked down and fixed'. This is the question being asked when people are asked to respond to month-to-month comparisons and accountant's 'variance'; for example, an individual difference between a predicted number (e.g. 'budget') and an achieved number (e.g. 'actual').

These reporting practices, although common, are very destructive of good business practice. They have people chasing smoke—wasting time investigating systemic causes of variation (e.g. trying to answer the stupid questions of the wobbling pen) and, through intervention in the situation, exacerbating the problem.

Useful questions

Consider some useful questions: 'Why is the pen wobbling?' or 'How can we stop the pen from wobbling—so much or at all?'. These questions are seeking information about the system that is producing wobbles.

In finding an answer to these questions, you have to understand the causes of the variation. Then you can get to a useful solution. To find a solution to this type of question requires you to change the process that causes the variation. For example, to stop the pen wobbling *so much*, you could have been seated and rested your hand on something. To stop the pen from wobbling *at all*, the pen could have been clamped. This is another illustration of Principle 4 ('To improve the outcome, improve the system')—in order to change this outcome (in this case the variation), we must change the process. In this case, to reduce the variation, we must understand its causes.

Special cause variation

If someone were to come up behind you and give you a push, the question, 'What caused that wobble?', is not stupid because there is a special cause—a push (Fig. 6.2). But how do we identify which is a special cause variation, and so worthy of the question, and which is not special?

Because of the strong interconnectedness between variability and systems, much of the discussion of Principle 4 ('To improve the outcome, improve the system') could be reproduced here—especially the sections on process capability. However, for Principle 6, only specific examples about variability will be discussed. Variability is probably the one area where people have most difficulty.

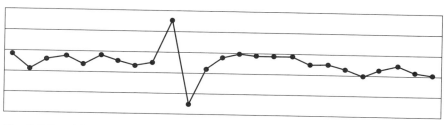

Fig. 6.2 Special cause variation—a push

Performance appraisal

Consider this finding in terms of performance appraisal. Everybody has good days and bad days. Suppose you had a policy of giving praise when someone did very well and delivering an admonishment when they did badly. Believe it or not, some bosses do have such policies. Let 'good' be 'up' and 'poor' be 'down' on the wobbling pen graph (Fig. 6.1). Immediately after poor performance, when an admonishment is delivered, performance usually improves. The policy clearly works—admonishments cause performance to improve. However, immediately after the good performance, when praise is delivered, performance usually goes down. Woops! You knew that praise did not work! Better to stick with the reprimands as they clearly work. Or, perhaps you should understand and expect variation in the performance and do neither.

Clearly, variation is an important consideration that should be considered as part of performance management but seldom is. Most (99%) people perform about average within the systems around them. Some days are good and they perform a bit better than average. Some days are bad and they perform a bit worse than average—overall, neither good (deserving praise) nor bad (deserving sanction). Just average. Ranking people who are all performing about average becomes nonsense.

Good practices

- Awareness sessions are conducted to improve understanding of data, information and variation.
- A performance management system based on an understanding of process capability and variation which seeks to: praise, celebrate and recognise success; identify system problems that prevent the employees from doing their best work; and provide the employees with the skills, knowledge, power and ability to further assist the company reach its goals.

179

Poor practices

- Rework is thought normal.

6.3 Data presentation shows variation

The method you choose to present data and information can help understand the variation in that data and help you understand your processes. Tabulated data is useless in showing variation and providing an understanding of what is happening. This also applies to all financial presentations.

Bar charts have little value and three-dimensional bar charts should be banned as they mask the variation. Wherever possible, the use of *control charts* is strongly recommended. These are described in section 6.4.

Financial variance and month-to-month comparisons

When talking about variation, this does not mean financial variance—the difference between actual and budgeted expenses and revenue. The terms 'variation' and 'financial variance' are quite different.

The common reporting procedures about financial variance contribute nothing to the understanding of the causes of variation and so contribute nothing to the control of the processes that cause it. The common practice of month-to-month comparisons of financial variance can be destructive of good business outcomes. They do not contribute to understanding the causes of variation, but cause the focus to be on minimising the variance (so that you do not have to report) and unnecessary knee-jerk reactions and unnecessary work to explain non-issues, and do not recognise the existence of variation. They are the equivalent of asking, 'What caused that particular wobble?' in the wobbling pen example.

Many people in companies (including executives and managers) point to last month's results (which is finally better than the trend or average) and say 'see, it is improving!'. This is very bad management. It is used to fend off criticism and prevent any serious attempt at systematic improvement. It will only stop when the CEO and other executives refuse to accept the excuse.

Month-to-month comparisons and financial variance are *bad measurements*. They should be replaced with reporting tools such as run or control charts.

Are these numbers different?

Are the numbers 111 and 112 different from each other? This type of question is at the heart of all discussion about variation.

Some would argue that 'Of course, they are different. How could they not be different? It is a stupid question! If they were the same, there would be no need for different numbers'.

To some extent the answer to the question 'are the numbers different?' depends on whether or not you want them to be. In some of the examples that follow, you may be saying, 'of course they are different'. In others, you may be saying, 'of course they are the same'.

The answer also depends on the scale. Scale tells you something about the size of the difference. What if they are 111 kilometres and 112 kilometres and you are walking. What if they are $1.11 and $1.12? Not a big difference if it was the price of your lunch. But what if that was the unit price and you had to buy 100 000 of them? What if they are $1.11 billion and $1.12 billion (a difference of $10 million) and it is your budget overrun? What if they are estimates of the distance to a star that is either 111 or 112 light years away? What if 111 seconds is the time of the first place winner in an Olympic event and 112 seconds is the time for the person who came last? What if they are the diameter of a part and 111 mm is the specifications and 112 is not?

What if it was 199 and 200? Is $199 different from $200? Retailers know the numbers are the same but our mind tells us $200 is much more. Is 84.9 cents per litre different from 85 cents per litre?

What about 6 and 7? And they are earthquake readings on the Richter scale! Now they represent very different indications of survival and the extent of the disaster.

These are not stupid questions. You have to make these judgment calls all the time. The trouble is that without the right tools, your response remains just that—a judgment call, gut feelings.

A difference is a difference only if it makes a difference

What you are really asking is 'are these numbers so different that I care?'. This means that there is some point beyond which you care about the difference between two numbers. A point beyond which you want to know because you care. Let's call that 'the caring point' (Fig. 6.3).

Another way of thinking about this is that as far as you are concerned, all the numbers close to one number are really the same as that number. It would be good to find that 'caring point'. One way to find the 'caring point' is to ask 'what if' questions, like above.

If the numbers are different and you say they are different, or if the numbers are the same and you say they are the same, everything is all right. There is no problem.

But what if you make a mistake? Do you care? If you fail to identify that the numbers are different, and you care, you have a problem. Remember that you only care when the numbers are different enough that it makes a difference to you. You may have failed to identify a problem that could cost you a great deal of money.

Fig. 6.3 The caring point

What if you made the other mistake and said the numbers are different when they are, in fact, the same? Usually when people care about something, they act. In this case, you thought you had to act, when in fact you did not have to do anything. A wasted effort—that can cost you a great deal of time and resources. Figure 6.4 is a decision matrix that shows the results of your decision—especially the errors. You need to prevent these two types of errors. To do that you must be much more certain about the 'caring point' than just 'gut feeling'.

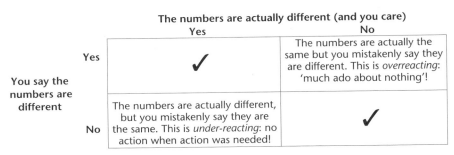

Fig. 6.4 The decision matrix

I care because my boss makes me care

An answer that 'I care because my boss makes me care' is *not* a good one. Bosses who make you care about things that you do not need to care about are being wasteful—of your time and resources, and the company's time and resources.

Shareholders should be wary about CEOs and senior executives who waste resources by fighting unnecessary fires and cannot find the real fires to fight. If the CEO and senior executives do not know how to find the 'caring point', they are probably wasting money chasing smoke or failing to act when they should be—overreacting and under-reacting.

Good practices

- The concepts of variation and trends are used to assist decisions based on measuring and monitoring of processes.
- A comprehensive set of essential measurements is built into the production process to ensure minimum variation and consistently high-quality products and services.

Poor practices

- Use of bar charts and three-dimensional bar charts to present data (these mask variation).
- Extensive use of tables to display data. Data displayed as masses of figures.
- Seeing trends where there are no trends; missing trends where there are trends.

6.4 Use control charts

To proceed further, you need to get into more detail about the numbers. Unfortunately, no-one can tell if 111 and 112 are different without more information.

- Firstly, you need to determine the *caring point*: this can be a specification, a break-even point, an answer to an important 'what if' question.
- Secondly, you need to know the *scale*: dollars or cents or millions of dollars; metres or millimetres or kilometres or light years; seconds or thousands of a second or hours.
- Thirdly, you need to know the *accuracy*: this becomes the critical issue.

You can never measure anything exactly

All measurements, whether of time or distance, can only be within a certain degree of accuracy. Everything you measure or count is only an approximation.

The accountants among you all cry 'not true, our accounting is dead accurate'. Think about that for a little longer. It usually does not take long to think of examples where the dollars are only approximate. Is there any foreign exchange in the calculations? The exchange rate is never exact. Is there any variable borrowing rate? Do you know *exactly* how much remains to be repaid? Do you and the lender agree, *exactly*? Do you have any shareholdings in other companies?

Do you know *exactly* what they are worth? How much did you make today on your shareholdings? *Exactly?* That is, to the cent not to the nearest thousand dollars. (Usually, the caring point is set a little way out so that 'exact' accuracy is not required as long as everything balances.)

Often companies (even quite small ones) do not even know exactly how many staff they have. How do you count Mrs Smith who works Tuesdays and Thursdays from 9.30 a.m. to 4 p.m.? What about Mrs Jones who shares work with Mrs Smith and works Wednesdays and Fridays? Is that one employee or two?

> **A fine point**
>
> In *Popper*, Bryan Magee discussed how if you order a piece of steel 6 millimetres long, you can have it made accurately to within the finest margin of which the best instruments are capable—millionths of a millimetre. But where the exact point of 6 millimetres lies within that tiny margin is something you do not know. It may be that your piece of steel is exactly 6 millimetres long, but you will not know it. All you know is that the length is accurate to within such and such a fraction of a millimetre. With the next improvement in measuring tools, an even smaller margin would be possible so your piece of steel would be closer to 6 millimetres. But you will never get one exactly 6 millimetres except by chance. And you can never know when you do.

Do they come from different populations?

Consider the following two sets of 30 data that each contain 111 and 112.

Example 1

111.0	111.1	111.5	111.2
111.0	111.2	**112.0**	111.4
111.3	111.4	111.3	111.5
111.3	111.1	111.2	111.4
111.2	111.2	111.4	111.2
111.3	111.3	111.1	**111.0**
111.3	111.2	111.2	111.5
	111.0	111.1	

Example 2

111.0	112.4	112.9	111.6
112.0	111.8	112.9	111.6
111.7	112.7	111.7	112.3
111.0	111.5	111.8	112.9
112.9	112.6	111.3	112.4
111.3	111.9	111.9	111.4
111.6	111.8	**111.0**	111.7
	112.6	111.7	

You probably cannot tell very much from these data sets so let's draw graphs. In this analysis, you need to know the 'average' and the 'standard deviation'. The graph should show the average and three standard deviations above the average and three standard deviations below the average (Fig. 6.5). (A good spreadsheet package will let you do this elementary calculation.)

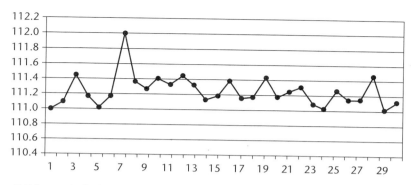

Fig. 6.5 Example 1: 112 is different

Out of control

Your question is, 'Does the number 112 belong to the same set of numbers as 111?'. In other words, 'Does it belong to the same population?'.

In Example 1, the answer is 'no'. Because 112 is more than three standard deviations away from the average of the points (see Fig. 6.5), 112 is beyond the caring point.

Three standard deviations are used because the probability of saying that 112 is different from 111 when they are really the same has fallen to 1%; that is, one chance in 100 of making that error.

This graph is an example of a simple control chart, which shows that 112 is 'out of control'. That is, it does not belong to the same data set as the other points.

In terms of Principle 4 ('To improve the outcome, improve the system'), think of your data points as having been generated from a process. The process that gave the value 112 was not the same as the process that gave the other 29 points. This is a very important finding. You now know that 112 really is different. It is significantly different. The reasons for the difference might be worth exploring.

To use this simple tool, you need at least 30 numbers that come from the set of numbers that you think are all the same. When you are calculating your estimate of the average and standard deviation, leave out the number(s) that you think are different. If the numbers are themselves averages (i.e. if 111 is actually the average of a few numbers), then you have a more robust tool.

Control chart rules

If these points are all measurements from a process, your process is 'out of control' when the control chart is divided into zones, as shown in Figure 6.6, and any of the following is true. Each zone is one standard deviation wide.

185

- One or more points fall outside the control limits (i.e. three standard deviations away from the average).
- Two points, out of three consecutive points, are on the same side of the average in zone A or beyond.
- Four points, out of five consecutive points, are on the same side of the average in zone B or beyond.
- Nine consecutive points are on the same side of the average.

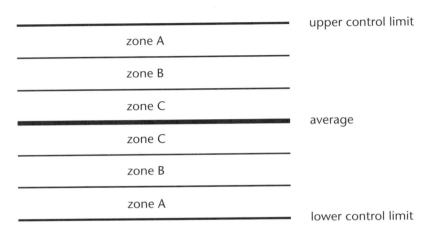

Fig. 6.6 Control chart zones

In control

In example 2, 112 is the same as 111 because all the points are within the three standard deviations (Fig. 6.7). When systems are 'in control', they do not react to the up and down fluctuations.

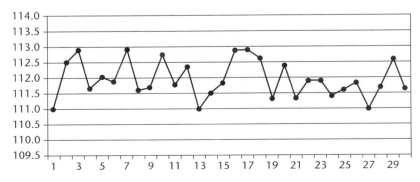

Fig. 6.7 Example 2: 112 is the same as 111

186

Good practices

- KPIs are presented using control charts that demonstrate an understanding of variation.
- Extensive use of control charts—which are understandable—to present and help understand data.

Poor practices

- Two data points used to indicate a trend.
- Using 'financial variance' as an indicator of variation.
- Month-to-month or year-to-year comparisons.

6.5 Reduce special cause variation

The first step in bringing your processes in control is to reduce or eliminate special causes of variation. Section 6.3 describes how to identify which 'wobbles' are special. The 'normal' wobble is due to the common causes of the system (e.g. an unsupported arm). A special cause was the push.

Faults inherent in the system are called 'common causes' of trouble. Faults from fleeting events are called 'special causes'. In *Out of the Crisis*, Deming estimated that 94% of problems are from common causes and belong to the system (and so are the responsibility of management—Principle 4, 'To improve the outcome, improve the system') and only 6% are due to special causes. People often make the mistake of assuming that every event (defect, mistake, accident) is attributable to someone (usually the nearest at hand) or is related to some special event. This is very rarely the case.

| | | Variation is due to: | |
		Special cause	Common cause
Assign blame to:	People and events	✓	The very common mistake of blaming people when the system fails (and is management's problem to fix).
	The system	The much rarer mistake of trying to find a system problem when the problem is not in the system.	✓

Fig. 6.8 The common and special causes of variation

187

Examples of special causes include:

- the push given in the wobbling pen example in section 6.2
- an employee is absent because he or she has been hit by a bus or has an ill child.

Special causes due to people are extremely rare.

Don't blame people, fix the system

Forget blaming any person. The problem is much more likely to be in your systems and you should look there first. Find what is causing the problem. Unfortunately, this approach is still very unusual. It is much easier to say 'we found the problem, sir, and he (or she) has been moved on. It won't happen again'. However, it is extremely unlikely that the person is a 'special cause' and so removing him or her is not the solution. It is much more likely that this is a 'common cause' issue and, unless you work on the common cause (be it hiring policy, inadequate training, inadequate knowledge to do the job, processes that cannot work), the problem will happen again. In a few months time you will be moving the next poor sap on.

Train derailment

In 1998 in Sydney, a train tipped over when its driver failed to slow at several warning signals and went into a corner too fast. The driver was injured. No-one else was on board the train. There was a public outcry and howls for the driver to be dismissed and castigated as 'a dangerous person who should never again drive a train' (i.e. the driver was a special cause). The employer took a very unusual position, which was, 'We learned a lot from this accident. We had put too much pressure on the driver by making him work alone. In those conditions, he could not actually see the warning signals because he was busy with other demands. This was clearly very dangerous. We have now changed the warning signals so they appear in the driver's cabin and are audible—not only visual. We have changed the staffing numbers so that the work is now possible to do'. In other words, the employer took the very unusual position of recognising the 'common cause' and fixing the system problems.

Good practices

- Special cause variation is identified.
- Working to make processes more stable by reducing special cause variation.

188

Poor practices

- No evidence that the concept of variation is understood (e.g. unthinking reactions to single points of data). Chasing one-off events.
- Deterministic models used to make decisions.
- Expecting 'averages' to be 'actual' performance.

6.6 Reduce common cause variation

When you reduce common cause variation, you reduce your major source of variation. You make your products and services more consistent. In other words, you deliver a more consistent product/service to your customers, who will be more satisfied because your products/services are more reliable.

Your costs go down because you have less rework. Your customers' costs go down because they have less work to do to make your products/services useable.

Your company is more capable of delivering what it said it would deliver. And you will be more able to tell if you are achieving your objectives. (With high levels of variation, you can do neither, even if you wanted to.)

The major improvement of all systems involves systematic reduction of common cause variation. No other path can succeed. To make your processes more capable, reduce your common cause variation.

Range and difference from target

When the output of any system is measured, it shows variation around an average result. We are interested in two components:

1. the difference between the average measurement and the target value
2. the 'range' in the measurements.

Improvement

What can you do to improve, to reduce the variation? You can try to reduce the 'range' in the measurements as well as move the system average closer to the target (i.e. reducing the 'difference between the average and the target'). In other words, you can make the system more 'stable' by making it more 'consistent', and then make it more 'capable' by moving it closer to your target.

Improving a process follows the path shown in Figure 6.9.

- Firstly, achieve stability (statistical control—this was dealt with in the previous section) by eliminating the *special causes of variation*—reduce the 'range'.
- Then improve the capability by working to reduce the *common causes of variation*—move the system average closer to the target.

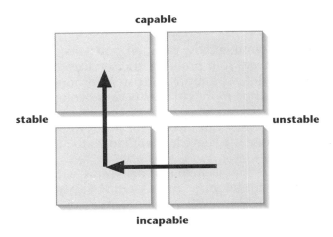

capable

stable **unstable**

incapable

Fig. 6.9 Making the process stable and then capable

Making systems more capable

You can only change common cause variation if you change the system—Principle 4 ('To improve the outcome, improve the system') again.

If there is a gap between the system average and the target, the only option is to move the system average towards the target or to change the target. Changing the target may be an option when it is technologically impossible to reach the target.

Improvement should proceed by first identifying processes and activities that contribute most of the significant variation. These are the 'low hanging fruit' and offer good opportunity for pre-emptive control design. Errors in early stages are amplified later. Therefore, the earlier you can intervene in the system the better. For example:

- We recruited 10 trainee managers five years ago. We didn't pay too much attention to our selection criteria at the time. Unfortunately, none of the 10 has proved to be up to our requirements and we have let them all leave. We are now very short on good management talent for our expansion.

How will you know that you have improved?

You have your process producing results that move nicely between the control limits of your control chart—all stable—and now you want to improve the process. You now want better results. How will you know that the process has improved? Answering that is an extremely difficult question.

Let us assume you want a 10% improvement. For example, your process produces 100 units per day and you now want to make 110 units per day. Let us also assume that you are not willing to be wrong more than 0.5% of the time (i.e. you want to be 99.5% confident that when you say the average has moved from 100 to 110, it actually has moved). (This is a very high degree of accuracy. When you use control charts that use three standard deviations for the control limits, this is the degree of accuracy you have chosen.)

The standard deviation of your process must be less than 3.33% of the process average for you to detect a change of 10% in the average. Or, around the other way, if the standard deviation of your process is more than 3.33% of the process average, you cannot pick up a change of 10% in the average. In our example with the process average at 100 units per day, if the standard deviation is 4 units, you cannot tell if the process average shifts to 110 units per day (100 + 3 x 4 > 110, so 100 and 110 are indistinguishably the same number even though you would like them not to be the same).

This shows another very good reason to reduce the variation of your process. A smaller variation will allow you to detect a change in the process average more quickly.

There is nothing magical about three standard deviations being used as control limits in control charts. It is just a convention. Its implied level of confidence (99.5%) can be a bit restrictive. What if you decide that you can tolerate a lower level of confidence? For example, 2.75 standard deviations would give 99% confidence (i.e. you are willing to make an error 1% of the time); 2.5 standard deviations would give 98% confidence (i.e. you are willing to make an error 2% of the time); two standard deviations would give 95% confidence (i.e. you are willing to make an error 5% of the time). (Statisticians often use 95% confidence levels. This comes from the early days of statistical research when the grandfather of statistics, R. A. Fisher, was researching agricultural products to determine if one product was better than another. He had 20 plots of land and decided that if one of the 20 was different, it was significant—1 in 20 or 5%.)

Table 6.1 shows the minimum percentage change that can be detected in the average with a variety of error tolerances and a variety of standard deviations.

Table 6.1 The minimum percentage change detectable in the average

Standard deviation (SD) as a percentage of the average	Change detectable by control limit width (tolerance for error)			
	3 SD (0.5%)	2.75 SD (1%)	2.5 SD (2%)	2 SD (5%)
1%	3%	2.75%	2.5%	2%
2%	6%	5.5%	5%	4%
3%	9%	8.25%	7.5%	6%
4%	12%	11%	10%	8%
5%	15%	13.75%	12.5%	10%
6%	18%	16.5%	15%	12%
7%	21%	19.25%	17.5%	14%
8%	24%	22%	**20%**	16%
9%	27%	24.75%	22.5%	18%
10%	30%	27.5%	25%	20%

For example, if the standard deviation is 8% of the average (in our example, 8 units per day compared with an average of 100 units per day) and you are comfortable with a 2% probability of error, then the smallest change in the average that you can detect is 20%. That is, you would have to be making more than 120 units per day before you would know there had been a change.

Thus, you need quite a big difference before you would find it. The good news is that the control charts do all the mathematics for you. You just plug in the numbers and the control chart tells you if a change has occurred.

Can we ask this question the other way around? How small must the standard deviation be for us to be able to detect a 10% change in the process average? Table 6.2 shows this.

Table 6.2 The minimum size of the standard deviation required to show a 10% change

Control limit width (tolerance for error)		Minimum standard deviation (SD)
3 SD	(0.5%)	3.33%
2.75 SD	(1%)	3.6%
2.5 SD	(2%)	4%
2 SD	(5%)	5%

For example, if you want to be able detect a 10% change in the average and you are comfortable with a 2% probability of error, then the standard deviation cannot be more than 4% of the average (in our example, 4 units per day compared with an average of 100 units per day).

In other words, you would need to have your processes well under control with very minimal variation before you can tell if those processes have changed.

(The other assumption made in these tables is that you have measured at least 30 points in your process.)

Everyone here is above average

People forget the simple message of the average. In a team of 20 people, no matter what, half (10) will be above average and half (10) will be below average. Two will be in the bottom 10%, and two will be in the top 10%. That is a law of nature—like gravity. If you chase, hassle or fire those who are below average, the bottom 10%, you are just fighting gravity. Another half will take their place and you will just have another 10 who are below average. 'Yes, but', you cry, 'I have raised the average by firing the bottom half and hiring better'. Maybe.

Unfortunately, because all systems dictate the ability of people to perform in them, you will probably never know who your really good and really bad performers are. Even your really top performers may need the support of people who may not be so visible. When you fire the support person (because they look to be below average), you may significantly weaken the star's ability to perform.

In *Out of The Crisis*, Deming reminded us about understanding the meaning of 'average'. Consider the nonsense of these statements:

- Everyone should come up to the average.
- Everybody in our company is above average.
- We have three distributors. One is below average and must go.
- Half our employees earn less than the average (of course they do!).
- Half the students at this school are below average (of course they are!).
- An education system puts children of age 15 through examinations and by design passes 50%. Job advertisements read 'School Certificate required'. The system of grading has generated half as unemployable.
- To solve this, the examination system is changed so that 80% now pass. Unemployment is solved. Now students can pass who have not achieved even minimum levels of competence. The School Certificate now has no credibility with employers who declare 'school leavers do not have the basic skills we want'.

Other examples include:

- My doctor's surgery is very busy. I am always reluctant to go because the doctor is always at least 1 hour late and it can be as long as 2 hours. I wouldn't mind so much if she was consistent. I could simply turn up late knowing that I only have to wait for a short time. It would be even better if she was on time.

- We are always in trouble with our budget performance. Every month we are way off the forecast, sometimes high and sometimes low. Our typical monthly performance is + or – 50%. As the year goes on, we seem to get further and further away from the expected year to date forecast. Over the last five years, we've been consistently more than 20% above our annual budget.

Good practices

- Common cause variation is identified.
- Working to make processes more capable by reducing common cause variation.
- Control charts used to determine if change has occurred.

Poor practices

- Only one or two indicators to indicate quality of product or service supplied (e.g. 'in full and on time').
- The only measure of success is results of surveys that have been averaged together (e.g. '75% of our customers report they are satisfied or very satisfied').

6.7 Reduce variation to reduce costs

Is there any benefit in getting your processes to the point where they are capable of consistently producing products (or services) better than what your customer specifies? Yes, there is. To understand this, you must consider the 'cost of quality' issue.

In the old thinking, the only importance of variation was the need to *force* the product to comply with its specifications. 'Cost of quality' was thought to be the aggregation of *all costs required to meet the specification*. It was assumed that there were no cost advantages, only additional costs, in having the product consistently better than the specification. The location of the midpoint of the range within the specification was incidental—'So long as you are within specification, it is okay'.

Taguchi, a Japanese statistician, developed an alternative approach to evaluating the cost of quality. Taguchi proposed that *all variation from the ideal result causes additional cost* at some point in time—to your company, to your direct customers, to your end-users, to the community. He proposed that *all* variation impacts on your costs and performance.

He also found that costs increase in proportion to the *square* of the deviation from the ideal result. This finding indicates that you should work aggressively to minimise your variation, even when you are well within specification.

Taguchi's finding means that there are competitive and cost advantages in reducing the spread of variation to be well within your customers' specifications. When you do, you reduce your costs, your customers' costs or both. When you reduce you customers' costs, you have a competitive advantage. Working aggressively to reduce variation in output gives a real win–win situation.

Reduction in variation was essentially the strategy that saw Japanese manufacturers gain such a considerable market share during the 1980s. At that time, American manufacturers were still supplying equipment that had a much higher failure rate than their customers wanted. The Japanese manufacturers recognised that customers really wanted a lower failure rate and worked aggressively to reduce their failure rate. The competitive use of tools such as 'Statistical Process Control' and 'Six Sigma' grew out of that strategy.

Measuring your cost of quality

Measuring your cost of quality is extremely useful. Most companies measure what they have put in place to catch poor quality—audits, quality assurance, inspection, standardisation. Important as this is, it is only part of the true cost. It fails to recognise Taguchi's equation. As well as those traditional measurements—which should be going down—you must add the cost of:

- your rework (in most companies, this is huge)
- having your customers annoyed because what you delivered took them five telephone calls to get fixed
- being stuck fixing old problems to your future income
- lost production when your system bottlenecks work on faulty material
- employing people just to fix things that should have worked in the first place (this is often a huge proportion of your support staff)
- having 'sales' staff work on solving customer problems (when they are fixing problems with old customers, they are not bringing in new ones)
- warranty pay outs
- 'money-back' guarantees to customers
- returned goods
- damages, claims and liability insurance
- your complaints department and public relations department
- lost sales due to perceived unreliability
- overtime due to production fluctuations

- scrapped parts and finished goods.

All these costs are incurred when you do not have consistent, reliable products and services. These costs should all be going down.

We don't need to be consistent

Service companies often say that 'This is manufacturing stuff. It does not apply to us. We are a service company'. Wrong! Much of the work done each day by support staff in service companies is rework—fixing problems for the second, third or tenth time that should have been done right to start with.

Examples of rework in the service sector include:

- Invoices with errors—never!
- Trains running on time—always!
- The doctor (dentist, lawyer, physiotherapist, accountant) seeing you at *exactly* the appointed time—always!
- Enrolments at college or university completed without error. Results distributed without error. Consistency in marking.
- A library can always find the books on its shelves. Interlibrary loans work without error.
- A bank never makes an error in a transaction or on your statement. There is no queue at the teller.
- At the fast-food counter, there is no queue. It takes 30 seconds to give your order and 2 minutes to get it. Your change is always correct.

Even if you think the direct service part of your business is already consistent, there will probably be problems in administration and support.

Good practices

- Reducing variation is seen as a direct way to reduce costs.
- Working to obtain consistent products and services.
- Cost of quality is reducing as confirmed by measurement.

Poor practices

- Reducing variation is seen as a waste of time.
- Working to reduce variation is seen as adding costs.
- 'We don't need to be consistent' attitude.

6.8 Measure consistency

How do you *know* that you provide products and services at consistent quality to your customers? How do you measure what you provide? An answer of 'we ask our customers if they are satisfied' is the wrong answer. You must measure your processes that make a difference to your customers *before* they get to your customers.

For example, most customers have a need for timeliness. You must constantly measure your response time. Even if your customer has never set a formal time, you must measure your response time and be constantly reducing it—identifying common cause variations and eliminating them one by one.

Customers also usually have need for accuracy. Measure your accuracy (or lack of it) with invoices and all transactions.

If you were a manufacturer of cement, your customers would have set specifications about the lime and silica content for different usages. These specifications are usually described in a 'standard'. You would have to monitor your processes to ensure you stayed within those specification limits. That is, you must *measure* to make certain that you can produce within the customer's specifications every time. In terms of our discussion from Principle 4 ('To improve the outcome, improve the system'), you *measure* to make certain that your process is capable of delivering within these specification limits.

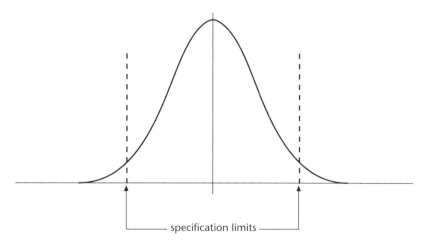

Fig. 6.10 Setting specification limits

Six sigma

As you work to reduce your rework, you have to work more and more to reduce the errors that are not detectable by eye. However, the methods you use to trap errors by eye break down when you have many transactions.

Six sigma is a methodology pioneered by Motorola. It is very useful for reducing the range of variation. Six sigma forces you to look at the different orders of magnitude that are necessary at each stage when reducing variation. Here are two examples.

Most of our systems work at the easy-to-do level. At these levels, you can use methods such as proofreading to find typing errors. The six sigma methodology approaches it like this. If you have one typing error in every six words, that is one sigma. It would be easy to find. Two sigma is an error every four lines—also easy to find. Three sigma is a typing error about every two pages—becoming more difficult. Four sigma is a typing error every 70 pages. Five sigma is a typing error every 20 books— a shelf full! Six sigma is a typing error every 5500 books—a library! Most of our systems work to find errors that occur as often as three sigma—a typing error every two pages. However, we cannot use the same methods when our errors are so infrequent as a typing error per library of books and we want to find and remove them. Who would care anyway?

Airline passengers do care when the errors are lost luggage rather than typing errors. Three sigma is one piece of luggage lost every two 747-sized aircraft. Four sigma is one piece of luggage lost every 90 aircraft (i.e. half a morning at Los Angeles airport). Five sigma is one piece of luggage lost every 10 000 aircraft. Six sigma is one piece of luggage lost every three million aircraft. Judging by the frequent use of lost luggage facilities, luggage handling systems work at about three or four sigma. Misplaced (rather than lost forever) luggage probably operates at one or two sigma.

It is clear from these examples that the solutions we use at one sigma level will not work at the next. Suppose we decide to reduce typing errors or lost luggage to the six sigma level. How would we go about it? Nothing we know about trapping or eliminating errors at our current level would help us at the next level down. How do we shift our thinking to the next level? Why would we want to?

Consider the banks. How many transactions a day does a big bank handle? Despite the huge transaction volume, most banks still operate at levels of two to three sigma—error trapping is done by eye. It is based on the old paper systems of 100 years ago. What is the risk to them of these errors? How much do they spend on error trapping and rework at this sigma level? What cost saving would they make if they could eliminate all that error trapping and move to the next level of sigma? Four sigma is an error every 31 000 transactions. Given the volumes of transactions involved, four sigma does not even sound extraordinary. It would be only an error every hour in most very large banks. However, it would need a huge change of thinking to even get to that level.

'Sigma' is based on the sigma symbol used by statisticians to represent 'variance' when they describe the normal distribution. The exact values are shown in Table 6.3.

Table 6.3 Sigma values

Σ (sigma)	1 error in:
1	6
2	44
3	741
4	31 574
5	3 488 556
6	1 013 594 863
7	782 010 701 054
8	2 251 799 813 685 250

Good practices

- Working in the levels of five or six sigma.
- The company makes processes easier and simpler to use or with less variation in their output.
- Working to reduce the variation in all major processes, products and services.

Poor practices

- Working at the levels of one, two or three sigma.
- Error checking is done by eye.

6.9 Calculate process capability

The concept of process capability was discussed in detail in Principle 4 ('To improve the outcome, improve the system').

Process capability is formally defined as the degree a process is or is not capable of meeting customer requirements. When variation is consistently in a range, the system is said to be stable. A stable system will provide outputs within a predictable range for long periods, changing only slowly as the elements of its processes deteriorate. Stable systems are predictable.

However, being stable still does not describe goodness or badness of the variation. Your process might be very stable and consistent but it may not be able to meet its targets. It might not be capable. To be capable the system output must be compared to some external reference—usually a specification. Process capability can be calculated mathematically from the variation compared with the specification.

You can represent a stable process by its variation or standard deviation. Process capability, C_p, uses six standard deviations of the process compared with the customer specification:

$$C_P = \frac{\text{upper specification limit} - \text{lower specification limit}}{6\hat{\sigma}}$$

where $\hat{\sigma}$ = your estimate of the standard deviation.

If the $C_P = 1$, the process is just capable of meeting its specifications. If the C_P is less than 1, the process is not capable and is producing rubbish (Fig. 6.11).

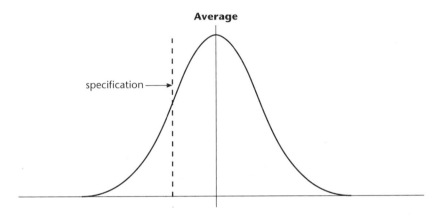

Fig. 6.11 Calculating process capability

Note that the C_P relates only to the spread of the process relative to the specification width. It does not consider how well the process average is centred relative to the target. The process capability index, C_{Pk}, defines when the location of the process average has been taken into account:

$$C_{Pk} = \min\left\{\frac{\text{process average} - \text{lower spec limit}}{3\hat{\sigma}}, \frac{\text{upper spec limit} - \text{process average}}{3\hat{\sigma}}\right\}$$

If the process is close to normally distributed and its variance is stable, the C_{Pk} can be used to estimate the expected percentage of defective material.

Example: ABC Lawyers

ABC Lawyers have entered into an agreement with their major client to always produce their initial advice within 14 days of receipt of instructions. This generous term was included in a tender response and so is a contractual obligation. The target was set by gut feelings, that is, 'we can easily meet a two-week turnaround so let's say 14 days!'.

But over 28 recent delivery times from ABC Lawyers, what are the facts?

Days to deliver by ABC Lawyers

33	22	38	20	9	17	22
16	17	40	6	10	28	22
21	36	25	19	33	17	20
41	11	16	35	17	24	6

The average of this is the sum of all observations divided by 28, which is 22 days. This means that, on average, ABC Lawyers miss the mark by eight days!! But wait, it gets worse.

Using the standard deviation formula in a spreadsheet package gives a standard deviation of 10 days.

If the upper specification limit is set at 14 days (i.e. the agreement with the client) and ABC Lawyers wants to allow damages claims on only one in 100 cases (i.e. 99% confidence level), the C_{Pk} is:

$$C_{Pk} = \left\{ \frac{\text{process average } - \text{ lower specification limit}}{3\hat{\sigma}} \right\}$$

$$= \frac{22 - 14}{3 \times 10}$$

$$= 0.27$$

Because this number is less than one, the process is not capable. ABC Lawyers will not be able to meet their obligations.

What is their risk exposure? To do this, first calculate Z, your estimate of how far, in standard deviation units, you are from the process average.

$$Z = \frac{\text{lower specification limit } - \text{ process average}}{\hat{\sigma}}$$

$$= \frac{14 - 22}{10}$$

$$= -0.80$$

We will assume that the data is normally distributed. We can then determine from statistical tables that with a Z value of –0.80, ABC Lawyers will meet its obligations only 21% of the time.

What if ABC's clients impose financial penalties for failure to meet this commitment? If the profit margin on each of the 28 matters is $1500? Of the 28, only six will be completed on time (i.e. $28 \times 21\%$). This means that 22 (i.e. $28 - 6$) will incur a penalty. If the penalty for each is $300, then the $6600 penalty takes a big chunk out of the expected $42 000 profit (i.e. $28 \times \$1500$). Failing to meet its obligations will also greatly annoy ABC Lawyers' clients. Initial advice is used to prepare for court action. Late advice may mean ABC Lawyers' clients could lose their cases. ABC Lawyers could expect to be sued by some of these customers that received late advice. Only one of the 22 needs to sue for $35 400 to wipe out all the profit.

Obviously, ABC Lawyers will just have to work harder to get the matters finished on time. The thing about process capability is that working harder is not a solution. Of course, you can put in an extra effort and get more done. But an extra effort is, by definition, 'extra'. You cannot sustain it. Process capability describes your 'average' ability to get the work done. As we see here, 79% of the time ABC Lawyers will not meet its obligations.

You frequently hear people say, 'That usually takes us two weeks, but we made a special effort and did it in three days'. The three days is not in the same data set as the two weeks. Different processes produced the numbers.

Taking the contract with the 14-day limit was clearly a mistake. The outcome is a long way short of the expected profit of $42 000.

If you were ABC Lawyers, what should you do? The customer clearly wants the work done in 14 days. If you don't do it, your competitors will. The answer is to fix your processes so that you are capable of doing the work in 14 days. You can do this by measuring and knowing your process capability and working to eliminate: errors in the data, reworking, waiting for information, the causes of strange outliers. Until that happens, this firm should not commit to the 14-day constraint.

Good practices

- A thorough understanding of process capability throughout the company.
- Process capability is calculated for all major processes, products and services.
- People at all levels of the company are comfortable in applying statistical thinking to daily work and decision making.

Poor practices

- No understanding of process capability. No sense of the capability of the systems.
- No training in statistical thinking.
- Expecting all people to be above average.

6.10 Eliminate early errors

All processes are complex networks of interconnected activities. Some activities have clear relationships with other activities, while with others, the relationship is obscure. Most systems are made up of many processes, each with many activities that interact and interrelate in complex ways.

The total variation of the system comprises all of the variation from all its processes. Variation accumulates from activity to activity and from process to process.

The most important intervention points are in the early stages of the system because reducing variation there will reduce variation overall.

Consider this simple system that combines the output from processes A, B and C, which are each a series of activities (Fig. 6.12).

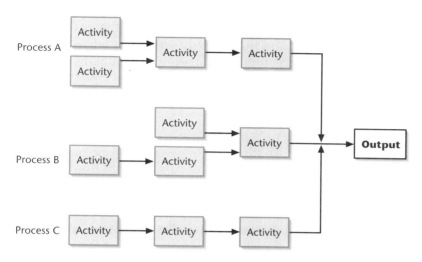

Fig. 6.12 Combining processes

Each activity in this system has variation in what it produces. This variation comes from machines, materials, people, methods, measurements, response times, reactions, moods, weather, supplies and so on.

In each case, the next activity in line receives this variable input, adds its own variation and passes the 'accumulated' variation to the next activity. That is, each activity accumulates variation from itself and all prior activities. Each process accumulates variation from every activity in the process. The whole system accumulates variation from all its processes.

In his book *The Goal*, Goldratt uses three examples to illustrate how the variations accumulate in dependent events in a process.

Scout troop example

The first example is a line of boy scouts walking on a hike. The scouts are analogous of dependent events in a process.

Each boy scout cannot walk the path until the person in front of him has walked it. The first in line must process the trail—to walk it—before the second can set foot on it. The entire troop must walk the trail before it is completed. If one scout is slow, that slowness accumulates. The scouts behind that person bank up and will not be able to complete the task (walked trail) in the required time (specifications). If one scout is consistently slow because of an injury, overweight or too much equipment, that is a common cause of variation for the process. However, other variations will occur as each person occasionally stops or stumbles.

Suppose the scouts are arranged in line from naturally fastest walker to naturally slowest walker. If a scout stumbles, he will not be able to catch up (without running), and the time lost will accumulate behind him. You could reduce the accumulated variation by arranging the line from slowest to fastest. However, such an arrangement may not be practicable.

Statistical fluctuation game

The second example is of a statistical fluctuation game. Arrange five bowls in a line (A, B, C, D, E). You also need a die (one half of a pair of dice) and some matches. The idea is to pass matches from one bowl to the next. You use the die to decide how many matches to pass, but—and this is the sticking point—you can only pass matches if you have them. On average (without that rule), you should be able to move 3.5 matches per cycle or 35 matches in 10 cycles. In practice, you will move far fewer.

- *Cycle 1.* A throws a two and puts two matches in bowl A (down 1.5 from the expected average). B throws a four but can only get two matches from A (so down 1.5 from the expected average). C throws a four but can only get two matches from B (so also down 1.5 from the expected average). D and E throw ones (down 2.5 from the expected average). So we get one instead of our expected 3.5. But don't worry. It will average out.
- *Cycle 2.* A throws a six and puts six matches in bowl A (up 2.5 from the expected average). B also throws a six and moves six matches to bowl B (up 2.5 from the expected average). That's looking better. C throws a three so can only get three matches from B (down 0.5 on the expected average). D throws a four and takes C's three and the one left from cycle 1 (up 0.5 from the expected average). E throws a three and moves three (down 0.5 from the expected average). So at the end of cycle two we have four matches when we should have seven.

Keep going? It just gets worse. You will find that matches move through the system not in a manageable flow, but in waves. This confirms the rule that:

In a linear dependency of two or more variables, the fluctuations down the line will fluctuate around the *maximum* deviation established by any preceding variables.

Dependent operations

Goldratt's third example goes on to show us that the maximum deviation of a preceding operation will become the starting point of a subsequent operation.

An order of 100 products is needed in 5 hours. Two machines are needed to make the product. The first machine passes parts to the second in batches at the end of each hour. The second machine can do a maximum of 25 parts per hour, the first slightly more, so it should be easy. Shouldn't it? The first machine makes 19, 21, 28 and 32 parts respectively in each hour. The second machine can, therefore, only make 19 parts in its first hour and 21 in its second hour because that is all it gets from the other machine. It makes 25 parts for each of the last 2 hours easily enough. However, because of the early backlog, it ends up 10 parts short.

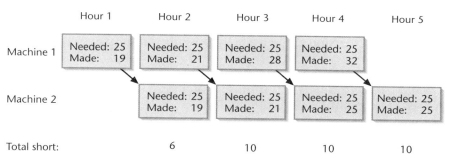

Fig. 6.13 Dependent operations

Insurance office example

What if those were files instead of widgets. What if you worked in an insurance office and your job was to process claims. On average, you can deal with 25 claims an hour. At the end of an 8-hour day, on average, you can process 200 files. Does that mean that the person downstream from you can also process an average of 200 claims a day as well? No, it does not! Many things happen to you during your day: interruptions, meetings, training, lunch, coffee breaks. Many things happen to your files: missing data, time on the telephone checking or confirming, or people are late getting back to you. As a result, in some hours, you get almost no work done but then you make up for it during other hours. Therefore, you complete 1000 claims in a five-day week, or 25 an hour on average. And the people downstream? Well, it's true they do not do anything much in the hour or so following those hours when you are not doing much. But it works out in the end, doesn't it? No, it does not. Everything downstream is impacted by the fluctuations upstream. Everything shows variation and this variation accumulates.

An average of 25 claims an hour might have a distribution of processed claims ranging from zero to 50. What is the cost of that variation? And the cost of its downstream effects? What are the costs of:

- idle time (on the part of those waiting when no files were being handled)?
- extra staff (or overtime) needed to handle the times when the log jam suddenly breaks and 50 files arrive?
- the errors and rework generated when 50 files are handled quickly, all at once?

Errors magnify in complex systems

Because of multiple dependencies between activities at the systems level, the real picture can be very complex. Processes inside real companies are usually not as discrete as the simple process shown so far. In practice, processes A, B and C usually influence each other. In reality, everything is connected to everything else, which is why simplistic solutions do not work.

For example, for the output characteristic 'service courtesy', process A could be 'recruitment and training', process B 'communication' and process C 'recognition'.

We have had several customer complaints about Debbie, who appears to lack courtesy. She appears not to like the job and tends to get upset easily. After we chew her out, she gets better for a few days, but then she slips back to her old ways. She resents being underpaid for what she does. Actually, she wasn't really suitable for the job originally, but she was the only applicant. We had a rush on when she joined, so she missed most of the orientation program. Her supervisor has not been able to do much on-the-job training for her. Her skills at handling angry customers are not good. She gets angry and resentful when they complain. She has been complaining to us that the procedure manuals she has to follow are badly written and do not accurately describe the job she does. Her supervisor does not appear to like her, and she does not like him. He has real problems also. He used to do Debbie's job. We promoted him into a vacancy. He was not an ideal choice and does not understand that he needs to coach and not shout.

Where does the variation in 'courtesy' originate? Can you find a single cause that can be fixed? The old thinking would be to 'fix Debbie'. Every element in this system is contributing to variation in 'courtesy'.

The activities and processes relate in complex ways and the amount of variation increases as we move through the activity/process sequence and with time. And as we saw from Goldratt's work, they accumulate at the rate of the maximum deviation—not the minimum. Which begins to explain why Murphy's law works so well.

Do you see the strong links back to Principle 4 ('To improve the outcome, improve the system')?

Good practices

- An understanding of how statistical fluctuation affects downstream processes.
- An understanding of how parts of the system affect each other.
- Identifying and fixing upstream causes of problems.

Poor practices

- No understanding that errors accumulate.

SUMMARY

- Variation can lead us to react inappropriately to random events, which uses time and energy unnecessarily and can make the situation worse.
- Errors accumulate and multiply from one step to the next. In complex processes, errors accumulate from many different sources. This means that the final product can (and will) have errors from many different sources.
- Variation means rework and rework is a waste of time, energy and resources.
- Most managers think that variation is abnormal and must be controlled. Traditional month-to-month management reporting, such as exception reports, budget variances and month-to-month comparisons, is typical of this old thinking. Staff are often asked to explain what has happened, especially when the variance is unfavourable.
- Month-to-month comparisons and financial variance are bad measurements. They should be replaced with reporting tools such as run or control charts.
- Faults inherent in the system are called 'common causes' of variation. Faults from fleeting events are called 'special causes'. Deming estimated that 94% of problems are from common causes and belong to the system and that only 6% are due to special causes. People often make the mistake of assuming that every event (defect, mistake, accident) is attributable to someone (usually the nearest at hand) or is related to some special event, which is very rarely the case.
- When you reduce common cause variation, you reduce your major source of variation and make your products and services more consistent. You deliver a more consistent product/service to your customers, who will be more satisfied because your products/services are more reliable. Your costs also go down because you have less

rework and your customers' costs go down because they have less work to do to make your products/services useable. Your company is more capable of delivering what it said it would deliver.

- The major improvement of all systems involves systematic reduction of common cause variation. No other path can succeed. To make your processes more capable, reduce your common cause variation.

WHAT WOULD YOUR STAKEHOLDERS SAY?

HOW WOULD YOUR EMPLOYEES RATE YOUR COMPANY ON THESE?

- This company understands that all systems and processes produce inconsistent results.
- This company understands that all systems and processes exhibit variability, which affects predictability and performance.
- The CEO and senior executives clearly understand and use Principle 6.
- Our managers never overreact or under-react.
- I understand variation.
- I have been given the skills to allow me to understand variation.
- Our managers clearly understand variation.
- Our managers have been given the skills to allow them to understand variation.
- Data is always presented in such a way as to allow interpretation of the variation.
- We work to make processes more stable by reducing special cause variation.
- We work to make processes more capable by reducing common cause variation.
- We are working to reduce the variation in all our products and services.
- Our managers do not ask 'Why are this month's results different from last month's?'.
- Our managers think variation must be controlled.
- We work to reduce the variation in the early steps of your processes.
- We do not use a deterministic model to make decisions.

HOW WOULD YOUR CUSTOMERS RATE YOUR COMPANY ON THESE?

- This company works to reduce the variation in its products and services.
- This company works to produce its products and services well within my specifications.

HOW WOULD YOUR SHAREHOLDERS RATE YOUR COMPANY ON THESE?

- The CEO and senior executives clearly understand and use Principle 6.
- The CEO and senior executives understand the major causes of variation within the company and are working to reduce them.
- The CEO and senior executives work to reduce the variation in all processes so as to reduce costs.
- When presenting data to us, this company makes extensive use of control charts to show variation.
- This company does not use month-to-month or year-to-year comparisons.

HOW WOULD THE COMMUNITY RATE YOUR COMPANY ON THESE?

- This company understands that the community must eventually pay the cost of quality.
- This company works to reduce the variation in its products and services.

Principle 7
Enthusiastic people

> *The potential of a company is realised through its people's enthusiasm, resourcefulness and participation.*

DR HAUSNER'S FINDINGS are that Principle 7 is in the group of Principles that correlate strongly with improvement in KPIs and business excellence scores. Companies that apply for National Business Excellence Awards already do it well.

Principle 7 forms one point of the major strategic triangle (Fig. 7.1). In order to make money now and in the future (the goal of most companies), you need customers who are so delighted with the value they get from you that they recommend you. You must also have employees who are so enthusiastic about working for the company that

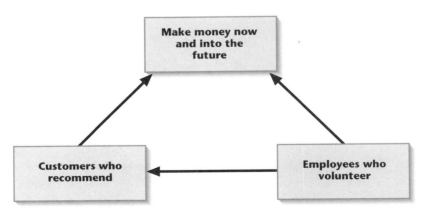

Fig. 7.1 The strategic triangle: the major driving forces. Influence also travels back along the arrows

they volunteer to help you make money by providing value to customers and by improving the company.

This makes the enthusiastic volunteering employee a major driver in the company, which is extremely important! Without the enthusiastic volunteering employee, you do not get customers who recommend you, you do not get a better company and you do not make more money. Which is why many argue that Principle 7 is *the* main driver for company improvement.

7.1 An environment where people volunteer

A company's success depends increasingly on the knowledge, skills, innovative creativity and motivation of its workforce.

Companies are increasingly realising that in competitive, dynamic environments, their people *are* their most important resource. People provide the brain and heart of the company. They provide the intellect for thinking, the emotional capacity for commitment, the enthusiasm to create and the energy for action. Only people can initiate and sustain the relationships that allow the company to function. The employees talk to the customers and work with alliance partners and community groups. The employees get the work done. There are no other resources available to the company to do this.

When people are truly involved, they become committed to what they are involved in. When people become committed, they want to become actively involved. Companies can use this energy to achieve whatever they wish to achieve.

> ### 'Harness' means 'control'
>
> Choose your words carefully. Words can accumulate considerable baggage and, thus, have very different meanings. For example, the word 'harness', as in 'companies can *harness* this energy', has the connotation of a horse being *controlled* by a 'harness'. Usually, when people use this word they might not mean control but they do imply it.

Principle 7 is concerned with:

- creating, maintaining and supporting an environment that enables people to reach their full potential
- aligning people's objectives with the company's objectives.

More than lip service must be paid to the concept that 'people (including their creativity and knowledge) are the company's greatest asset'.

211

- How do you enable your people to grow and contribute?
- How do you free your people to aspire to high ideals?
- How do you generate goodwill within the company?
- How do you develop professional capabilities that are consistently applied?
- How do you enable personal growth and encourage difference?
- How do you enable learning and its exchange?

This is another thinking shift. The old thinking was that employees are inherently lazy and unreliable, and need close supervision in order to achieve the company's goals. The new thinking is in two parts:

1. Almost all employees would like to do good work. They want to bring their hearts and minds to work. They want to volunteer.
2. As we have seen in Principle 4 ('To improve the outcome, improve the system'), the system people work in—its rules, procedures, power structure—usually prevents people from being able to do their best work. When you enable your employees to fix the systems, processes and procedures that prevent them from doing their best work, you get a better company. However, because the employees have the knowledge of what is wrong with the system but not the power to fix it, bosses must work to improve systems—with active, enthusiastic, volunteering help from employees.

Treat employees with respect

To quote the title of his book, Rosenbluth suggests that 'the customer comes second'. Second behind the employees, that is. However, employees will treat your customers in the same way as they are treated by the company. If you want your employees to treat your customers with respect—valuing their needs—then you must first treat your employees with respect—valuing their needs.

Good practices

- Employees are prepared to try new ideas, experiment, innovate and take reasonable risks, to take initiative and be proactive.
- In unusual circumstances, people can confidently take actions that fit the company's needs.
- People work with few rules and can make decisions.
- An attitude of trust from senior executives so that people are trusted to work towards the benefit of the company—'Keep going until I tell you to stop'—and few approvals are necessary.

- A clear process for all employees to contribute to developing company values. (Employees have a tendency to make the values stronger than the managers would.) This is enabled by providing the necessary skills, knowledge, power and 'space' to contribute to the stated values.
- All staff can articulate the values of the company and how they are based on the 10 Business Excellence Principles, and can give examples of how the values are used to drive behaviour (especially by the senior executives).
- People have pride in what the company stands for.
- People delight in telling how things have improved—and their stories demonstrate they are discerning about ethics and innovation.
- A high degree of ownership of the company's image and activities.
- Staff indicate that values are integrated throughout the company.

Poor practices

- No systems to encourage and ensure increased internal responsiveness.
- A culture of blaming people when things go wrong—scapegoats. (This significantly discourages risk taking and innovation.)
- Blaming people when innovations do not work.
- A culture that equates working long hours as a demonstration of real commitment to the company.
- Staff do not take initiative to find out how to solve problems—difficulties are simply passed up the hierarchy.
- A culture that uses people up.
- Overuse of overtime.
- People do just enough to get by, arrive just on time, leave on time, contribute minimum effort (grudging compliance).

7.2 Form a partnership with employees

You should form an alliance partnership with your employees—each party working for the benefit of the other.

A partnership relationship is very different from the traditional adversarial relationship between employees (and their unions) and managers. Do employees in adversarial relationships with a company still volunteer enthusiastically to do what is best for that company?

Like it or not, employees and management should be in a partnership to do the best for the company. If either party thinks otherwise and works against the other or against the company, there might not be a company to work for in the future.

Employees are your major suppliers

If you like, you can be very hard-nosed about this. You can consider your employees as suppliers. Employees supply their time, energy, knowledge and experience so that the company can make money.

Just as for all of your other suppliers, you should establish partner relationships with your *employees* to ensure that the quality and level of what is supplied is satisfactory to the company. This means that you have the same types of partnership obligations to your employees as you have with your external suppliers. In the case of employees, the supplier is part of your company.

Taking the position that the company and its employees are in a supplier partnership establishes that there are considerable obligations for both partners, as there are in all partnerships:

- on its part, the company must show it cares about its people
- the employees' obligation in the partnership is to volunteer their enthusiasm and resourcefulness.

The most important resource is people—their creativity and knowledge

Before going any further down the path of how to turn your employees into enthusiastic volunteers, let us look at how it is in the company's best interest.

In the mechanistic, industrial world, people were treated as redundant, interchangeable and disposable parts. In that world, the boss needed robots that could do repetitive tasks without thought. But the world has changed due to changes in technology. Now, the workplace is so complex that we cannot have the boss making all the decisions.

From a purely practical viewpoint, the boss cannot be everywhere or involved in all decisions. The boss would be an unnecessary bottleneck if all decisions had to go to him or her. And, as we saw in Principle 4 ('To improve the outcome, improve the system'), the boss does not know as much as the staff about what is going on, and as a result, his or her decisions are not always good ones. Companies find that they must spread the decision-making load.

In order to have this happen effectively, people must be trained and educated to be multiskilled and allowed to be flexible so that they can be involved in the management of their work areas.

You can certainly tell the difference between a world-class manufacturing plant and a traditional company. In the world-class plant, much more authority and responsibility is given to the shopfloor operators and supervisors: for the quality of their own work, for scheduling the production cells, for team composition, for hiring and firing, and for customer satisfaction levels.

We shall see in Principle 8 ('Innovation') that some companies are attempting to define in dollar terms the value of employees' knowledge, resourcefulness and creativity and how this translates directly into earnings. This is radically different to thinking of people as just a cost in the financial reports—interchangeable and disposable.

Knowledge and learning

In Principle 8 ('Innovation') we will see the importance of knowledge and learning. The capacity for a company to increase its intellectual capability represents the *new capital* for companies to sustain themselves successfully in this era of sophisticated information systems.

People are the source of that learning and knowledge. Knowledge only becomes available to the company through the efforts of its people. Education and on-the-job training are essential to increasing intellectual capacity.

For example, Carlzon found that Scandinavian Airline Systems (SAS) had to rely on the knowledge, responsiveness and creativity of its people to solve customer problems: 'We can not rely on rule books and instructions from distant corporate offices. We have to place responsibility for ideas, decisions and actions with the people who are SAS during those 15 seconds'.

Respect each other's knowledge

Employees have a huge wealth of knowledge and learning that they have accumulated through working. That knowledge and learning is usually not available to their companies. Employees may withhold it or not volunteer it. This is because employees are usually not asked to share their knowledge and learning. It is often assumed they know nothing useful. After all, the bosses know everything that is useful. Usually, employees receive no training in how to deliver their knowledge.

In other words, you must develop a situation in which:

• employees are willing to share their knowledge
• you ask (and are willing to listen to) employees to share their knowledge
• you provide employees with skills so that they can share their knowledge.

Of course, managers also have a huge wealth of knowledge. The trouble is that each party, the managers and the employees, deny the validity or usefulness of the other's knowledge.

A useful thinking shift happens when both parties realise that the other has something to offer. When this happens, companies find that the combination of the employees' and the bosses' knowledge can be very valuable.

A conflict resolution model

Partnerships and relationships do not always run smoothly. In all relationships, each party must represent their own interests as well as the interests of the relationship. So when another person begins to act self-interestedly, that is not a fault. It is normal for both parties.

We can assume that both parties want the same objective—in this case, the success of the company. In private companies, this is usually for the company to make money now and into the future. Even the acknowledgment that each party has a common objective can be a breakthrough in conflict resolution.

Each party is usually striving to achieve the objective in their own way. When each does that, he/she often makes assumptions that his/her way is the 'right' (and often the 'only') way to go about it, as well as making assumptions about the other party, his/her motivations and the rights or wrongs of his/her approach.

Goldratt suggests that the way to break the conflict is to challenge those assumptions. In Principle 5 ('Improved decisions'), we presented Goldratt's model to identify the conflict and to break it. Figure 7.2 uses the same terms to describe the conflict in this case.

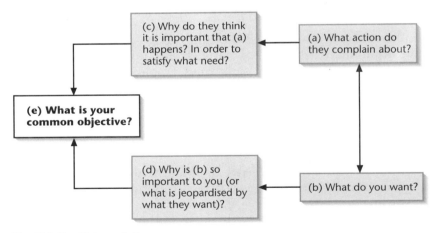

Fig. 7.2 Conflict resolution process

You should read it like this: In order to have (e), they must have (c). On the other hand, in order to have (e), I must have (d). Next, in order to have (c), they must have (a). But in order to have (d), I must have (b). The conflict should be clear. And no compromise is possible between (a) and (b).

Uncover the assumptions. Read the diagram again. This time, add the word 'because' and answer the implied question, as follows: 'in order to have (e), I must have (d) because...?',—do all five arrows, including, '(a) is mutually exclusive to (b) because...?'. The list of things you get when you ask 'because' for each arrow is your assumptions. There is often more than one assumption per arrow. Find as many as you need.

Examine the assumptions. Can you break an arrow by finding something to destroy the assumption? Is there an assumption that is nonsense?

Some useful hints are:

- Concentrate on the arrow with the assumptions that irritate you most.
- Find a solution at the (c) and (d) level; do not argue at the (a) or (b) level.
- For each assumption ask, 'Is there another result?' Keep challenging the implications of the assumptions. You are looking for a thinking shift.

If you can find a different approach for a major assumption, the problem disappears.

Often when you go through this process, the futility of the assumptions that you (or the other person) are making jumps out. Often the assumptions are so ridiculous that you can discard the original conflict and begin to work on the real issues.

Often the bloody-mindedness that you see in employee–management negotiation is because the employees assume that the bosses do not care and the bosses assume that the employees have stopped volunteering.

A major cause of employees withdrawing their enthusiasm, creativity and resourcefulness is due to such conflicts, especially when known dissatisfiers are not addressed or when bosses appear to be acting in their own best interest rather than the best interest of the company.

Downsizing—obligations and dangers

In the partnership agreement, the company's obligations include 'creating and maintaining a safe and secure workplace'.

Remember the necessary conditions from Principle 2 ('Focus on achieving results'). The first necessary condition to achieve your goal is to 'provide a secure and satisfying environment for employees now as well as in the future'. This 'necessary condition' carries considerable responsibility not to lay people off. Goldratt argues in *The Goal* that getting yourself into the position where you must downsize indicates poor strategy and lack of care by the owners/senior managers.

This obligation is being broken more and more with corporate downsizing. It is hypocritical to expect employees to care for a company that demonstrates it does not care about them. How do you expect employees to volunteer their enthusiasm for your company when you demonstrate that you do not care about them and their security? Companies may save $2.50 in wages and salaries but will destroy employee volunteering—is that a good deal? Little wonder that companies now find that downsizing does not work.

Downsizing has been common for the last 20 years. We now know it is unlikely to bring any long-term benefit for three main reasons:

1. Employees stop volunteering their enthusiasm to improve processes (why would employees volunteer their enthusiasm to improve processes when the result of their effort will see them dismissed?).
2. Knowledge and often core competencies are lost.
3. Capability is lost.

Goldratt says the temptations to downsize are enormous. For many companies, changes in their environment force restructuring and downsizing. Most downsizing is a result of major changes in products, services, markets, technology, automation or computerisation. Where there is major misalignment between market reality and workforce numbers or capabilities, survival of the company may demand radical change.

However, ...

- Do not consider lay offs as a parachute because of poor cash flow. This leads to a vicious cycle of lay offs that do not ever seem to improve profits. You must fix the problem that led to the poor cash flow. Most often, the problem is caused by poor throughput because of poor strategy.
- Many companies downsize *before* they undertake to process improvements to make it possible for the smaller workforce to do the work. The result is that products and services can't be delivered and customers don't get what they value. This is almost always followed by a downward spiral of a succession of staff cuts and the eventual destruction of the company.

Shareholders should be very wary about companies that promise they will make more money by downsizing. There is no compatibility between Principle 7 and corporate downsizing.

We have seen a few examples, however, where the employees were extremely enthusiastic about downsizing—both the employees that stayed and those that left. In those very few cases, the companies worked to enable their employees into new enterprises. The picture appeared to be one of caring. The company was seen by everyone to care about the future of people, and was obviously trying to do the right thing by employees in seeing their needs taken care of. This approach is very different from the 'fire them' approach or even the 'redundancy payment' approach.

Good practices

- A strong people focus throughout the company.
- People are involved in the decisions that affect them. Staff surveys show that staff are satisfied with their level of involvement.
- Simple yet comprehensive methods of involving employees in planning and communicating plans.
- A strong commitment by senior executives to maintain staff morale.
- Staff are involved in developing strategic and operational plans.
- Small flat structures locally that enable total involvement in the consideration of strategy and so enable participation in the decisions of the company.
- People are happy to contribute ideas for the company's benefit.

Poor practices

- Bosses think they are customers.
- A culture that implies people are basically 'screw-ups' who just need a good boss to keep them in line.
- Employees are seen as the enemy—them and us.
- 'Leadership' is confined to particular levels of the hierarchy. 'Management' makes all decisions.
- Cultural change is not given strategic importance—it should be the subject of high-level decisions on equal terms with other business strategies.
- Extensive use of downsizing. People are treated as commodities— 'get rid of them, we can always get some more'.

7.3 Give people space to volunteer

You must keep your promises, give your employees space to have their say and show that you care. Companies need enthusiastic, volunteering employees. What can you do to ensure that employees actually do volunteer their enthusiasm and resourcefulness?

Your employees can contribute to helping the company reach its goals and objectives, if you:

- create and maintain an environment in which your employees can do their best work
- enable them to contribute—provide skills, knowledge, resources, power and authority so they can contribute
- actively work to fix systems and processes that prevent people from doing their best work
- show you care.

People need considerable encouragement to continue to volunteer their hearts and minds. In Principle 1 ('Role models'), we saw in Figure 1.4 that people volunteer when:

- they are given space to have their say
- they feel appreciated for who they are
- they have a cause.

Leadership

It is a major part of the job of leadership to keep people in the top right quadrant of Figure 7.3 so that they feel they want to keep volunteering.

When people are not given space to have their say, feel they are not appreciated or do not have a cause, they withdraw to varying degrees. The old thinking of dealing with employees put people into the left-hand side of the matrix and tended to keep them there.

Remember, many of the detached employees who you may see as just coming to work to pick up their pay have very active lives away from your work place. Their 'active lives' are in an environment where they are allowed to volunteer and where they feel appreciated.

As a leader in the new thinking, your job is to keep people in the top right quadrant of the matrix. Keeping them there is a lot easier than getting them back. Depending on how much damage was done during the old thinking, you may have to do a lot of work to encourage people out of their various states of withdrawal.

Even if you are the best boss in the world and walk your talk on this concept very well, you usually have a lot to overcome to keep people in the top right quadrant—experience with previous bosses, broken promises, failed trust, myths about bosses (e.g. the shadows).

Teams

The team approach is an excellent way of encouraging volunteering, creativity and resourcefulness. It delivers because, by their nature, teams begin to break down the old thinking that Principle 7 is trying to address. The team approach is highly recommended. Almost all winners of the National Business Excellence Awards have followed the team path in their approach to Principle 7.

Enthusiasm

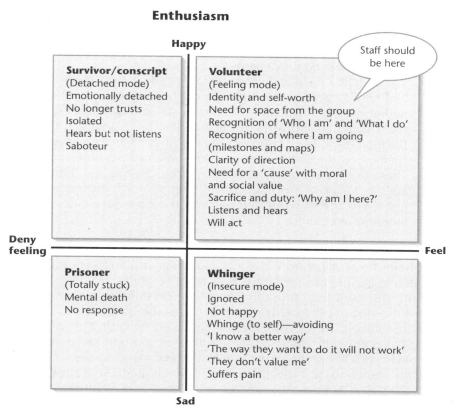

Fig. 7.3 The enthusiasm matrix

Although teams are a very useful way to generate the volunteering, enthusiasm, innovation and resourcefulness that the company wants, teams usually fail. Companies appear to think that the team structure by itself will do all these things. It will, if a complete transfer of authority to the team accompanies the team structure. If an old-fashioned hierarchy still exists (and it usually does), the team will fail. If you try to boss the team, forget it.

- *Give teams a real job to do.* Most team celebration days and team competitions show the huge amount of energy that is generated by the people by the process of being on a team. What is constantly amazing is the smallness of the projects: 'This team of six met eight times and after huge effort and cleverness has saved the company $18 000'. Without trying to offend anyone, who cares? If that much energy was generated, why not work on the real issues for the company and save $18 million or generate $25 million

> in increased revenue, instead of saving just $18 000 and generating a good time. Teams without real jobs to do fail in the long term. Team members see that they have not done anything useful and stop volunteering their energy.
>
> - *You must give the team proper authority to do its work.* Frequently you see so-called self-managed work teams where there is no authority to do anything. All authority still rests with the boss or team leader. Teams without the authority to do anything fail in the long term. Team members see that they cannot do anything useful, become disillusioned and stop volunteering their energy. These failures are difficult to recover from. People feel duped— another failure of trust. Companies often relaunch the team with just a change of name but without the necessary change in authority structure.

A useful definition of a team is 'all the people needed to do the work'. This helps break away from the artificial team structures so often seen when five people are formed into a team to solve problem X. This definition should help those five people understand that they are just one of the steering committees working with the team.

Also, someone in the team already knows the answer. This is true for a team as it exists at any time. Although cynics might say that, when combined with the point above, you just keep expanding the team until you find someone with the answer, in reality, a member of the existing team does already know the answer or knows where to find it.

Alignment

When you have all these people volunteering, you want them working creatively, enthusiastically and with resourcefulness *on things that are important to the company.* Human beings are naturally creative and resourceful. Often when these energies are released, people begin working full time (or part time) for themselves. You need alignment of people's activity. The importance of alignment of focus on achieving company goals and objectives was described in Principle 2 ('Focus on achieving results').

When you are successful at creating space for people to volunteer their enthusiasm, creativity and resourcefulness, it is like starting a stampede. You then have to manage it like a stampede:

- You can set its direction by keeping it within very well-defined boundaries.
- You can nudge it into different directions but cannot change direction suddenly.
- It has a power of its own.
- You do not know where it will end up.

To create alignment, the company's leaders have a responsibility to:

- set the direction and let everyone know what the direction is and how they can contribute
- be consistent in that direction (not to change direction every 10 minutes)
- create, maintain and support an environment in which people want to volunteer their creativity, enthusiasm and resourcefulness to the company's benefit.

From Principle 3 ('Customers'), you also need alignment with what customers value. You frequently see companies whose employees are so focused on themselves that they give little attention to customers' needs—music played at 200 decibels in retail stores, chatting about themselves and their own interests while supposedly looking after customers. The discussion in Principle 3 ('Customers') is about focusing the alignment of everything the company does with providing value to the customers.

Good practices

- People at all levels throughout the company are expected to take a leadership role regardless of formal position.
- Team structures are implemented—'natural work teams' work as a team (rather than a hierarchy); 'self-managed work teams'; 'semi-autonomous work teams'; 'process improvement teams'. These teams are adequately resourced, and provided with the required skills, data, information, knowledge and authority. Authority and responsibility boundaries are well defined.
- Teams are balanced by including people of, for example, different psychological types, different ethnic backgrounds, different genders. Considerable effort is made to show that the opinion of all people in the teams is valued and sought after. Differences of opinion are valued.
- Leadership is encouraged at all levels.
- Leadership depends more on role than on position.
- All people throughout the company who show an aptitude for leadership are given leadership skills and development so they can perform better as leaders.
- People are actively encouraged to share ideas and try new methods.

Poor practices

- Plans decided without participation from the people who will implement them. (Few things turn people off more than not being allowed to participate in decisions that affect them.)

- Fake participation—involving people to determine their goals within the constraints decided elsewhere in the company.
- Punishment of those who raise problems and questions—these people are called negative, sidelined and ostracised.
- Fear of saying what is on one's mind or criticising the opinions and demands of management.
- Emphasis on compliance with norms. Put downs and quashing of those who behave differently from the norm.
- A fear of failure.
- Risk aversion—like a tortoise withdrawing into its shell. It is better to take no risks, that way you cannot get into trouble. Many government companies are very risk averse, seeking to eliminate risk no matter what the cost.

7.4 Let employees know what their job is

Your employees need to know:

- what you are trying to achieve—what are the goals and objectives—and to be even more effective, where you are at in achieving those goals and objectives
- what their job is and what you expect from them—and to be even more effective, how that job contributes to the goals and objectives of the company
- how to do that job—they need training and education—and to be even more effective, access to the 'knowledge' of the company
- whether what they are doing is what you want—feedback.

Knowing what the company is trying to achieve

Employees need to know what the company is trying to achieve—its goals and objectives. The old thinking was that employees would not understand, so why waste their time. The new thinking is that you should keep employees informed and up to date with what you are trying to achieve. They will then at least have a chance of achieving it for you. This allows them to focus on achieving the goals (Principle 2, 'Focus on achieving results').

Principle 1 ('Role models') discussed how you get people to share your dream, your picture of success. It is your job to communicate what you are trying to achieve in terms that others can understand. If people do not understand or do not appear to want to understand, it is your fault—not theirs.

Letting employees know what you want to achieve is a statement of trust as well as a call for help. People usually respond to a call for help—until they are hurt or abused when helping.

Companies often find that their employees are very cynical about what the company is trying to achieve and calls for help. Cynicism can mean a lack of trust, a history of broken promises or lack of care for employees, a disparity of values between employees and the company's senior managers.

Employees might also consider the company's approach impractical—possibly because there is no defined process to achieve it, or no method to make the process capable except by working harder (Principle 4 'To improve the outcome, improve the system').

How do I contribute?

A question that employees often struggle to answer is, 'Do I know how what I do contributes to the success of the company?'. If employees do not know how they contribute to the success of the company, they are unlikely to be able to make 'good' decisions about what needs to be done and they will probably not be as 'enthusiastic' or 'volunteering' as they could be.

Delegation

Industry can learn from the military about delegation. The following format is commonly used. (The terminology has been modified to make it slightly more 'business' oriented.)

- *Situation*: A short summary of the background leading to the project.
- *Desired result*: What is to be achieved (not details or tasks or how to achieve the result—all that is to be determined by the team being tasked). The reason for the action. Why it needs to be done. How it links to other projects. How it will benefit the business.
- *Steps to take*: What is to be delivered, by whom for whom and to whom, by when and where. What the known milestones and deadlines are. Which groups are to be consulted. How big the task is. Specification of the boundaries. Are there restrictions and limitations—of policy or other units, any formidable restrictions? Details of coordination. (During the briefing, none of this is about what to do—that is to be determined by the team.)
- *Resources*: What resources can the team draw on: people, technical, organisational, budget, equipment, overtime.
- *Command and communications*: Who is in charge and how often will he/she report and to whom. What will be the reporting arrangements (oral briefing, written overview of current status, detailed examination with recommendations for change). How much detail is needed (half a page of notes or a detailed report). What power and authority is being delegated.

- *Consequences*: How will performance be assessed? How will success be assessed? What performance indicators will be used? What are the consequences of failure—to the business, the team and individuals? How will individuals be held to account for the outcome and decisions taken—to act or not to act? What are the rewards for success—to the business, the team and individuals?

Knowing what their job is

Employees need to know what is required of them in their daily work lives to meet the needs of the company and fulfil the needs of their part of the company. This was covered in detail in Principle 2 ('Focus on achieving results').

The box on delegation above shows the minimum information needed by people to do their job. None of this should have to be guessed, yet most companies do not take the trouble to do even this.

It is usually best if employees design their own jobs—in mutual agreement with their manager/supervisor.

The power of stating 'why'

Stating why you need something done is the single most important piece of information when you give someone a task. When people know why they are to do something, they can then go on and make decisions that fit with the situation. Adding 'the reason for the action' to military briefing practice was a significant change to what occurred 70 years ago. Unlike 70 years ago, the intent of present-day military missions is to have your people come back unharmed. This requires initiative by the people involved and less 'command' by the bosses. In fact, the bosses' role has become much more one of coordination with other units to arrange necessary resources.

The 'why' is still often left out in companies. Most companies have not yet achieved this change of role and tell only 'how to do' or exactly 'what to do' when delegating. This is too controlling and usually removes initiative and the chance to 'volunteer'.

Knowing 'when'

Knowing the time frame is a critical piece of information that people often leave out when delegating. If you know the task is to be completed in half a day, you approach it in a different way from the way you would if you know it is expected to take a month. Time frames—like budgets—tell you how much you have to do, the level of detail, the expected effort.

Useless feedback

People need to know how they are going but they dislike 'feedback'. Feedback usually has very negative connotations. Saying 'I'm going to give you feedback on your performance' usually turns people cold. Why?

People know that their ability to do their work, their performance, is totally dependent on 'the system' around them. Yet 'feedback' is almost never based around the system's performance. Feedback is usually given at the individual level. If the system is included, it is usually an afterthought, a reason for excuses.

This may be because 'the system' is the boss's responsibility. Discussion that includes 'the system' may be too close to the boss's performance. You probably have very few people who come to work each day with the idea of doing a bad job. Your advice on what they can do better is probably irrelevant. You are probably a major part of their problem.

What is it that prevents you doing your best work?

One of the most useful questions to ask employees is 'What is it that prevents you doing your best work?'. This usually uncovers system problems. The company must then act on the answers to improve processes. Most companies do not ask this question. It is easier to assume the employee is to blame.

When we understand the concept of process capability and the Principle of variation (Principle 6), we know that a person's performance will vary each day, depending on what 'the system' does with him/her that day.

The only reason for a feedback session is to find out what else the person needs in order to do his/her job better. In other words, what the employee and the boss each need to do, together and separately, to get a better outcome.

Well done

Try praise instead of criticism. Saying 'well done', regardless of what the employee has done, is a good beginning. You need to be constantly looking for opportunities to find people doing things right. You need to find opportunities to praise, to say 'well done'.

In the old thinking, bosses would try to find people doing the wrong thing, then 'kick their arse'. Many bosses think their job is to look for the opportunity to chew out, to kick butt, to fire, to chastise, to bully, to show who is boss. These are all the wrong approach. People hate them. Instead, your only feedback should be 'well done'. Use it as often as you can.

Good practices

- People know what their job is and how they contribute to the company.
- Job descriptions exist that are designed by the employees, that show the boundaries of responsibility and authority and show how the employees contribute to the company's goals.
- People know how their daily work contributes to the company's goals and strategic direction.
- Feedback sessions are devoted to 'what can the company and its management do to improve systems and processes so the employee can do the work?' and 'what other enablement factors (e.g. skills, knowledge, resources, authority) does the employee need to do the work?'.
- Working at catching people 'doing things right' and reinforcing positive values-based behaviour. 'Well done' is the most common form of feedback.
- Continuous feedback of praise and joint action plans for improvement.
- Use of 360-degree feedback or similar systems.
- Employee performance is assessed in a context of systems thinking and knowledge of process capability.
- Staff performance goals are jointly set with management and these goals are monitored by staff and management.
- Staff development plans are based on feedback from the performance management system. Staff and management agree on any education and training needed for staff to have the necessary competencies to do their jobs.

Poor practices

- People engaged in mindless work—the purpose of which they do not understand and whose outcome and process they cannot control.
- People feel like they are helpless against the 'system'. 'The system' is anonymous and undefined.
- Large amounts of energy are expended to 'beat the system'.
- Feedback given to people on how to improve their performance. No reference to systems or processes that affect performance. No recognition of process capability.
- Induction training not given to *all* employees (including executives and managers) on customer focus and company's context and ethics.

7.5 Enable your employees

You should make certain your employees are properly enabled to carry out their work (i.e. provided with sufficient skills, knowledge, resources and authority).

In order for employees to be able to be enthusiastic volunteers, they need:

- knowledge of what is expected of them
- skills and resources
- desire.

Only when someone knows what to do and why, has the skills of how to do it and the desire to want to do it, is that person enabled.

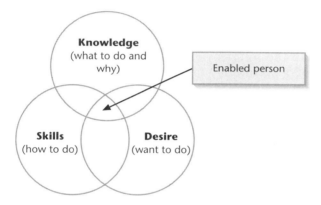

Fig. 7.4 Enabling employees when knowledge combines with skills and desire

Skills development

How can you expect employees to do their work if they do not have the minimum skills for that job? The old thinking was 'I can't afford to train them'. Can you afford not to train them and yet have them deal with your customers? Or work with your processes?

New employees need training in the technology and processes they will now have to use. Existing employees will need training whenever you change your process or technology. You cannot assume that people will know how to use the new process or the new technology. The best ways of doing things are often unused because people are not shown how to do it that way.

You should invest in the development of your workforce through education and training and by providing opportunities for continuing growth. Employees increasingly need opportunities to learn, practise and demonstrate new skills. Development must meet the ongoing needs of employees and the company.

Education and training should provide the knowledge and skills that employees need to meet their work and personal objectives, as well as meeting the company's need for skilled employees. Employees' education and training requirements will depend on the employees' responsibilities and stage of development.

Examples of development programs include: leadership, knowledge sharing, communications, teamwork, problem solving, interpreting and using data, meeting customer requirements, process analysis, process simplification, waste reduction, cycle time reduction, error-proofing, priority setting based upon cost and benefit, and other training that affects employee effectiveness, efficiency and safety.

Your developmental plans also might include:

- basic skills, such as reading, writing, language and arithmetic
- initiatives to help knowledge sharing and cross-functional interactions throughout the company
- creation of opportunities for employees to learn and use skills beyond current job assignments
- developmental assignments to prepare future leaders, executives and managers
- individual development or learning plans
- formation of partnerships with educational institutions to develop employees or to help ensure the future supply of well-prepared employees.

On-the-job training offers a cost-effective way to train and to link training to work processes.

Customer-contact employees

Specific training is usually required for customer-contact employees. For example, training is required in:

- product and service knowledge
- selling skills
- how to listen to customers
- how to solicit comments from customers
- how to anticipate and handle problems or failures (recovery, diffusing anger)
- retaining customers
- effectively managing expectations.

Resources

Employees need adequate and appropriate resources to be able to carry out their job. Resources can include all those things that make a mess of the job when they are not available, for example:

- the right number of people on the team with the right skills
- the right equipment—digging a hole with a bulldozer instead of a shovel
- the right technology
- the right funding—the boss decided you could do it for half the $100 000 that you estimated
- the right amount of time—trying to do it in two days when you needed six weeks.

All of these things directly affect the capability of the process. All relate to the part of the process that the boss controls. They are all scarce. There are trade-offs between all of them.

Data and information as motivation

Data and information help to provide alignment with company goals and objectives and are a very useful source of employee motivation.

The old thinking was to keep people in the dark. But, when people know how the company is tracking, this can provide the stimulus to modify processes, find out what is or is not working, or to work harder to reach the goals and objectives. You can achieve significant change by focusing on the results achieved or not achieved.

If people do not know how the company is tracking, how do they know that there is a need to do anything differently? Why would they modify processes, find out what is or is not working, or work harder?

Data should be tied to indicators of company or work unit performance, for example, on process outputs, customer satisfaction, customer retention and productivity (Principle 5, 'Improved decisions').

You should provide data and information to employees that they think is useful and of value. Employees are the customers of most of the data used internally. Because they are customers, their needs must be included.

- The data and information should be useful to them—not a waste of their time.
- Principle 4 ('To improve the outcome, improve the system') tells us that we should make collection and distribution of the data easy so collecting and using it does not become a distraction.
- Principle 6 ('Variation') tells us that presentation should display the variation in the data.
- Employees will need skills in how to interpret and use the data.

You also need effective systems for collection and transfer of data and information so it is useable.

Desire

People have to *want* to volunteer, to contribute, to be resourceful, to be enthusiastic. Most of the discussion in Principle 7 is about how to provide this desire—this motivation.

For many employees, the opportunity to 'have fun and do neat stuff' is what creates the desire to volunteer—to keep on having fun and doing neat stuff. Having an exciting place in which to work and having their needs met is extremely motivating to people.

Empowered and enabled to fix processes

As we saw in Principle 4 ('To improve the outcome, improve the system'), employees know most about the details of the processes they work in. They also know most about what is wrong with them. When you enable people by providing the necessary skills, knowledge, power, resources and authority to fix those systems, you unleash enormous energy.

As we also saw in Principle 4, although it is the employees that know most about the processes of the company, it is the bosses that control almost every aspect of the process that will make a significant difference— the technology used, the resources, the capital. Employees may be able to change a few steps in the process and save a few dollars. However, the boss controls and, therefore, constrains the process.

Most team-based projects fail because the boss has limited the scope of the project so much that the team can only fiddle at the edge of meaningful change.

Managers are responsible for processes and must form partnerships with their employees in order to fix those processes. Each party cannot do it without the other. The employee has knowledge but insufficient power, and the manager has power but insufficient knowledge of the process. The manager has knowledge of coordination and of getting things done.

Building these partnerships unleashes huge energy from enthusiastic employees and managers, and gets the changes made that significantly improve the company.

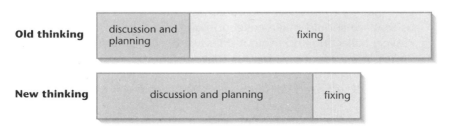

Fig. 7.5 Time taken to implement changes

Discussion helps implementation

Extensive discussion during planning can be the crucial difference between good and bad implementation.

Successful companies find that when they give space for discussion and debate up front, this can iron out impracticalities. The discussion phase brings together the knowledge of each of the implementation stakeholders, which makes implementation much easier. Total implementation time can be more than halved. This can be crucial in meeting the need for shorter and shorter cycle times.

Deliberately go out of your way to find what is wrong—what will not work. Then you can work out how to overcome those problems. It is always easier and less expensive to do that before you launch the product than after.

Good practices

- Induction for all employees (including managers and executives) includes details on values, ethics, role, expectations, company direction and purpose, skills, safety, health and well-being.
- Staff at all levels are enabled, empowered and encouraged to take initiatives to achieve company goals.
- Confidence that employees will take actions that fit the company's needs in unusual circumstances.
- Troubleshooting by staff beyond the call of their responsibility to nurture customer relations.
- Employees believe they are empowered and enabled.
- Authority and responsibilities are delegated at all levels to support customers.
- Heavy investment in training.
- Leaders, at all levels within a company, increase their skills through continuous learning and from formal training and development.
- The company provides coaching and mentoring resources to all people.
- People are constantly given challenging roles to achieve goals beyond their known potential.
- People are given skills and knowledge beyond those required for their existing roles.
- People are given experience in a variety of roles, functions and jobs.

Poor practices

- Don't enable employees (by not providing adequate skills, knowledge, power, resources or authority) to actively participate in the workplace or to make decisions.
- Not enabling process workers to improve processes (by not supplying skills, knowledge, resources and authority).

7.6 Provide value to your employees as well as customers

You should work to ensure your work environment provides value to your employees. If you provide what your employees perceive to be valuable, then they will enthusiastically volunteer their creative contribution.

Each person will have a different perception of what is valuable to him or her, at different times of their career and for different reasons. It can be money, power, influence, the excitement of creativity or being part of a team, being responsible, doing their duty, being practical, the social structure, meeting and dealing with customers or their fellow employees, solving problems, solving world problems, having fun, doing neat stuff. All together, it is what people find satisfying from work.

More and more companies are finding that the way forward for their employees is to use the same value proposition process that they use for their customers. The skills the company has established for finding out what its customers value and building value propositions around those wants and needs can be extended to find out what its employees want from work and the company. Value propositions for employees are then built around those wants and needs.

Just as a company should find out what customers don't like about the products and services the company offers, the company should find out what its employees don't like about working for the company. The company should then work to eliminate those dissatisfiers.

However, you need to be clear about the difference between 'values' (or beliefs) that people hold and what they think is of 'value' (or useful) to them. Much of Principle 7 is concerned with beliefs and 'values'. In this section, we are concerned with what people find useful or 'value'.

What employees value

Below is a list of what employees appear to value. It has been assembled by considering the major issues that cause employees to be dissatisfied so that they withdraw their enthusiastic volunteering.

- Being respected.
- Being appreciated.
- A climate of trust.
- Recognition.
- Honesty.
- Space to have their say.
- Security of tenure and of their person.
- Knowing where they are going (and a map of how to get there).
- Being told why something needs to be done.

- Being enabled to do their work (receiving sufficient skills, knowledge, resources and authority).
- Learning new skills and obtaining knowledge.
- Being part of a team (or work family).
- Being involved in decisions that affect them.
- Being able to demonstrate competence.
- Being cared for.
- Status.
- Being able to do their duty and act responsibly.
- A work place that shares their values (or where they can fulfil their values).
- Safety.
- Having fun and doing neat stuff.
- Being creative.
- Not being blamed.
- A balanced life—with family and health needs heeded.

People want to feel valued in all of their interactions

In building value propositions, it is useful to have a picture of what employees perceive to be of value. Here is a model about what people value at work. It applies regardless of situation. There are four dimensions.

1. *Sense of purpose.* The more consistent the company's purpose is with the individual's, the better. The higher the purpose, the better. The higher the perceived value of the individual's purpose and role, the better. The more coherent it is with their values, the better. The more it extends personal endeavour, the better. People like a 'just cause'.

2. *Sense of control or 'choice'.* The degree that individuals can exercise control over their situation. The amount of discretion they can exercise in the pursuit of purpose. The strictures that deny them the opportunity to 'do what is best'. The extent they can contribute their ideas and act on their ideas. The degree they can make a free and informed choice.

3. *Sense of achievement.* The degree they see the results of their action. Personally acquired feedback—not the stuff directed at them, but the stuff they learn through inquiry and direct interaction. The closer the relationship with the end-user, the better. The greater the freedom to inquire, the better. The greater the pursuit of learning new skills and the refinement of skills and knowledge, the better. The greater the degree of freedom to act on the learnings, the better.

4. *Sense of affiliation or 'belonging'.* The greater the consistency of contribution, the better. The greater the alignment of what the

235

person wants to do with what the organisation wants to do, the better. The greater the alignment between the person's values and the company's values, the better. The greater the focus on humanness, the better. The greater the listening systems, the better. The more inclusive, the better. The more diversity is prized, nurtured and coalesced into surprising actions, the better.

Just cause

Employees lose their motivation to volunteer when they think there is a gap between what the company says it is doing and what they are being asked to do. If people think that the company has a 'just cause', they volunteer. If they think that the company is not committed to its 'just cause', they withdraw.

Alignment with the 'just cause' is crucial to liberate creative and emotional energy.

Misunderstandings and misinterpretations can cause employees to believe that the company is not acting in accordance with espoused values. Senior managers must work hard to dispel misconceptions by using active dialogue to reach realistic understanding of the situation. Often, it is only by using active dialogue that clashes with values can be straightened out and practical implications for policy implementation can be found.

As we saw in Principle 1 ('Role models'), it is crucial that the most senior managers demonstrate their belief in the spirit of company values. Senior managers should take every opportunity to show they care about the values and the Principles.

Undiscussable dilemmas

Most companies have forbidden topics—things people just don't talk about if they want to stay in favour and keep their jobs. These are often the latest failed scheme by one of the bosses or incentive schemes that work against the best interests of the company (i.e. rewarding A while hoping for B).

You should encourage discussion and dialogue on such topics— painful as it is for the people involved. Out of the discussion can come learning that can help prevent recurrence of similar mistakes. Such dialogue should be based around available facts and data (including feelings) and how they have informed the decision process.

Trompenaars and Hampden-Turner's *Riding the Waves of Culture* and Senge et al.'s *The Fifth Discipline Fieldbook* make a useful contribution to this area.

Relationships and networks

People need information about what is going on. A company is a social organism with social purposes and interactions as well as business purposes and interactions.

Most managers forget this. We are a social species that has spent most of our up to 400 000-year history in small family groups and very small villages. Because we are a social species, social interaction is critically important to us. Failure to understand its importance is to overlook a major cause of system failure.

It may help to think of the company as a huge family with its ongoing likes, dislikes, misunderstandings, feuds, hatreds, infatuations, loves and fads. More often than not, this history drives the daily behaviour of the company more than any vision or purpose.

Like it or not, even in large corporations, we still have the needs of villagers. We need to know what is going on with people in our village. Now, our village is likely to be our work group, or the 20–30 people that make up our 'work family'. (Don't forget that most people in the work place spend more of their waking time with their 'work family' than with their real family. The social contact with the 'work family' is, therefore, at least as important as that with the real family.) Around the 'work family' is 'the network'—the often-large numbers of people that each person can draw on to mutually help each other.

Many people spend more work time trying to keep up their relationships with their 'work family' than they do on work for the company. The temptation is to try to stifle this 'unproductive non-work'. That is a mistake. Relationship building is natural for people. The networks and relationships are what make the company function.

All work groups need processes to make the social interaction quicker and easier. You can acknowledge that it happens and work with it to the company's benefit. Some suggestions include:

- find ways to bring the work group together so that the social interchange can happen with minimum disruption to the work flow
- team days
- have the team discuss its relationship building and networking in terms of the values, mission, vision, goals and objectives of the company.

Good practices

- The company has processes to understand what its employees see as providing value to them and seeks to provide them.
- Formal and informal systems of management to listen to the needs of employees.

- Providing time and sponsorship for healthful activities so people have the opportunity to look after their own health, safety and well-being.
- Two-way communication strategies have been developed and implemented.

Poor practices

- No process measurements to indicate what drives perception of value.
- A token attempt to 'listen' to employee opinion—no action is taken.
- The effect on people not considered.

7.7 Pay fairly and well

The current thinking in almost every company worldwide is that you must pay for performance. That is, you need to offer monetary incentives for people to work; that people are motivated by monetary reward to perform for the company. This approach is destructive and does *not* work. However, it remains a persistent thinking that is extremely difficult to break.

The most basic flaw in the thinking is found by looking at the assumption that 'people are motivated by monetary reward to perform *for the company*'. The monetary reward does cause people to work harder—for *themselves*. They do things that will increase *their* monetary input. The emphasis has changed from doing things that will benefit the company to doing things to cause monetary benefit to themselves. This is especially so at the top of large companies where the size of the incentive is so large that it can cause behaviour that is very destructive to the good of the company. The most obvious of these behaviours is the 'notice me and how good I am' behaviour. When engaged in this, the person takes credit for other people's work and discredits anyone else who may look good.

All incentive schemes stop good performance

In the previous section, we described a considerable list of issues that people value, need and want in their workplace before they volunteer. Money is not usually high on this list. You cannot buy enthusiasm.

There is plenty of anecdotal evidence that managers are dissatisfied with the 'motivational' programs in their companies. A veritable herd of consultants waits with new gimmicks for manipulating people, new variations on the same old rewards theme. Unfortunately, the problems are not due to the way any one program has been implemented so much as to the simplistic premise of all pay-for-performance schemes. Here are eight reasons why incentive plans cannot succeed (these concepts were presented in Alfie Kohn's excellent book *Punished by Rewards*).

1. *The system people work in controls their productivity.* From Principle 4 ('To improve the outcome, improve the system'), we know that everyone is under the control of the system. The system they work in, and its processes, determine the quality and quantity of our work. Incentive plans are really disguised work-harder schemes. Working harder is not a long-term solution to better performance. Dollar motivation assumes that effort is being withheld and is waiting to be bribed out. That is, it assumes that working harder does work and if people are bribed enough they will break their lazy ways and do the right thing by the company. 'If I give you another $20 000 a year, will you work harder? If so, why are you withholding that effort? I always knew you were a lazy slob!'

2. *You cannot motivate people with money.* Although giving extra money does not produce extra effort, taking money away will produce a withdrawal of enthusiastic contribution. You can demotivate people by taking money away. When people do not get the rewards they were hoping for (e.g. an expected bonus), the effect of this is, in practice, indistinguishable from being punished. The more desirable the reward, the more demoralising it will be to miss out. A result is the alteration of company KPIs so employees (especially the senior managers) look good even when the company is not doing so well.

3. *Rewards rupture relationships.* Research and experience increasingly show that excellence depends on effective teamwork, both because of the exchange of ideas that occurs and the climate of social support that is created. However, the scramble for rewards—particularly when they are made scarce, creating competition—destroys cooperation. Relationships between supervisors and subordinates, too, can collapse under the weight of incentives.

4. *People dissemble, cheat and lie in order to look good.* If a supervisor issues penalties, employees will probably be as glad to see that person coming as they would be to glimpse a police car in their rear-vision mirror. Even if he or she is seen as a rewarder, the effect is essentially the same. Employees will be tempted to conceal any problems they might be having and present themselves as infinitely competent. Rather than asking for help, they may try to flatter that person and convince him or her that everything is under control. Very few things are as dangerous to a company as a collection of incentive-driven individuals trying to reassure the incentive dispenser.

5. *Rewards discourage risk taking and destroy creativity.* Whenever people are led to think about what they will get for doing something, they are very inclined to protect their income by being overly cautious. Consequently, they are less inclined to take risks or explore

possibilities; to play hunches that might not pay off or to attend to anything whose relevance to the problem at hand is not immediately evident. The number one casualty of rewards is 'creativity'. Excellence pulls in one direction, encouraging employees to think about how well they are doing, and what they will earn as a result pulls in another. The proof: a dozen psychological studies showing that the more people are led to think about rewards, the more they prefer easy tasks. Challenge is typically avoided not because of laziness but because incentive systems encourage concern about what one is going to get. A 'do this and you'll get that' approach makes people focus on the 'that' (the incentive) and not the 'this' (doing their jobs well). This means that prompting employees to focus on how much will be in their pay envelopes is about the last strategy we ought to use if we care about innovation and creativity.

6. *Rewards often produce threats and coercion.* We know that fearful and threatened employees withdraw their enthusiastic voluntary contribution. 'Whippings will continue until morale improves' is a saying that usually evokes a smile. The reality is that it is very common and takes the form of 'coercion and fear will be enforced until performance improves'. The fear is often fear of not getting the bonus or of being fired. Coercion comes from all those who have an interest in the bonus. The result is a climate of fear and coercion, which certainly gives a performance result that is far from the optimum. This is the same stimulus response thinking of the 'do this and you will get that' approach, which produced the incentive reward approach. Again, the reward approach causes the exact opposite result to the one intended.

7. *Rewards undermine interest.* Artificial incentives are much less effective than intrinsic motivation at ensuring interest in the company—they tend to undermine it. Incentives create self-interested employees. The more a manager gets employees to think about what they will earn for doing their jobs well, the less interested they will be in what they are doing. Again, a 'do this and you'll get that' approach makes people focus on the 'that' and not the 'this'. Rewards turn play into work and work into drudgery.

8. *All incentive schemes fail.* Scores of experiments have replicated the finding that people who are promised rewards for doing something are less likely to continue doing it when they have a choice as compared with people who are not promised anything.

If the question is, 'Do rewards motivate people?', the answer is, 'Absolutely! They motivate people to get rewards'.

Changing the incentive will not work

Kohn gives several practical conclusions that follow from the analysis above:

- It is not enough to change the type of bribe we offer (T-shirts versus trips versus cash), or the criteria for getting it, or the level at which it is offered (e.g. for teams instead of individuals). The problem is relying on bribes at all. Of the eight explanations above for how incentives impede performance, not one will disappear just because we manipulate people a little differently by using a different type of bribe.
- The problem is not with compensation per se, but with turning compensation into a reward—that is, pushing money into people's faces by offering more of it if they do what they are told. The more closely compensation is conditioned on achievement, the more damage is done.
- We have to stop asking how motivated employees are, and start asking *how* employees are motivated. And this is the heart of Principle 7. We want enthusiastic employees who volunteer their creativity. We need to know what people value. Motivation is not a single entity, such that rewards can create more of 'it'. Rather, intrinsic motivation (loving what you do) is completely different from extrinsic motivation (doing something to get a goodie)—and more of the latter often means less of the former.
- If 'recognition' of employees is intended to control their future behaviour, it will backfire as surely as programs involving tangible rewards. If recognition is intended only as a respectful acknowledgment of a job well done, an appreciation, then it should be done privately, non-competitively and in the context of a two-way conversion rather than as a patronising pat on the head.
- The actual money paid is both a status symbol and a statement of appreciation. It allows thoughts of 'people think I am worth this much'. When the status aspect dominates, it can lead to a scrabble for more status—and more money to prove it. Unfortunately, this scrabble is seldom to the benefit of the company and its other stakeholders.

Pay fairly and well

Kohn recommends that business owners pay employees fairly and well, and then do everything possible to help them forget about money. Manipulating behaviour by offering inducements, although a sound approach for training the family pet, can never bring excellence to the workplace. Attempts to improve a company by fiddling with the compensation system are doomed to failure.

What should replace the carrot-and-stick thinking? The quick answer is that there are no quick answers. Kohn suggests three 'Cs' that offer a good framework: choice, collaboration and content.

1. *Choice* means that employees should be able to participate in making decisions about what they do every day.

2. *Collaboration* concerns the need to structure effective teams so that the team *does* include *all* those needed to do the work.
3. *Content* refers to the tasks on which people work; as Frederick Herzberg put it, 'If you want people motivated to do a good job, give them a good job to do'.

Successfully attending to these three factors is much more difficult than offering dog biscuits to people for jumping through your hoops.

Adjusting the KPIs

When the rewards are high enough, you often see senior employees 'modifying' reports and 'adjusting' KPIs so that they continue to look good and look as though they are achieving their performance targets.

Falsification of KPIs is not uncommon. It is very destructive to the company and its shareholders, who are kept from the true picture. The practice of falsification of KPIs is a direct consequence of extremely high money incentive schemes.

Paid volunteers

It is helpful to think of employees as 'paid volunteers'. Think of how you behave as a volunteer in your local community group. No-one makes you go there. You go because you get something out of it. Fulfilment, being appreciated, social belonging, helping, contributing, giving, meeting people, having fun, doing your duty. It is an endless list of what you value and get in return for volunteering. None of the reasons can be about the money you receive. If you do not get value for your time, you stop volunteering. At first, you withdraw your enthusiasm. Eventually, you leave and do something else with your time.

In the workplace, the same value-for-time equation is working. However, leaving can be more difficult. Employees are usually dependent on their pay cheque. Throughout history, employers have taken advantage of that to demand work. That approach achieved work but not volunteering, enthusiasm or resourcefulness.

Each person works for him or herself

More and more employees are realising that everyone works for him or herself. It is the responsibility of each person to obtain as much value for his or her time as possible. In the old thinking, this would have said, 'It is the responsibility of each person to obtain as much *money* for his/ her time as possible'. We now know that to be only part of the equation—although an important part.

Each person forms a picture of his or her self-worth. This is made up of two distinct parts—monetary and non-monetary things of value. The old thinking considered only the monetary side. The monetary side says, 'If the money is less than my picture of my monetary self-worth, I am undervalued by this company and I will search for a better match'. This is where the reward thinking has focused. Reward thinking helps with status, but not much else. The non-monetary side says, 'If what I get out of work is less than what I value, I will withdraw'. The new thinking is to give much more emphasis to the second of these. It helps with volunteering.

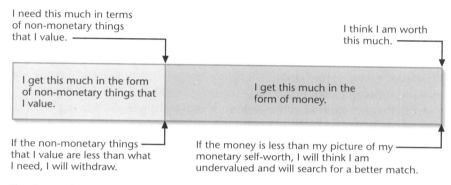

I need this much in terms of non-monetary things that I value.

I think I am worth this much.

I get this much in the form of non-monetary things that I value.

I get this much in the form of money.

If the non-monetary things that I value are less than what I need, I will withdraw.

If the money is less than my picture of my monetary self-worth, I will think I am undervalued and will search for a better match.

Fig. 7.6 Each person works for him or herself

Good practices

- A performance management system based on an understanding of process capability and variation, which seeks to: praise, celebrate and recognise success; identify system problems that prevent the employees from doing their best work; and provide the employees with the skills, knowledge, power and ability to further assist the company reach its goals.

Poor practices

- Rewarding A while hoping for B.
- Performance appraisal systems used instead of management of process.
- Work harder reward structures and incentive schemes.
- Rating systems and rewarding practices that contradict teamwork.
- Blaming people for problems over which they have no control, or giving credit to those who are lucky.
- Performance management does not include job simplification, enrichment and coaching.

7.8 Eliminate what employees dislike

You should actively search for what dissatisfies your employees and work to overcome those dissatisfiers for the same reasons as providing value to customers. The best way to provide more value is to find what your customers/employees dislike and eliminate those dissatisfiers. This method prevents you from having to guess. In both cases, your customers/employees tell you what you should be working on. You just have to listen to them and work to fix the problem to their satisfaction—not yours.

Below is a list of what causes employees to be dissatisfied and so withdraw their enthusiastic volunteering. It was used to build the 'what employees value' list on page 234. It is not in order of priority. Different personality types will have different priorities of dislikes.

- Not being respected.
- Not being appreciated.
- Not being trusted.
- No recognition of achievement or of themselves as individuals.
- Criticism of all kinds (constructive included).
- Dishonesty and broken promises.
- Not allowed to have their say or having their say dismissed.
- No security of tenure.
- Lack of safety.
- Not knowing where they are going (and no idea how to get there).
- Being told in detail how to do the job.
- Not receiving sufficient skills, knowledge, resources and authority, but still being expected to do their work.
- No opportunities to learn new skills and knowledge.
- No recognition of the role of the work family and work relationships.
- Not being involved in decisions that affect them.
- No opportunity to demonstrate competence.
- Not cared for.
- No chance to show their status, no place in a hierarchy.
- Prevented from doing their duty and acting responsibly.
- Cowardly, gutless behaviour. Expediency.
- Being forced to do things contrary to their values and beliefs.
- Not working for a 'just cause'.
- Not able to live a meaningful life.
- No chance to have fun or do neat stuff.
- No opportunity to be creative.
- Being blamed unfairly.
- Time away from the rest of their interests—family, hobbies.
- Put downs.
- Their self-esteem damaged. Challenges to their picture of their self-worth.

No sense of being valued or doing something useful

Let us look at the four dimensions of the model in this context. It paints a very bleak workplace. Like it or not, most workplaces, including yours, look like this to employees. To have a workplace where people volunteer their enthusiasm, creativity and resourcefulness, you must overcome these dissatisfiers. Obviously! That is what we have been talking about.

1. *No sense of purpose.* Poor consistency between the company's purpose and the individual's. An 'unjust cause'. No higher purpose than making a bundle of money for someone who already has a bundle. An expendable role. Forced to act contrary to their beliefs and values. No sense that it extends them personally.
2. *No sense of control or 'choice'.* The individual can exercise no control over his or her situation. Decisions that affect them are made without their knowledge or input. They can exercise no discretion. Not allowed to do what they think is best. Not allowed to contribute their ideas or act on their ideas. Information and knowledge withheld. No free choice. No freedom to act.
3. *No sense of achievement.* They do not see the results of their work. The only feedback they get is criticism from a boss. No 'well done' praise, only 'do better'. No relationship with the end-user. No freedom to inquire. No opportunity to learn new skills or refine skills.
4. *No sense of affiliation or 'belonging'.* No feeling of contribution. No alignment of what the person wants to do with what the organisation is doing. No alignment between the person's values and the company's values. No respect for humanness. No-one listens. Diversity of thought and action is punished. Surprises are punished.

Value diversity

Diversity is about respect for individuals and valuing and seeking different perspectives. It is best managed through deliberately building your teams so that they are made up of people with a variety of perspectives, encouraging people to see things differently and to speak up. Different perspectives can come from people of different ages ('dotcomers' versus generation X versus baby boomers), different ethnic groups, different psychological types (thinkers versus practical doers; feeling versus impersonal), different work functions (*gemba* versus finance versus marketing versus design), different genders, different countries.

If you surround yourself or build up teams with people who all agree with you and with each other, you are setting up a very great risk. For example, you may miss the huge hole in the practicability of your idea. You may overlook that it is a product that no-one wants, or that the 'solution' does not address the problem, or that consumers will not understand or will hate the product, or that you can't make it or deliver it, or that your staff won't know how to sell it.

People often get a reputation for picking holes in the boss's good idea. And the boss stops asking for their opinion. Wrong! You need people on your team who are willing to challenge. You must do everything you can to encourage them—even if it hurts your ego and no matter how much it stings. You must withstand the pressure by others to get rid of the troublemakers. Cultivate them. Get your ideas out to as many of these people as you can.

No put downs

Have a 'no put downs' workplace. Do not say anything that is a put down to other people. Many people (and most bosses) think they have to put everyone down. This shows low self-esteem. They are essentially saying, 'I need that person to be below me. I need to show I am better and they are worth less than I am. The only way I will achieve it is to put them down'.

Much workplace chat and most jokes are aimed at putting people down. Put downs are a major withdrawal of trust. They are a major invasion of space. They often cause an instant withdrawal of volunteering enthusiasm. Do not use them at all. No jokes and no put downs.

Good practices

- People are not blamed when things go wrong.
- People's ideas are respected, no matter what position they hold or at which level they sit.
- The company can handle ambiguity and conflict.
- The company creates value from the diversity of its workforce—'oddball' ideas are encouraged and used.
- Valuing and encouraging different points of view within the company—especially from 'oddballs' and eccentrics.
- Valuing and enhancing diversity through language and literacy courses in multilingual companies.
- Employment arrangements, working arrangements, dress and employment policies support diversity.
- Methods to give people greater freedom and flexibility (e.g. teleworking).
- Employee support services (e.g. counselling, sports, child-care, gymnasiums, entertainment, social events and personal

development) exist and are well publicised. Staff are actively encouraged to use these services.

Poor practices

- Not acting on employee dissatisfiers.
- Difference and diversity is not valued. Subtle punishment of those who break cultural rules (e.g. senior executives say the company is 'family friendly' but staff who need to take time off are excluded from decision-making processes. This tells staff what the real rules are).
- Token examples of diversity in the workforce (e.g. token disabled person, Asian, woman) rather than real integration.
- Part-time workers treated differently.

7.9 Measure how employees feel

You should measure how your employees feel about your company. You need to know what their perceptions of value are, what their dissatisfiers are (in order of importance) and how well you are going at addressing those dissatisfiers. You should measure all the dissatisfiers listed previously (p. 244). You need to know that:

- your employees get value from being part of the company
- they are provided with sufficient skills, knowledge, resources and authority to carry out their work
- they are given space to have their say
- you show you care and keep your promises
- there is a climate of trust.

Measuring safety

Safety is often a workplace issue that goes unaddressed. Because it shows lack of caring, it is a huge dissatisfier.

Most companies have a policy to kill or maim a specified number of their employees each year. Are you shocked? You can easily recognise these companies. They keep statistics on lost time accidents and are trying to reduce them. What is wrong with that? This approach, regardless of its best intentions, says that 'accidents happen when people come to work, some of them get hurt, nobody means it to happen, they are accidents'. However, when you consider it from a systems viewpoint, those 'accidents' are generated by the system. Put another way, most companies have designed (albeit inadvertently) their systems to kill or maim so many of their employees each year.

So what should you be doing? Your picture must be *no* accidents, incidents, near misses or work-related illness! A huge ask? Or a different picture? Many companies give it up as too hard. It is hard because we have had the thinking for so long that death and injury are normal in the workplace and it is not our fault.

Beware when you measure your progress towards this picture. Let's face it, you can't get those systems that generate the deaths and maiming fixed overnight. While you are fixing, death and maiming will still occur. Companies have found that if you measure 'numbers of incidents', especially deaths, people give up when the first one happens. A better measurement is time between failure—measure the time between incidents. The goal is to make it as long as possible. Some companies have hundreds of thousands of hours between near misses and hundreds of millions of hours worked between incidents.

Another goal is to send employees home in better condition than they arrived at work. If you do this, you will certainly have enthusiastically volunteering employees who may not want to ever go home. If you don't try to send them home in better condition than they arrived, you are showing that you don't care and your employees will stop volunteering.

This includes that plague of the modern office worker—*stress*. Most companies have created such stressful environments with respect to time and performance demands that employees leave the workplace far more stressed than they arrive. Companies that do this are failing their duty to care for their employees. Their employees know it and withhold their enthusiasm. It is difficult to be enthusiastic when you are stressed.

Good practices

- Employee opinion surveys measure the company's resourcefulness.
- Improvements are made based on survey results and other learning sources.
- Improving results on staff opinion polls, cultural audits and self-assessments.
- Results from employee surveys are published and distributed throughout the company.
- Existence of mechanisms to collect data (numbers and qualitative) on culture.
- Employee surveys show that employees feel valued, are enthusiastic about their work and want to volunteer.
- Regular measurements are made of 'fear' and morale, how employees feel 'valued' by the company, employees' perception of their senior executive's 'trustworthiness' and belief in the 10 Business Excellence Principles—the gap is measured and the results acted on.
- Staff are motivated, flexible—and display high morale levels.
- Staff surveys show people are delighted with communication—they know what is going on and they know they are listened to.

- Sick leave and staff turnover statistics are used as indicators of morale.
- A picture of zero lost time incidents and a process to eliminate workplace accidents, incidents and near misses.
- People go home in better condition than they arrive in.
- Occupational health and safety goals are established and strategies developed to achieve them.
- Staff develop the occupational health and safety strategies and systems to achieve a safe workplace, long-term health and happiness. Occupational health and safety strategies are visible and well publicised. Staff well-being and safety programs go well beyond compliance.
- Methods to evaluate workplace stress and seek solutions.
- Work areas are environmentally friendly and meet or exceed occupation health and safety regulations (e.g. well ventilated, well lit).

Poor practices

- Expecting to kill or maim x people per year in work-related incidents.
- Expecting workplace accidents to happen. They are normal. Expecting so many per year.
- No process of systematically eliminating all causes of workplace harm to all employees and managers.
- Measurement of lost time accidents and workers compensation payments without a thorough approach to fix the systems that generate them.
- Signs and slogans exhorting people to think about 'safety first'.
- Stress and sick leave are normal.

7.10 Measure effectiveness of training and education

You should measure the effectiveness of your training and education (e.g. that it changes what employees do).

Many companies devote a significant amount of time and money to education and training—10% of revenue being spent on education, training and development is not unusual. Most companies provide training and education without giving any thought to whether it was worth the effort.

How do you know that the education and training you are providing is a good use of the time and money? How do you measure the effectiveness of training and education?

The only reason to have someone undertake training and education is to change behaviour—to do things differently or to be able to do things differently. This definition applies to all training and education—- for issues as diverse as keyboard skills, product knowledge, selling skills, customer contact skills, skills with equipment, interpersonal relations, strategic planning or working to within budget.

> - If you want people to do things differently, you have to give them some training, education or development.
> - If you want to know if the training and education was effective, measure the behaviour change.

It should be in that order—know what change you want, do the training and education and then measure to see that you get it.

Effective companies actually stipulate the behaviour they want to see and the benefits to the company of that behaviour *before* they agree to the education or training program. Effectiveness is measured by the extent the desired behaviour is achieved.

Many companies do a cost–benefit analysis before approving any education or training program—'We want this benefit to the company and it will cost this much'. Your evaluation should determine if you actually did receive the benefit—in behaviour change or increased company performance.

This does not imply that you should have education and training programs so that everyone 'behaves' themselves. Your education and training program should be aimed at valuing individual differences, not at eliminating them. Nor should you read into this anything about stimulus-response training to achieve a specific behavioural outcome.

What you need not measure is whether everyone had a good time at training, if the educator smiled or told good jokes. Yet those are usually the only measurements you get from most training programs and they are useless.

You must put your education and training effort into the context of process capability and 'the system'. If the constraints are in the system, all the education and training in the world will not help.

Consider this example of a 100-metre foot race. Why does it take 10 seconds? Why can't those people run it in 8 seconds? If we put them through a truly effective education and training program, could they do it in 8 seconds? Should we measure the effectiveness of our education and training program by the ability of the athletes to run 100 metres in 8 seconds? Of course not! The system (in this case the human body) is not capable of doing it. But, companies sometimes do that. In this case, the approach is faulty. It does not have a chance of success.

Training and working harder will never resolve a problem caused by a system constraint.

Potential

What is the potential of your employees? People generally behave in accordance with others' expectation of them. The way you regard and treat others greatly influences how they shape their lives. People act like your image of them. (Psychologists call this the Pygmalion Concept after the Greek legend of Pygmalion, who fell in love with a statue he had made.)

If you believe you are surrounded with people full of potential, you will find that you are. If you think they are idiots with no potential, they will behave as such. Even if they did not, you would not be able to recognise it. If you want them to be great, act as though they are great. Treat them as though they are the best in the world with infinite potential to do anything, and they will respond by being that. We know that children treated as smart act smart. The same applies for adults.

Companies repeatedly find that ordinary people do extraordinary things when they are properly enabled, trusted and *believed in*. You do not have to go to the ends of the earth to find extraordinary people. They are already in your company. Too often bosses are dismissive of their staff and cannot see their capability.

When you constantly seek outside for 'better' people, you imply that you are surrounded by incompetent dummies.

Good practices

- The effectiveness of training is measured and monitored.
- The company identifies the competencies needed for all its strategic jobs and assists people to achieve those competencies.
- Human resources plan describes career path planning.
- The 'next generation' of leaders is identified and developed for seamless transitions.

Poor practices

- Not measuring the effectiveness of training or know what they want to achieve with training.

SUMMARY

The two books by Byham and Cox, *Zapp! The Lightning of Empowerment* and *Heroz*, give an excellent summary of the thinking of Principle 7 and how to implement it. (Both are set as novels about a workplace. Zapp is the lightning people feel that creates enthusiastic employees who volunteer their creativity. Sapp is its opposite. Byham and Cox describe it as being wrapped up in mummy tape or working in a green fog.)

When you have been Zapped, you feel like:

- your job belongs to you
- you are responsible

- your job counts for something
- you know where you stand
- you have some say in how things are done
- your job is part of who you are
- you have some control over your work.

These things Zapp people:

- Responsibility
- Knowing why you are important to the company
- Trust
- Flexible controls
- Being listened to
- Direction (clear key result areas, measurement, targets)
- Being part of a team
- Knowledge (skills, training, information, targets)
- Solving problems
- Support (approval, coaching, feedback, encouragement)
- Praise
- Resources readily available
- Recognition of ideas
- Upward and downward communications

For Zapp to work people need:

- direction (key result areas, targets, goals, measurements)
- knowledge (skills, training, information)
- resources (tools, materials, facilities, money)
- support (approval, coaching, feedback, encouragement).

Management's role in spreading Zapp:

- To create an environment where Zapp can happen.
- To protect people from the Sapping things that the company might attempt to put upon them; while at the same time supporting and encouraging the Zapping things the company can offer.
- To be sure that subordinate managers have the skills required to Zapp (and if they don't, get them trained).
- To model Zapp.
- To coach subordinate managers in how to use and improve their Zapp skills.
- To reward performance resulting from Zapp.

THE FOUR STEPS OF ZAPP!

1. Maintain or increase self-esteem.
2. Listen and respond with empathy.

3. Ask for help in solving problems and encourage involvement.
4. Offer help without taking responsibility for action is the soul of Zapp!

THINGS THAT BOOST THE ZAPP VOLTAGE

- Learning more about the job.
- Give the team a say in who works on the team.
- Establish a mission for the team.
- Provide time and places for the team to meet.
- Provide technical training at 'the teachable moment'.
- Provide 'people' skills for interacting, solving problems, making decisions and taking action.

ZAPP COACHING

- People learn more from success than from failures.
- Explain purpose and importance of what you are trying to teach.
- Explain the process to be used.
- Show how it is done.
- Observe while the person practises the process.
- Provide immediate and specific feedback (coach again or reinforce success).
- Express confidence in the person's ability to be successful.
- Agree on follow-up actions.

CONTROLS

- A boss who over-controls Sapps his/her people.
- A boss who abandons controls Sapps his/her people.
- A boss who uses situational control Zapps his/her people.
- People only respond negatively to controls when they are inappropriate for the situation.

RESPONSIBILITY

Sharing responsibility with people does not mean abandoning responsibility. Through Zapp, people gain responsibility in their individual jobs, but managers still have responsibility to:

- know what is going on
- set the direction for the department
- make the decisions staff can't
- ensure that people are on course
- offer a guiding hand—open doors to clear the way
- assess performance
- be a smart manager.

WHAT WOULD YOUR STAKEHOLDERS SAY?

HOW WOULD YOUR EMPLOYEES RATE YOUR COMPANY ON THESE?

- I am valued (appreciated) by this company.
- I feel secure.
- I am respected.
- What stops me from doing my best work?
- I do my work without fear.
- I trust the company.
- I trust my bosses.
- The company demonstrates values that I like.
- I know what is expected of me in my job.
- I know what my job is.
- I know how my job contributes to the goals and objectives of the company.
- I know how my job contributes to the success of the company.
- I am given adequate skills, knowledge, authority and resources to be able to do my job.
- When people give me a task to do, they tell me *why* it needs to be done.
- I know what the company is trying to achieve—its goals and objectives.
- I know that what I am doing is what is wanted.
- I get useful feedback on how I do my job that focuses on helping me, not blaming me.
- All my bosses appreciate the knowledge and experience that I have about my job.
- I am always provided with training when I am expected to use new processes and technology.
- I have been given training in how to improve processes. This is updated as I need it.
- This company provides a safe working environment (physically and mentally and free of harassment).
- My union never needs to be adversarial in representing my interests to the company. There is trust on both sides.

HOW WOULD YOUR CUSTOMERS RATE YOUR COMPANY ON THESE?

- The employees of this company receive considerable training in how to handle customers and meet their needs.
- I find it easy to deal with the employees of this company.
- Customer-contact employees have been carefully selected for their customer-caring skills.

- Employees of this company care about their customers.
- I have the impression that employees of this company want to take my problem and make it theirs.
- The employees of this company show a huge degree of enthusiasm about their work.
- The employees of this company show a huge degree of enthusiasm about their company.
- The employees of this company show a huge amount of resource-fulness in getting things done.

HOW WOULD YOUR SHAREHOLDERS RATE YOUR COMPANY ON THESE?

- This company has not followed a downsizing path.
- This company does not use incentive schemes that put pressure on executives to falsify KPIs and other reports to us.
- This company does not use confidentiality as a habit.
- I am confident that this company does not hide information from me or falsify KPIs and other reports to us.
- The employees of this company show a huge degree of enthusiasm about their work.
- The employees of this company show a huge degree of enthusiasm about their company.
- The employees of this company show a huge amount of resource-fulness in getting things done.
- The enthusiasm, creativity and resourcefulness of all employees of this company are aligned with making the company successful (rather than their pay packets).
- The enthusiasm, creativity ad resourcefulness of all senior executives of this company are focused on making the company successful (rather than their pay packets).
- This company does not return to us as 'profits' funds that should have been used to train, educate and develop the workforce.

HOW WOULD THE COMMUNITY RATE YOUR COMPANY ON THESE?

- This company has followed a downsizing path.

Principle 8
Learning, innovation and continual improvement

Continual improvement and innovation depends on continual learning.

THIS IS PROBABLY the single most important Principle for long-term sustainability of the company. If you do not continually improve (by constantly saying 'what we do is not good enough, we can and must do it better'), you have little chance of long-term sustainability. If you do not continually innovate (adapt, generate new concepts, provide new products and services, do things differently), you have little chance of long-term sustainability. If your company does not do both these things, it will be overwhelmed, crushed and become just another case history.

Continual improvement and innovation are, therefore, both critical to a company's long-term success. Principle 8 goes on to say that continual improvement and innovation will happen *only* when there is continual learning. If you do not continually learn (from others, from what you do and have done, from your mistakes, from your successes, from your customers, from your competitors, from your employees, from technology), you have little chance of long-term sustainability. This means that continual learning is vital.

Dr Hausner's research does not put Principle 8 in the group of seven Principles that have most influence on improving KPIs. For the time period covered by Dr Hausner's research, Principle 8 was not directly addressed in the business excellence frameworks but was included later.

However, learning and continual improvement were (and still are) heavily implied across all the categories during the application process. Learning and continual improvement are heavily implied in a high business excellence score. It is not possible to get a high business excellence score unless the approach and deployment have been subjected to a regular review, learned from and improved.

256

From this, we infer that Principle 8 is already strongly implied in the strong alignment with success shown in Principles 1, 2, 4, 5, 6, 7 and 10. Principle 8 is a higher order Principle in that it depends on the other Principles for it to be able to work. For example, innovation will not happen unless you: have trust (Principle 1, 'Role models'); have enthusiastic volunteering (Principle 7, 'Enthusiastic people'); add value to your customers (Principle 3, 'Customers'); improve your systems (Principle 4, 'To improve the outcome, improve the system'); and focus on your objectives (Principle 2, 'Focus on achieving results').

8.1 Create an environment of continuous learning

If you stand still in the current world, you will probably not survive for long. Just to keep up requires an almost headlong rush. The rush is to improve constantly—in terms of both products and services that customers will value (Principle 3) and processes that are more efficient (i.e. cost less) and effective (i.e. better meet your goals and objectives).

Principle 8 says that you will have to be innovative in that rush for improvement. You should not be satisfied with the status quo. It also says that your ability to do well in the rush of constant improvement and innovation depends on your ability to learn continuously—to grow your knowledge and make use of it.

We need to see innovation not as a fad but as an essential area of attention. Innovation brings a vitality that comes from finding new ideas and using them to develop and grow. Without innovation, systems—even 'perfect' systems—become drab, uninteresting and eventually irrelevant.

Continuous improvement, whether it is through continual incremental improvement, innovation, breakthrough or invention, means that you are changing the status quo in order to reach your goal. Continuous improvement is crucial for all companies in today's marketplace.

Effective companies know that innovation is more than spontaneity or serendipity. Innovation is purposeful. It must be treated as the essential internal business attribute of the company. This used to be called 'research and development' and was often restricted to a department with that name. The new thinking takes it much further and has it as the province of everybody.

Adaptation—a natural act

Innovation is a natural act. In nature we call it evolution—the gradual unfolding of new forms through the constant interaction of organisms (all of which exhibit variation in all their characteristics) with their environment. In *The Same and Not the Same*, Nobel-prize winning Hoffmann says, 'Nature is a tinkerer...Anything that works is co-opted, banged into shape by (myriad) natural experiments'. Major shifts—new species and extinction—are excited by major shifts in the environment. 'Major shifts' do not simply mean climate change or some cataclysmic event—but also perhaps the arrival of a new form, a competitor, or the chance establishment of a more viable strain.

The history of all species is one of adaptation—to new conditions. Those that adapt best do best. Every adaptation and its relationship with its environment is always very thoroughly tested.

Iteration over billions of years—an infinity of failed experiments—has led to intelligent humans and the world in which we find ourselves. In nature, iterations that fail are not 'learnings'. However, all viable forms discovered through the process are taken up, and these emerging forms continually change the nature of the experiment. *Viability* is always the goal.

Imperfect fit

This natural iteration—the chance establishment and improvement of viability and resilience—has its parallels and differences in the human-made world. Intelligent, curious, learning humans short-circuit these myriad iterations.

From synthetic chemistry, Hoffmann presents images of the chemist as the architect/discoverer. The chemist brings discipline and thinking to the iteration process: fast-tracking—reducing the iterations; setting up conditions in which viability can be established and improved. By inducing and designing, the chemist exploits and guides the iterations. He/she applies learning, selectively experiments, reduces the iterations, finds viability that suits and exploits this knowledge to define the next experiment.

Think of the tens of thousands of iterations that Thomas Edison tried in his 'experiments' while searching for filament material that would produce the best light.

The central notion is Russell's 'imperfect fit'—'that things "fit" well rather than "perfectly". This allows trial and failure, and trial and refinement—often followed by breakthrough and new theory'.

'Imperfect fit' is used to draw attention to the fact that we live in a dynamic world—always searching to improve viability—whether the search is conscious or by design.

We seek order and new experiences

Our nature is to seek comfort: we seek to impose order and to repeat pleasurable experiences. Yet we also seek the novelty that only diversity can deliver. These two ideas are in tension—between what we are used to and what is new; between satisfaction with what we know and dissatisfaction with the old.

Novel stuff that appeals is drawn into our current way and is improved. We are driven to experiment, to understand concepts and the relationships between them. But we are averse to failure. Novel stuff that does not appeal we call a 'mistake' (and are so presented with the opportunity to learn). Each step gives a platform that allows us to reach a little further.

The more extensive the diversity of alternatives, the richer the mix of relationships. The greater our skill and our 'feel' for the desired result, the more likely we are to arrive at viable innovation.

Poetry

Chris Russell gives this example: A poet has an idea or emotion to present in an appealing form. To make it 'appealing' causes certain rules to be applied. These might be the rules of metre, rhyme and logic—but any set will guide iteration as the poet searches hundreds of combinations for the right solution. The tension between discipline and aesthetics will drive the iterations. The quality of the iterations themselves will be regulated by the poet's ability to exploit the diversity of language and style—and commitment to stay with the process. This process can and often does lead to ideas that surprise the poet. In the world of purposeful innovation, we would call this surprise a 'discovery'—or 'invention'.

Good practices

- Senior executives have created an atmosphere that accepts and welcomes innovative change that benefits the customer and the company and makes processes easier and simpler to use or with less variation in their output.
- A climate is created whereby an entrepreneurial approach is encouraged, new opportunities and prospects are sought, outstanding attributes are recognised and there is no fear of failure.
- Employee survey results show employees believe their creative ideas are sought and used and that innovation really is an essential internal business attribute of the company.
- People have pride in what the company stands for.
- A high degree of ownership of the company's image and activities.

Poor practices

- A culture of blame when things go wrong. Blame when innovations do not work. (This significantly discourages risk taking and innovation.)
- Apparent uniformity of thought across the company—usually manifested as an unwillingness to challenge management.

8.2 Continuously innovate

You must continually innovate (adapt, provide new products and services, do things differently). You must seek new ways of doing what you are good at now. If you do not, you will not keep up with your marketplace and you will not be capable of providing the goods and services at the quality and price demanded.

You must be constantly adapting and copying new ideas from everywhere that you can—from competitors, from other industries, from customers, between processes, from other technologies.

Steal ideas shamelessly

Keep looking outside of your company and your industry for new ideas. Many of the real breakthrough ideas have come from adapting the practices, products or service offerings from one company or industry into another.

How have other industries reduced their response time? For example, if response time means getting there quickly, all the following industries would have much to learn from each other: police, fire, ambulance, taxis, road-side service, couriers, fast-food delivery. This is benchmarking in its broadest sense.

Borrow ideas from others. Externally, the company acquires ideas through its interaction with its environment and its capability to extract ideas of value. Thus, your customers, alliances, industry, science, technology and competitors are all valuable sources of ideas.

If the benchmarking process is not well established, if a company begins to believe it cannot learn from anyone else, if it is not willing to look outside at what other companies or even other parts of its own company do, then innovation will not happen. It will remain stuck.

Often when people practise benchmarking, they are much more interested in proving to themselves and everyone else how good they are. You see constant examples of so-called benchmarking tours whose participants appear only to want to tell what they are doing rather than find out what the place they are visiting is doing. Wrong! Put your ego on hold. You can learn from these people, regardless of how good you think you are. Listen and ask questions! Suck their brains dry!

Battle analogy

Many writers describe the 'battle of the marketplace'. It is a good analogy. In 'battle' and in the marketplace, the problem is about positioning, applying force and developing the capability to win. The military approach says we work on ourselves to be ever more capable—to improve our viability in the world around us. The battle view leaves no option but to ensure plans and actions do have external application and internal bite.

Companies are imperfect. They rely on fallible people and operate systems that they know need improvement. Without clear knowledge of the future, they create a vision and then watch the future close in around it. This 'closing in' creates the need for viability. The closing in is rarely benign. Competition and other enormous forces of change in a turbulent transforming world bring great uncertainty and insecurity. Globalisation, accelerating change and the shifting nature of competitiveness all mean that innovation is now a battle imperative rather than just a good thing to do.

As in warfare, the contestants have two issues to face: the first is to keep up with current play and the second is to find ways to increase their capability more comprehensively than the opposition. The military analogy is valid across the huge array of business strategy.

Invent, innovate, improvise and imitate

Chris Russell has identified four levels of continuous improvement and innovation (Fig. 8.1):

- imitation and improvisation (the lower levels), which both imply a continuation of the current outcome or process, continuous improvement
- innovation and invention (the upper levels), which imply novelty, something new.

The two lower levels deal largely with the refinement of what already exists. The risk is low, the time to do them in is short and the benefits are commonly low. However, results can be substantial and important; for example, massive improvements in the performance of processes, in aircraft safety and in heart valves. The innovativeness, enthusiastic volunteering and resourcefulness described in Principle 7 ('Enthusiastic

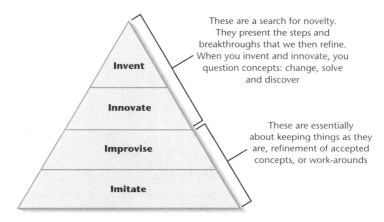

These are a search for novelty. They present the steps and breakthroughs that we then refine. When you invent and innovate, you question concepts: change, solve and discover

These are essentially about keeping things as they are, refinement of accepted concepts, or work-arounds

Invent

Innovate

Improvise

Imitate

Fig. 8.1 The improvement–innovation triangle

people') are essential ingredients to the solutions we can generate at these levels. But it is at the higher levels that you search for the new.

Innovation sees the introduction of new concepts, the introduction of new models or substantially different ways. The upper levels are distinguished from the two lower levels in that at these levels you are very dissatisfied with what exists and believe that current concepts limit you from finding alternatives.

The dominant idea behind distinguishing 'innovation and invention' from 'improvising and imitating' is that at the upper levels, it is the concepts that are up for grabs or unknown. They create instability. You prospect, trial, dismiss and overturn. At the lower levels, you are more accepting of the concepts and seek to refine.

Ideas cluster

Invention, whether by purposeful endeavour or by surprise/discovery, opens new possibilities. Similar ideas fly and cluster to this new knowledge. New relationships are tried. Some are viable. Those that are viable fire the processes of imitation and improvisation. And you begin again.

Invention presents you with a window on new possibilities and innovation sees you exploit that condition as established concepts begin to migrate to it.

In Russell's words 'Ideas cluster, iterate and sort into higher levels of viability. Each brings new value, novelty and complexity. For example, we see the car and the aircraft as different in almost every respect from their original inventions because of innovation. Often this is done by way of importing an idea or technology already established in some other field. Importing ideas or technology is constrained by awareness of them, receptivity of the candidate processes to change, the capability to integrate them and the effect on current operations and markets. We usually innovate with our feet firmly on the ground'.

Risk

Invention carries higher risk than innovation because not all inventions are viable. The risk is high because most inventions fail to deliver a valued, viable result. Indeed, some concepts needed for the viability of the invention may not be known.

The improvement–innovation triangle (Fig. 8.1) also presents the idea that we spend most of our energy working in the existing world—the lower levels. This is our stable foundation. Russell notes 'at these levels, there is little risk or cost of failure. Commonly, improvements are in small increments. Most "experiments" at these levels have high chances of success because we are dealing with "knowns". At the top, the triangle is small—representing the idea that few of the experiments will deliver viable results.

'In pursuing all these levels—particularly the upper ones—we apply imagination, inquiry and initiative. Thus, innovation is a natural act that we induce and guide. It is driven by imagination ("the readiness to redefine what could be"), inquiry ("curiosity, discovery and learning") and initiative ("the readiness to do"). The notions of imperfect fit, iteration, viability and imperfect knowledge make risk and failure likely. Risk also plays its role in the external environment where competition, innovations that are more appealing and our sense of aesthetics and values all play their role. Against this relative simplicity, companies deal with people and mess'.

Innovation is hard work

Innovation is natural for humans. But why don't we see more of it? Roald Hoffmann, a Nobel Prize winner in Chemistry, notes 'The intriguing thing about creation is that it is so intellectual and so down-to-earth practical. Creation is such hard work'. Hoffmann's personal experience gives a valuable insight—curiosity and adventure live hand in hand with perseverance and knowledge, with intensity of effort, persistence and an often huge number of iterations.

In a company, the innovation process needs to be nurtured. Although it is clearly necessary, innovation has many enemies.

Good practices

- Innovation and creative ideas are actively sought. People are happy to contribute ideas for the company's benefit.
- Employees are encouraged to try new ideas, experiment, innovate and take reasonable risks. People are encouraged to take initiatives and to be proactive. Creative problem solving is encouraged.
- People can decide things and work with few rules.
- There is a willingness to experiment, albeit cautiously, with different technological and human resource systems.
- Recognising the value of innovation for the vitality it brings to the drab push for reliability.

Poor practices

- Customer needs not considered in the generation of innovation opportunities.
- No innovation in highly task-focused companies (or parts of companies), which claim not to have the resources to pursue alternative ways.

8.3 Use tools to generate ideas

You should use tools and techniques to generate new concepts. Because of the large number of iterations possible and to help you break out of your current thinking, it is a good idea to use tools and techniques to guide your process of idea generation and reduce the number of failed iterations.

Here is a list of tools in common use (the reference in brackets provides more information on them):

- Brainstorming (Brassard & Ritter (1994), *The Memory Jogger II*)
- Affinity diagram (Brassard & Ritter (1994), *The Memory Jogger II*)
- Lateral thinking (de Bono (1985), *Six Thinking Hats*)
- Mindmapping (Buzan (1977), *Make the Most of Your Mind*)
- Fishbone, Ishikawa or cause and effect diagrams (Brassard & Ritter (1994), *The Memory Jogger II*)
- TRIZ (a very good Russian problem-solving tool, based on patents, for reducing iterations; Kim, *TRIZ: The Theory of Inventive Problem Solving*, www.ddj.com).

There are three more sophisticated tools in use:

1. de Bono's 'six thinking hats'.
2. Assumption breaking—this is a Goldratt tool and is detailed in Principle 5, 'Improved decisions', and Principle 7, 'Enthusiastic people', and is not repeated here. It allows you to ignore tradition and find simple, powerful solutions that are based on commonsense but which may not be common practice.
3. Goldratt's 'current reality tree'.

Six thinking hats

Early in the 1980s, Dr de Bono invented the sophisticated brainstorming tool—the 'six thinking hats' method. The method is a framework for thinking and can incorporate lateral thinking.

Companies such as Prudential Insurance, IBM, Federal Express, British Airways, Polaroid, Pepsico, DuPont, and Nippon Telephone and Telegraph, possibly the world's largest company, use this method.

The six hats represent six modes of thinking and are directions to think rather than labels for thinking. The thinker can put on or take off one of these hats to indicate the type of thinking being used. This putting on and taking off is essential. The hats must never be used to categorise individuals, even if their behaviour may seem to invite this. Judgmental thinking has its place in the system but is not allowed to dominate as in normal thinking. The hats are used proactively rather than reactively. When done in a group, everybody wears the same hat at the same time.

1. *White hat thinking—facts and figures*. This covers facts, figures, information needs and gaps. 'I think we need some white hat thinking at this point' means 'Let's drop the arguments and proposals, and look at the database'.
2. *Red hat thinking—intuition and feelings*. This covers intuition, feelings and emotions. The red hat allows the thinker to put forward an intuition without any need to justify it. 'Putting on my red hat, I feel this is a terrible proposal. It makes me upset that...'. Usually feelings and intuition can only be introduced into a discussion if they are supported by impersonal logic. Usually the feeling is genuine but the logic is spurious. The red hat gives full permission to a thinker to put forward his or her feelings on the subject.
3. *Black hat thinking—logical negative and caution*. This is the hat of judgment and caution. It is a very valuable hat. It is not in any sense an inferior or negative hat. The black hat is used to point out why a suggestion does not fit the facts, the available experience, the system in use, the policy that is being followed, or is not practical. The black hat must always be logical.
4. *Yellow hat thinking—suggestions*. This is the logical positive. Why something will work and why it will offer benefits. It can be used in looking forward to the results of some proposed action or it can also be used to find something of value in what has already happened.
5. *Green hat thinking—creativity*. This is the hat of creativity, alternatives, options, proposals; what is interesting, provocations and challenges.
6. *Blue hat thinking—organising the thinking process*. This is the overview or process control hat. It looks not at the subject itself but at the way you are 'thinking' about the subject. 'Process check! Putting on my blue hat, I feel we should do some more green hat thinking at this point.' In technical terms, the blue hat is concerned with metacognition.

The method promotes fuller input from more people. In de Bono's words, it 'separates ego from performance'. Everyone is able to contribute to the exploration without denting egos as they are just using the yellow or whatever hat. The six hats system encourages performance rather than ego defence. People can contribute under any hat even if they initially support the opposite view.

The essential point is that a hat is a direction to think rather than a label for thinking. The main theoretical reasons for using the six thinking hats are to:

- encourage parallel thinking
- encourage full-spectrum thinking
- separate ego from performance.

Current reality tree

In his book *It's Not Luck*, Goldratt claims that problems are not independent of each other—there are usually strong links of cause and effect between them. Until the cause and effect is established, you do not have a clear enough picture to know which problem to solve. It is very likely that all the seemingly unrelated problems come from one or two core problems—that one or two core problems are the cause of all the others. If you can identify the core problems, it gives you real direction for action and stops you wasting your time on what are annoying but irrelevant symptoms. You can direct your efforts at the core problems, not the symptoms. Follow the steps below to clearly identify the core problem.

The symptoms are called 'undesirable effects'—unavoidable derivatives of the core problems. Begin with a list of five to 10 undesirable effects—these may be common excuses. To determine the undesirable effects, some suggested questions are: 'What is preventing you from getting what you want?'; 'What are the major complaints of your customers?'; 'What demands do your customers make?'; 'What do they demand in order to place an order with you?'; 'What are the major problems in your market or industry?'.

The next step is to build a current reality tree—a diagram of the cause and effect relationships that connect all the problems prevailing in a situation. You need intuition and the willpower to do the meticulous work needed. It takes about 5 hours—a small investment for a serious problem.

Example: How to increase sales

1. Write down the undesirable effects (UDEs):
   - Competition is fiercer than ever (UDE # 1).
   - There is increasing pressure to reduce prices (UDE # 2).
   - In more and more cases the price the market is willing to pay doesn't leave enough margin (UDE # 3).
   - More than ever the market punishes suppliers who don't perform according to expectation (UDE # 4).
   - Managers are trying to run their companies by striving to achieve local optima (i.e. lack of overall vision). As a result this gives ad hoc solutions, fire fighting, but no sound overall strategy backed up by a reasonable detailed, tactical plan (UDE # 5).
   - Various functions inside the company blame each other for lack of performance (UDE # 6).
   - There is unprecedented pressure to take actions that will increase sales (UDE # 7).
   - There is the need to launch new products at an unprecedented rate (UDE # 8).

- The constant introduction of new products confuses and spoils the market (UDE # 9).
- Most new outlets and most new/improved products eat into the sales of existing outlets/products (UDE # 10).
- A large percentage of the existing sales force lacks sufficient sales skills (UDE # 11).
- Salespeople are overloaded (UDE # 12).
- Production and distribution do not improve fast/significantly enough (UDE # 13).
- Engineering is unable to deliver new products fast or reliably enough (UDE # 14).
- Companies don't come up with sufficient innovative ideas in marketing (UDE # 15).

2. Find a cause and effect (an 'if...then' relationship) between at least two of the undesirable effects listed:

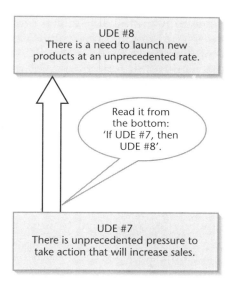

Fig. 8.2 Cause and effect relationship of undesirable effects (UDEs)

- Write each undesirable effect on a post-it note.
- Do not prioritise the undesirable effects.

3. If necessary, add clarity by inserting intermediate steps.

4. If something is missing, an insufficiency, write an 'if...and...then...' set.

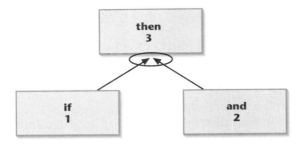

Fig. 8.3 Read it from the bottom as 'if **1** and **2**, then **3**'

5. If the bottom of the tree is general and the top of the tree is specific, add an entry at the bottom that accounts for the specific entry.

6. Read aloud what you have written, and change and clarify your wording as you go.

7. Using the solid nucleus established by connections made in the steps above, add the remaining undesirable effects one by one:
   - It is not difficult, it just requires meticulous work. Usually there is a long period of floundering.
   - Initially, many connections pop into your mind, but when you try to put them on paper, none is substantiated. If this happens, use Goldratt's categories of legitimate reservations (i.e. converting an intuitive connection into something so solid that everyone will refer to it as commonsense).
   - Go slowly. The process cannot be rushed.
   - Expect to find at least one loop (where an undesirable effect feeds itself) when the effects are getting worse (unprecedented, bigger and bigger, increasing).
   - Don't brush aside nagging 'trivialities' as they often let you connect more undesirable effects and lead to breakthrough solutions. However, tracking down all the trivialities can lead to paralysis. Don't forget, you are looking for a solution that will make a difference.
   - Logic by itself is not enough. You must have intuition as well. The logical diagrams force you to verbalise your gut feelings and so enable true unleashing of your intuition, and the ability to check it. Intuition is a necessary condition for finding solutions but it is far from sufficient. The diagrams give you a method to unleash, focus and study your intuition so you can arrive at practical, simple solutions.

8. Work down the arrows to the root cause issue—the core problem. It will be towards the base of your tree.

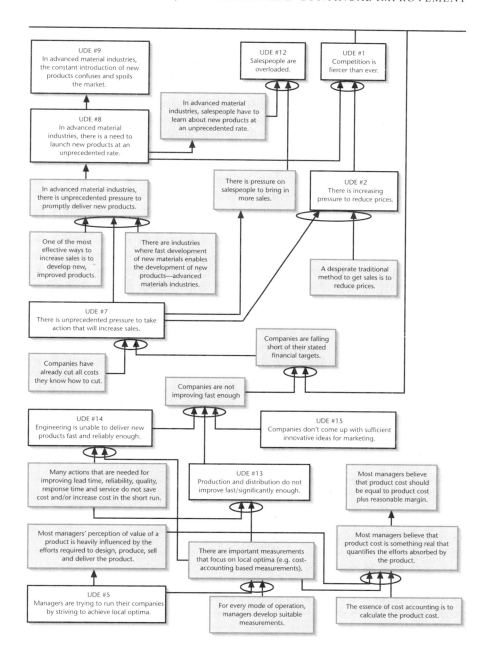

Fig. 8.4 A current reality tree—read it from the bottom

Don't forget what customers value when you innovate

Your innovation and continual improvement must be aimed at providing better products and services to your customers/stakeholders.

Most companies are caught up in the technological chase of their industry. Consequently, most think that the only innovation worth thinking about is a technical change to the product or service. Or, a clever change to the process design to make it more efficient. Although these are, without doubt, important (and often receive the most publicity), they are not where the most successful innovations come from.

The innovations that have the most leverage are those that directly address your customers' dissatisfiers. Recall from Principle 3 ('Customers') that what your customer sees as your product and service offering is much broader than the physical product or that actual service. Your customer sees things about your product and service that they do not like—especially those things that inconvenience them, cause them extra work or how they pay you.

Very high leverage innovations can come from addressing these dissatisfiers. They have high leverage because they can often be achieved with little cost or inconvenience to you and at the same time give you a much more satisfied customer.

For example, here is a common set of customer dissatisfiers. You can often get a considerable increase in customer satisfaction by addressing them:

- payment terms and conditions
- access to be able to purchase
- advice on how to use the product
- how the product is delivered
- response time
- perceived status from using your product or service
- reliability
- accuracy
- the number of times they have to contact you to be able to get the product to work to their satisfaction.

Science or serendipity

Brilliantly creative ideas are rarely, if ever, a result of an exact, scientific procedure.

- Most revolutionary inventions and great ideas were thought up while sleeping or in the shower.
- Many adaptations are planned as described above.
- Many adaptations are serendipity (making desirable but unsought changes).

Other adaptations are very puzzling. The macaque monkeys of Japan wash their rice in the sea. They all do it. Washing the rice separates it from stones and adds a bit of salt for flavour. How did they adapt to do this? It is certainly learned. Where did this invention come from? Was this serendipity?

Some adaptations look as though they happen by good luck. For example, Art Fry invented the 3M Post-it note. He was looking for a way to hold his bookmarks in place. At about the same time a colleague had developed a glue that did not stick too well. The eventual result was the Post-it note.

There is often the impression of 'good luck' about these innovations. Isn't 'good luck' the intersection of preparation and opportunity?

Good practices

- 'Thought leaders' are encouraged and provided with skills and knowledge to assist them.
- Business intelligence used to evaluate new techniques and technology.
- Common systems are used to exchange important customer information across the company. These systems are easy to use and highly accessible, making customers' input accessible to staff in all areas of the company—especially product design.
- Customer comments are seen as 'opportunities for improvement' and shared across the company using a variety of media.

Poor practices

- Ad hoc approach to innovation. Expecting people to be innovative, without any of the necessary support.

8.4 Eliminate barriers to innovative ideas

In order to get innovative ideas, you must systematically eliminate the enemies of innovation (e.g. structures, traditions, politics, fear in the workplace). Innovation is natural for all people. It's in your genes. Many people are naturally very creative. But we still don't see much innovation. Why not? Why don't we see more of it?

Innovation is very fragile. It is very easily destroyed. It belongs in the high ground of imagination, inquiry and initiative—all of which rely on freedom, independence, absence of fear, difference, high autonomy and mistakes. In most companies, the environment is very different from that picture. If inventiveness and innovation are to thrive, they need a considerable helping hand.

Principle 7 ('Enthusiastic people') covers some of this—you actually have to work quite hard for people to volunteer their enthusiasm and resourcefulness. Structures, traditions, politics and fear in the workplace all act to counter people's natural innovation. And this would get you only to the lower levels of the triangle (Fig. 8.1). You often see bosses demanding that their people be innovative or creative and at the same time actively discouraging such innovation. The following are further examples of why the creative process does not often happen in the workplace. Perhaps, fortunately, your competition has to deal with the same issues.

Control and reward

Most companies establish control and reward systems to ensure reliable performance. These are good things. However, they can work against your need for innovation. Beware that you are not saying 'we want you to innovate' but then rewarding only behaviour that sticks to the status quo and punishing behaviour that asks questions—rewarding A while hoping for B.

Most researchers believe offering rewards for creativity and innovation cannot and does not work effectively. This is despite the common practice of offering or withholding rewards to try to stimulate creativity. When the planned 'improvement' produces 'more of the same', the normal response is to vary the reward system or to have yet another search for new ideas.

Unsupporting environment

In most companies, the necessary supporting environment is absent for Principles 1 ('Role models') and 7 ('Enthusiastic people') to work. Senior managers have not worked to establish an environment of trust or to set direction adequately. The supporting environment necessary for employees to enthusiastically volunteer their resourcefulness and consequently innovation is absent. Offering a few rewards is of little help if all the supporting environment is absent or is working against you. Having Principles 1 and 7 in place is a prerequisite for Principle 8 to work.

No space

When people have become emotionally detached robots who just come to work to pick up their pay, they do not innovate (see Fig. 7.3). Principle 1 ('Role models') and Principle 7 ('Enthusiastic people') discussed people's need for space and how barging into or invading that space will cause people to cease to volunteer.

Scarce resources

People don't have time. One of the common mistakes companies make is to downsize to the point of efficiency. Everyone is busy to the point that they have no time for anything beyond dealing with the here and now, the daily grind. If you are constantly fighting crocodiles, you just don't have time to think of new ways to drain the swamp.

You need to have time and space to be able to think of new ways of doing things. You need the actual time as well as the emotional space to want to do so. To do this, you need adequate resources.

You have to be looking

Before you can find something, you have to be looking for it. The problem must be clear. Each of us has a part of his or her brain (the reticular activating system) that filters out information that you do not want. This filter is a very good thing. If you did not have it, you would be swamped with 'junk'. Your senses would be overwhelmed with so much information you would not be able to function. Because of this filter, you let in only information that you want. The filter's job is to let only important information through. The downside of this is that your filters can take out too much.

Before you can find something, you have to be looking for it. Until you want it, even if it is right in front of you, you will not be able to see it. The first step to finding anything is to know that you need it. Only then do you open your awareness to opportunities around you.

This is one of the keys to innovation. The process is actually quite orderly. Firstly, you need to identify a problem that needs solving. Then you can begin to look for solutions.

Of course, the problem must be very clearly defined for this to work to your advantage. Otherwise, you will find the solution to the wrong problem.

No pressure

If there is no pressure, there is no need to change. Pressure can be essential. Pressure can range from gentle disquiet with the status quo through to 'solve this or you die'. The disadvantage of pressure of the 'you die' magnitude is that many people become paralysed or are less able to identify which problem needs to be solved. They frequently lock onto the wrong problem and so come up with the wrong solution.

It would be good if the pressure were a bit less than that and if the problem was clear. Good—but not always possible.

Lack of good tools

In general, the tools available to assist thinking are fairly poor. We can go through the iterations described by Hoffmann. However, it would be very much better if tools existed to take shortcuts. The six thinking hats and current reality tree tools allow some of that. However, their use is very limited.

Comfort zones and conservatism

People get very comfortable being able to fight the fires they know. They develop skills in dealing with the problems of yesterday. Often, those skills were very hard won. There is always the fear that those fire-fighting skills will not work in the new world. People don't want to learn new skills by getting new bruises. It is easier to pour scorn on the new idea—don't let it get off the ground.

People in companies have seen it all before. The boss comes out with some new idea that will save the world and make us all rich. Six months later, that one is dead but he now has a bigger and better one. Or, with the churn in companies, you probably have a new boss who is pouring scorn on the previous boss's ideas. Why get interested in any of them?

It is likely that inertia, conservatism (i.e. the limitation of our current intellectual and technological reach), causes us to stick with the past.

Rigorously enforced standards

Standards are very good for controlling your processes and reducing variation in products and services. However, often they are so rigorously enforced that people are not allowed to even think about a new way of doing something—even if mounting pressure from changing technology, customer demand or market forces would suggest that new ways are imperative.

Inertia

There appear to be three parts of inertia:

1. People become stuck in past technology and the way they have always done things and just don't want to find a new way. For example, when a company invests in a technology, it usually becomes locked into that technology (until it gets its money's worth)—even if technology used by others in its industry has far surpassed that old technology.
2. It is usually not possible to take too big a step. In complex systems and in a competitive environment you can only innovate to the extent that resources, technology, market forces and current physical or structural complexity will allow. For example, you cannot innovate faster than technology will allow or than you can persuade your customers to buy the strange product or service. You cannot have ideas today that you will not have the knowledge for until tomorrow.
3. People become caught in the thinking of how they were taught. Then, when they go to teach, they apply exactly the same approach. Unfortunately, the technology has probably moved on. (This applies in almost all fields.) For example, in the case of skiing, we now have

shaped skis. We no longer have grooves down the middle of the ski that were there in the 1960s. However, the techniques that were necessary for grooved skis are still the ones insisted on by the ski instructors' certifying body. This means that because of standards' inertia, teaching skiing is lagging 30 years behind the technology. Such a large change in technology will mean a completely new training manual.

Poor ability to use information

You must have a viable process to make intelligent use of information. A customer's suggestion that a product could solve a much richer problem will not be exploited in a company that cannot communicate the suggestion in a way that develops the necessary political and technical momentum.

Psychological temperament

Not everybody is good at finding new ways of doing things. The work on psychological temperament suggests that large numbers of people in companies will resist change. 'Guardians' make up almost 40% of the community and are even more strongly represented in many companies. Guardians are practical, commonsense people who see their role as being responsible and doing their duty. They usually do not want to change. The need to change suggests that what they have been doing so far has not been good enough. Guardians will improve and refine (the lower levels of the triangle) to make things more practical and useful. Guardians are very, very good at this continual improvement work. They will seldom innovate or invent.

Innovation or invention is usually left to the 'independent rationalists'. Most companies have very few of these and because they are often very independent they may not feel the need to be seen to fit in with the rest of the company. They are often viewed as eccentric or arrogant and their new ideas discounted or ignored.

This is an interesting paradox. Most people in the company are not able to innovate and the few who are able to do so are ignored.

Good practices

- People's ideas are respected no matter what position they hold or at which level they sit. The value of an idea does not depend on its source.
- Continuous practice of effective change management. Continual search for best or better fit.
- Bosses prize surprises.

- People delight in telling how things have improved—and that the stories demonstrate they are discerning about ethics and innovation.
- Regular measurements of employees' perception of 'trust-worthiness' of the senior executives, 'fear' and overall 'morale'.

Poor practices

- Company 'think tanks' that are the only source of new ideas generation.

8.5 Change old structures

When you implement new ideas, you must change all the old structures that the new will impact on (e.g. reward and recognition systems, performance management systems, technology, standard operating procedures, standards systems, communications systems, company structure, performance indicators, resources, job descriptions, performance agreements, organisation values, audit systems).

Things do not just happen. It is often astounding to the person with the new idea, which to them is so logical, exciting and will solve the problems of the world, that everyone does not immediately jump on it and do it. The innovator often dismisses those who reject the wonderful idea as stupid, lazy or negative. Wrong!

We will now move on to the issue of implementing those ideas—turning them into new products, services or new processes. Two models for implementing innovations are offered.

James Carlopio from the Australian Graduate School of Management proposed the first model. Carlopio takes the perspective of how people will be affected by and react to the proposed change—an issue most often omitted entirely or dealt with only superficially by those planning the change. Failure to consider how people will react to the change is the number one reason for project implementation failure.

The second model is from Goldratt, who looks at other issues often overlooked.

A five-step implementation process

Carlopio gives a five-step process and extensive checklist for implementing anything.

1. *Knowledge and awareness*: create awareness, conduct research and development, gather information, identify needs, conduct initial planning.
2. *Matching and selection*: match solutions/innovations to problems, initial sorting.

3. *Decision*: choose innovation(s) to be implemented.
4. *Implementation*: roll-out—put the innovation or new technology to use.
5. *Confirmation*: modify, test, evaluate—the 'innovation' becomes normal.

The fourth step—implementation—is not a simple 'just do it' step. The implementation step, itself, consists of five parts, all of which must be done—although not necessarily in a linear order. However, you will not be successful with the last two until the first three have been fulfilled.

The implementation steps mirror the generalised five-step process above. Do not rush through them. Each one is important. This is a very useful checklist as it shows that there is a fair amount of work needed to implement a good idea. Regardless of how good it is, it will not work unless this work is done.

Implementation: knowledge and awareness

- People have to be comfortable about the new innovation.
- You have to fill the rumour gap—that gap in information in which rumour thrives.
- You must deal with emotions and the ghosts of the past. This is very important. You must counter the 'here comes another one' syndrome. You must acknowledge past failures and say how this implementation will be different. If jobs are at stake because of the innovation— acknowledge it. You cannot expect people to be enthusiastic about losing their jobs or being lied to about it. You are attempting to deal with an attitude of 'It wasn't what was done, it was how it was done'.
- You must answer the fundamental question 'What's in it for me?'— WIIFM.
- People want to know the five Ws—'what, when, why, how, who'.
- You must provide education and training about the innovation (what it means, where it fits in, how it will work, how people will use it), so you need: course content, types of training and education, sources of training.

Implementation: facilitating structures

- You must have in place (or modify) all those systems that will allow the implementation to work. Because the implementation of the innovation is, by definition, new, it will run up against all the previously installed systems. You will need to modify these where necessary so the innovation can coexist (and does not run counter to) existing systems. You may even need very new systems. Depend on it, if there is nothing to support the new wonderful idea, or if people get punished for using it, or if your company is set up to keep looking after the old ways, the new way will fail.

- Facilitating structures that you must consider include: reward and recognition systems; performance management systems; technology; education and training; standard operating procedures; standards systems; communications systems; company structure; performance indicators; resources; job descriptions; performance agreements; peer pressure; company values; personal values; audit systems.
- You will also need these facilitating structures: detailed implementation plan; cultural analysis; innovation analysis; innovator analysis; union agreement; change agreement; working groups; discussion groups; committees.
- You are working to counter the fallacy of supporting (or rewarding) the old way while hoping for the new way.

Implementation: persuasion, decision, commitment

- Cost justification: economic evaluation; cost–benefit analysis; evaluation of tangible and intangible benefits; determining costs.
- Determining the costs of unintended side-effects—internally and to customers and the community. Also, changes to your cost of quality.
- Decision-making: rational and non-rational methods.
- Obtaining commitment from senior managers—overcoming resistance. You need a senior person to sponsor the innovation, to demand compliance with the new way, to talk it up, to obtain resources, to coordinate and to not tolerate use of the old.

Implementation: roll-out

- Training.
- Conversion: slow migration from the old to the new, or run parallel systems, or quick switch from the old to the new.
- Project termination—know when roll-out of the new is finished and the maintenance phase commences.
- Plan the evolution of the new—how to milk the most possible from the new way and modify and improve it.

Implementation: confirmation and routinisation

- Individual level measurements: What are people's attitudes to the new? Are people doing it or using it? Is everyone doing it or using it who should be?
- Group level measurements: Is there conflict between the needs of different groups? Are there unintended side-effects (good and bad)? Does the information flow work? Do the supporting structures provide the necessary support? Are the process customers satisfied? Does it reduce (or increase) your customer's costs? Does it provide value to the employees?

- Company level measurements: Is the innovation effective? Does it deliver the benefits promised? Does it provide value to the company, its customers and other stakeholders? Are the costs what were estimated? Is it always available when needed (up time/down time)?
- Societal level measurements: How does this effect the community and society? Are there societal benefits? Are there any bad (or good) side-effects?
- Review: Is it still what you want to do? What have you learned during implementation? How can you use that knowledge?

This is quite an extensive checklist. It is clear that all or most points on the list are essential. It is also clear that most companies do not bother with these points at all. This would explain why the vast majority of companies report that their innovations fail—even if they were good ideas that should have worked. Many bosses continue to think that when they have a good idea (or approve one), it is instantly implemented everywhere.

If you want your innovation to be successful, you must work at it and follow most of the points on James Carlopio's checklist.

How to cause the change

Goldratt approaches this issue in a very different way from Carlopio. In doing so, he fills in some important gaps. In *It's Not Luck* and *The Goal*, Goldratt suggests that these questions are critical and fundamental for leaders of companies:

- What to change?
- What to change to?
- How to cause the change?

Many people in almost every company have many innovative, bright ideas. Which ideas are the 'right' ones—the ones that will solve the current and future problems? Most innovative solutions address only symptoms and fail to address the causes—the underlying problems. As Goldratt says, how do you know what you need to change? Then, when you have found the underlying problem, how do know what you need to change to? And when you know that, how do you go about causing the change to happen?

The process of innovation can learn a lot from the tools Goldratt presents to address these three core issues. The tools are extremely rigorous and significantly help the innovation process. Their main drawback is the rigour, which is off-putting to many. However, if you are serious about innovation, you will need to be rigorous, otherwise you are probably wasting your time and money on half-baked ideas or solutions to the wrong problems. If the idea is worthwhile, it is worth your while to treat it seriously and analyse it properly. The details of the techniques are well beyond the scope of this book and can be found in Goldratt's work and Scheinkopf's *Thinking For a Change*.

In overview:

- Create the current reality tree to identify the core problem. The current reality tree answers the question 'What to change?' by listing the undesirable effects, describing the causalities that exist between them and identifying a core problem that is keeping the undesirable effects in existence (see p. 266).
- Create an 'evaporating cloud' (see section 5.4 and Fig. 7.2) to identify a systemic conflict in your assumptions that is perpetuating the core problem. Brainstorm solutions to the core problem and select the initial elements of a solution. This was discussed in Principle 5 ('Improved decisions') where it was established that every problem is a conflict between assumptions. We should be able to articulate every core problem as a conflict—the core conflict. The 'evaporating cloud' technique will help verbalise the assumptions that are maintaining the conflict.
- To answer the question 'What to change to?', create a 'future reality tree' to develop a robust solution to the core problem. Use the starting point found in the evaporating cloud—the initial solution—as your 'injection'. The process calls for you to list the positives and all negatives of the injection. Eliminate all the undesirable effects and block all undesirable side-effects that you can think of. The process also calls for you to do a 'negative branch reservation analysis', whereby you look for and find solutions to everything you and your team can think of that can go wrong. You should test the negative branches to destruction. It is far better to find solutions to problems during this stage than when you are in production. When you begin this analysis, your initial solution may seem as impossible as getting pigs to fly. The beauty is that this process provides a way to get them to fly.
- Create a 'prerequisite tree' to determine the necessary conditions (immediate objectives) for implementing the injections (objectives) and the sequence in which they should be accomplished to overcome all the obstacles you can think of. This is the first step in answering the question 'How to cause the change?'. Obstacles can include all the enemies as well as 'hiring freeze, no staff, no money, no advertising'.
- Create 'transition trees' to define the detailed specific action plans to accomplish the intermediate objectives and injections of the prerequisite tree.

Although that sounds complicated and long, it does not have to be. If you know the answer, don't follow all the steps. But the full process is there, when you need it, for an important innovation. It is rigorous and it certainly gives focus on real problems, real solutions and problems that you need to overcome along the way.

The rigour involved—that few companies or bosses have the patience to follow—is another clear indication of the work needed to have innovations implemented successfully.

Good practices

- The company is agile—able to respond quickly to opportunities, technological change and changing stakeholder needs. It keeps its 'ear to the ground' to keep informed of these changes.
- The company has guidelines for overcoming inertia. It recognises that each change in technology, each change in stakeholders' needs and each time it wants to do something differently, it must break the ties with the past—the old ways of doing things. They are no longer valid.
- Research and development plans exist to turn innovative ideas into products.

Poor practices

- Programs that generate many ideas but fall short of turning those ideas into products and services that are brought to the market.

8.6 Overcome barriers to implementing innovations

In order to implement new ideas, you should systematically overcome the barriers that prevent you from implementing your innovations (e.g. existing stock, past investment, no time or budget).

It should be obvious by now that if you do not work to implement the innovation, it will not happen by magic or by goodwill. There are many reasons that companies do not take up new ideas. Here are a few of them.

It is natural to push back

We saw in Principle 2 ('Focus on achieving results') that is natural for people to push back when they think they are being pushed into something. New ideas are often presented as a challenge to the old. The holders of the old ideas will naturally push back. You might have the solution to world hunger, or a cure for cancer or heart disease, but the established order will naturally push to defeat you. The problem is not new. Machiavelli says in *The Prince*, 'It must be considered that there is nothing more difficult to carry out, nor more doubtful of success, nor more dangerous to handle than to initiate a new order of things. For the reformer has enemies in all who profit by the old order, and only lukewarm defenders in all those who would profit by the new'.

Existing stock and investment in the past

Every new product idea means that existing stock is made obsolete. There will always be considerable pressure to make every dollar possible from previous investment—either of money, time or effort. New ideas threaten to cut short the reaping of these rewards. Companies must plan development and release of products to make the most of these past investments. That process is usually well cared for. However, innovation is the enemy of carefully planned development and release programs, which are operating at the bottom levels of the triangle (Fig. 8.1).

Consider just one path in the recorded sound industry, which began in 1878 when Edison invented the phonograph. It progressed from cylinders, to wind-up gramophones, to record players, tape recorders, cassette tape recorders, to compact disc players and eventually arrived at today's digital versatile disk players. Each of those stages had its product development cycle—gradual improvements on existing products—miniaturisation, new features, the planned obsolescence of this year's new model.

However, there are distinct jumps—when the thinking changed and the entire product range had to be scrapped. There is always pressure from the status quo to prevent that from happening. As we have seen in Principle 3 ('Customers'), everything about the company might be directed to delivering the *old* product to its customers: including customer and staff training, career development, strategies for takeovers up and down the supply chain, strategic alliances. All this alignment is at risk from the new thinking.

There are a thousand reasons not to take up the new thinking. However, you see what happens when you do not accept the new with open arms. As an example, think of the failure of the Swiss watch industry to see the potential in the electronic watch. They invented it and gave it away. It had so little in common with their old business that it was pushed away with ridicule. Consequently, the Swiss watch industry died, as did the phonograph makers and buggy whip makers before them.

If you do not have processes to counter the push back from the existing old thinking, your new competitors will grab it and you will get creamed.

Budget

Where do people with good ideas go to get them funded in your company? Are you tied to budget processes that are based on ideas and proposals that are two years old? How is a new idea funded if you have already allocated your entire budget to admirable projects by your capital allocation process in your budget cycle? Do you say, 'If you have a new idea, put in for it in next year's budget'? Next year!? Too late!!

You should set aside seed funding to grow your new ideas. If the idea is good enough and has enough potential, you should be flexible enough to interrupt the budget cycle. You should not do this lightly because it sounds like instability. However, sometimes you are forced to be flexible by market forces.

Time

'Who has got time to work on the new stuff? We have so much work to do just to do our daily job.' Many companies are so bound up in their current processes that they do not make time to fit in innovations.

No outlet for unbounded creativity

What do you do when your creative technical people come up with a new idea that is way out in left field? Often when you get the creative juices really romping along, they find and develop products that just don't fit with what you do—at all. Solution? 3M use the 'new company' solution. Provide the creative geniuses who made the invention with a new company. Pack skills around them (that they probably don't have) to make failure less certain (e.g. management, marketing, development, financing). Keep the ownership in place back to the parent but break the main shackles with the old company—the old way of thinking. Such freedom has often turned out to be a significant incentive.

Control, habit, training and standards

We are driven by habit (the way we do things now and are comfortable with), training and standards and standard operating procedures. These and other controls not only stop new ideas emerging but they lock the old ways in place and make change very difficult. Implementation must address changes to standards, training procedures and methods of enforcing them, such as audits. As Carlopio has pointed out, we must apply systems thinking to the implementation and address all the issues that affect the innovation or that it affects.

Persuasion

The story about zippers is a good one—true or not. The story is that soon after the invention of the zipper, a bright young man thought it would be a good idea to replace the fly buttons in men's trousers with a zipper. He made this suggestion to his boss—who did not see the potential but only lawsuits resulting from caught anatomy. He rejected the idea.

It was of course later taken up by a competitor. Possibly, a better presentation of the idea would have been to make up a pair of trousers with the zipper and let the boss use them. The convenience of the zipper would have made it the boss's idea.

Trouble-free implementation needs good design

The trouble-free implementation of new products and services requires good design. Design should include:

- merging external and internal customer requirements into the product or service
- taking advantage of the most recent stable technology
- designing production/delivery to provide the quality and operational performance requirements of external and internal customers
- following Carlopio's five-step implementation process
- finding and addressing all the reasons the new approach will not work (Goldratt's negative branches)
- making time for an orderly changeover to the new procedures and supporting structures.

The amount of design needed will depend on the nature of the products and services, including whether the products and services are entirely new, variants, or require major or minor process changes. You must consider:

- health and safety (of employees and customers)
- long-term performance of the product and the company
- environmental impact of the product, your waste stream and your raw materials
- unintended consequences
- how you will measure quality, performance to specification, meeting objectives
- process capability
- manufacturability
- marketability
- commercialisation
- maintainability
- obsolescence
- supplier capability
- documentation
- cycle time
- delivery processes
- effect on existing products and services (for both production and sales)
- effect on all stakeholders in the value chain (including suppliers, strategic alliances, business partners, employees and the community)
- redesigning ('re-engineering') existing processes.

Coordination of design and production/delivery processes should involve all work units and individuals involved in production/delivery and whose cooperation and performance will affect the outcome. This might include groups such as research and development, manufacturing, production, distribution, marketing, customer service, sales, design and engineering.

Measure effectiveness of the innovation

You should measure the effectiveness of the new idea. You need to see if the new idea is successful. For example, measure to determine if:

- the innovation is effective
- it delivers the benefits promised
- it provides value to the organisation, its customers and other stakeholders
- the costs are what were estimated.

Good practices

- Discussion about proposed changes is encouraged. Processes exist to test new ideas to destruction before they are implemented. As many negatives as possible are found and solutions devised. Questions about the practicality of proposed solutions and the logic of the proposed approach are valued and sought after.
- Customer input is sought when converting innovative processes to marketable products/services.
- Innovations are widely canvassed with stakeholders during development to ensure wider take-up.
- Collaborating with customers for innovation and joint innovation.

Poor practices

- Innovation is not well translated into active programs and strategic links.
- Uncoordinated duplication of effort in development. Different groups working on the same things without contact or knowledge of what the others are doing or that they exist.

8.7 Have a strategic approach to innovation

You must take a strategic approach to innovation, implementation and continuous improvement (e.g. innovation and implementation objectives, resources provided to assist innovation and implementation, including seed funding and champions).

The turbulent marketplace suggests the need to:

- achieve viability faster—just to keep up
- reach further into the future
- seek predictability in your innovation activities.

You must think strategically about your innovation processes. Is the innovation proposal consistent with your direction? Is your direction right? Is your rate of innovation appropriate for your industry and market? Are you being left behind?

- Borrow ideas from other companies that are successful at innovation. Exploit your networks—especially the global ones. Exchange information on the development and diffusion of new and unusual technical solutions.
- Grow innovation alliances. Share information on how your innovation and change programs work, not just at the technical level. Which innovations should you pursue independently? Which innovations should you pursue with established partners? Which need establishing new partnerships?
- Enter the formal planning process every six months—not yearly. This provides a path for significant innovation proposals to enter the formal planning process without having to wait another year, by when the window of opportunity may be shut.
- Establish a seed-funding process to hold money aside specifically to explore innovations and get them under way. This accelerates commercial advantage and gives extraordinary motivation to individuals.
- Include a business case methodology in your innovation process that tests the proposal against your key result areas (KRAs) and prepare a cost–benefit analysis.
- You need sufficient flexibility to accommodate product/service proposals that would fail strict tests against KRAs. (KRAs describe the company's current thinking—e.g. 'make buggy whips'. The innovation may be a gateway to a new business. Five years ago, few companies had an 'e-commerce' KRA.)
- Measure your rate of innovation. Compare yourself against other companies that are successful at innovation.
- When you choose among competing innovations, think strategically. It is an investment decision. Choice should not be driven by the appeal of the innovation itself.
- Perseverance remains an important aspect of the innovation strategy—essentially every step will have issues to be decided. You need to resolve the issue of how busy people, when confronted by an idea out of left field, can cherish it and work with it.

Suggestions from Honeywell

It is clear from the above that you need formal and informal processes to sustain the innovation effort—to encourage, support and coax the good ideas, to weed out the unsuccessful ones while encouraging the heart of the people whose good ideas were weeded out. This section has a few suggestions from Honeywell that companies may wish to adopt. However, you must recognise that if Principle 8 were truly adopted, you would not need these props.

- Establish an innovations manager to institute an integrated approach to innovation, to lift awareness and to champion/support innovation efforts.
- Develop an improvement system—'opportunity for improvement'—that enables all staff to notify improvement opportunities under four classifications: customer dissatisfiers: environment, health and safety; procedural conformance/improvement; and suggestions for improvement. Importantly, this system should not collect ideas in some central repository. Instead, originators should send opportunities for improvement directly to the person he/she thinks is best placed to achieve a solution. Aggregations should be made of the data to identify emerging themes and assist in developing system-wide improvements. The improvement system could also be Intranet based.
- The opportunity for improvement should be available to all employees and could be extended to customers and suppliers. As a matter of principle, all opportunities for improvement should be accessible by all people.
- Use your innovations manager as a reference point for matters of uncertainty regarding the expression and treatment of ideas.
- Major unprogrammed innovation proposals stemming from opportunities for improvement, workshops, business opportunities and customers should be supported or championed by the innovations manager. This is a coordination role but it also gives the idea a home where the process can start with some certainty.
- Direct individual contact often proves to be the primary method of championing an idea. Listening and the ability to integrate various views seem to be essential skills. Measure your opportunity for improvement referral rate—the majority of opportunities for improvement should be resolved by direct action.
- Beware of the way you use extrinsic reward. Reward could include education, development or technical skills training associated with the innovation.
- As a matter of principle, originators should remain influential throughout the life of their innovation.
- Place emphasis on the need for a rapid (although considered) response to opportunities for improvement. Measure response and resolution times.

- Introduce an 'empowerment card', which emphatically presents the CEO's personal message to 'challenge the status quo and to innovate'.
- Establish an 'innovation champions network' to provide local contact and support in each region and business unit. The 'champions' can be selected by peer review and carry this role as additional to their operational role.
- Procedures should be deliberately simplified to allow greater use of discretion during normal work.
- Introduce a 'concept explorers' initiative.
- Workshops can be used to generate and build ideas.

Continuous improvement

Continuous improvement can be small or large—affecting a small part of one process or re-engineering of the whole company. Improvements could include:

- providing increased value to customers through new and improved products and services
- developing new business opportunities
- increasing throughput
- reducing errors, defects, waste and related costs
- improving responsiveness and cycle time
- increasing efficiency in the use of all resources
- improving the company's performance in fulfilling its responsibilities as a good citizen
- reducing environmental impact or unintended consequences.

As Goldratt suggests, you should concentrate your efforts on improving processes that affect throughput. It is very common to see companies that work on 'improvement' but fail to 'improve'. This is an error. This was discussed in detail in Principle 4 ('To improve the outcome, improve the system').

A continuous improvement philosophy should be 'embedded' in the way the company operates. That is, continuous improvement must be a regular part of daily work, practised at individual, work unit and company levels. It must be driven by having the space and opportunities to innovate, increase throughput and do better, as well as by problems that must be corrected. Problems must be eliminated at their source.

Good practices

- A deliberate innovation strategy with innovation champions throughout the company. Innovation champions are self-managing—outside the control of hierarchy, peer-review and funding approvals systems.

- A dynamic mechanism, such as a central database, is used to capture and record innovative ideas from all sources and to make them available to the company. Its existence is well known and it is used.
- Total visibility of all suggestions, with each suggestion going directly to the person who can implement it. (A central assessment of suggestions implies people cannot be trusted to work for the best of the company.)

Poor practices

- Do not see innovation as a process that needs nurturing and resources—but rather as 'good ideas'.
- Innovation not included as an important success factor.

8.8 Continually learn

You must be continually learning (from others, from what you do, from your mistakes, from your varied success, from your strategies and approaches, from your customers, from your competitors, from your employees, from technology, from each new idea you implement). Principle 8 gives you the concept of a 'learning company'—that is, a company that creates better solutions by using its ability to:

- use its knowledge and core competencies to create superior value
- use the individual learning and experience of its staff
- undertake meaningful reflection
- use the tension of unresolved dilemmas.

Principle 8 goes further than saying that learning is a 'good idea', a good thing to do. According to Principle 8, continuous improvement and innovation (which has been described as essential to company success and sustainability) is *dependent* on the company continually learning. In terms of the previous discussion, lack of a process of continual learning by the company is a significant barrier to innovation and the company's success and sustainability—a huge barrier that is worthy of its own discussion.

'Company learning' is not synonymous with 'individual learning'. Company learning is about how the company uses and grows its base of knowledge in pursuit of its business results. It requires capturing and using the learning and knowledge of individual members. A learning company is skilled at creating, acquiring and transferring knowledge, and at modifying its decisions and behaviour in response to new knowledge and insights.

Peter Senge and others have described this 'learning organisation' in books such as *The Fifth Discipline Fieldbook* and *The Dance of Change*.

Stages of competence

There are four stages of competence. All of us are at one stage or another about everything:

1. unconscious incompetence—you don't know you don't know
2. conscious incompetence—you know you don't know
3. conscious competence—you have only recently learned and have to think about it
4. unconscious competence—you know it so well you can do it in your sleep.

Learning to drive a car is an example. When you were very young, you did not even know what a car was. In your early teens, you knew you wanted to learn but couldn't yet. When you were learning to drive and had recently obtained your licence, you had to think about what you were doing. After you have been driving for 20 years, no thought is needed, except when conditions change—icy or slippery road, mud—and you suddenly go back to stage 1 or 2. There are hundreds of other examples of learning that you can relate to: skiing, walking, e-commerce, video games, sex.

All of your skills and learnings fall into those categories. For many of them, you stay in the unconscious incompetence stage. For others, you progress to the unconscious competence stage. The stage you are in can suddenly change as the thinking is suddenly overturned, revealing yet another unconscious incompetence—where most people are for most things.

Cycle of learning

The 'cycle of improvement' is also a 'cycle of learning'. It requires you to stand back from the process and review it—to reflect, to take stock: 'What have we learned from what we have been doing and what has happened to us?', 'Is it still appropriate?', 'Is it achieving what we wanted it to achieve?', 'Could we do it better?', 'Are there unintended and unforeseen side-effects that we should address?', 'Have changes occurred in the market, technology and customer needs that would cause us to make a different decision if we made it today?', 'Are our assumptions and decisions still valid?'.

This questioning sets us off in a new round of improvement, which, in turn, leads to another. This cycle amalgamates Senge's double loop learning process with the 'plan, do, check, act' (PDCA) cycle originated by Shewhart. Figure 8.5 shows the steps in the process. The essential difference from the PDCA cycle is that the cycle initiates from the perceived need to close a performance gap. A realisation that you cannot keep going with what you are doing creates the essential tension to stimulate action.

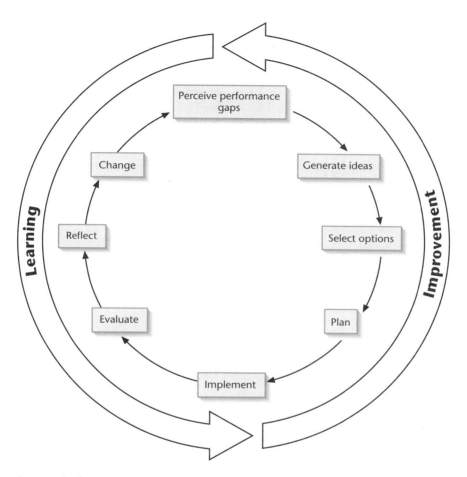

Fig. 8.5 The learning–improvement cycle

Learn from your mistakes

A sign of stupidity is to keep doing the same thing while hoping for a different result. Yet you see it all the time. People and companies follow exactly the same path they have followed in the last several relationships or product releases, none of which has worked in the past, but now hope for a different result.

People learn most from mistakes. One theory of learning is that people *only* learn from making mistakes. This implies that people do not learn from having someone (an expert or boss) tell them what to do. People only learn from making the mistake *themselves*. The role of the expert or coach is to guide them through their learning—to get the most out of it. In an educational setting, the teacher sets up harmless opportunities for learning through making errors. A company must do the same—set up a lot of opportunities for failure—however, because this is the real world, not all will be harmless. You can reduce the harm by risk analysis and practice. A role of the manager is to guide the learning.

Make a lot of mistakes for two reasons. Firstly, 'nothing ventured, nothing gained'. If you do not take risks, you do not gain ground. If you are too complacent and only do what you have done before, you will be left behind by the market and customer demands. If you do things you have not done before, there is a good chance you will be making mistakes. Good executives have large numbers of low risk failures behind them. Unfortunately, most company cultures punish mistakes. People who make mistakes are 'moved on'. Other companies (often competitors) pick up that experience and learning.

Secondly, make a lot of mistakes so that you have a lot of mistakes to learn from. And have in place coaches and mentors to guide people at all levels in the company so they make the most of the learning—a role for leaders!

Every day do something that scares you!

Good practices

- A growing program of learning (e.g. formal and informal study, discussion groups, brainstorming sessions, conferences, trips) with a record of the progress.
- Learnings from reviews are shared throughout the company.
- Mechanisms for understanding 'what we don't know' by exposure to businesses outside the company's area of operations, benchmarking and so on.
- A willingness to make mistakes—and a process to learn from them. People at all levels are actively encouraged to share ideas and try new methods.

Poor practices

- Not standing back and reviewing approach and deployment.
- No systemic work to avoid common pitfalls like 'fixes that fail'.

8.9 Make time to reflect and practise

You should make time to reflect on what has happened, or is happening, and why it is happening. Learning does not happen without reflection, without thinking about what has happened or is happening, about why it is happening. People need to discover things for themselves. That probably applies to everything—a journey of self-discovery.

Reflection

Learning is fundamentally associated with conscious changing of the status quo—leading to new goals, decisions and ways of doing things. At the level of the individual, this means changes in beliefs, assumptions and values that influence attitudes and behaviours.

True learning only occurs through a process of reflection as the individual takes time to challenge his or her beliefs, assumptions and values. At the level of the company, learning is about changes in the assumptions, norms and rules (implicit and explicit) that underpin the culture, decisions and behaviours of the company's people.

It is important for companies to create and develop their own reflective awareness. How do you do it? Senge suggests that we should use the 'left-hand column' to help us reflect. Divide your page in two. Use the right-hand side to make your notes about what is being said— facts. Use the left-hand side to record your thoughts, your feelings, what you were thinking but did not say.

Double loop learning

Double loop learning is the process of questioning your deep assumptions, your beliefs, your picture of how the world works and why. This is very hard to do. We all 'know' things about the world and about people. We all make assumptions and have prejudices. It is very difficult to challenge our assumptions because we are usually not aware we make them.

How do you do double loop learning?

- Reflection.
- Dialogue, especially with people who hold different views, can help to challenge and possibly uncover assumptions—another reason for diversity in the workplace and in your network of friends and contacts. However, your company must be a long way down the path of implementing Principle 7 ('Enthusiastic people') before dialogue will work. Fear will be too strong otherwise.
- Use Goldratt's assumption breaking tools (e.g. the evaporating cloud, see Figs 5.2 and 7.2).
- Whenever you find yourself saying 'we must do this because…', you are probably making an assumption about the 'because'. Challenge it.
- Ask yourself questions about 'Why did it happen?', 'What can we learn from what happened?', 'How can we do better next time?'. If you find that you are blaming a person (e.g. 'It is Bill Blogg's fault'), you are making a poor assumption. You must look for the deeper meaning behind what was and is happening.

Practice

It is amazing that companies try to do things without practising first. It is amazing that they think they can—the arrogance of thinking that says 'we do not need to practise'.

Compare this with the enormous amount of practice in almost every other human endeavour. In any sport you can think of, do people who are very good at it (experts) get good at it the first time they do it—or do they practise, and practise and practise until moderate skills become excellent skills? If it is a team sport, do they not practise doing it together? Think of all the learning they have made—learning from mistakes, doing the hard bits over and over and over, finding better ways. In music, haven't all musicians practised for hours alone and together to get as good as you see them?

Why, then, do companies think they do not have the need to practise? You don't have time? Too busy? Very probably, you are too busy fighting fires caused because you did not practise.

You must make time to practise. If it is important—make time to practise. Work out what a practice session would look like and do it.

Tiger Woods

When a professional golfer such as Tiger Woods hits off in a tournament, is his shot from the first tee his first for the day? No way! He actually begins several days before, thinking about the course—its layout, who designed it, its difficulties and so on. On the day of the tournament he does an intensive warm-up (swimming, weights). He goes to the practice range. He begins with his 7 iron, hitting balls till he can hit a frisbee five times in a row. Then the 5 iron. Then the 3 iron. Then the 2 iron. Each until he can hit the frisbee five times in a row. Then he works through the woods—5, 3, 1. Then to the putting green. Does he begin with 25-metre putts? No. He works out from 1 metre to 5 metres, then 10 metres, then 15, 20 and 25 metres.

It's quite a warm-up. Do you do something similar? Every day?

Match game

This game was used in training by Peter Wildblood recently to illustrate a number of issues about knowledge and learning. Each person in the group is given 24 matchsticks to be arranged as shown (Fig. 8.6). The instructions are to 'remove eight matches to leave two squares not touching. When you have it, raise your hand. If you are right, you will be tapped on the shoulder. Those tapped can, if they wish, coach others. Coaching is to take the form of silence if wrong and clapping if right'. In this game, people learnt in three ways:

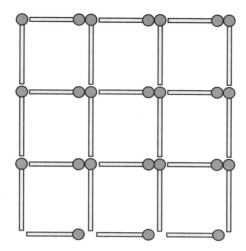

Fig. 8.6 Remove eight matchsticks

1. Many people would not let anyone else see their solution—either breaking it up or covering it when it was complete—hoarding knowledge.
2. Many people had to solve it themselves and ignored the coaches, ignoring existing knowledge—refusing to learn from others.
3. Other people did not attempt to solve it by themselves and simply touched each match in turn and removed it if the coach clapped. Very efficient. However, they did not learn a solution, just an efficient way of working—for them. They remained totally dependent on the coach.

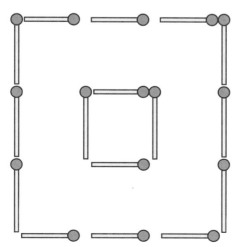

Fig. 8.7 The matches solution

In the workplace you see tension between these three groups. The first, conditioned by that damaging environment for learning and sharing knowledge—schools—don't want cheating or cheats to benefit. Many behave as though marks are being allocated and only a few will be awarded.

Surely, in the workplace 'cheating' should have little meaning. So long as it is legal, 'copying' is encouraged. We call it benchmarking. (You need to draw a distinction between stealing a piece of intellectual property and copying a piece of learning—a good idea. If you intend to use someone else's intellectual property, ask permission and acknowledge their contribution.)

The third group are always calling on the coaches to help them—'I can't do this, please help', 'My computer won't work, please help'. Help is usually gladly given but it ties the second group down to being a permanent helper and may prevent both groups from being able to do their real work, which they may resent.

Does the third group need to increase their skills? Do they actually need those skills or do they need them so infrequently and would not be able to get to a useful level without significant time devoted to the skill? Most people are in that third category about computers—the technology is moving so fast that it is almost impossible to keep up. Should the arrangements be formalised between the two groups about what skills and knowledge they share and how?

Good practices

- The company can handle ambiguity and conflict. Dialogue is encouraged about all issues, including difficult issues and past failures.
- The company creates value from the diversity of its workforce—'oddball' ideas are encouraged and used where appropriate.
- The company places value on and encourages different points of view—especially from 'oddballs' and eccentrics.

Poor practices

- No reflection and learning from actions.
- The senior executives do not think reflectively about what they and the company are doing.

8.10 Take a strategic approach to learning

You should take a strategic approach to learning (i.e. you should have learning objectives and strategies to grow your core competencies and knowledge). Principle 8 states that your ability to innovate, to develop and implement new ideas, depends on your capacity to learn. The marketplace has a frenetic rate of change. All companies have to adapt rapidly and be very innovative just to keep up. Innovation itself should be a strategic issue. Because innovation depends on learning, learning must be a strategic issue as well.

You must develop your ability to learn and develop knowledge. Make it a key result area. Build your core competencies, work systematically to overcome the barriers to learning.

Core competencies and learning

Remember the core competencies described in Principle 2 ('Focus on achieving results'). Your core competencies are what the company is very good at doing—what makes the company special and different from other companies. You support them by your underlying skills, learning, knowledge and experience. The core competency is what defines the difference between a bank and a law firm. Each has developed skills, knowledge and experience in different competencies. The bank has core competencies in finance; the law firm has core competencies in law. Even where their interests appear to coincide, they take their own approach. The bank's legal branch is not a core competency of the bank.

A company's core competency is usually earned in the school of hard knocks—learning is accumulated through mistakes and successes, learning what works and what does not work, experience. When a company tries to change its core competency (from, say, steel making to mining), it has to go back to square one in its learning. All of the learning it gained in the previous competency is worthless.

Companies should seek to make the most of their core competencies—increase them. They should not be sold off—doing so is selling what makes the company work. Yet, you often see examples of companies failing to think strategically about their core competencies and selling them off in their downsizing activities. Selling your core competencies is selling what makes the company work. When they are sold, it implies a major change in direction—hopefully to meet an emerging, more lucrative market—or stupidity.

A rule of thumb for investors is that when you see a company sell off its core competencies as part of a downsizing or a change of direction, sell your shares.

Barriers to learning

The barriers to learning include all the barriers to innovation described above.

1. *Trust and a learning environment.* In particular, it must be emphasised that the foundations to learning are laid by a full implementation of Principle 7 ('Enthusiastic people') and creating an environment of

trust with Principle 1 ('Role models'). If these are not in place, people in the company are more interested in survival than in passing their wisdom on to others in the company.

2. *Systems to retrieve knowledge.* Learning is a process whose output is knowledge. You need systems and processes so that you can find the knowledge. You do not know something unless you can retrieve that information. Knowledge is lost when you don't know what you have learned, when you can't find the policy document you issued last month, when the right hand does not know what the left hand is doing, when you continue to make the same mistakes or when you continue to do the same things expecting a different result. Given the importance of continual improvement and innovation, and how much they depend on continual learning, you had better be able to find what you know.

3. *People hoard knowledge.* Players in companies have known this since Machiavelli's time and withheld or dealt in knowledge—often to their own advantage and the detriment of the company.

4. *People will not cheat.* Most school systems come down hard on people who cheat—a lesson that most people take with them into the workplace. Unfortunately, in the workplace, cheating (or bench-marking or copying) are very good qualities. As said above, steal ideas shamelessly. If it is someone else's intellectual property, ask permission and acknowledge his/her contribution, then add to it and adapt it. The growth in knowledge and learning is to everyone's advantage.

Good practices

- The core competencies of the company (i.e. those things that it does very well compared with other companies) are understood, protected and developed through deliberate strategies.
- A pool of knowledge to create sustainability.
- Processes to assign value to non-balance sheet assets, such as intellectual property, intellectual capital, image capital, knowledge and core competencies. Documented increases in these 'self-created assets'.
- Processes to manage knowledge and intellectual property assets to ensure that they create value for the company.
- Knowledge is retained during downsizing.

Poor practices

- When asked, 'What assets does this company have?', no mention of intellectual capital, people, knowledge or core competencies.
- Companies with a strong ethos to 'promote from within' do not always have ways to acquire new knowledge and alternative thinking.

SUMMARY

- Innovation is fragile and very easily destroyed. It relies on freedom, independence, absence of fear, difference, high autonomy and mistakes. In most companies, the environment is very different from that picture. If inventiveness and innovation are to thrive, they need a helping hand.
- You have to work quite hard for people to volunteer their enthusiasm and resourcefulness. Structures, traditions, politics and fear in the workplace all act to counter people's natural innovation. You often see bosses demanding that their people be innovative or creative and at the same time actively discouraging such innovation.
- When you implement new ideas, you must change all the old structures that the new will impact (e.g. reward and recognition systems, performance management systems, technology, standard operating procedures, standards systems, communications systems, company structure, performance indicators, resources, job descriptions, performance agreements, organisation values, audit systems).
- You must take a strategic approach to innovation, implementation and continuous improvement (e.g. innovation and implementation objectives, resources provided to assist innovation and implementation, including seed funding and champions).
- You must be continually learning (from others, from what you do, from your mistakes, from your varied success, from your strategies and approaches, from your customers, from your competitors, from your employees, from technology, from each new idea you implement).
- Principle 8 gives you the concept of a 'learning company'—a company that creates better solutions by:
  — using its knowledge and core competencies to create superior value
  — using the individual learning and experience of its staff
  — undertaking meaningful reflection.
- You should take a strategic approach to learning (e.g. you should have learning objectives and strategies to grow your core competencies and knowledge).
- Principle 8 states that your ability to innovate, to develop and implement new ideas, depends on your capacity to learn. The marketplace has a frenetic rate of change. All companies have to adapt rapidly and be very innovative just to keep up. You must develop your ability to learn and develop knowledge. Make it a key result area. Build your core competencies, work systematically to overcome the barriers to learning.

WHAT WOULD YOUR STAKEHOLDERS SAY?

HOW WOULD YOUR EMPLOYEES RATE YOUR COMPANY ON THESE?

- Senior executives of this company demonstrate a commitment to innovation and learning.
- This company places importance on and encourages learning.
- This company places importance on experience.
- This company places importance on and encourages innovation and continual improvement.
- This company constantly searches for a better way (tries new concepts, ideas, products and services).
- This company is continually learning (from others, from employees, from customers, from competitors, from technology).
- This company keeps up with changing technology.
- This company is not satisfied with the status quo.
- This company constantly grows its knowledge base.
- This company makes use of and uses the leverages of its knowledge base.
- This company constantly searches for a better way.
- This company encourages taking risks.
- I am encouraged and enabled to question concepts and assumptions.
- We have very good tools to assist us generate new ideas.
- Our recognition and reward systems encourage innovation rather than to stick with the 'tried and true'.
- Our performance management systems encourage innovation rather than to stick with the 'tried and true'.
- We have enough time to think of new ways of doing things.
- We have enough time to implement new ways of doing things.
- I can make suggestions without fear.
- I trust the company.
- I trust my bosses.
- When new ideas are to be implemented, I get enough information through formal channels about when, where, what, why, who and how.
- When new ideas are implemented, I don't have to rely on rumour.
- When new ideas are implemented, I know what is in it for me.
- When new ideas are implemented, I get adequate training.
- When new ideas are implemented, all the old structures that the new will impact on are also changed.
- Before new ideas are implemented, they are talked through by all those whom will be affected to iron out any bugs and problems.
- Before new ideas are implemented, all those who will be affected are involved in discussion and planning of the implementation.

- When new ideas are implemented, we measure people's attitude to the new, whether people are doing it or using it, whether everyone is doing it or using it who should be.
- When new ideas are implemented, we measure if the innovation is effective, if it delivers the benefits promised, if it provides value to the company, its customers and other stakeholders, if the costs are what were estimated.
- This company takes a strategic approach to innovation and learning.
- Inertia (comfort with the way things are) prevents us from innovation or implementation.
- Existing stock does not prevent us from innovation or implementation.
- The budget does not prevent us from implementing innovations when we need to.
- This company is skilled at creating, acquiring and transferring knowledge, and at modifying its behaviour to reflect new knowledge and insights.
- This company builds on, grows and protects its core competencies.
- When this company downsizes, it protects its core competencies.
- People in this company do not hoard knowledge.
- People in the company copy from one another a lot.
- We often make time to practise doing things when they are important.
- We make time to undertake meaningful reflection—thinking about what has happened or is happening, why it is happening.
- This company learns from its mistakes.
- People in this company are respected for skills and knowledge acquired outside the workplace.
- This company shares its knowledge with others.

HOW WOULD YOUR CUSTOMERS RATE YOUR COMPANY ON THESE?

- This company innovates continually (tries new concepts, ideas, products and services).
- This company is continually learning from its customers.
- This company is continually innovating to meet my changing needs.
- The employees of this company show a huge degree of enthusiasm about innovation.
- The employees of this company show a huge degree of enthusiasm about their company.
- The employees of this company show a huge amount of resourcefulness in getting things done.
- When new ideas are implemented, this company measures to see if the innovation provides additional value to its customers.
- This company takes a strategic approach to innovation and learning.

HOW WOULD YOUR SHAREHOLDERS RATE YOUR COMPANY ON THESE?

- When this company implements new ideas, it measures if the innovation is effective, if it delivers the benefits promised, if it provides value to the company, its customers, the shareholders and other stakeholders, if the costs are what were estimated.
- This company has sufficient resources to generate and implement new ideas.
- When this company implements new ideas, I get enough information through formal channels about when, where, what, why, who and how. I don't have to rely on rumour.
- This company takes a strategic approach to innovation and learning.
- This company protects, builds on and grows its core competencies.
- When this company downsizes, it protects its core competencies.
- This company learns from its mistakes.
- The employees of this company show a huge degree of enthusiasm about their company.
- The employees of this company show a huge amount of resourcefulness in getting things done.
- This company does not return to us as 'profits' funds that should have been used for innovation and implementing innovations.

HOW WOULD THE COMMUNITY RATE YOUR COMPANY ON THESE?

- When new ideas are implemented, this company measures to see if the innovation provides additional value to the community and society.
- When new ideas are implemented, this company measures to see if the innovation caused any unintended side-effects (good and bad) to the community and society.

Principle 9
Corporate citizenship

The company's action to ensure a clean, safe, fair and prosperous society enhances the perception of its value to the community.

TO A LARGE EXTENT, Principle 9 is the long-term view of sustainability. It is also about your right to operate, in that if companies (and the people in them) do not work to what are thought of as 'good rules', their licence to operate is revoked.

In Dr Hausner's analysis, Principle 9 is significantly correlated with KPI improvement and with a high overall business excellence score. However, of all the Principles it has the lowest correlation with both. This low correlation does not give a true indication of its importance, though. It is a binary operator, a minimum condition. If you keep your licence to operate, you do have a chance to be successful. If your licence is withdrawn, there is no chance.

On all the 10 Business Excellence Principles, Principle 9 is the one most often disregarded. However, there is growing evidence that disregarding the needs of the community will no longer be tolerated in the twenty-first century. More and more companies are feeling the wrath of the community through the courts and regulation.

Principle 9 is made up of five parts. These are not about doing things to feel good or for altruistic reasons. This is good hard business.

1. The community withdraws the 'licence to operate' from companies that pollute or have unacceptable standards or ethics. Or, the community imposes regulations to enforce companies to work to acceptable standards of practice. Companies should discontinue unacceptable practices and adopt acceptable practices.
2. Seek competitive advantage by adopting 'community friendly' practices, practices that are perceived to 'add value' to the community in general.

3. Work to reduce the waste and pollution your company produces in order to keep the community clean.
4. Work to reduce the unintended consequences (side-effects) to the community of your actions and policies. Keep the community safe, or do no harm—intentionally or unintentionally.
5. Share your knowledge with others to help them prosper on their journey to adopt the 10 Business Excellence Principles. At a very minimum, this should be with your stakeholders: owners, suppliers, customers, employees and community.

9.1 Operate by acceptable ethical standards

In Principle 1 ('Role models'), we saw that employees will not follow untrustworthy 'leaders'. In Principle 3 ('Customers'), we saw that the market punishes companies that do not perform according to expectation. In Principle 7 ('Enthusiastic people'), we saw that employees withdraw their enthusiasm and resourcefulness from companies that are not working towards a 'just cause'.

The community does not tolerate it either. You repeatedly see the community, in one way or another, withdraw a company's (or its executive's or director's) right to continue to operate. This happens when the community perceives that the company (or its executives or directors) have broken Principle 9 by behaving in a way that endangers the community's prosperity, health, safety or cleanliness.

There still appear to be many exceptions—that is, companies that have dispensed with Principle 9 and remained successful in the long term. In the past, many companies have for a long time avoided punishment for flouting Principle 9. However, the days when the community will tolerate such behaviour—profit by few at the expense of most—is now long past.

The tobacco industry is an excellent example. In the tobacco industry, prosperity of a few companies and their shareholders has, for generations, used strategies and actions that knowingly and callously endangered and took the lives of hundreds of thousands in the community. We are now seeing the inevitable community backlash. 'Withdrawing the right to operate' can take the form of fines, gaol, regulations, lawsuits and litigation.

Much of the current community attention grew out of the excesses of the 1980s, when the words 'business ethics' began to appear in the media. The world community grew to understand that it had been raped in the name of expedient profit and began to demand it be stopped. Twenty years ago, this was not an important Principle. It is now.

No company or person is beyond scrutiny. Over the last 20 years, we have all seen politicians, presidents, CEOs, company directors, public officials, executives all come under intense scrutiny. And are frequently kicked out of office, frequently fined and sometimes sent to gaol.

At the boundary

There is considerable potential for short-term gain at the boundary between legal and illegal, between ethical and unethical. As a result, many people and companies are drawn there.

Twenty years ago the boundary was not well patrolled. There appeared to be an attitude that companies would do nothing to harm us and a helplessness when they did. No more! The media now constantly patrols the boundary. Investigative journalism and nightly 'current affairs' programs with time slots to fill and a public demand for scandal and outrage all mean that journalists are constantly picking at the boundary looking for the next outrage—looking for the next official to haul before the lens of scrutiny. The greater the outrage that can be whipped up, the better the story.

The boundary area can be very tricky. It is not stable or fixed. The community's concept of what is and is not ethical will vary from community to community and over time.

People have an innate concept of right and wrong, which is not defined by laws. It depends on our values. In the past, our parents and close community shaped it. It now also comes from our peers, the media, our company's values. It changes as concepts of right and wrong are questioned, proved impractical, unfair or unlawful. The 'political correctness' movement made rapid changes to the boundary for a number of issues. The position of the boundary is now changing at an unprecedented rate. One hundred years ago the boundary was not changing much. In the last part of the twentieth century, it galloped along.

Be aware and keep up. Be aware that much of what you were brought up believing is no longer true. Be aware that much of what you thought to be ethical is no longer considered ethical. Be aware that when you operate in another country or another culture, right and wrong might not be the same as what you grew up with in your own community.

Good practices

- A clear framework of ethics for decision making.
- Senior executives pay explicit attention to ethical issues pertinent to the company's situation/industry.
- All staff can articulate the values of the company and how they are based on the 10 Business Excellence Principles, and can give

examples of how the values are used to drive behaviour (especially by the senior managers/owners).
- Plans reflect the company's values and basic beliefs.

Poor practices
- No concern about ethical behaviour. Fraud is considered okay. A 'Make me rich, bugger the world' attitude.

9.2 Add value

What you do should add value to the community, rather than cost the community money in the long or short term. Companies must ensure that they are seen to 'add value' to society as well as delivering particular goods and services. You should use practices that the community perceives as friendly and that appear to 'add value' to the community in general. Companies succeed by their relevance and the value they add to the community they serve.

If the community perceives that the company does not add value, is causing harm or is taking value from the community, the community will act to withdraw the company's right to operate. This is a logical extension of the value proposition concepts described in Principles 3 ('Customers') and 7 ('Enthusiastic people'). In those Principles, if the value proposition is not to the customer's (or employee's) liking, the customer (or employee) withdraws support. Depending on the extent of the mismatch, the customer can go so far as to buy from someone else (a failure to return or to show loyalty). The employee can go so far as to leave and/or to sabotage (indirectly by inaction or directly by deliberate action against the company).

In the context of Principle 9, the company must build its value propositions so that it provides what the community thinks of as value. In fact, it does not appear to work so much from the positive perspective—that is, expecting value added. The community is not there yet. Principle 9 operates more from the negative context of the community becoming more and more intolerant of companies that take value from the community, or that operate in a way that will impose an additional cost to the community or society. Now or in the future.

Increasingly, the community expects the full cost of production to be covered by the company and so included in the product or service price to customers. This includes the cost of air and water that were once considered free.

- If the process of production contaminates them, the community demands the cost of decontaminating them to pre-production levels be covered by the company and so included in the price to customers.

- If excess energy or greenhouse gases are released into the atmosphere, the community expects the cost of removal of these to be covered by the company and so included in the price to customers.
- If a company releases products that harm the health of product users or others in the community, the community expects the company to pay the cost of rehabilitation.
- Although we have not reached this next one yet, it will not be long before we see the community punish companies that do not use their depreciation allowance to replace equipment (as intended by governments) but instead pass those funds on to shareholders (as 'profits') and then cry poor when the equipment is obsolete and sack its workforce. Similarly, for companies who distribute employees' pension funds to shareholders as 'profits'. Shareholders should all be wary of companies that have such practices. Profits will not be as high for long.

This is why we see a continued backlash against *globalisation*—a strategy that pays no tax (and so does not support community infrastructure) and pays poverty level wages in Third World communities. The globalisation strategy may look good for shareholders but it is seen to take from the community.

Companies that operate close to the boundary of unacceptable practice must work very hard to keep the community's perception on their side. The risks of community backlash are high.

Principle 9 significantly challenges the concept that shareholders are the only stakeholders that matter. This issue is taken up further in Principle 10, 'Value for all stakeholders'.

Regulation

The boundary is often defined in the form of regulation or legislation. You have all heard the constant cry that 'my industry is over regulated. If only those regulations were not there I could make a decent living—I could before'. Possibly. However, regulation and legislation is the community's way of positioning the boundary—often as a response to unethical behaviour. Regulations are, and will continue to be, a fact of life. They are Principle 9 in action. They are the community's way of having their say in 'market forces' and making certain that companies do no harm.

This does not mean that all regulation is good. Because there is more and more regulation, there is more need for it to be up to date—to reflect *current* community needs. Unfortunately, too often regulation is out of date and so is of no practical use. Poor or out-of-date regulation is an actual hindrance to the community it is supposed to serve and imposes unnecessary costs on suppliers. It is, therefore, up to the regulators to make certain they are up to date. Most often, however, regulations are imposed on companies so that they do not harm the community.

Good practices

- A deliberate community involvement strategy—including sustainability and respect for the environment.
- The company's environmental and community initiatives are widely known in the community.
- Work is refused if accepting it will compromise the company's ethics or values, even if the work is very lucrative. A clear framework for such decisions exists and is understood by all.

Poor practices

- No involvement in the community other than normal business operations (an 'in and out' mentality).

9.3 Do no harm

You should do nothing that will endanger the community's prosperity, health, safety or cleanliness. Increasingly, now, the community expects companies to do no intended or unintended harm to the environment in which that community lives.

We can predict that, over the next 20 years, community concerns for its prosperity, health, safety and clean environment will result in a shift in the ethical boundaries yet again. Just as we saw a progressive hardening of community attitudes towards companies that pushed ethical boundaries during the 1980s and 1990s, over the next two decades we will see a progressive hardening of attitudes towards companies that seek to take significantly more from the community than the perceived value they add, especially towards those companies that appear to do harm or endanger the health, safety or prosperity of the community.

Safety

The fourth part of Principle 9 is that the community expects to be kept safe and not harmed by any company's activities. The community's expectation with respect to Principle 9 has been increasing with each passing year. A company's failure to do so can bring significant repercussions—for the company, its directors and executives. This responsibility is being increasingly acknowledged and tested through the courts in many countries.

- Employees expect the company to provide a safe working environment (physically and mentally and free of harassment).
- Customers expect the products and services to be safe and delivered in a safe way.
- The community expects the company, its employees and its products to be safe, behave safely and not harm the community or its environment—intentionally or unintentionally.

Most of this was not evident 20 years ago.

Consider the interfaces where the community holds the company responsible for safety, which are shown in Figure 9.1. The community holds the company responsible when:

- one of the company's products injures someone
- an employee provides a service or advice that endangers someone (e.g. a bar worker serves alcohol to someone who subsequently is injured or injures someone else)
- a company sells something (such as a gun) that is subsequently used for harm
- a company knowingly or unknowingly causes harm to the environment that will in turn harm the community.

We have already seen examples of all of these. There will be more and more examples as the community makes its feelings known and tests them in the courts.

Shareholders should ask, 'Are the company's profits real? Or will they be taken up in litigation costs? Or is the company using shareholders funds to defend criminal behaviour by executives?'.

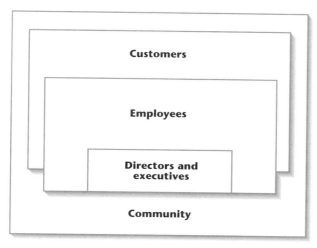

Fig. 9.1 Whom the community holds responsible

Good practices

- Company strategies make reference to environmental and community responsibility.
- Community input to the strategic direction and strategies is actively solicited.
- The community gives feedback to the company and this feedback is valued and acted upon.
- Employees are caught by the idea that they are an icon for others.

Poor practices

- Policies of exploitation in developing countries to increase profits—especially policies that are illegal or unacceptable in the home country (e.g. in Australia). Exploitation of child labour in developing countries.

9.4 Reduce harm to the environment

You should be working strategically to reduce the harm you do to the environment (e.g. your dependence on mining and fossil fuels, your dependence on persistent, unnatural substances, and your dependency on nature-consuming activities). You should always try to do more with less.

With the continuing rapid increase in the earth's human population over the next few decades, there will be greater demands for food, water and other resources needed to support the additional people. There will also be increased pressures on the capacity of the ecosphere to absorb waste. In the face of such growing demands, and in a world of limited resources, fundamental societal changes are necessary.

The earth's human population has reached six billion people. Due to the collective actions of the current population, life-supporting systems, such as crop lands, wetlands, the ozone layer, forests, fisheries and ground water, are in decline. An increasing amount of waste is being generated, which includes visible garbage, such as that which is placed in landfills, as well as invisible forms of molecular garbage, such as greenhouse gases and chlorofluorocarbons (CFCs), which are accumulating in the atmosphere.

Paul Hawken, author, environmentalist and director of the US branch of The Natural Step, which is concerned with organisational sustainability, notes, 'We are far better at making waste than at making products. For every 100 pounds of product we manufacture in the United States, we create at least 3200 pounds of waste. In a decade, we transform 500 trillion pounds of molecules into non-productive solids, liquids and gases'. The 'non-productive garbage' produced by our linear way of living and working never finds its way back into the cycles of society or nature to be reused or absorbed.

What happens if we do not begin to live more sustainably? 'As we busy ourselves with tearing down more than we rebuild', founder of The Natural Step, Dr Karl-Henrik Robèrt notes, 'we are racing toward world-wide poverty in a monstrous, poisonous garbage-dump. The only thing that can save us from the consequences is the restoration of cyclical processes, where wastes become new resources for society or nature'.

The primary components of the environmental situation can be viewed as the walls of a giant funnel where societal demand for resources is one wall of the funnel and resource availability is the other side. As aggregate societal demand increases, and the capacity to meet those demands decreases, it is as if, as a society, we are moving into the narrower portion of the funnel.

It is possible to change this situation. Sustainable and restorative behaviour opens the walls of the funnel and moves the sides further apart.

The Natural Step

According to Dr Robèrt, eventually our businesses and our communities around the world will 'hit the wall'. If humans can recognise the limits of the ecosystem in which we live, and target activities within the parameters of The Natural Step's four system conditions (see box on p. 312), we may be able to avoid hitting the walls of the funnel and create a sustainable society.

Today in Sweden, The Natural Step is a household word and has transformed the way individuals, schools, communities and businesses think about the natural world and sustainability. More than 70 municipalities have adopted the framework and 60 corporations (e.g. IKEA, Electrolux, McDonald's, Scandic Hotels and OK Petroleum) are actively using The Natural Step's conditions to change the way they do business.

The Natural Step framework helps individuals and companies address important environmental issues from a systems perspective, reduce the use of natural resources and develop new technologies. The system conditions are used by business corporations, municipalities and other companies as an instrument for strategic planning for sustainability and as a shared mental model for problem solving and for developing consensus documents (e.g. sustainable practices for metals, energy, agriculture and forestry). They give people a common language and guiding Principles to help change existing practices and decrease their impact on the environment.

When making investment decisions, assess the investment in terms of:

- How can we reduce our dependence on mining and fossil fuels?
- How can we reduce our dependence on persistent, unnatural substances?
- How can we reduce our dependency on nature-consuming activities?
- How can we do more with less?

The Natural Step was founded in Sweden in 1989 by Dr Karl-Henrik Robèrt, an oncologist who was concerned that so much of the environmental debate was focused on downstream issues and so little on systemic causes of problems. He had noticed a significant increase in childhood leukemia cases and witnessed first hand the connection between human illness and toxins. On a cellular level, he observed limits within which a living cell will properly function.

With the help of 50 Swedish scientists, Dr Robèrt developed a consensus document that describes the basic knowledge of the biosphere's functions. The document describes how society influences natural systems, and acknowledges that humans are a part of natural systems and that they are threatening themselves by causing natural systems to deteriorate.

It is possible to change the situation into an attractive, sustainable society. In the early 1990s, Dr Robèrt worked with Swedish physicist John Holmberg to define a set of system conditions for sustainability which are based on the laws of thermodynamics and natural cycles (see box).

The Natural Step's four system conditions

1. Substances from the earth's crust must not systematically increase in nature

In a sustainable society, human activities such as the burning of fossil fuels and the mining of metals and minerals will not occur at a rate that causes them to increase systematically in the ecosphere. There are thresholds beyond which living organisms and ecosystems are adversely affected by increases in substances from the earth's crust. Problems may include an increase in greenhouse gases leading to global warming, contamination of surface and ground water, and metal toxicity, which can cause functional disturbances in animals. In practical terms, the first condition requires society to implement comprehensive metal and mineral recycling programs and decrease economic dependence on fossil fuels.

2. Substances produced by society must not systematically increase in nature

In a sustainable society, humans will avoid generating systematic increases in persistent substances such as the insecticide DDT (dichloro-diphenyl-trichloroethane), PCBs (polychlorobenzenes) and freon. Synthetic organic compounds such as DDT and PCBs can remain in the environment for many years, bioaccumulating in the tissues of organisms, causing profound deleterious effects on predators in the upper levels of the food chain. Freon and other ozone-depleting compounds may increase the risk of cancer due to increased ultraviolet radiation in the atmosphere. Society needs to find ways to reduce economic dependence on persistent, human-made substances.

3. The physical basis for the productivity and diversity of nature must not systematically be diminished

In a sustainable society, humans will avoid taking more from the biosphere than can be replenished by natural systems. In addition, people will avoid systematically encroaching upon nature by destroying the habitat of other species. Biodiversity, which includes the great variety of animals and plants found in nature, provides the foundation for ecosystem services that are necessary to sustain life on this planet. Society's health and prosperity depends on the enduring capacity of nature to renew itself.

4. We must be fair and efficient in meeting basic human needs

Meeting the fourth system condition is a way to avoid violating the first three system conditions for sustainability. Considering the human enterprise as a whole, we need to be efficient with regard to resource use and waste generation in order to be sustainable. If one billion people lack adequate nutrition while another billion have more than they need, there is a lack of fairness with regard to meeting basic human needs. Achieving greater fairness is essential for social stability and the cooperation needed for making large-scale changes within the framework laid out by the first three conditions.

To achieve this fourth condition, humanity must strive to improve technical and company efficiency around the world, and to live using fewer resources, especially in affluent areas. System condition four implies an improved means of addressing human population growth. If the total resource throughput of the global human population continues to increase, it will be increasingly difficult to meet basic human needs. Human-driven processes intended to fulfil human needs and wants are systematically degrading the collective capacity of the earth's ecosystems to meet these demands.

Gaining momentum and the recognition of the King of Sweden, The Natural Step received support from business and political leaders, many of whom subsequently participated in workshops designed to teach The Natural Step framework. Major Swedish companies began incorporating the system conditions into their business practices. Twenty independent, professional networks for the environment (e.g. Scientists for the Environment, Doctors for the Environment, Farmers for the Environment) were initiated and supported by The Natural Step. These networks share the core knowledge, or system conditions, for sustainability and build consensus from this common structure.

The Natural Step advocates a step-by-step implementation strategy. Companies are not expected to achieve long-term goals immediately. On the contrary, they are encouraged to move systematically by making investments that will provide benefit in the short term, while retaining a longer term perspective. They can use The Natural Step process to map out a series of steps that will eventually lead to full sustainability. Companies using The Natural Step framework are encouraged to start with the 'low hanging fruit'—those steps that are easiest to take and will achieve results that help move a company closer to its goals. The Natural Step is not prescriptive and does not judge. Instead, it serves as a guide.

Good practices

- Competitive advantage is sought by adopting The Natural Step's and other 'green' policies.
- The company has convincingly linked its mission to higher-order social needs. (Examples include Red Earth and The Body Shop, who have developed reputations for high levels of integrity with respect to not testing cosmetic products on animals. This gives them a considerable competitive advantage. They then live and trade consistently in support of that position. Several other companies focus on environmental issues, one or two on the child labour exploitation issue and others on animal liberation.)

Poor practices

- Risk management strategies ignore risk to community.
- A 'this does not apply to me' attitude.

9.5 Reduce waste

You must work to systematically reduce the waste and pollution your organisation produces. Over the next 20 years, we will see a significant shift in the way companies think about products and waste. We can see the beginnings already in that people are aware of waste management and that pollution is considered 'not a good thing'. However, the thinking shift from 'our waste must be managed so we meet our regulations' to 'our systems thinking about the relationship between waste and our products gives us a competitive advantage' is not yet here—except for a few companies.

A systems approach

Currently, most companies have at least moved to the 'regulation obeying, good corporate citizen stage'. Few are adopting the full systems approach.

Here is an example. Is your waste water good enough to use as input to your plant or factory? If not, why do you think it is good enough for the next person? de Bono's famous solution in *Lateral Thinking* for a highly polluted river is to take your input from downstream of your waste. This forces a systems solution. (We could extend this problem to human waste and suggest the solution as sewage treatment being upstream of potable water catchment reservoirs. This solution may possibly be required eventually and will need considerable systems thinking to implement—especially at no increased cost.)

That is impractical

You may scoff that 'All that greenie stuff is impractical. People might say they want it, but we can't afford it. We will take our profits now. That is what our shareholders want. Not this expensive, greenie gobbledygook!'. However, that take-it-now-and-damn-the-environment approach is not sustainable. The 10 Business Excellence Principles consistently argue for the company's sustainability—that is, that the company will be around for a long time, at least 100 years. Even if your day-to-day pressures and worries stop you from seeing that far, it is not logical or practical to conduct actions that you know will stop your company being sustainable. If all your customers are dead, or suing you for harming them, your company will not be sustainable.

By 2010, if you are not enforcing good environmental solutions within your business, large or small, you will no longer be sustainable. This is realistic.

Turn waste into profit

You can now see more examples of companies that turn their waste stream into a profitable product, for example, restaurants and abattoirs that turn waste food or animal wastes into vermicast (i.e. worm casts) that is then sold.

You often hear the argument that 'if we do this greenie stuff, we die'. That assumes the 'greenie stuff' will add costs. It does not have to. That was the same argument that was applied to improving quality—'If we improve quality, it will increase our costs'. The reality is that if you improve quality, you reduce rework and waste (which are very expensive) and increase sales because of increased customer satisfaction. But that is an old message. Implementing environmental solutions has similar advantages.

It is worthwhile for all companies to work out how to sell their waste stream or turn the waste stream into a profitable product.

Good practices

- 'Green policies' are used to acknowledge the wider community as an important stakeholder.

Poor practices

- No effort to reduce waste or pollution. Not following regulations. Careless discharge of waste. A 'Let someone else clean it up, it's not my cost' attitude.

9.6 Use environmental performance indicators

To make sure that your environmental strategy is implemented throughout the company and that your environmental work gets results for you, you should develop a set of environmental performance indicators. For example, you could monitor:

- the environmental impact of your production sites
- the average environmental standard of your products
- your energy usage
- your waste
- your paper usage and recycling
- the profitability of your most environmentally sound products.

You need environmental performance indicators because what gets measured gets done. If you do not have environmental performance indicators, you will not be able to measure if your environmental strategies are having an effect. This will help you prove that your environmental work is not only good for the environment, but is good business.

You should also develop a 'recycling value index' to help with decisions about trade-offs between increased production costs and increased recycling value. The recycling value index should include the value added or value lost throughout the entire product life cycle—at each stage of production, use, disposal or recovery. Optimal 'recycling value' can then be included as part of your design process and help decisions to make product recovery a profit centre in a future where product take-back is the norm, as it currently is in Europe—that is, the manufacturer must 'take the product back at no cost to the customer when the customer is finished with it'. Be it a refrigerator, radio, freezer or table, it is the manufacturer's job to recycle it, not the community's job to handle the landfill.

Shareholders should ask questions such as 'Does this company really consider long-term sustainability? Or, are the profits you see today obtained at the expense of tomorrow's cash flow?'.

Good practices

- Staff surveys indicate widespread support for the company's approach to the environment and the community.

Poor practices

- No measurement of environmental factors.
- A 'This does not apply to me' attitude.

9.7 Reduce unintended consequences

You should work to reduce the unintended consequences (side-effects) to the community of your actions and policies. The community expects that you will keep it safe and do no harm—either intentionally or unintentionally. Most companies do not consider the 'unintentional harm' aspect of their business. 'We made a mistake, sorry' may have worked in the past. It does not work now. Unintended harm can result in expensive and damaging court cases.

Most companies deal with 'unintended injuries' and 'unintended harm' as one-offs, as special events. They are sometimes hard to spot because they are often far removed in time and space from the original decision. However, they are directly attributed to the company's actions—'unintended consequences' of the way the company does things—and the courts increasingly agree. An injury or harm does not have to be intended for the company to be held responsible.

Here are some examples.

- Police are pursuing a speeding driver of a stolen car. 'Very good', you say. 'That is their job'. But…the speeding driver ran a red light and crashed into another car, killing the family. No-one meant it to happen—it was an unintended consequence of the chase.
- A woman undergoes an operation that relieves the pain from which she has been suffering. But…she gets a killer infection and dies. No-one meant it to happen—an unintended consequence.

- In the 1970s, computer memory was expensive—'Why don't we save space by using only two characters to store the date?'. What a good idea! In the 1990s, millions of dollars were spent on the Y2K 'bug'.
- Space for housing is scarce. Pressure is put on town planners to release marginal land. Twenty years later hundreds of people are killed in landslides and mud slides. No-one meant it to happen—an unintended consequence.
- A railway company decides to save costs by reducing the number of crew in the engine. The driver now has so much to do that it is not always possible to look out for signals. Six years later, two trains collide when one does not stop at a signal. No-one meant it to happen—an unintended consequence.

For legal firms, the unintended consequences include:

- getting crooks off on technical aspects of the law but the crooks then go on to re-offend—more rape and murder
- giving poor (or erroneous) advice because of a multitude of different possible interpretations that cause clients and the community to make unsafe decisions
- acting unethically—following the letter of the law but not its intent
- during family law matters, causing extreme stress that causes family break up or continued violence.

The military call them collateral damage—'A few civilians were killed, but we took our target'.

Like it or not, *all* of your unintended consequences are designed—yes, designed—into your current processes. This inadequate design has resulted in increasing insurance costs as companies struggle to protect themselves against a more litigious community. You can depend on the community becoming more litigious and the courts supporting its litigation. If you want the unintended consequences to diminish, you must redesign your processes (Principle 4, 'To improve the outcome, improve the system').

You should anticipate adverse effects from production, distribution, transportation, use and disposal of your products and from the behaviour of your employees in carrying out your policies and required activities. You should anticipate and prevent problems, provide a practical response if problems occur and provide information and support in order to maintain public awareness, safety and confidence. If you have to recall a product, do it early, don't lie, and provide useful information to the community.

Good practices

- Processes exist to examine and deal with the unintended consequences of activities and policies.

- Risk management is used for community and environmental impact and unintended side-effects.

Poor practices

- No concept that unintended side-effects of actions can be harmful to stakeholders.
- No strategies to address the unintended side-effects of current strategy.
- No measurements of the unintended side-effects of current strategy.
- Failure to consider that there are unintended side-effects of policies and actions.

9.8 Improve your industry

You should constantly work to improve your industry: its code of conduct, how its operates, sharing of knowledge on what does and does not work well, regulations that affect you, regulators and community perceptions. Each company has a responsibility to lift the average ability of the companies in its industry.

Many companies think they have no role in this. This is not true. If the community or regulators think badly of your industry and that affects your profitability, change the perception and the regulations. You can't sit back and moan and blame the mythical 'them'. It is in your hands.

If you are too small to do it by yourself, get together with others in your industry. Is there an industry association? If not, make one. Is there an industry code of practice? If not, make one. If you do not like the industry association or its code of practice, then work to change them.

Leadership as a corporate citizen entails influencing other companies, private and public, to join together to address the community need. Individuals and companies can and should lead efforts to define the obligations of their industry to its communities.

You should influence your trade or business association to engage in beneficial cooperative activities, such as sharing best practices to improve the overall performance. No company is too small to be involved in such activities.

What about competition? Isn't it the job of all companies to drive their competitors into the dirt? Drive them out of business? The trouble is that the mud sticks. If a company in your industry (a competitor) is producing poor quality products or harming the community, to some extent that damage comes back to you. (Politicians have been slow to learn this. When they throw mud at each other in their efforts to discredit each other, they all just look bad.)

319

Good practices

- There is active sharing of knowledge and technology with suppliers, customers and trade allies.
- Executives interface with other companies to expand and develop for the common good. They encourage participation in conferences and tours of facilities.
- Executives establish workshops with dedicated facilitators to promote relationships and communication.

Poor practices

- Attitudes of 'We go it alone', 'What we know, we know', 'We share it with nobody'.

9.9 Share your knowledge

You should share your knowledge about the 10 Business Excellence Principles with others to help them prosper. At a very minimum this should be with your stakeholders: owners, suppliers, customers, employees and community.

You should share your knowledge of these Principles so that other companies—competitors or not—should benefit. Sharing knowledge about the 10 Business Excellence Principles is a huge contribution to your community and your industry.

The expectation for 'sharing knowledge' requirement is different from the other four parts of Principle 9 as there is not yet a community punishment for companies that do not do it. The community will think better of you if you do it but will not punish you if you do not. This is about improving the general prosperity of your community.

Improving prosperity

Many believe that Principle 9 also extends to sharing prosperity with the community. This means that the company should extend its resources to assist in the community's infrastructure. It would, therefore, include:

- paying taxes so that the infrastructure of the community (on which everyone in it depends) can grow and further support the community
- keeping jobs in your country by not establishing offshore manufacturing at the expense of jobs in your community
- helping the less well off members of the community.

Good citizenship would include community service by employees. For example:

- employing disabled people
- funding community projects
- company child-care facilities not restricted to employees
- employees encouraged to participate in voluntary community activities (e.g. community associations, emergency services)
- assisting local schools and your trade and industry associations to adopt practices that are in line with the 10 Business Excellence Principles.

Good practices

- Assisting other companies to adopt the 10 Business Excellence Principles and practices. Providing a role model for other companies.
- Community outreach activities are conducted to share knowledge with the community.
- Accepting responsibility for (and involvement in) community-related projects and activities. Activities such as community involvement and support are beyond the normal business interests.

Poor practices

- An attitude of 'We don't share what we know with anybody'.
- Policies of tax avoidance. These mean that the company does not make its contribution to community infrastructure.

9.10 Be a good corporate citizen

You should take a strategic approach to your corporate citizenship. For example, you should plan your approach to all aspects of Principle 9 and measure your success as a good corporate citizen.

Principle 9 is important. However, it can be easily overlooked in the daily bustle that means that urgent jobs take priority over the important jobs—the ones that make a huge difference in the long term.

To make certain that you address Principle 9, you should include it in your strategic work. Make plans that address all aspects of the Principle, implement those plans and measure your success at being a good corporate citizen. Make corporate citizenship a key result area. Include your corporate citizenship measurements in your KPIs.

The motivation for such changes is often external, sometimes internal. For example, in Germany, the packaging 'take-back' regulations and the threat of further product take-back requirements have been the driver of environmental design and business strategy innovations for many companies. The inescapable logic of The Natural Step is a catapult for others. A personal commitment to crack the disparity between the dispassionate businessperson looking just at the numbers and the loving grandparent looking at a child's future has turned the tide for still others.

For Electrolux, the immediate prospect of a significant economic impact focused and shifted the company's attention, and the prospect of significant competitive advantage has held it there. In many cases, it is a combination of all these factors and others. The good news is that it works!

Electrolux and sustainability

Gil Friend points out that for Electrolux (see box below), The Natural Step funnel became an important part of the company's strategic landscape. Electrolux made a strategic decision to aim its company towards the narrowing throat of that funnel rather than to drift haplessly, like most companies do, towards the sloping walls.

This hard-nosed business decision embedded 'sustainability' at the heart of business strategy and moved the 'environment' from an obscure operational function to a core strategic driver of everything from business strategy to product design.

To do this, Electrolux moved compliance obligations to line and general managers, and had environmental managers and departments focus on strategy and design issues. This has served two purposes: it put an environmental orientation more deeply into the operating company, and it focused 'environmental' work on business problems, business solutions and strategic competitiveness, that is, on real areas where sustainability-oriented thinking can lead to major breakthroughs for companies.

Electrolux case study

Electrolux AB of Sweden didn't eagerly choose The Natural Step path towards sustainability. Apparently, the company faced a multimillion dollar contract loss when a major customer who had been working with The Natural Step turned it down because Electrolux products violated The Natural Step's four 'system conditions' for sustainability. Electrolux executives angrily demanded a meeting with The Natural Step's founder, Dr Robèrt. 'What are you doing?', they demanded. 'You've cost us millions!'

Dr Robèrt, as he typically does in the face of such confrontation, returned to the basic thermodynamics and evolutionary biology underlying the Natural Step framework. The Electrolux executives, good scientists and engineers that they are, found the non-negotiable scientific Principles...well...non-negotiable!

With no choice but to acknowledge their validity, the Electrolux executives moved on to the challenge of how to steer their company's operations to be in line with the laws of nature. Now, seven years later, Electrolux calls their billion krona-plus investment in The Natural Step initiatives the best financial investment they've ever made.

Source: Friend, Gil (1997), 'Strategic sustainability—dragged kicking and screaming to where we really want to go', *New Bottom Line* 6.2 January 14, www.natlogic.com.

Good practices

- The community knows and respects the company and learns from the company.
- Employees are proud to talk about their company because of what it stands for.

Poor practices

- No strategic corporate citizenship or leadership in the community, including the environment, industry standards and community support of a more general nature.

SUMMARY

- The community withdraws the 'licence to operate' from companies that pollute or have unacceptable standards of ethics. Or, the community imposes regulations to enforce companies to work to acceptable standards of practice. Companies should discontinue unacceptable practices and adopt acceptable practices
- Companies must ensure that they are seen to 'add value' to society as well as delivering particular goods and services. You should use practices that the community perceives as friendly and that appear to 'add value' to the community in general. Companies succeed by their relevance and the value they add to the community they serve.
- You should be working strategically to reduce the harm you do to the environment (e.g. your dependence on mining and fossil fuels, your dependence on persistent, unnatural substances, and your dependency on nature-consuming activities). You should always try to do more with less.
- Work to reduce the unintended consequences (side-effects) to the community of your actions and policies. You should do nothing that will endanger the community's prosperity, health, safety or cleanliness. Increasingly, now, the community expects companies to do no intended or unintended harm to the environment in which that community lives.
- You should anticipate adverse effects from production, distribution, transportation, use and disposal of your products; from the behaviour

of employees in carrying out your policies and required activities. You should anticipate and prevent problems, provide a practical response if problems occur, and provide information and support in order to maintain public awareness, safety and confidence.

- Share your knowledge with others to help them prosper on their journey to adopt the 10 Business Excellence Principles. At a very minimum this should be with your stakeholders: owners, suppliers, customers, employees and community

WHAT WOULD YOUR STAKEHOLDERS SAY?

HOW WOULD YOUR EMPLOYEES RATE YOUR COMPANY ON THESE?

- This company operates ethically.
- This company operates well within standards of ethics considered acceptable by the community.
- This company does nothing that will endanger the community's prosperity, health, safety or cleanliness.
- This company works hard to keep up with changing community mores and what the community thinks is acceptable behaviour.
- This company uses 'community friendly' practices that 'add value' to the community in general.
- This company works to reduce the waste and pollution it produces.
- This company works to reduce the unintended consequences (side-effects) to the community of its actions and policies.
- This company keeps the community safe and does no harm—intentionally or unintentionally.
- This company does nothing that might endanger its right to operate.
- This company shares its knowledge with others to help them prosper on their journey to adopt the 10 Business Excellence Principles.
- This company systematically decreases its economic dependence on underground metals and other minerals.
- This company does not release greenhouse gases or excess energy into the atmosphere.
- This company's waste products are decontaminated to pre-production levels.
- We are working strategically to reduce our dependence on mining and fossil fuels, our dependence on persistent, unnatural substances and our dependency on nature-consuming activities. We always try to do more with less.
- This company systematically decreases its dependence on fossil fuels.
- This company systematically decreases its dependence on persistent synthetic substances.

- This company systematically decreases its activities that encroach on productive ecosystems.
- This company uses a set of environmental performance indicators to monitor environmental impact at production sites, the average environmental standard of its products and the profitability of its most environmentally sound products.
- We have pushed well beyond the traditional notions of recycling to rigorously design our products for optimal 'recycling value'.
- We use a recycling value index to guide decisions regarding trade-offs between increased production costs and increased recycling value.
- This company provides a safe working environment (physically and mentally and free of harassment).
- We constantly work to improve our industry: its code of conduct, how it operates, sharing of knowledge on what does and does not work well, regulations that affect us and regulators and community perceptions.

HOW WOULD YOUR CUSTOMERS RATE YOUR COMPANY ON THESE?

- This company shares its knowledge with others to help them prosper on their journey to adopt the 10 Business Excellence Principles.
- This company does nothing that will endanger the community's prosperity, health, safety or cleanliness.
- This company designs its products for optimal 'recycling value'.
- This company's products and services are safe and delivered in a safe way.

HOW WOULD YOUR SHAREHOLDERS RATE YOUR COMPANY ON THESE?

- This company operates ethically—well within the standard of ethics considered acceptable by the community.
- This company seeks competitive advantage by adopting 'community friendly' practices, practices that are perceived to 'add value' to the community.
- This company does nothing that will endanger the community's prosperity, health, safety or cleanliness.
- This company works to reduce the waste and pollution it produces.
- This company works to reduce the unintended consequences (side-effects) to the community of its actions and policies.
- This company does no harm—intentionally or unintentionally.
- This company's products and work practices are safe and do no harm to employees, customers or the community.
- This company shares its knowledge with others to help them prosper on their journey to adopt the 10 Business Excellence Principles.
- There is no question of this company's right to operate being continued indefinitely.

- This company does not return to us as 'profits' funds that will subsequently have to be made up by the community (e.g. not paying a reasonable level of taxation).
- This company does not follow strategies of paying poverty level wages in developing countries.
- This company works strategically to reduce its dependence on mining and fossil fuels, its dependence on persistent, unnatural substances and its nature-consuming activities. It always tries to do more with less.
- This company uses a set of environmental performance indicators to monitor environmental impact at production sites, the average environmental standard of appliances and profitability of its most environmentally sound products.
- This company designs its products for optimal 'recycling value'.
- This company uses a recycling value index to guide decisions regarding trade-offs between increased production costs and increased recycling value.
- This company does not have to spend shareholders' funds to defend criminal behaviour by executives or to defend accusations of harm in the courts.
- This company works constantly to improve its industry: how the industry operates, its code of conduct, sharing knowledge on what does and does not work well, changing regulations that affect it and perceptions of regulators.

HOW WOULD YOUR SUPPLIERS RATE YOUR COMPANY ON THESE?

- This company shares its knowledge with us to help us prosper on our journey to adopt the 10 Business Excellence Principles.
- This company does nothing that will endanger the community's prosperity, health, safety or cleanliness.
- This company designs its products for optimal 'recycling value'.
- This company uses a recycling value index to guide decisions regarding trade-offs between increased production costs and increased recycling value.
- This company works constantly to improve its industry: how the industry operates, its code of conduct, sharing knowledge on what does and does not work well, changing regulations that affect it and perceptions of regulators.
- This company makes a significant contribution to its industry.

HOW WOULD THE COMMUNITY RATE YOUR COMPANY ON THESE?

- This company works to ensure a clean, safe, fair and prosperous society.
- All of this company's actions enhance the value it adds to the community.

- This company has an acceptable standard of ethics.
- We willingly extend this company's right to operate.
- This company does nothing that will endanger the community's prosperity, health, safety or cleanliness.
- This company uses 'community friendly' practices that 'add value' to our community.
- This company works to reduce the waste and pollution it produces.
- This company does not release greenhouse gases or excess energy into the atmosphere.
- This company's waste products are decontaminated to pre-production levels.
- This company works to reduce the unintended consequences (side-effects) to the community of its actions and policies.
- This company does no harm—intentionally or unintentionally.
- This company shares its knowledge with others to help them prosper on their journey to adopt the 10 Business Excellence Principles.
- This company works to reduce its dependence on mining and fossil fuels, its dependence on persistent, unnatural substances and its nature-consuming activities. It always tries to do more with less.
- This company systematically decreases its dependence on under-ground metals and other minerals.
- This company systematically decreases its dependence on fossil fuels.
- This company systematically decreases its dependence on persistent synthetic substances.
- This company systematically decreases its activities that encroach on productive ecosystems.
- This company uses a set of environmental performance indicators to monitor environmental impact at production sites, the average environmental standard of appliances and profitability of its most environmentally sound products.
- This company designs its products for optimal 'recycling value'.

Principle 10
Value for all stakeholders

> *Sustainability is determined by an organisation's ability to create and deliver value for all stakeholders.*

I**T IS NOT DIFFICULT TO ARGUE** that Principle 10 is one of the most important of the 10 Business Excellence Principles. In Dr Hausner's research, Principle 10 has the highest correlation with KPI improvement. It is one of the four Principles that show a high correlation with good business excellence scores. It is done well by winners of the National Business Excellence Awards.

To some extent, that level of importance is expected. Principle 10 is a high order, summary Principle. Three of the 10 Principles (3, 'Customers', 7, 'Enthusiastic people' and 9, 'Value to the community') describe designing the company to provide value to different stakeholder groups. When you combine those already important Principles, you get a very powerful Principle. When you then add the other stakeholders (i. e. the owners, the company itself and alliance partners), it is extremely powerful indeed.

Principle 10 says 'create and deliver value for *all* stakeholders'. The emphasis is on '*all* stakeholders'. Principles 3, 7 and 9 each insist that the company must be designed to provide value to a particular stakeholder group. If the stakeholder groups are not aligned in what they want from the company, and there is no reason that they should be, then the company must find ways to resolve any conflicts.

If you choose *not* to provide value to *all* stakeholders, this means that you have chosen to give less than an expected share to one or more stakeholders. This usually results in a less than optimum result for that company and can seriously harm its long-term sustainability.

10.1 Create value for all stakeholders

Principle 2 ('Focus on achieving results') discussed the goals of the company and the necessary conditions to achieve that goal. In *It's Not Luck* and *The Goal*, Goldratt described the goal for most companies as *to make money now and in the future*. There are three necessary conditions for success in reaching your goal:

1. Provide a secure and satisfying environment for employees now as well as in the future.
2. Provide satisfaction to the market now and in the future. (This condition comes from the idea that the market punishes companies that do not satisfy the market perception of value.)
3. Provide value to the community now and in the future. (This is Principle 9—the community punishes companies it considers are not good corporate citizens and takes away their right to operate.)

In Principle 10, we look at achieving a balance between these 'necessary conditions' and balancing the needs of all stakeholders in relation to the company's goal.

Government-owned companies and not-for-profit companies

The main difference between government-owned and not-for-profit companies and other companies is the type of goal. For government-owned and not-for-profit companies, making money now and in the future is usually not the goal. It is more likely to be to provide a valuable service to the community's infrastructure.

In government-owned organisations, the government provides money in the form of taxpayer's funds. Taxpayers expect their money to be spent well and for value to be provided in exchange for the money. For example, the government and its taxpayers expect:

- infrastructure to be built and services delivered to the community
- government agency customers to get value from the services provided
- the government agency to maintain itself
- government agency employees to be resourceful and enthusiastic
- the community's interest to be looked after and the community protected from harm from the activities of the government agency
- the government agency to form alliances with partners in order to achieve its objectives.

This is a different goal to that of companies and consequently there is no dividend stream. However, if the government does not provide enough funds, the government-owned companies will not be able to fulfil those expectations. The same applies to not-for-profit organisations, who also have no dividend stream.

Stakeholders

In most companies the important stakeholders are:

- owners (shareholders)
- customers
- the company itself
- employees
- the community
- alliance partners.

Principles 3 ('Customers'), 7 ('Enthusiastic people') and 9 ('Value to the community') described in detail why it is important to design the company around three of those stakeholder groups—customers, employees and the community.

There is already an implied conflict between Principles 3, 7 and 9 in that each claims that the company must be designed to provide value to *its* particular stakeholder group. The implied conflict occurs if each stakeholder group wants the design for them to exclude value for the others. For example, employees may insist the company be designed for them to the exclusion of customers or community needs.

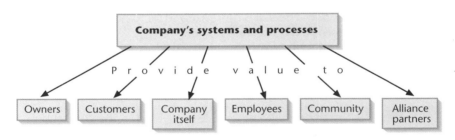

Fig. 10.1 The company must provide equal value to the various stakeholders

When we add the remaining three stakeholders (owners, the company itself and alliance partners), the potential for conflict is huge. It is clear that each of these stakeholders has a major call on the company to design itself so that each stakeholder receives sufficient value. How does the company resolve this conflict?

Solving that conundrum while ensuring the company's sustainability is the heart of Principle 10. The company must be designed to deliver value to all its important stakeholder groups in proportions that those stakeholders consider appropriate.

Objectives, strategies and plans

The company should know the needs, expectations and objectives of each of its major stakeholder groups. You should determine your company's short and long-term objectives with respect to each stakeholder group (and these should be in line with meeting your own objectives and goals). You should ensure that your actions and plans explicitly address the different stakeholder needs. You should assess and resolve any conflict between the different stakeholders' needs and the company's needs and objectives.

You need to determine the balance you want to achieve between the interests of the stakeholder groups and negotiate a position that is acceptable to all stakeholders. You should find a balance that best meets most stakeholder needs. You must avoid adverse affects to any stakeholders.

The needs of the stakeholder groups are constantly changing. Although the stakeholder groups will tend to remain fairly constant, the composition of each group will constantly be changing—as owners and shareholders change; as customers are added and lost; as managers join, are promoted and leave; as employees join and leave; as suppliers are added and discontinued; as members of the community change.

Even if the composition of the groups did not change, the needs and expectations of the group change over time—as ways of doing business change; as products and service types change; as competition offers different ways of delivery, service, terms of payment; as workplace conditions change; as salary ranges and payment methods change.

- You need to review your objectives and strategies for each group constantly.
- You should set targets for these objectives, develop strategies and carry out activities to meet your objectives with respect to each stakeholder group.
- The company should measure the success of those strategies in meeting its stakeholders' and its own objectives, and in carrying out the activities.

Good practices

- Short- and long-term objectives for each stakeholder group and the company's strategies for each are clearly stated in the strategic or corporate plan.
- Objectives and strategies are in place for all major stakeholder groups (i.e. owners, customers, the company itself, employees, the community and alliance partners).

- Everyone in the company has a clear idea of who the company's stakeholders are and what value the company creates for each stakeholder group.
- The company tries to increase the value it provides to all its stakeholders.
- Plans are examined for unintended side-effects and modified to avoid them.
- Indicators reflect what is important to all stakeholder groups.

Poor practices

- Not recognising and balancing the needs of the six main stakeholder groups (owner, customer, the company itself, employees, community and alliance partners) and not measuring success in meeting those needs.
- Executives and employees only point to owners and customers as stakeholders of the company and do not mention employees or the community.
- No measurement of progress towards achieving the mission, vision, values and goals.
- KPIs bear little or no relationship to strategic plans.
- Not acknowledging that the goal is to make money.
- KPIs not linked to company objectives.

10.2 Invest to meet stakeholders' needs

You must invest (funds and effort) to meet the needs of each major stakeholder group. These should be deliberate investment decisions in which you apportion the potential retained earnings to the six major stakeholder groups to reach your goals and objectives and to meet their needs. There should be so much:

- for owners in the form of dividends
- for customers in the form of product development and improvement
- put back into the company in the form of maintenance, risk protection, growth, innovation, research and diversification
- for employees in the form of increased payments, development, education and training, working conditions
- for the community in the form of taxes, environmental and community programs and helping others
- towards alliance partnerships.

Owners require dividends. Customers will not buy unless the company invests in providing products and services they value. The company invests in its own maintenance and growth. Employees will not contribute their enthusiasm, resourcefulness and innovation unless they get value (and are valued and trusted) in return. The community will withdraw the company's right to operate or impose restrictive regulations if it thinks the company is doing harm or taking more than it should from the community. Alliance partners will stop being partners if they are not getting value from the partnership.

For each stakeholder group, the company forgoes money now for increased value later—an investment. Companies are accustomed to making capital investment decisions. These are cost–benefit, capital-rationing decisions.

Owners and shareholders

As stated, the goal of the company is to make money now and in the future. Because owners and shareholders put up the money and take the risk, they have the main call on the money generated by the company. However, the company must balance the owners' call on the money generated *now* against money to be generated in the *future* and against the demands by the other stakeholders.

The owners take their value from the company in the form of dividends. The size of the dividend stream is an indicator of company health. However, to keep the dividend stream healthy, some of the owners' equity must be diverted away from the dividend stream. That is, it is in the best interest of the owners to give up some of the dividend stream now in order for the dividend stream to continue and possibly increase in the future. It is an investment decision.

This particular investment decision is at the heart of the long-term success of the company. If the owners do not get enough 'value', they withdraw their support and funds, causing the company to have difficulty in reaching its goal and possibly causing it to collapse. If owners take too much money out now and do not reinvest it into the company, the company also has difficulties in reaching its goal and the owners may get reduced value in the future.

Owners should be suspicious of companies that do not invest in the other stakeholders. If companies do not invest in the other stakeholders, the future dividend stream is seriously under threat.

Many companies appear to think that these 10 Business Excellence Principles do not apply to them because they appear to remove the owner from a position of total control. However, it is clear that the owners did *not* have total control anyway, and that when the company fully adopts Principle 10, the owners (and all the other stakeholders) get more value.

Customers

The company's money mainly comes from its customers. It is the customers who actually provide money (in the form of revenue) and they want value for that money. You have to satisfy your customers to provide what they value—Principle 3 ('Customers'). The more you do that, the more they buy and the more money you make.

It takes money (and effort) to provide what your customers value. You must work out what they value (and do not value) and continue to improve and modify your products to provide it. You must spend the money and effort now to get more revenue later. It is an investment—a sharing of value between stakeholders. The company gives value to the customers now in order to get more money later.

The company itself

Good owners have always known that there is a very definite limit to what they can take out of the company. If you want to be sustainable, every year you must plough a goodly part of the profits back in. This use of funds takes several forms. You must constantly be diversifying (to protect yourself against a calamity in your market). You must be conducting maintenance by improving what you do well (to build your core competency)—and trying to improve (or dropping) what you do less well. You must protect yourself against risk, you should innovate and do research. If you decide to grow, you must invest money in it.

These all take funds. If the company chooses not to make these investments, sustainability is compromised.

Home ownership is a useful analogy. To keep your home sustainable as a place you wish to inhabit, you need occasional investments in furniture, landscaping in the garden, an extension, a pool, a major redecoration. These are infrequent but all take effort, funds and planning. You also need to do maintenance chores, sometimes daily—washing up, cleaning the bathroom, the kitchen and the pool, clearing away odds and ends, vacuuming, mowing the lawn, weeding the garden. These maintenance tasks are done frequently. They also need effort, funds and planning. Although less than the major investments, they are still investments. If you decide not to make these investments and use your efforts and funds elsewhere, the value of your home declines.

Employees

The company's employees are the ones who provide the products and services to the customers. If your employees are not fully enabled, then they will not be able to do their jobs properly. If they are not resourceful or enthusiastic, they will not do all the things necessary to make the company's products and services more exactly what the customers need or value. For employees to be enthusiastic about the company's business, the employees themselves must feel valued. Employees need: education and training in processes, technology, products and service; development so that they become better at their jobs and able to meet their career; space to have their say; time to reflect and practice; time to develop relationships with their work family, their customers and their alliance partners; pay; and to be safe.

These are investments. The company must invest in enabling its employees and providing what its employees value in order for the employees to provide what its customers value—Principle 7 ('Enthusiastic people'). This is another example of sharing of value between stakeholders. The company gives value to the employees now in order to get more money later.

Community

The community expects the company to contribute to its infrastructure. The most obvious way is by paying tax—which is a direct payment by the company to the community for infrastructure. The community also expects the company to spend (or forgo) funds in order to meet its expectation of a clean, safe and prosperous environment. As we discussed in Principle 9 ('Value to the community'), the community has begun to have more of a voice (via the media and courts) in calling to account companies that behave unethically or have broken social and environmental mores that are considered important.

Providing work practices and processes that are safe and clean may add additional costs. Once again, this is an investment. But this is an investment made now so as to be allowed to keep operating in the long term.

Alliance partners

This is in two parts. The first is an old one. Most companies take an input of some form and do something to it to turn it into something more valuable. This is not just manufacturing companies. Most companies have suppliers. In non-manufacturing companies, the input is often information.

As you get better and better at running your processes, it soon becomes very apparent that the quality of the goods and services provided by your suppliers is crucial to your ability to make money. If you get junk from your supplier, it costs you more to produce a product or service that is valuable to your customers. Companies found it was to their advantage to establish win–win partnerships with their suppliers in order to help them improve the quality of their goods and services.

Secondly, just as you are courting your customers, your suppliers are courting you. You are their customer. You have and must demand all the rights and claims for value that your customers make on you.

Because almost every company is in the middle of someone's supply chain, when company A was establishing partnerships with its suppliers, company A's customers were establishing supplier partnerships with it. You might not seek out an alliance partnership with your customer. However, from your customer's viewpoint, you are a supplier. If you are important enough to that customer, he or she will want to establish an alliance partnership with you.

Another type of alliance partnership occurs when two (or more) companies form an alliance to do something together. You probably have partnerships everywhere. All have been established for mutual benefit.

However, each partnership has a cost, even if it only means having to do things in a different way from the company's preferred way. Partnerships are often dissolved if one of the partners is not satisfied with the benefits obtained from the partnership—compared with the cost of being in the partnership.

Therefore, when it has alliance partnerships, the company is, in part, working with the outside company. All 'working' involves some form of investment. Establishing alliance partnerships means that the company is investing some of its funds in those partnerships (so that the company benefits in the end). However, the money generated by the company is spread a little more thinly.

Good practices

- A deliberate policy to invest in each stakeholder group. Plans and strategies are developed and implemented to invest and measure this investment.
- Cost–benefit analyses are conducted to assist investment decisions. Decisions to invest in all stakeholder groups are given similar treatment.
- Success of investment is measured.
- The company identifies strategically important partners and other alliances.

Poor practices

- Failure to make time to work to improve the business (at all).
- 'Business improvement' is separate from 'the business'.
- Cultural change not given strategic importance—it is not the subject of high-level decisions on equal terms with other business strategy.
- Cutting funds to other stakeholders to support the dividend stream to owners.
- Unbalanced perceptions of stakeholders—in particular, a focus on meeting short-term needs of shareholders or political masters.

10.3 Negotiate a balance

You should negotiate a balance with representatives of all your major stakeholder groups. It is clear that the company must be designed to provide value to each of the six stakeholder groups. You need to establish a balance between what the company can provide to each group and the value each stakeholder wants. This balance is crucial.

How do you find a balance? You should negotiate it.

All six of these stakeholders to some extent require value from the company. Principles 3, 7 and 9 say that the company should be designed to provide value to three of them (customers, employees and community). Yet two others (the owners and the company itself) have a very logical right for the company to be structured for their benefit.

Each stakeholder group has its own needs and expectations. Negotiating a way through that quagmire of conflicting needs and demands is a major task for executive management. Doing it formally and with structure is rarely achieved.

Representatives

Because all six stakeholder groups require value from the company, and five of them expect the company to be designed for them, they all expect to have some input into the running of the company. Companies that are doing this well include representatives from each stakeholder group in strategic decision making, strategic planning, products and service design, process redesign and company design.

This very revolutionary stuff is often met with serious opposition. Most companies only have representatives from the owners (the board) and the company itself (the executive managers). Those who are clinging to the old thinking see no reason to allow any stakeholder other than the owners and executive managers to have their say in the company.

Although it is always up to the executive managers to negotiate the balance between the needs of the stakeholders and to make the decisions, it is clear that all stakeholder groups must be represented at senior level and have input at major decision points. This does not mean that they should be poking into every decision every day. However, all decisions every day must consider their interests and the balance between them.

In the stakeholders' interests

Sustainability of the company is in the best interest of all stakeholders. They all want the company to keep going. Look at it from the stakeholders' side. Think of the unwanted effects on the stakeholders if the company goes bankrupt:

• the owners lose income

- the customers see good products lost—good products and services that might not be available from another source
- the company itself disappears
- the employees see jobs lost—loss of income and loss of the work 'family'
- the community sees loss of employment opportunity and taxation income
- the suppliers lose a customer.

Unions

Some unions also appear to cling to the idea that companies must be designed for union members alone. This is just as unsustainable as the senior managers insisting that the company must be designed for themselves. Unions must recognise that in order for the company to survive, it must make money now and in the future, or else there will not be a company to employ the union members.

There is no place for bloody-mindedness. Both sides have a legitimate role—provided both are working for the good of the company and not just playing power games. Employees need their say in the way the company is designed so that they receive value. The company needs efficient work practices. The employees need the company and the company needs the employees.

Unfortunately, most companies and their employees have a downward spiral of ill will and lack of trust built over many years by both sides bluffing, lying and breaking promises. It usually takes considerable time and effort to restore that destroyed trust—as described in Principle 1 ('Role models').

It is in the company's best interest for employees to volunteer enthusiastically—Principle 7. If the company is designed so employees think they are valued and receive value, there is probably no need for a union. Active union action usually indicates that Principles 1 ('Role models'), 7 ('Enthusiastic people') and 10 ('Value for all stakeholders') are being violated.

On the other hand, a union can be an excellent representative of employees' needs. A union can have a very active role in representing these needs even when trust exists and the employees are extremely satisfied with the company. It is a different role.

Providing value to each stakeholder group

There is a logical reason to include each of the stakeholders. Each has a significant call on the value of the company. In each case, value to the owners is given up in exchange for promised value in the future—an investment.

As well as the benefits that each stakeholder group brings, it is useful to look at the effect on the company of the stakeholders not getting what they value from the arrangement.

Table 10.1 If they think they do not get enough value:

Owners	Customers	Employees	Community	Partners
Sell shares, so decrease share price	Do not buy, so decrease revenue	Are not enthused, so show decreased innovation, creativity	Increase regulations	Break partnership, so you have to fix it (do it) yourself

Good practices

- Consultation with customers and suppliers as part of the planning process.
- Customer representatives are included in strategic planning.
- Community input to strategic direction and strategies actively sought.
- Alliance partnerships are considered as matters of strategic significance with senior executive involvement.
- Strategic alliance partnership relationships are developed with major suppliers and customers.
- Key suppliers are invited to participate in process improvement and product development activities.

Poor practices

- Only including owners and managers when determining company objectives and strategies.
- No concept that unintended side-effects of actions can be harmful to stakeholders.
- No strategies to address the unintended side-effects of current strategy.
- No measurements of the unintended side-effects of current strategy.
- Failure to consider that there are unintended side-effects of policies and actions.
- Risk management strategies ignore risk to community.

10.4 Focus on the best interest of the company

Your reward and recognition systems should focus on the long-term best interest of the company (rather than the short-term interest of the executives).

Senior managers have to determine how to split the company's investment between the six stakeholder groups. Unfortunately, pressures from the owners for money now and the reward structures for managers to keep dividends flowing may cause the managers not to act in the long-term best interests of the company.

For example, managers are often rewarded according to performance of the share price. The share price is usually very strongly influenced by the dividend stream. Managers may be tempted to increase the share price by investing too much into the dividend stream. This can mean cuts in maintenance, innovation, research, customer service, product development, education and training, diversification or knowledge retrieval systems. This keeps the dividend stream going—for a while. Does it help the company and the owners in the long term? No!

You expect senior managers to do the best possible for the company and its stakeholders. Unfortunately, reward schemes often put senior managers in a conflict between their own best interests and the best interests of the company. The conflict occurs because the rewards at the top are now so huge that they cause the people at the top to look after themselves first. When they are looking after themselves first, they are not always acting in the best interest of the company.

Huge pay packets cause considerable political infighting and diversion of attention away from the main game. Too much is personally at stake for the players to be seriously interested in the company, its customers or its other stakeholders. With the competition so fierce for the highly paid top jobs, most people get sucked into highly destructive back-stabbing tactics—they do anything to undermine their fellow executives, the real competition.

Owners hope that the best interest of the individual aligns with the best interest of the company. However, it is almost as though reward according to share price performance is guaranteed to give less than optimum distribution of funds among stakeholders and hence less than optimum performance of the company. Another case of rewarding A while hoping for B.

Good practices

- Senior management sees its main job is to provide value and reach its objectives for all stakeholders.
- Management reward schemes that give equal focus to providing value to all stakeholder groups.
- Management objectives are to provide balanced investment to all stakeholder groups with the intention of providing acceptable value to all.

Poor practices

- Reward structures overemphasise looking after owners.
- Investment in other stakeholders is punished.

10.5 Use innovative ways to deliver value

You should be seeking to find innovative and inventive ways to create and deliver value for all your major stakeholder groups. This follows the process described several times already.

- Find out what your stakeholders want, need and value. Ask them. Don't assume that you know.
- Work out what you will do (if anything) to meet those needs. Set objectives and have plans to reach those objectives for each major stakeholder group. Make certain that those objectives help you meet your own objectives.
- Carry out the plan.
- Measure to see if the plan was carried out. Did you do what you said you were going to do?
- Measure to see if what you did helped meet the stakeholders' objectives and your objectives.
- Review what you did to see if you can do better or if you need to do something differently.

It is important to know what your stakeholders want, need and value and how you will meet those needs because:

- it is easy to *assume* that you know what your stakeholders want, need and value but what you assume may have no relationship to what they actually want, need and value
- you need to work out if and how you will respond to those specific needs
- you need your objectives for those stakeholders to contribute towards your own objectives
- you may need to be innovative and inventive to meet those needs.

Competition for stakeholders

Most companies are used to thinking about competitors for the customer stakeholder group. Unfortunately, you have competitors for the other stakeholders as well.

- *Owners* can choose to buy their shares from other companies or allow their funds to be invested in other companies in an expectation of better reward.
- *Customers* can choose to buy products and services from other companies.
- The *company itself* can choose to concentrate on a different set of core competencies or to diversify away completely or partially from its existing business mix.

- *Employees* can choose to work for other companies (or for themselves by withdrawing their volunteering).
- The *community* can choose to allow other companies to operate and deny you permission to operate, or to operate only with very restrictive regulations.
- *Suppliers* can choose to sell to different companies and exclude you from being able to use their particular products and services.
- *Alliance partners* can choose to form alliances with different companies and exclude you from benefits that the partnership could bring to your company.

The company is constantly competing for players from each group. You need to determine what the players in each stakeholder group want and set out to woo them.

Stakeholders want sustainability

All stakeholder groups usually want the company to be sustainable into the future. Owners want the continued income stream, customers want the continued supply of the useful products and services, the company and employees want continued employment with its financial, social and other rewards, the community wants the continued benefits the company brings in terms of infrastructure, employment and so on, and suppliers want you to continue to buy their products.

Of course, there are exceptions, such as a company formed to complete one project and whose intention was to close when the project was completed (e.g. a company formed to stage the Olympic Games). However, usually the intention is for the company to continue indefinitely. It would be rare for a company to plan to fail.

The plan for the future may be to be taken over. Many small companies have just such a plan. In this case, their main product is the company itself and their main strategy is to maintain or grow the company until it is attractive to a buyer. Thus, the company still continues—albeit as part of another company.

Unfortunately, few companies articulate their plans for the long term. Is there a plan for the company's end game in three, five or 20 years? Or, is there a 300-year plan?

Good practices

- There is active sharing of knowledge and technology with suppliers, customers and trade allies. Leaders interface with other companies to expand and develop for the common good. They encourage participation in conferences and tours of facilities. Executives

establish workshops with dedicated facilitators to promote relationships and communication.
- The company engages regularly in 'imagineering' its future using input from all stakeholder groups.
- The company extends beyond its commercial partnerships and alliances to find other areas of mutual interest (e.g. values, information technology).

Poor practices
- Doing the same old thing. Doing what has always been done.
- No attempt to achieve unique positioning for sustainable competitiveness.

10.6 Measure your investment in each stakeholder group

You should measure the investment you make in meeting the needs of each major stakeholder group. You should measure the apportionment of investment between your major stakeholder groups. The balance of investment of funds between the different stakeholder groups is one of the most important measurements made by a company. Most companies do not record or monitor what is invested in each group. How much are you investing in each of these stakeholders? Just what is it costing you?

We often see companies that constantly wander down the path of a latest fad—customer service, or looking after employees, or waste management—without any understanding that these are strategies or investments. No effort is made to determine what is invested, what benefit is expected, what success of the strategy/investment would look like or how they would measure it.

Here are some examples of investment funding decisions for each stakeholder group. Each should be measured and ongoing cost–benefit analyses conducted.

Owners
- Dividends paid

Customers
- Surveys, focus groups, market research to find what customers need and want
- Research
- Product and service development
- Funds spent on innovation, inventions, new products and services
- Customer functions
- Promotions, advertising

- Customer-related data storage and retrieval
- Systems to make customer contact easy for customers
- Customer satisfaction and perception measurements

Company

- Salaries paid to senior managers
- Maintenance expenditure
- Capital expenditure
- Diversification, mergers and acquisitions
- Restructuring
- Investment in and growth of knowledge and core competencies
- Company improvement, process improvement
- Risk management
- Cost of quality, quality control, audit, complaint handling, rework, scrap
- Compliance with standards, standard operating procedures and company policy
- Litigation, insurance
- Workers compensation
- Measurement and reporting systems, management information systems, KPIs
- Benchmarking, competitive comparisons

Employees

- Surveys, focus groups to find what employees need and want, determination of morale
- Increases in salaries and wages
- Education, training and development
- Safety
- Workplace improvement
- Internal newsletters, social functions and networks

Community

- Tax paid
- Waste stream quality improvement
- Compliance with regulations and laws
- Public relations, media, 'company as good guy' advertising

Suppliers and alliance partners

- Systems to evaluate suppliers
- Tendering processes
- Quality control on your input stream from suppliers
- Time and funds spent fixing your suppliers' processes
- Quality and process variation in your processes caused by your suppliers
- Time and funds spent working for an alliance partner

This is a list of investment decisions. In each case, there is a cost and a received benefit. An investment in improving the organisation returns benefits in terms of better profitability.

It is clear that for some the costs can be small compared with the benefits. For example, an investment in improving quality of processes is usually rewarded with huge benefits in terms of significantly reduced cost of production.

Good practices

- Investment in each stakeholder group is indexed and measured.
- The expected benefit for each investment is widely known within the company.
- Performance against plans is reviewed regularly. A user-friendly set of performance indicators is used to gauge the level of implementation and performance against plans.
- Improvement indices are constructed for all key, core and support processes.
- Process improvement data is collected. Measuring the outputs of all key, core and support processes.
- The rate of improvement is measured for all key, core and support processes.

Poor practices

- Not keeping track of specific investments made to each stakeholder group.
- Burying the investments in general expenditure. Not differentiating investments.
- Not measuring process outputs.

10.7 Measure success for each stakeholder group

You must measure your success in meeting your objectives for all your stakeholder groups. You must measure your success, including and beyond financial performance, by determining how you are achieving success for each of your stakeholders by integrating and balancing their needs.

You will need to measure in order to find out if your investment is paying off. Are you getting value for money for your investments? Are you getting the promised benefits?

For example, for your owners, are revenue, return on net assets and return on investment increasing? Are earnings per share increasing? Do your customers and employees think the value they get is increasing?

Are customers and employees increasingly satisfied? Does the community think it is increasingly safe and prosperous? Are alliance partners increasingly satisfied with the partnership? To find out, you must ask, and ask often.

You need to measure your progress by obtaining results for all indicators. You should present your results in a way that shows trends, comparisons with competitors or best in class and allows meaningful interpretation of variation.

You should be confident that you:

- have significantly improved
- can show a connection between what you did and a change for the better in the data
- have knowledge of the performance of the best players in this field
- are among the best that you can find when you look very hard.

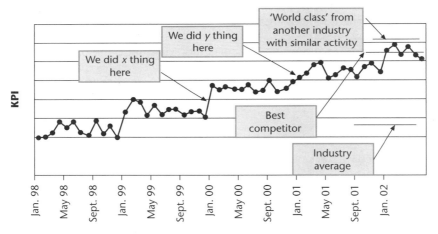

Fig. 10.2 XYZ company performance

In order to assess its performance to date and its sustainability, the company should collect results about the following issues.

Owners' results

- Return on investment, return on net assets, return on equity.
- Net margin, operating margins, pre-tax profit margin.
- Dividends paid per net assets, present value of projected future dividends, earnings per share, price-to-earnings ratio.
- Profit forecast reliability.
- Cash flow.
- Liquidity and financial activity measurements.

- Comparative data for these measurements, which might include industry best, best competitor, industry average and appropriate benchmarks from outside your industry.

Customer results

- Customer perception of value, for example, customer satisfaction, customer dissatisfaction, customer satisfaction relative to competitors, and product/service performance.
- Other indicators of the company's performance as viewed by the customer might include retention, gains and losses of customers and customer accounts; positive customer referrals; customer complaints and warranty claims; competitive awards, ratings, recognition from customers and independent companies; product and service performance measurements, especially those related to customer specifications.
- Product/service field performance assessment based upon data collected by the company or for the company; or customer surveys on product and service performance. It should include attributes that cannot be accurately assessed through direct measurement (e.g. ease of use) and customer's perception of value received relative to quality and price.
- Marketplace performance could include market share measurements, business growth, new product and geographic markets entered and percentage of new product sales.
- Measurements of the success of product and service features are also useful 'listening posts'. Improvements in features should show a clear, positive correlation with customer perception of value and other marketplace indicators. Using such correlations focuses the company on essential customer requirements and helps identify what differentiates product and service in the marketplace. The correlation might reveal emerging or changing market segments, the changing importance of requirements, or even the potential obsolescence of products and services.

Company improvement results

These are needed to assess the success of the company investing in itself through strategies, capital investment, innovation, diversification, maintenance. For example:

- improvement in responsiveness indicators, such as throughput, cycle time, lead times, set-up times
- reduction in inventory
- reduction in rework; cost of quality (including rework and variation from standards and averages); scrap and waste reduction; product/ process yield; complete and accurate shipments

- investment in standards and process assessment results, such as customer assessment or third-party assessment (e.g. ISO 9000)
- innovation rates, innovation effectiveness, cost reductions through innovation, time to market
- measurements of strategic goal achievement
- profitability and operational effectiveness in all important areas.

Employee results

These are needed to assess the employees' perception of value. For example, how the company tracks employee well-being, satisfaction, development, motivation, work system performance and effectiveness. For example:

- employee perceptions of well-being, safety, morale, motivation and job satisfaction
- employee satisfaction with pay, recognition, benefits, compensation
- employee views of leadership, executives and management
- employee satisfaction with development and career and promotion opportunities; equality of opportunity
- perceptions of improvement in job classification, job rotation, work layout and changes in local decision making
- employee perceptions of effectiveness of employee problem or grievance resolution
- employee view of preparation for changes in technology or introduction of new products, service or work practices
- employee perception of work environment; workload; cooperation and teamwork; communications
- employee perception of job security
- employee perception of capability to provide required services to customers
- effectiveness of training
- dissatisfaction index of departing employees
- safety; time between lost time incidents and near misses; numbers of lost time incidents and near misses, workers compensation payments
- absenteeism, turnover, turnover rate for customer-contact employees, grievances, strikes
- comparative information so you can evaluate your results meaningfully against relevant external companies including competitors; for some measurements, such as absenteeism and turnover, local or regional comparisons are appropriate.

Community effectiveness results

These are needed to assess the company's contribution to a safe and prosperous community. For example:

- environmental indicators (emission levels, waste stream reductions, by-product use, recycling)
- compliance with regulatory/legal requirements
- using external rating systems, such as ISO 140001, International Safety Rating System or International Environmental Rating System
- community satisfaction index
- reduction in regulatory requirements; increase in community confidence in self-regulation
- reduction in negative media attention
- comparative information so you can evaluate your results meaningfully against competitors or other relevant external measurements of performance, which might include industry best, best competitor, industry average and appropriate benchmarks from outside your industry; such data might be derived from independent surveys, studies, laboratory testing or other sources.

Supplier and alliance partner results

These are needed to assess the success of your supplier and alliance partnership arrangements. The focus should be on the most important requirements from the point of view of your company—the 'buyer' of the products and services. For example:

- data that shows improving results from suppliers and alliance partners because of selection of better performing suppliers and alliance partners and assisting suppliers and alliance partners improve their work practices
- measurement of suppliers' and alliance partners' contributions to your company's performance goals
- measurements and indicators of major purchasing factors (e.g. quality, delivery and price)
- cost savings; reductions in scrap, waste or rework; improved cycle time and productivity
- supplier and alliance partner satisfaction with the arrangement; satisfaction and dissatisfaction indices
- an index of your perception of your satisfaction with each major alliance partnership; satisfaction and dissatisfaction indices
- comparative information so that you can evaluate your results meaningfully against competitors or other relevant external companies.

Good practices

- Clearly defined measurements of success in terms of KPIs for each stakeholder group. Stakeholder KPIs are linked to company objectives.

- Clear and simple KPIs measure the success of strategies, plans and actions.
- Comparative data for 'best in class' and 'best in region' for all KPIs.
- Measurements in place to measure success in achieving the mission, vision and objectives and behaving in accordance with the values.
- Clear cause and effect relationships between company strategy, action and results are shown in KPIs.
- Positive trend data on major indicators that the company uses to judge its success, in combination with a rational explanation about what the company is doing to ensure the positive trends continue.
- Trend data is used to identify successes or opportunities for improving strategies.
- Improving results on staff opinion polls, cultural audits and business health assessment.

Poor practices

- Not measuring the success of the company (at all) and not measuring achievement of the mission, vision and strategic objectives.
- Not measuring to see if strategies and plans (i.e. 'experiments' to reach objectives) are successful.
- Mistaking action for success.

10.8 Measure the balance

You must use a balanced set of performance indicators. You need to develop indicators to track your progress in:

- implementing your strategies and plans
- reaching the balance required between the stakeholders' objectives and the company's objectives
- reaching your own objectives.

The modified balanced scorecard presented in Principle 5 ('Improved decisions') emphasises the balance needed. The use of a balanced composite of performance measurements:

- offers an effective means to show how value is added to both the company and its stakeholder groups
- provides an opportunity to pull together the strands of the holistic management system required to meet the needs of each of the stakeholder groups.

Good practices

- Use of a balanced scorecard or similar methodology to present and help balance the needs of the major stakeholder groups (owners, customers, the company itself, employees, community and alliance partners).
- Indicators developed for the customer specifications for all major processes, products and services. At a minimum, these include timeliness, on-time delivery, number of times any rework was necessary, anything deliberately specified by the customer, anything that customer research has identified as important to the customer and the company controls (or should control).
- Extensive measurement of the satisfaction gap between what the customers value and what the company provides.
- Suppliers (and focus groups) surveyed to identify level of deployment, satisfaction and dissatisfaction with the partnership relationship. These results have been acted on through several cycles.

Poor practices

- Financial KPIs not included in assessment of business health. This would indicate that business excellence is an 'add on' and the real business of making money is done elsewhere by the real people.
- KPIs relate only to financial performance.
- Only interested in standard balance sheet assets.
- No links between operational and financial measurement.

10.9 Use leading indicators to predict sustainability

You should use lead indicators and other measurements to predict your long-term sustainability. You have KPIs that tell you that you have been successful up to now. You want to answer the question 'will the company continue to be successful?'.

Most KPIs in use by companies today are very poor predictors of the future (as anyone knows who has had to predict sales revenue from past sales figures). Most KPIs describe history—they tell you what has happened in the past. This does not mean that KPIs are useless and should be abandoned. Quite the opposite. Useful KPIs are essential. You need them. However, when you try to predict the future, you cannot rely solely on the past.

Lead indicators are indicators that you can measure today to give a clue about tomorrow. Here are some simple examples. KPIs that rely solely on historic data are like indicators that say 'the clothes on the line are wet so it must have rained'. If we try to use these as predictors of the future, it is like looking at the wet clothes on the line and trying to work out if it will rain—only partially useful as a predictor. This is like trying a drive a car while looking only in the rear-vision mirror. You need a different type of indicator to predict the future.

On the other hand, an indicator that says 'clouds brewing and winds are getting stronger, it will rain soon and wet the clothes' could be a very useful predictor. We call such indicators 'lead indicators'.

In your battery of KPIs that you use to make decisions about your company, you need lead indicators (predictors of the future) as well as *lag* indicators (descriptors of what has already happened).

Indicators of sustainability

Indicators you can use to predict the company's ongoing success, long-term viability, competitiveness and sustainability of its success into the future are outlined below.

1. Investment in stakeholder groups—these are strong lead indicators:
   - the amount of investment in each stakeholder group
   - the balance in investment between stakeholder groups.
2. Focus on 'creating and providing value' for stakeholders.
   - Measure and track over time your estimates of the value you provide and create for each stakeholder group. Compare this with your estimate of their target.
   - Measure and track over time your estimates of the value you remove from each stakeholder group (i.e. how much its costs them or their business to do business with you).
   - Measure the balance in value you provide to your different stakeholder groups. Is this acceptable?
3. Stakeholder perception of value. This should be obtained for each stakeholder group because if stakeholders perceive that they have received value, they are less likely to jump ship. It is a complement of the indicator above.
   - Have each stakeholder group make an assessment of the value it perceives it receives from your company.
   - Have each stakeholder group make estimates of the value you deduct from it—their estimates of what it costs them to do business with you.
4. Describe the future.
   - Paint word pictures of what you think the future will look like.
   - Predict the future for several likely scenarios.
   - Make plans to achieve the futures you want to happen.
   - Develop indicators so you can tell which scenarios are emerging.
   - Track your scenario predictions.
5. Influence the future—what the company is doing to influence its important stakeholders (especially the owners, shareholders, community, political, government, media, customers, alliance partners) to ensure its future viability.

- Develop an index to summarise the perceptions these major stakeholders have of your company: their perceptions of the value you provide to them; the value your company provides to society and the community; your values. Subtract any major negatives (e.g. bad media coverage).
- Develop an index to summarise your activity to influence the above index. For example, lunches, breakfasts, meetings, knowledge exchange with your stakeholder groups; your advertising, positive media activity, public relations, press releases, your attempts to influence the media and the community to have a positive view.

6. Management of major risks.
   - Assess your company's major strategic risks (e.g. the risks to it being able to achieve its mission, vision and objectives or to its values or core competencies). These may include risks due to changes in technology; social mores; political situation; financial situation of your customers, supplier or host country; government policy or regulations; industry structure; competitive mix, competitor offerings or ways competitors do business; natural environment or decisions of parent company.
   - These risks should be tabulated and their effect and the likelihood of each occurring objectively assessed. For example, if x happens it will reduce our revenue by $200 000; however, the likelihood of x happening is low at 10%. Multiply the effect by the likelihood. In our example, $200 000 multiplied by 10% is $20 000. Total all the risk likelihoods.
   - Develop and implement plans to mitigate or eliminate the negative consequences of these risks. Turn your negative risks into opportunities.
   - Estimate the residual risk likelihoods, that is, all the risk likelihoods that remain after you have implemented your plans.
   - Graph and track the residual risk likelihoods. If you have done the analysis objectively and if you have found all the risks, this is a good estimate of your company's sustainability.

7. Relevance.
   - Measure and assess whether the company will continue to be relevant to stakeholders in the future.
   - Predict your ability to continue to create valued products and services for future customers.

8. Core competencies and company capability—how you measure existing core competencies and capability and compare yourself with your competitors.
   - Your predictions of your core competencies and capabilities necessary over time; how you will acquire these competencies and capability (i.e. knowledge, skills and resources); comparison with competitors.

9. Responsiveness and innovation indicators. Indicators for the company's:
    - responsiveness to change
    - rate of knowledge acquisition
    - innovation rate
    - ability to cope with new technology
    - willingness to embrace new technology
    - competitive, innovative, responsiveness and technological capabilities
    - capability with its core competency.
10. Self-assessment against the 10 Business Excellence Principles—the Principles themselves are indicators of future success and sustainability.
    - Your estimate of how well you are performing on each of the Principles is a significant indicator of future success and sustainability. Use the Business Health Assessment questionnaire (p. xxvii) and the questionnaire in Appendix 1.
    - Measure the extent to which your company is aligned to each of the Principles.
11. Self-assessment against one of the national business excellence frameworks.
    - Each of the business excellence frameworks is an assessment tool for the Principles. Make your own 'self-assessment' of your company against one of the frameworks.
    - Alternatively, you could have an assessment made by an external organisation or make a formal application for an Award.
12. Extrapolations—these are weak lead indicators.
    - Extrapolate historical lag KPI trends into the future (e.g. project historical financial data, cost or revenues into the future as predictors).

Warning. Never build a strategy based on a market forecast—it is like trying to capture the wind. Depending on sales forecasts is a sure recipe for non-sustainability. You should do it the other way around. Build strategies and plans to reach the target forecast. When you get a sales forecast, verify it (if you can) and build and implement plans to reach it. A sales forecast is just another target—albeit an important one. And, like all targets, you must put in place very good plans to reach it.

Good practices

- A set of indicators that measure the health of the company.
- A scenario planning process that leads to new strategy. Several probable futures are identified and likelihoods and tell-tale signposts determined. These are tracked. People at all levels of the company

are aware of the scenarios, talk in terms of them and track the likelihood of them being the actual future.
- Strategies are developed to achieve desired outcomes. Strong strategic planning processes. Strategies and actions are put in place to achieve futures that are most advantageous for the company.
- Making time in the present to plan for and influence the future. Balancing the effort between present realities and future concerns.
- Attempts made to predict the future using data and information.
- An ability (at senior levels) to articulate a clear strategy for growth of the company—how much, when and why the business will grow. A clear path for that growth and the risks associated with that growth.
- Processes to identify and respond to risks (e.g. economic, social) and to likely changes to its environment (positive and negative).
- Thorough strategic risk assessment of the risks and threats to achieving success (mission, vision and objectives) conducted and acted upon.
- Plans include overcoming risks to the company (e.g. risks to revenue, achieving mission and vision, market share, assets, knowledge, safety, environment; risk of technology change; threat to values).
- The core competencies of the company (i.e. those things that it does very well compared with other companies) are understood, protected and developed through deliberate strategies.
- Developing a pool of knowledge as a strategy for sustainability.
- Lead indicators for rate of knowledge acquisition, innovation rate.
- Recognition of the relationship between improved company performance (i.e. the KPIs) and the application of the 10 Business Excellence Principles.
- Business improvement (in line with an acknowledged business excellence framework) is a company level objective with strategies that are given high priority and acted upon.

Poor practices

- Inability to articulate a clear view of several possible futures.
- Over-reliance and emphasis on a single view of the future across the company.
- Lack of strategic intent or supporting strategies to achieve or support new futures.
- No evidence of measurement of rate of improvement and no understanding of its importance.
- Learnings from overall performance analysis not deliberately developed and not directly reflected in plans.
- Not recognising and building on business excellence strengths.

10.10 Keep stakeholders informed

You should keep your stakeholders informed of your progress. This is important so that they know that you have listened to them and taken them seriously enough to do something about it. Keeping people informed about what you are doing for them and what you have achieved for them is a very important way to build perceptions of value and trust.

You need to communicate these results to the stakeholder groups in a manner that is meaningful to them so as to provide them with details about what you are doing on their behalf and how your efforts are progressing. This information on actual performance allows all parties to negotiate from a position of knowledge. This helps achieve a shared understanding of the company's objectives and values and a shared understanding of its KPIs. Again, you should present your results as trends and include comparisons with targets, competitors or best in class companies (see Fig. 10.2).

Exactly what information you share with your stakeholder groups should be negotiated with each group. There is obviously information that you do not want your competitors to have. However, the minimum information you should supply is:

- what you are doing for the stakeholder group—your activity and investment
- the results you have achieved for them.

Stakeholders should be wary of companies that do not provide this information. For example, just as investment is very often a lead indicator of future profitability, lack of investment can be an indicator of reduced future profitability.

Shareholders (owners) should be kept informed of all significant investment decisions for all stakeholder groups. Although this is usually true for major capital investment in the company, it is usually not true for the non-capital investment. Investment in non-capital such as training and employee development, knowledge acquisition, product and service development, innovation, process improvement, work environment and knowledge, community safety and infrastructure, and alliance partnerships should be dealt with in the same rigorous manner used for capital investment.

Owners (shareholders) should be informed when investment is carried out, postponed or cancelled in any of them. Information about investment in all of these is as important to shareholders as is any capital project. They should be treated the same.

Although it may appear that the number of stakeholder groups making a claim on the company's value chain has gradually increased, that is not true. The claim has always been there. It is just that companies have not always recognised the claim. Many still do not. However, the better ones do.

Good practices

- Progress on all these KPIs is measured automatically each month, quarter or year and the results published internally.
- Performance indicators are measured and reported regularly across the company. Corporate data is charted and made readily accessible to staff. Everyone in the company has a clear sense of 'how we're going'.
- Trend data using KPIs is communicated to stakeholders to indicate how well the company is doing.
- Regular company self-assessment (using a business excellence framework) is seen as a strategic measurement tool that feeds strategy. This is used to indicate business priorities or to gauge the pace of change required for maintaining competitiveness. The results of self-assessment are published for stakeholders.

Poor practices

- Stakeholder groups not informed of rationale for decisions.
- Stakeholder groups not kept informed of investment decisions or successes achieved.

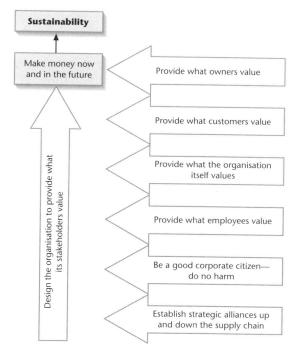

Fig. 10.3 How to be a sustainable business

SUMMARY

Your indicators should:

- be 'big picture' indicators that provide evidence of success in achieving, coordinating and integrating the needs of your stakeholder groups
- measure benefits you have achieved for each of your stakeholder groups
- allow you to interpret company performance in a broad, holistic sense—including and beyond financial performance
- allow you to determine how you are achieving success for each of your stakeholders, and integrate and balance their needs
- allow you to interpret these results in terms of the company's past and future performance and in terms of the balance between the needs of the stakeholders
- show how your initiatives contribute to achieving the company's purpose, vision and goals
- allow you to ensure that all work contributes to the company's long-term success and adds value to both the company and its stakeholders.

Interpreting these measurements and acting on your findings is essential to achieve the balance. Success in the old thinking was measured purely in terms of share price, return on investment and profit levels. That approach was too one-sided and often led to a disregard of the needs of customers and employees, and the other stakeholders.

You need 'real-time' information (measurements of progress) so you can evaluate success of strategies, improvement of processes, products, and services, and alignment with overall company strategy.

You need to act to address any problems or opportunities revealed by the indicators and your interpretation of them. You actually need to do something. For example, the information on the well-being, satisfaction and motivation of employees should be used to identify dissatisfaction priorities—and these must be acted on in the context of overall performance and the balance between stakeholders needs.

WHAT WOULD YOUR STAKEHOLDERS SAY?

HOW WOULD YOUR SHAREHOLDERS RATE YOUR COMPANY ON THESE?

- This company will be around in 100 years.
- This is a fantastic company. I intend to keep my shares and advise others to do likewise.
- This company is increasing in value.

- This company looks after my needs.
- All things considered, I get value from this company.
- This company takes my needs into account when developing strategy and plans for the future.
- I understand the balance being achieved between my needs and those of the other stakeholders (customers, the company itself, employees, suppliers and alliance partners and the community).
- This company has objectives, strategies and plans to address the needs of and to create and deliver value for all the company's stakeholders (owners, customers, the company itself, employees, suppliers and alliance partners and the community).
- I believe I am given a say in this company.
- This company protects the dividend stream by investing (funds and effort) in meeting the needs of each stakeholder group.
- This company has diversified to reduce its risk from each part of the market.
- This company has huge pay packets for executives.
- This company has reward and recognition schemes focused on the long-term interest of the company (rather than the short-term interest of the executives).
- This company does not have political infighting and one-upmanship among its executives.
- This company invests in maintenance.
- This company invests in building its core competencies.
- This company has established partnerships with its major suppliers and distributors.
- I am kept informed when investment is carried out, postponed or cancelled in customers, products and services; employees, training, work environment and knowledge; community safety and infrastructure; alliance partnerships.
- This company measures its success in meeting its objectives for all its stakeholder groups.
- This company develops objectives that are vital to its success, sets targets for these objectives, develops strategies to achieve the targets, implements plans to address the strategies, and measures its progress at implementing the plans and their success in reaching those objectives.
- This company determines the objectives of each of its stakeholder groups and determines its short- and long-term objectives for each stakeholder group.
- This company determines the balance it wants to achieve between the interests of the stakeholder groups and negotiates a position that is acceptable to all stakeholders.
- This company develops strategies and plans to achieve that position of balance.

- This company uses indicators to track its progress in implementing those plans and in reaching the balance required and reaching its objectives.
- This company measures its progress by obtaining results for all indicators.
- This company presents its results in a way that shows trends and comparative data with competitors or best in class, and allows meaningful interpretation of variation.
- This company interprets these in terms of the balance between the needs of the stakeholders.
- This company uses 'big picture' data for evidence of success in achieving, coordinating and integrating the needs of the stakeholders.
- This company can cite benefits achieved for each of its stakeholder groups (owners; customers; the company itself; employees; suppliers; and the community).
- This company interprets company success, determining how it is achieving success for each of its stakeholders by integrating and balancing their needs.
- This company measures the extent to which it is aligned to each of the Principles.
- This company communicates its results to me in a manner that is meaningful to me.
- I can negotiate with this company from a position of knowledge.
- This company takes action to address any problems or opportunities revealed by its indicators.

HOW WOULD YOUR CUSTOMERS RATE YOUR COMPANY ON THESE?

- This is a fantastic company.
- This company looks after my needs.
- The value I get from its products and services is increasing.
- All things considered, I get value from this company.
- This company takes my needs into account when developing strategy and plans for the future.
- I am represented in major decisions affecting strategic planning, products and service design, process redesign and company design.
- This company is designed to deliver what I need and value.
- I understand the balance being achieved between my needs and those of the other stakeholders (owners, the company itself, employees, suppliers and alliance partners and the community).
- I believe I am given a say in this company.
- This company invests time and money to find out about my needs.
- This company invests time and money to meet my needs.
- This company will be around in 100 years.
- This company has good products and services. I will continue to buy.

- This company communicates its results to me in a manner that is meaningful to me.

HOW WOULD YOUR EMPLOYEES RATE YOUR COMPANY ON THESE?

- This is a fantastic place to work.
- I recommend it to all my friends.
- I want my children to work here.
- This company looks after my needs.
- All things considered, I get value from working for this company.
- The value I get from working here is increasing.
- This company takes my needs into account when developing strategy and plans for the future.
- I am represented in major decisions affecting strategic planning, products and service design, process redesign and company design.
- This company is designed to deliver what I need and value.
- I understand the balance being achieved between my needs and those of the other stakeholders (owners, customers, the company itself, suppliers and alliance partners, and the community).
- I believe I am given a say in this company.
- This company does not have political infighting and one-upmanship among its executives.
- This company invests time and money to find out about my needs.
- This company invests time and money to meet my needs.
- This company has diversified to reduce its risk from each part of the market.
- This company invests in maintenance.
- This company invests in process improvement and process re-engineering.
- This company invests in building its core competencies (i.e. what it does very well).
- This company helped me diversify my skills to reduce the risk to my employment from a downturn in my part of the market.
- This company has established partnerships with its major suppliers and distributors.
- This company is a good employer.
- This company will be around in 100 years.
- This company communicates its results to me in a manner that is meaningful to me.
- My union never needs to be adversarial in representing my interests to the company. There is trust on both sides.
- I can negotiate with this company from a position of knowledge.
- This company takes action to address any problems or opportunities revealed by its indicators.

HOW WOULD YOUR SUPPLIERS RATE YOUR COMPANY ON THESE?

- This is a fantastic company to be in partnership with.
- I wish all my other customers were this good.
- I am increasingly satisfied with the partnership.
- This company is responsive to my needs.
- All things considered, I get value from this company.
- This company takes my needs into account when developing strategy and plans for the future.
- I am represented in major decisions affecting strategic planning, products and service design, process redesign and company design.
- I understand the balance being achieved between my needs and those of the other stakeholders (customers, the company itself, employees and the community).
- I believe I am given a say in this company.
- This company invests time and money to find out about my needs.
- This company invests time and money to meet my needs.
- This company has established partnerships with its major suppliers and distributors.
- This company will be around in 100 years.
- This company communicates its results to me in a manner that is meaningful to me.
- I can negotiate with this company from a position of knowledge.
- This company takes action to address any problems or opportunities revealed by its indicators.

HOW WOULD THE COMMUNITY RATE YOUR COMPANY ON THESE?

- This is a fantastic company.
- This company looks after my needs.
- All things considered, I get value from this company.
- This company takes my needs into account when developing strategy and plans for the future.
- I understand the balance being achieved between my needs and those of the other stakeholders (owners, customers, the company itself, employees and suppliers and alliance partners).
- I believe I am given a say in this company.
- I am represented in major decisions affecting strategic planning, products and service design, process redesign and company design.
- This company invests time and money to find out about my needs.
- This company invests time and money to meet my needs.
- This company pays sufficient tax to contribute to the community infrastructure.
- This company is good for the community.
- This company is a good employer.

362

- This company consistently self-regulates itself.
- I do not need to impose regulations to keep them in line.
- This company communicates its results to me in a manner that is meaningful to me.
- I can negotiate with this company from a position of knowledge.
- This company takes action to address any problems or opportunities identified.

Appendix 1
Employee questionnaire

THIS QUESTIONNAIRE IS DESIGNED to test your company's alignment with the 10 Business Excellence Principles. It does this by having you assess how well your company applies the 10 Business Excellence Principles. Companies that apply these Principles usually perform significantly better than those that do not.

For each question, give your rating out of 10 for how well it is done in your workplace. Answer from your experience of your immediate workgroup. (If you are part of a large organisation, you will also need to consider the relations between your workgroup and the rest of the organisation.) The scores are:

- 0: never-ever
- 1: never
- 2: starting—just
- 3: starting
- 4: sometimes—rarely
- 5: sometimes
- 6: oftenish
- 7: often
- 8: always—almost
- 9: always
- 10: fantastic at doing it

Employee questionnaire

	Actual performance (out of 10)
1. Can you do your work without fear? (P1)	
2. Do you trust the company? (P1)	
3. Do you feel secure? (P1)	
4. Do you trust your bosses? (P1)	
5. Does this company have fantastic internal communications? (P1)	
6. Does the company demonstrate values that you like? (P1)	
7. Are the senior managers open and honest? (P1)	
8. Do you feel that you are supported? (P1)	
9. Do you have access to managers/team leaders when you need decisions made? (P1)	
10. Is this a company where you can do your best work? (P1)	
11. Are you all treated equally? (P1)	
12. Does this company know where it is going and have plans to get there? (P2)	
13. Do you contribute to the planning process in a meaningful way that you are very comfortable with? (P2)	
14. Are you represented in major decisions affecting strategic planning, products and service design, process redesign and company design? (P2)	
15. Are you given a say in this company? (P2)	
16. Are there any surprises for you after the planning process is completed? (If surprises, score 0; if none, score 10.) (P2)	
17. Do all parts of the company work together to achieve the company's objectives? (P2)	
18. Does this company have political infighting and one-upmanship among its executives? (If infighting, score 0; if not, score 10.) (P2)	
19. Is this company focused on achieving its goals and objectives? (P2)	
20. Do you know what this company is trying to achieve? (P2)	
21. Do you know how you are going (i.e. do you have clear indicators of success that you have access to)? (P2)	
22. Do you know how you contribute to the company's success? (P2)	
23. Is this company proactive rather than 'knee jerk'? (P2)	
24. Do you understand what your customers value? (P3)	
25. Are you actively trying to find out what your customers *dislike* about your products and services? (P3)	
26. Do you use customer input in product and service design? (P3)	
27. Do you use customer feedback/complaints to improve your service? (P3)	
28. Are your products and services of value to your customers? (P3)	
29. Is everything about this company focused on providing what your customers value? (P3)	

Employee questionnaire (*continued*)

	Actual performance (out of 10)
30. Does this company understand what its processes are capable of delivering (its process capability)? (P4)	
31. Does this company deliberately work to improve its processes? (P4)	
32. Are you enabled (provided with skills, knowledge, authority and power) to change processes in which you work? (P4)	
33. Do your managers spend considerable time working to improve processes (i.e. making it easier for you to do your work)? (P4)	
34. Are systems improved when things go wrong and people are not blamed? (P4)	
35. When processes need to be improved, do your managers/team leaders draw on the experience of all people who have knowledge of the processes? (P4)	
36. Is your performance management system based on the capability of the *processes* to deliver? (P4)	
37. Do you have plans to reach all targets? (P4)	
38. Are your managers team members rather than 'bosses'? (P4)	
39. Are your needs as an internal customer of the process considered and met? (P4)	
40. Does this company base all its operational decisions on facts—data and information—rather than rumour and gut feelings? (P5)	
41. Does this company gather data that it does not use? (If it gathers much data that is not used, score 0; if it uses all data collected, score 10.) (P5)	
42. Does this company demand reports that no-one uses? (P5) (If it produces many reports that are not used, score 0; if it uses all reports, score 10.)	
43. Does this company evaluate its performance using indicators of success such as key performance indicators (KPIs)? (P5)	
44. Does this company have KPIs and measurements that force you to work against the company's best interests? (If it has many such KPIs, score 0; if no such KPIs, score 10.) (P5)	
45. Does this company make comparisons with other companies to find better ways of doing things? (P5)	
46. Does this company make good use of the knowledge held in the company? (P5)	
47. Does this company understand that all systems and processes produce inconsistent results? (P6)	
48. Do your managers overreact or under-react? (If they overreact or under-react often, score 0; if seldom or never, score 10.) (P6)	
49. Have you been given the skills to allow you to understand variation? (P6)	
50. Do your managers clearly understand variation? (P6)	

Employee questionnaire (*continued*)

	Actual performance (out of 10)
51. Do your managers ask 'why are this month's results different from last month's'? (If ask, score 0: if don't, score 10.) (P6)	
52. Have your managers been given the skills to allow them to understand variation? (P6)	
53. Is data always presented in such a way as to allow interpretation of the variation? (P6)	
54. Do you work to make processes more stable by reducing 'special cause' variation? (P6)	
55. Do you work to make processes more capable by reducing 'common cause' variation? (P6)	
56. Are you working to reduce the variation in all your products and services? (P6)	
57. Are you valued (appreciated) by this company? (P7)	
58. Are you respected? (P7)	
59. Do you know what is expected of you in your job? (P7)	
60. Are you given adequate skills, knowledge, authority and resources to be able to do your job? (P7)	
61. When people give you a task to do, do they tell you *why* it needs to be done? (P7)	
62. Do you get useful feedback on how you do your job that focuses on helping you and not blaming you? (P7)	
63. Are you always provided with training when you are expected to use new processes and technology? (P7)	
64. Does this company provide a safe working environment (physically and mentally and free of harassment)? (P7)	
65. Does your union ever need to be adversarial in representing your interests to the company? Is there trust on both sides? (P7)	
66. Is this company continually learning (from others, from employees, from customers, from competitors, from technology)? (P8)	
67. Does this company constantly search for a better way (tries new concepts, ideas, products and services)? (P8)	
68. Does this company encourage taking risks? (P8)	
69. Are you encouraged to question concepts and assumptions? (P8)	
70. Can you make suggestions without fear? (P8)	
71. Do your recognition and reward systems encourage innovation rather than stick with the 'tried and true'? (P8)	
72. Before new ideas are implemented, are they talked through by all those who will be affected to iron out any bugs and problems? (P8)	
73. Do you have enough time to implement new ways of doing things? (P8)	
74. When new ideas are to be implemented, do you get enough information through formal channels about when, where, what, why, who and how? (P8)	

Employee questionnaire (*continued*)

	Actual performance (out of 10)
75. When new ideas are to be implemented, do you get adequate training? (P8)	
76. When new ideas are to be implemented, do you also change all necessary structures and systems (e.g. reward and recognition systems; performance management systems; technology; standard operating procedures; standards systems; communications systems; company structure; performance indicators; resources; job descriptions; performance agreements; company values; audit systems)? (P8)	
77. When new ideas are implemented, do you measure: if the innovation is effective; if it delivers the benefits promised; if it provides value to the company, its customers and other stakeholders; if the costs are what were estimated? (P8)	
78. Does existing stock prevent you from innovation or implementation? (If prevented, score 0; if not, score 10.) (P8)	
79. Does the budget prevent you from implementing innovations when you need to? (If prevented, score 0; if not, score 10.) (P8)	
80. Is this company skilled at creating, acquiring and transferring knowledge? (P8)	
81. Does this company build on, grow and protect its core competencies? (P8)	
82. Do people in this company hoard knowledge? (If hoard, score 0; if not, score 10.) (P8)	
83. Do people in the company copy from one another a lot? (P8)	
84. Does this company share its knowledge with others? (P8)	
85. Do you make time to undertake meaningful reflection—thinking about what has happened or is happening, why it is happening? (P8)	
86. Does this company operate ethically? (P9)	
87. Does this company 'add value' to the community in general (e.g. it does nothing that will endanger the community's prosperity, health, safety or cleanliness)? (P9)	
88. Does this company work to reduce the unintended consequences (side-effects) of its actions and policies? (P9)	
89. Does this company work to reduce the waste and pollution it produces? (P9)	
90. Does this company systematically decrease its economic dependence on underground metals and other minerals? (P9)	
91. Does this company systematically decrease its economic dependence on fossil fuels? (P9)	
92. Does this company systematically decrease its economic dependence on persistent synthetic substances? (P9)	

Employee questionnaire (*continued*)

	Actual performance (out of 10)
93. Does this company use a set of environmental performance indicators to monitor the environmental impact at production sites, the average environmental standard of appliances and the profitability of its most environmentally sound products? (P9)	
94. Do you constantly work to improve your industry: its code of conduct, how it operates, sharing of knowledge on what does and does not work well, regulations that affect you and regulators and community perceptions? (P9)	
95. Is this a good place to work? (P10)	
96. All things considered, do you get value from working for this company? (P10)	
97. Is the value you get from working here increasing? (P10)	
98. Does this company invest time and money to meet employees' needs? (P10)	
99. Does this company invest in maintenance? (P10)	
100. Does this company invest in process improvement and process re-engineering? (P10)	
101. Does this company invest in building its core competencies (i.e. what it does very well)? (P10)	
102. Has this company helped you diversify your skills to reduce the risk to your employment from a downturn in your part of the market? (P10)	
103. Is this company a good employer? (P10)	
104. Does this company communicate its results to you in a manner that is meaningful to you? (P10)	
105. Will this company be around in 100 years? (P10)	
106. Describe what you enjoy (or like) most about your workplace.	
107. Describe what stops you from doing your best work.	
108. If you could change one thing about this company, describe what it is.	

Appendix 2
Relative importance of questions

THE TABLE OPPOSITE lists the top 10 and 25 most important questions in the Business Health Assessment questionnaire and the Employee Questionnaire (Appendix 1) in numerical order (but not in order of importance). These questions address the 10 and 25 most important issues to address for any company. If you get a low score on any of these questions, you must address the issue as your most important. (This gives a relative importance, it does *not* imply that the other questions are not important.)

| Business Health Assessment | | Employee questionnaire | |
Top 10 questions	Top 25 questions	Top 10 questions	Top 25 questions
1.5	1.1	1	1
1.8	1.3	3	2
4.3	1.5	33	3
4.6	1.8	34	8
6.5	2.4	47	16
6.6	2.5	48	22
6.7	3.2	51	27
6.8	3.4	56	29
10.1	4.3	95	31
10.7	4.4	96	32
	4.5		33
	4.6		34
	4.7		36
	6.5		47
	6.6		48
	6.7		51
	6.8		54
	6.9		55
	6.10		56
	7.3		57
	7.5		59
	10.1		95
	10.2		96
	10.7		98
	10.9		100

Appendix 3
Award winners

Malcolm Baldrige National Quality Awards

3M Dental Products Division (1997), www.mmm.com/dental
ADAC Laboratories (1996)
Ames Rubber Corporation (1993)
Armstrong World Industries Building Products Operations (1995)
AT&T Consumer Communications Services (now part of the Consumer Markets Division of AT&T) (1994)
AT&T Network Systems Group—Transmission Systems Business Unit (now Lucent Technologies, Inc., Optical Networking Group) (1992)
AT&T Universal Card Services (1992)
BI (1999)
Boeing Airlift and Tanker Programs (1998), www.boeing.com
Cadillac Motor Car Company (1990)
Corning Telecommunications Products Division (1995)
Custom Research, Inc. (1996)
Dana Commercial Credit Corporation (1996)
Dana Corporation—Spicer Driveshaft Division (2000)
Eastman Chemical Company (1993)
Federal Express Corporation (1990)
Globe Metallurgical Inc. (1988)
Granite Rock Company (1992)
GTE Directories Corporation (1994)
IBM Rochester—AS/400 Division (1990)
KARLEE Company, Inc. (2000)
Los Alamos National Bank (2000)

Marlow Industries, Inc. (1991)
Merrill Lynch Credit Corporation (1997), www.ml.com/woml
Milliken & Company (1989)
Motorola Inc. (1988)
Operations Management International, Inc. (2000)
The Ritz-Carlton Hotel Company (1992)
The Ritz-Carlton Hotel Company, L.L.C. (1999)
Solar Turbines Inc. (1998), www.cat.com
Solectron Corporation (1991 and 1997), www.solectron.com
STMicroelectronics, Inc.—Region Americas (1999)
Sunny Fresh Foods (1999)
Texas Instruments Incorporated—Defense Systems & Electronics Group
    (now part of Raytheon Systems Company) (1992)
Texas Nameplate Company Inc. (1998), www.nameplate.com
Trident Precision Manufacturing, Inc. (1996)
Wainwright Industries, Inc. (1994)
Wallace Co., Inc. (1990)
Westinghouse Electric Corporation—Commercial Nuclear Fuel Division
    (1988)
Xerox Corporation—Business Products & Systems (1989)
Xerox Business Systems (1997), www.xerox.com/XBS
Zytec Corporation (1991)

European Foundation for Quality Management Award recipients

Beko Trading Co Award Subsidiary SMEs (1998)
BEKSA (1997)
BRISA (1996)
Burton-Apta Refractory Manufacturing Ltd (Hungary) (2000)
D2D (Design to Distribution) Ltd (now called: Celestica Limited) (1994)
Danish International Continuing Education (DiEU, Denmark) (1999)
Inland Revenue, Account Office Cumbernauld (UK, Scotland) (2000)
Milliken European Division (1993)
Nokia Mobile Phones, Europe & Africa (Finland) (2000)
Rank Xerox Ltd (1992)
Schindlerhof Award Independent SMEs (1998)
Servitique Network Services (France) (1999)
SGS-Thomson (1997)
St Mary's College Northern Ireland (2001)
Texas Instruments Europe (1995)
TNT United Kingdom Ltd Award Large Businesses (1998)
Volvo Cars Gent (Belgium) (1999)
Yellow Pages (UK) (1999)
Zahnarztpraxis (Switzerland) (2001)

Australian Quality Awards for Business Excellence

ABB Power Transmission Pty Ltd (1993)
Abbott International (division of Abbott Australasia Pty Ltd) (1996)
ABM Electronic Engineering (Aust) Pty Ltd incorporating Amalgamated
    Business Machines (1994)
Australia New Zealand—Direct Line (1998)
Australia New Zealand—Direct Line (Award Gold 2000)
Australian Pacific Airconditioning Manufacturing (1994)
Avis Australia (1992)
Baxter Healthcare Pty Ltd (1991)
BHP Building & Industrial Products Division (Tubemakers of Australia
    Limited) (1991)
BHP Building and Construction Products (formerly Lysaght Building
    Industries) (1993)
BHP Research (1996)
BHP Wire Products (formerly BHP Steel High Carbon Wire Products
    Division) (1991)
Bilcon Engineering Pty Ltd (1995)
Britax Rainsfords Pty Ltd (1999)
Building & Construction Industry (Portable Long Service Leave) Authority
    (1998)
ENERGEX (formerly The South East Queensland Electricity Board) (1991)
EnergyAustralia (formerly Sydney Electricity) (1994)
Enhance Systems Pty Ltd (1993)
Ericsson Australia Pty Ltd (1996)
Ericsson Australia Pty Ltd Supply Division (1995)
Ford Motor Company of Australia Limited (1993)
Honeywell Limited (1997)
Honeywell Limited (Australian Quality Prize Winners 2000)
ING Funds Management (Award Gold 2000)
Integral Energy (Award Gold 1998)
Integral Energy Australia (formerly Prospect Electricity) (1995)
Kodak (Australasia) Pty Ltd (Australian Quality Prize Winners 1992)
Mercantile Mutual Funds Management (1997)
NEC Australia Pty Ltd (1994)
Noyce Lawyers (1999)
PanBio (1997)
SmithKline Beecham Consumer Healthcare (formerly Sterling Winthrop
    Pty Ltd) (1993)
South East Water (1998)
South East Water (Award Gold 2000)
Southern Pathology (1999)
The National Roads and Motorists Association (NRMA) (1992)
The TVS Partnership Architects (1993)

The Wesley Hospital (1996)
Toyota Motor Corporation Australia Limited (1991)
Venture Industries (formerly The Ford Motor Company of Australia
    Limited, Plastics Plant) (1992)
Wollongong City Council (1997)
Zeneca Pharmaceuticals Australia P/L (formerly ICI Pharmaceuticals)
    (1996)

References, resources and recommended reading

Websites

Alfie Kohn: www.alfiekohn.org
AQC: www.aqc.org.au
Curious Cat Management Improvement: www.curiouscat.com/guides/qlist
European Foundation for Quality Management: www1.efqm.org
Goldratt Institute: www.goldratt.com
Malcolm Baldrige National Quality Award: www.quality.nist.gov
Peter Scholtes Consulting: pscholtes.com
The Natural Step: www.naturalstep.org

Recommended reading

Brassard, M. & Ritter, D. (1994), *Memory Jogger II*, GOAL/QPC, Methuen, MA.
Buzan, T. (1977), *Make the Most of Your Mind*, Pan Books, London.
Byham, W. C. & Cox, J. (1988), *Zapp! The Lightning of Empowerment*, Fawcett Columbine, New York.
Byham, W. C. & Cox, J. (1994), *Heroz*, Fawcett Columbine, New York.
Carlopio, J. (1998), *Implementation: Making Workplace Innovation and Technical Change Happen*, McGraw-Hill, Sydney.
Carlzon, J. (1989), *Moments of Truth*, Harper & Row, Sydney.
Covey, S. R. (1990), *Principle-Centred Leadership*, Simon & Schuster, New York.
Covey, S. R. (1990), *The 7 Habits of Highly Effective People*, Simon & Schuster, New York.
de Bono, E. (1967), *Lateral Thinking*, Penguin, London.
de Bono, E. (1985), *Six Thinking Hats*, Penguin, London.

Deming, W. E. (1982), *Out of the Crisis*, Cambridge University Press, Cambridge.

Deming, W. E. (1994), *The New Economics*, Massachusetts Institute of Technology, Cambridge, MA.

De Vries, M. F. R. (1993), *Leaders, Fools and Imposters: Essays on The Psychology of Leadership*, Jossey-Bass, San Francisco.

Firth, D. (1998), *The Corporate Fool*, Capstone, Oxford.

Goldratt, E. M. (1990), *The Haystack Syndrome: Sifting Information Out of The Data Ocean*, North River Press, New York.

Goldratt, E. M. (1992), *The Goal*, North River Press, Great Barrington, MA.

Goldratt, E. M. (1994), *It's Not Luck*, North River Press, Great Barrington, MA.

Goldratt, E. M. (1997), *Critical Chain*, North River Press, Great Barrington, MA.

Goldratt, E. M. (2000), *Necessary but Not Sufficient*, North River Press, Great Barrington, MA.

Goldratt, E. M. (2000), *Essays on the Theory of Constraints*, North River Press, Great Barrington, MA.

Hausner, Alexander (1999), 'Business Success and ABEF Evaluation Results: on the Nexus between Manufacturing Results and Frameworks for Business Excellence' (PhD thesis), University of Wollongong, Wollongong.

Herzberg, F. (1968), 'One More Time: How Do you Motivate Employees?', *Harvard Business Review*, January–February.

Hoffmann, R. (1995), *The Same and Not the Same*, Columbia University Press, Columbia.

Kaplan, R. S. & Norton, D. P. (1996), *The Balance Scorecard*, Harvard Business School Press, Massachusetts.

Kim, Eugene Eric, *TRIZ: The Theory of Inventive Problem Solving*, www.ddj.com.

Kohn, A. (1986), *No Contest. The Case Against Competition*, Houghton Mifflin, Boston.

Kohn, A. (1993), *Punished by Rewards*, Houghton Mifflin, Boston.

Kouzes, J. M. & Posner, B. Z. (1993), *Credibility*, Jossey-Bass, San Francisco.

Magee, B. (1973), *Popper*, Fontana Press, London.

Maskell, R. H. (1991), *Performance Measurement for World Class Manufacturing—A Model for American Companies*, Productivity Press, Cambridge, MA.

Maynard, H. B. Jr & Mehrtens, S. (1993), *Redefinitions of Corporate Wealth*. In M. Ray & A. Rinzler (eds), *The New Paradigm in Business—Emerging Strategies for Leadership and Organisational Change*, G. P. Putnam's Sons, New York.

Mink, O. G., Shultz, J. M. & Mink, B. P. (1991), *Developing and Managing Open Organisations*, Somerset Consulting Group, Texas.

Porter, M. E. (1980), *Competitive Strategy*, Free Press, Macmillan, New York.

Rosenbluth, H. F. & Peters, D. M. (1992), *The Customer Comes Second*, Quill William Morrow, New York.

Scheinkopf, L. A. (1999), *Thinking for a Change*, St Lucie Press/APICS, Florida.

Scholtes, P. R. (1988), *The Team Handbook*, Joiner, Madison, WI.

Scholtes, P. R. & Ackoff, R. L. (1997), *The Leader's Handbook*, McGraw-Hill, New York.

Senge, P. (1990), *The Fifth Discipline: The Art and Practice of the Learning Organisation*, Currency Doubleday, London.

Senge, P., Kleiner, A., Roberts, C., Ross, R. B. & Smith, B. J. (1994), *The Fifth Discipline Fieldbook: Strategies and Tools for Building a Learning Organisation*, Nicholas Brealey, London.

Senge, P., Kleiner, A., Roberts, C., Ross, R. B., Roth, G. & Smith, B. J. (1999), *The Dance of Change: The Challenges of Sustaining Momentum in Learning Organizations*, Nicholas Brealey, London.

Senge, P., McCabe, N. H. C., Lucas, T., Kleiner, A., Dutton, J. & Smith, B. J. (2000), *Schools That Learn: A Fifth Discipline Fieldbook for Educators, Parents, and Everyone Who Cares About Education*, Doubleday, London.

Shewhart, W. A. (1939), Statistical Method from the Viewpoint of Quality Control, Graduate School, Department of Agriculture, Washington (Dover 1986).

Taguchi, Genichi & Yokoyamá, Yoshiko (1994), 'Taguchi Methods: Design of Experiments', *Quality Engineering*, vol 4.

Tice, L. (1995), *Smart Talk for Achieving your Potential*, Pacific Institute Publishing, Seattle.

Tice, L. (1997), *Personal Coaching for Results*, Pacific Institute Publishing, Seattle.

Trompenaars, F. & Hampden-Turner, C. (1998), *Riding the Waves of Culture*, McGraw-Hill, New York.

Walton, M. (1989), *The Deming Management Method*, The Business Library, W. H. Allen & Co, London.

Index

measuring effectiveness of, **285**, 286, 354
outlets for, **283**
pressure &, **273**
psychological temperament &, **275**
questionnaire on, **xxxv**
resources &, **272–3**, 274
reward &, **272**, 287
senior executives &, 7, 23, **278**, 279–80
strategic approach to, **285–9**
using tools to encourage, **264–71**, 273
value &, **341–3**, 348, 354
see also adaptation; persuasion
innovations managers, 287
intangible assets, **43–4**
integrity, 6
intellectual property/capital, 43, 44
interconnectedness, **xxiv**, xxvi
International Standards Organisation, 122, 349
Internet lead indicator, 121
invention, **261**, *261*, **262–3**, 270, 275, 341
inventory, 123, 160, 347
inventory dollar days, 124
investment, **332–6**, 339–40, 352, 356
investment analysts, xxiii

job descriptions, 45–6, *46*, *104*, 226, 228
job satisfaction, *104*
judgment calls, 181
judgmental thinking, 264
just cause, **236**, 244, 245

key customers, 37
key performance indicators, xxii, xxiii, *xxiii*, 2,
40, 51, 52, 54, 60, 113, 130, 133, **149–50**, *151*,
152, *153*, **156**, 160, 170, 174, 187, 210, 239,
242, 303, 321, 328, **349–50**, **351–2**, 356, 357
key result areas, 113, 149, 150, 286
knowledge, 43, 44, 46, 53, 71, 72, 79, 98, *104*, 128,
137, **158–66**, *164*, 175, **215–17**, 218, 229, 276,
277, 289, 297, **298**, 304, 319, **320–1**, 324, 355
knowledge sharing, 163, 215, 230, 342
Kohn, A., **239–42**

lag indicators, **156**, 352
lateral thinking, 264, 315
lead indicators, 121, **156**, **351–5**, 354, 356
lead times, 118, 347
leadership, **220**, 223, 319
leadership style, 7, **8–9**, 10, *11*, **12**, 20
learning, 23
  barriers to, **297–8**
  continuous nature of, **xxxv**, 256, **257–9**,
  289–92, 299
  core competencies &, **297**, 298, 299
  cycle of, **290**, *290*
  employees &, **215**, 229–30, 289
  environment &, **257–9**
  knowledge &, 162, 297, **298**
  mistakes &, 256, 259, **291–2**, 299
  practice &, **294–6**

questionnaire on, **xxxv**
reflection &, **292–3**
strategic approach to, **296–8**
see also adaptation; innovation; training
learning-improvement cycle, 290, *291*
location, 164, *164*

Malcolm Baldrige National Quality Award, xix,
xx, **xxi–xxii**, 38, **372–3**
managers and management, 97
  chain analogy &, **125–6**, 147
  customer values &, 60, 69, 71
  customers from, **81**
  data management &, **168–9**
  decision-making &, **159**
  deterministic models &, **175–6**
  failures &, **292**
  feedback from, **227**, 245
  improving the outcome/ system &, **107–14**,
  130–1
  job of, **107–14**
  knowledge of, **22–4**, 215, 216, 232
  new-style, 7, **9**, *11*, 20, **108**, *108*, 109, 110
  old-style, 7, **8–9**, 10, *11*, 20, 28, **107–8**, *107*,
  109, 110, 120
  processes &, 81, 91, **111–12**, 232
  put downs by, **246**
  rewards for, **19–21**, **339–40**
  role of, **110–11**, **112–13**
  understanding of work &, **108–10**, *109*, 232
  variation &, **176–80**, 207
  see also bottlenecks and constraints;
    incentive schemes; senior executives
management by fact, **134–6**
managerial capability, 26
market forces, 307
market forecasts, 354
market perception of value, 30
market segments, 37, **73–4**, *75*, 77, 85, 158
market share, 160, 161
match game, **294–5**, *295*
media, 305, 348
Memory Jogger II, 146
mergers, 61
milestone tracking, 54
mind set, 142
mindmapping, 264
mistakes, 256, 259, 271, **291–2**, 299
moments of truth, 80
money-back guarantees, 195
month-to-month comparisons, 177, *180*, 207
morale, 6, 9, 80, 104, *104*, 149, 219, 248, 276, 348
multivoting, **147**

National Business Excellence Awards, 90, 210,
220, 328
National Business Excellence frameworks, **xix–
xx**, xxiv, 35
National Institute of Standards and Technology,
xx

35315199